READING THE AMERICAN PAST

Selected Historical Documents
Volume II from 1863

READING THE AMERICAN PAST

Selected Historical Documents
Volume II from 1863

MICHAEL P. JOHNSON, EDITOR
Johns Hopkins University

Bedford Books ⚘ Boston

For Bedford Books

President and Publisher: Charles H. Christensen
General Manager and Associate Publisher: Joan E. Feinberg
History Editor: Katherine E. Kurzman
Developmental Editor: Louise Townsend
Managing Editor: Elizabeth M. Schaaf
Production Editor: Patricia Bergin
Copyeditor: Barbara Sutton
Text Design: DeNee Reiton Skipper
Indexer: Steve Csipke
Cover Design: Wanda Kossak
Cover Art: Colbar Art, Incorporated, Long Island City, New York

2   1   0   9   8   7
f   e   d   c   b   a

For information, write: Bedford Books,
75 Arlington Street, Boston MA 02116 (617–426–7440)

ISBN 0–312–13909–8

Acknowledgments

PREFACE FOR INSTRUCTORS

Designed specifically to accompany *The American Promise: A History of the United States, Reading the American Past* aims to help instructors make history come alive for students in the survey course. The documents in this collection give students compelling first-hand accounts that provide depth and breadth to the discussion of important events, ideas, and experiences found in *The American Promise* and other comprehensive United States history textbooks. Organized chapter by chapter to parallel *The American Promise*, these sources offer teachers many educational options. Above all, *Reading the American Past* seeks to ignite the sparks of historical imagination that every teacher hopes to see in students' eyes.

Reading a textbook discussion of Columbus's arrival in the New World, for example, gives students basic, up-to-date information that has been collected, sorted out, and synthesized over the last 500 years. But reading the words Columbus wrote in his log shortly after he stepped ashore in the western hemisphere (see Volume I, Chapter 2, page 14) recaptures as no textbook can that moment of immense, mutual surprise when fifteenth-century Europeans and the people they called Indians first encountered each other. As every historian knows, primary sources bridge from the present, when they are read, to the past, when they were written. They encourage students to venture across that span connecting present and past and to risk discovering a captivating and unexpected world.

Three basic principles guided the selection of documents. First and foremost, the sources highlight major events and significant perspectives of a given historical era. Second, documents were chosen and carefully edited to be accessible, interesting, and often surprising to survey course students. Third, I have sought sources that lend themselves to analysis in classroom discussion and writing assignments, sources that vividly portray controversies that marked a particular historical moment and that offer multiple avenues of interpretation.

FEATURES OF THE DOCUMENTS SELECTION

A wide variety. The documents assembled here provide students a generous cross-section of the diverse experiences that comprise the American past. The reflections of women and men, politicians and thieves, generals and privates, reformers and reprobates can be found here, along with those of the nation's countless ethnic and religious minorities. Classic sources such as John Winthrop's *Arbella* sermon, George Kennan's "Long Telegram," and Ronald Reagan's "Evil Empire" speech disclose the perspectives of influential leaders. Bottom-up views of common people are revealed by such documents as seventeenth-century witchcraft depositions, testimony by slaves accused of conspiring to rebel, and letters from working people to New Dealers. Diaries and court cases convey the immediacy of history as lived experience. Reminiscences and oral histories illuminate the past with memories of participants. Speeches, manifestos, congressional testimony, and White House tape recordings spotlight the ends and means of political power. Essays, addresses, poems, and passages from books offer the considered opinions of cultural leaders, whether captains of industry, novelists, poets or social critics.

Allows instructors flexibility in the classroom. The selections in *Reading the American Past* allow instructors to choose documents that best serve their teaching needs. Teachers might, for example, ask students to read documents in preparation for lectures, then refer to the assigned selections as they explain, say, Puritanism or the Civil War. An instructor might devote a class to explicating a single source, such as a Mexican account of Spanish Conquest (see Volume I, Chapter 2, page 17) or Reinhold Niebuhr's probing reflections about the meaning of Christianity in Detroit of the 1920s (see Volume II, Chapter 23, page 134). The documents are ideally suited for provoking discussions in section meetings. Students can be asked to adopt and defend the viewpoint of a given source, to attack it from the perspective of an historical contemporary, to dissect its assumptions and evasions, or to compare and contrast it with other sources. Selections might also be used for brief writing assignments, longer papers, or examinations. The documents open these and many other possibilities for inspiring students to investigate the American past.

EDITORIAL FEATURES

Consistently user-friendly editorial features will help students read and interpret the sources. These features have been kept brief, providing just enough information to allow students to explore the sources and make their own discoveries. By minimizing editorial interventions, I hope to encourage students to focus on the documents and to experience the excitement of being astonished and perplexed by what they read.

An Introduction for Students. A short introduction at the outset explains the significance of documents for understanding history and suggests key questions that students should ask themselves in order to decipher any primary source.

Useful chapter apparatus. A brief paragraph begins each chapter, setting the documents in the larger historical context detailed in the corresponding chapter of the textbook. A headnote precedes every document, identifying the source, explaining when it was produced, by whom, and why it presents a revealing point of view. Rather than cluttering documents with numerous explanatory notes, I have assumed that students will — and should — refer to a textbook for basic information about the people and events that appear in the sources.

Questions that help students get the most out of the sources. To guide students toward crucial passages and central ideas, a few questions follow each document. They are intended to help students identify fundamental points, consider what a document says, and think about its larger historical significance. Comparative questions at the end of each chapter direct students toward important similarities and differences among the ideas, observations, and viewpoints expressed in the chapter's documents.

To see more clearly along the many angles of historical vision offered by the documents, students rely on the guidance, insight, and wisdom of their teachers. Ideally, *Reading the American Past* will give instructors numerous opportunities to entice students to become active collaborators in the study of American history. Perhaps these documents will help persuade students that the American past is neither frozen in time nor entombed in books, but instead shapes their present and prefigures their future. Perhaps they will come to see that they do not simply read American history; they live it.

ACKNOWLEDGMENTS

I am indebted to my fellow coauthors of *The American Promise* — James L. Roark, Patricia Cline Cohen, Sarah Stage, Alan Lawson, and Susan M. Hartmann — for invaluable suggestions of pertinent and provocative documents. Motivated by their idea and by the enthusiasm of Chuck Christensen and Joan Feinberg for a documents collection that aspired to the high standards readers have come to expect from Bedford, I combed the stacks of the Milton S. Eisenhower Library of The Johns Hopkins University where I soon located many more excellent documents than could possibly be included here. After repeated consultation, particularly with Jim Roark, I winnowed the list, regretting all the great ones left in the chaff, but prizing the keepers still more. The beneficiary of the advice and support of my colleagues, I am nonetheless solely responsible for the final selection of the documents and the edited passages in this anthology.

Many others contributed their energy and creativity to bring this project to completion. Sarah Elizabeth Johnson compiled a small mountain of copies from unwieldy volumes to allow thorough checking and proofreading. Louise Townsend pored over the manuscript with the sympathies of an historian and the instincts of an experienced editor. At Bedford, Patty Bergin, supervised by Assistant Managing Editor John Amburg, shepherded the book throughout the production process; Barbara Sutton expertly copyedited the manuscript, attentive to the documents' numerous idiosyncrasies of spelling and phrasing; and DeNee Reiton Skipper designed the volumes, transforming typescript into book pages. Arrangements that made all this possible were put in place by Gerry McCauley. And Anne Johnson lovingly tolerated another of my disappearances into the company of books and bytes.

INTRODUCTION
FOR STUDENTS

Documents allow us to peer into the past and learn what happened and what did not happen, crucial beginning points for understanding how and why the present came to be. It would be convenient if we did not need documents, if we could depend instead upon our memory to tell us what happened. Unfortunately, memory is far from perfect, as we are reminded every time we misplace our keys. Not only do we forget things that did happen, but we also remember things that never occurred, such as putting those keys right there on the shelf. Mark Twain once quipped, "When I was younger I could remember anything, whether it happened or not; but my faculties are decaying now, and soon I shall be so [old] I cannot remember any but the things that never happened."

Twain's witticism points to another important property of memory: it changes over time. Every good trial lawyer knows that memory is fragile, volatile, and subject to manipulation by our desires, intentions, and fears. Spin artists routinely perform not just on witness stands and at press conferences but whenever memory is reshaped to serve the needs of the present. Compounding the unreliability of memory are two stubborn realities: most of the people who might remember something about what happened are dead, their memories erased forever; and no person, no single memory, ever knew all of what there is to know about what happened.

These flaws of memory might cause us to shrug wearily and conclude that it is impossible to determine what happened. But that conclusion would be wrong. Documents make it possible to learn a great deal —although not every last thing—about what really happened. Since they are created by humans, documents are subject to all the frailties of memory, with one vital exception. Documents do not change. Unlike memory, documents freeze words at a moment in time. Ideas, perceptions, emotions, and assumptions expressed in a document allow us to learn now about what happened then. In effect, documents are a kind of bridge from the present to the past. They allow us to cross over and to discover how we got from there to here.

Today you can stand where the audience stood in 1863 to listen to Abraham Lincoln's famous speech at the dedication of the cemetery for the Union soldiers killed at the battle of Gettysburg. Of course you can't hear Lincoln's voice, but you can read his words because the Gettysburg Address exists as an historical document; you can literally read this portion of the American past. The Address transports the reader back to that crisp November day more than a century ago, the outcome of the war very much in doubt, when the president and commander in chief of more than a million men in blue uniforms explained in a few words his view of the meaning of the war for the nation and the world. Lincoln spoke of the immense sacrifice made by the soldiers at Gettysburg and evoked the nation's highest ideals in words that continue to inspire Americans long after the Civil War was over: "Four score and seven years ago our fathers brought forth on this continent, a new nation, conceived in Liberty, and dedicated to the proposition that all men are created equal. . . . [W]e here highly resolve that these dead shall not have died in vain—that this nation, under God, shall have a new birth of freedom—and that government of the people, by the people, for the people, shall not perish from the earth." Because the Gettysburg Address survives in Lincoln's handwriting, we know not only what Lincoln said, but also what he did not say: for instance, that the thousands of dead soldiers at Gettysburg proved that the price of war was too high and it was time to negotiate a peace settlement. The Address captured Lincoln's thoughts at that moment and preserved them, much like an historical snapshot. All documents have this property of stopping time, of indelibly recording the views of somebody in the past.

Documents record far more than the ideas of presidents. They disclose, for instance, Mexicans' views of conquering Spaniards in the sixteenth century, accusations New Englanders made against witches in the seventeenth century, the testimony of slaves on trial for conspiring to rebel against their masters in the nineteenth century, the reminiscences of Vietnamese immigrants in the twentieth century, and much, much more. These views and many others are recorded by the documents in this collection. They permit you to read the American past from the diversity of perspectives that contributed to the making of America: women and men, workers and bosses, newcomers and natives, slaves and masters, voters and politicians, moderates and radicals, activists and reactionaries, westerners and easterners, northerners and southerners, farmers and urbanites, the famous and the forgotten. These people created historical documents when they stole a spare moment to write a letter or record thoughts in a diary, when they talked to a scribbling friend or stranger, when they appeared in court or made a will, and when they delivered a sermon, gave a speech, or penned a manifesto. Examples of all these kinds of documents are included in *Reading the American Past*. Together, they make it possible for you to learn a great deal about what really happened.

From the almost limitless historical record I chose documents that clearly and vividly express an important perspective about a major event or a widespread point of view during a certain historical era. I selected documents that are not only revealing but also often surprising, controversial, or troubling. My goal is to bring you face to face with the past through the eyes of the people who lived it.

Reading the American Past is designed specifically to accompany *The American Promise: A History of the United States*. Each chapter in this volume parallels a chapter in *The American Promise*. The documents provide eyewitness accounts that broaden and deepen the textbook narrative. Chapter 16, for example, supplements the textbook discussion of Reconstruction with selections from the 1865 Mississippi Black Code, resolutions of a black convention in Alabama in 1867, testimony of an African American Republican before the congressional committee investigating the Ku Klux Klan in 1871, and the report of a prominent white Republican about conditions in the South in 1875. As a rule, each chapter contains four documents; occasionally there are more shorter ones or fewer longer ones. To help you read and understand the documents, a brief paragraph at the beginning of each chapter sketches the larger historical context explained in more detail in your textbook; a headnote precedes each document identifying its source, explaining when it was produced, by whom, and why it is revealing; and questions follow each selection, pointing you toward key passages and fundamental ideas and asking you to consider both what a document says and what it means.

Making the most of these documents requires reading with care and imagination. Historians are interested in both what a document says and what it suggests about the historical reality that is only partly disclosed by the document itself. A document might be likened to a window through which we may glimpse features of the past. A document challenges us to read and understand the words on the page as a way to look through the window and learn about the larger historical context of the time.

Lincoln's Gettysburg Address, for example, hints that he believed many loyal Americans wondered whether the war was worth the effort, whether all those soldiers, as he said, "have died in vain." Lincoln's words do not explicitly say that many people thought the human tragedy of the war was too great, but that seems to be one of their meanings. His Address attempted to answer such doubts by proclaiming the larger meaning of the war and the soldiers' deaths. Behind his public statement of the noble ideals of the Union war effort lay his private perception that many Americans had come to doubt whether the war had any meaning beyond the maiming or death of their loved ones.

To see such unstated historical reality in and through a document, readers must remain alert to exactly what the document says. The first step is to learn something about the era in which the document was written by reading *The American Promise* or another textbook of American history.

The next step is to read the document, keeping in mind three important questions: Who wrote the document? When was it written? Who was the intended audience? To help answer these questions, you will find useful information in the brief headnote and the questions that accompany each document, as well as in the concluding comparative questions that draw attention to similarities and differences among the documents in the chapter. But these editorial features are merely beginning points for your investigation of the documents. You should always take the next step by asking who wrote a document, when, and for what audience.

Obviously, a document expresses the viewpoint of its author. Different people had different views about the same event. At Gettysburg, for example, the Confederacy suffered a painful defeat that weakened their ability to maintain their independence and to defend slavery. If Jefferson Davis, the President of the Confederacy, had delivered a Gettysburg Address, it would have been very different from Lincoln's. Documents also often convey their authors' opinions of the viewpoints of other people, including those who agree with them and those who don't. You should always ask, then: What does a document say about the viewpoint of the author? What does it say about the author's opinion about the views of other people? Does the document suggest the author's point of view was confined to a few people, shared by a substantial minority, or embraced by a great many Americans?

A document conveys valuable information about the time when it was written as well as about the author's point of view. Frequently, a person's point of view changes, making it critical to know exactly when a document was written in order to understand its meaning. When Lincoln delivered the Gettysburg Address, the outcome of the Civil War remained in doubt; seventeen months later, in April 1865, he was certain of northern victory. The Address expresses the urgency and uncertainty of the wartime crisis of 1863 rather than the relief and confidence of 1865. As you read every document, you should ask: How does the document reflect the time when it was written? What does it say about the events underway at the time? What does it suggest about how that particular time was perceived by the author and by other people?

In addition to considering who wrote a document and when, one must think about the intended audience. A politician may say one thing in a campaign speech and something quite different in a private letter to a friend. An immigrant might send a rosy account of life in America to family members in the Old Country, one at odds with many features of life in the New World. The intended audience shapes the message an author seeks to send. The author's expectations of what the audience wants to hear contribute to what a document says, how it is said, and what is left unsaid. Lincoln knew that his audience at Gettysburg included thousands of family members mourning the death of loved ones who "gave the last full measure of devotion" on the battlefield; he hoped his remarks would soothe the heartache of the survivors by ennobling the Union and those who died in its defense. To decipher any document, you should always ask: Who is the intended audience? How did the audience shape what the author says? Did consideration of the audience lead the author to emphasize some things and downplay or ignore others? How would the intended audience be likely to read the document? How would people who were not among the intended audience be likely to read it?

The meanings of words, like the viewpoints of individuals, also reflect their historical moment. For the most part, the documents in this collection were written in English; several have been translated into English from Spanish, Latin, German, Swedish, or one of several Native American languages. But even documents originally written in English require you to translate the meaning of English words at the time the document was written into the meaning of English words today. Readers must guard against imputing today's meanings to yesterday's words. When Lincoln said "this nation" in the Gettysburg Address, he referred to the United States in 1863, a vastly different nation from the one founded four score and seven years earlier and from the one that developed a century later. The word is the same but the meaning varies greatly.

Although the meaning of many words remains relatively constant, if you are on the lookout for key words whose meanings have changed, you will discover otherwise hidden insights in the documents. You can benefit simply from exercising your historical imagination about the changing meaning of words. To Lincoln, the phrase "all men are created equal" did not have the same meaning that it did for women's rights leaders at the time, or for slaves, or slaveowners. You should always pay attention to the words used in a document and ask a final set of questions: How do the words in the document reflect the author, the time, and the intended audience? Would the same words have different meanings to other people at that time? Does the author's choice of words reveal covert assumptions and blindspots along with an overt message?

Historical documents provide readers not only with indelible markers of historical changes that have occurred. They also illuminate the role that human beings played in making those changes. Documents instruct us about the achievements and limitations of the past as they inspire and caution us for the future. Documents also instill in us a strong sense of historical humility. Americans in the past were no less good and no more evil, no less right and no more wrong, than we are today. Their ideas, their experiences, and their times were different from ours in many respects. But they made the nation we inhabit. Ideally, the documents in *Reading the American Past* will give you an appreciation of what it took, and will continue to take, to make American history happen.

CONTENTS

CHAPTER 16

RECONSTRUCTION
1863–1877

During the turbulent years of Reconstruction, the character of freedom for former slaves was the subject of intense debate within the South and across the nation. Most southern whites sought the most limited form of freedom for African Americans, as the black codes passed by several states suggested. Most former slaves sought to exercise their liberty to the full, as black conventions repeatedly declared. White vigilantes resorted to murder, lynching, and other acts of brutality to force blacks to limit their horizons. In the end, most northern Republicans concluded that, once former slaves had the vote, the South—not the North or the federal government—should determine how best to define freedom and preserve order.

DOCUMENT 1

Black Codes Enacted in the South

After the Civil War, the legal status of former slaves was defined by state legislatures throughout the South. In the months following General Lee's surrender at Appomattox, white legislators devised laws to regulate and control former slaves. Known as black codes, these laws defined freedom for African Americans in terms that resembled slavery in many respects, as revealed in the following provisions of the Mississippi black code, enacted in November 1865.

Mississippi Black Code, November 1865

AN ACT to confer Civil Rights on Freedmen, and for other purposes.

Be it enacted by the Legislature of the State of Mississippi. That all freedmen, free negroes and mulattoes may sue and be sued, . . . in all the courts of law and equity of this State, and may acquire personal property . . .

Laws of Mississippi (1865).

1

by descent or purchase, and may dispose of the same, in the same manner
. . . that white persons may: Provided that the provisions of this section
shall not be so construed as to allow any freedman, free negro or mulatto,
to rent or lease any lands or tenements, except in incorporated towns or
cities in which places the corporate authorities shall control the same. . . .

– That all freedmen, free negroes and mulattoes may intermarry with
each other. . . . That all freedmen, free negroes and mulattoes, who do
now and have heretofore lived and cohabited together as husband and
wife shall be taken and held in law as legally married, and the issue shall
be taken and held as legitimate for all purposes. That it shall not be lawful for any freedman, free negro or mulatto to inter-marry with any white
person; nor for any white person to intermarry with any freedman, free
negro or mulatto; and any person who shall so intermarry shall be
deemed guilty of felony, and on conviction thereof, shall be confined in
the State penitentiary for life. . . .

That . . . freedmen, free negroes and mulattoes are now by law competent witnesses . . . in civil cases . . . and they shall also be competent witnesses in all criminal prosecutions where the crime charged is alleged to
have been committed by a white person upon or against the person or
property of a freedman, free negro or mulatto. . . .

That every freedman, free negro and mulatto, shall, on the second
Monday of January, one thousand eight hundred and sixty-six, and annually thereafter, have a lawful home or employment, and shall have
written evidence thereof; as follows, to wit: if living in any incorporated
city, town or village, a license from the mayor thereof; and if living outside of any incorporated city, town or village, from the member of the
board of police of his beat, authorizing him or her to do irregular and job
work, or a written contract . . . which licenses may be revoked for cause,
at any time, by the authority granting the same. . . .

That all contracts for labor made with freedmen, free negroes and
mulattoes, for a longer period than one month shall be in writing and in
duplicate, attested and read to said freedman, free negro or mulatto, by a
beat, city or county officer, or two disinterested white persons of the county
in which the labor is to be performed . . . and if the laborer shall quit the service of the employer, before expiration of his term of service, without good
cause, he shall forfeit his wages for that year, up to the time of quitting. . . .

That every civil officer shall, and every person may arrest and carry
back to his or her legal employer any freedman, free negro or mulatto,
who shall have quit the service of his or her employer before the expiration of his or her term of service without good cause, and said officer and
person, shall be entitled to receive for arresting and carrying back every
deserting employee aforesaid, the sum of five dollars, and ten cents per
mile from the place of arrest to the place of delivery, [to] be paid by the
employer. . . .That upon affidavit made by the employer of any freedman,
free negro or mulatto, or other credible person, before any justice of the
peace or member of the board of police, that any freedman, free negro or

mulatto, legally employed by said employer, has illegally deserted said employment, such justice of the peace or member of the board of police, shall issue his warrant or warrants . . . directed to any sheriff, constable or special deputy, commanding him to arrest said deserter and return him or her to said employer . . . and it shall be lawful for any officer to whom such warrant shall be directed, to execute said warrant in any county of this State . . . and the said employer shall pay the cost of said warrants and arrest and return, which shall be set off for so much against the wages of said deserter. . . .

That if any person shall . . . attempt to persuade, entice or cause any freedman, free negro or mulatto, to desert from the legal employment of any person, before the expiration of his or her term of service, or shall knowingly employ any such deserting freedman, free negro or mulatto, or shall knowingly give or sell to [him] any food, rayment or other thing, he or she shall be guilty of a misdemeanor, and upon conviction, shall be fined not less than twenty-five dollars and not more than two hundred dollars and the costs. . . .

An [A]ct to regulate the relation of Master and Apprentice, as related to Freedmen, Free Negroes, and Mulattoes.

Be it enacted by the Legislature of the State of Mississippi:

That it shall be the duty of all sheriffs, justices of the peace, and other civil officers of the several counties in this State, to report to the probate courts of their respective counties, semi-annually, at the January and July terms of said courts, all freedmen, free negroes and mulattoes, under the age of eighteen, within their respective counties, beats or districts, who are orphans, or whose parent or parents have not the means, or who refuse to provide for and support said minors, and thereupon it shall be the duty of said probate court, to order the clerk of said court to apprentice said minors to some competent and suitable person, on such terms as the court may direct. . . . Provided, that the former owner of said minors shall have the preference. . . .

That . . . the said court shall require the said master or mistress to execute bond and security, payable to the State of Mississippi, conditioned that he or she shall furnish said minor with sufficient food and clothing, to treat said minor humanely, furnish medical attention in case of sickness; [and to] teach or cause to be taught him or her to read and write, if under fifteen years old. . . . Provided, that said apprentice shall be bound by indenture, in case of males until they are twenty-one years old, and in case of females until they are eighteen years old. . . .

That in the management and control of said apprentices, said master or mistress shall have power to inflict such moderate corporeal chastisement as a father or guardian is allowed to inflict on his or her child or ward at common law. . . .

That if any apprentice shall leave the employment of his or her master or mistress, without his or her consent, said master or mistress may pursue and recapture said apprentice, and bring him or her before any justice of the peace of the county, whose duty it shall be to remand said apprentice to the service of his or her master or mistress; and in the event of a refusal on the part of said apprentice so to return, then said justice shall commit said apprentice to the jail of said county. . . .

That if any person entice away any apprentice from his or her master or mistress, or shall knowingly employ an apprentice, or furnish him or her food or clothing, without the written consent of his or her master or mistress, or shall sell or give said apprentice ardent spirits, without such consent, said person so offending shall be deemed guilty of a high misdemeanor, and shall, on conviction thereof before the county court, be punished as provided for the punishment of persons enticing from their employer hired freedmen, free Negroes or mulattoes. . . .

AN ACT to amend the Vagrant Laws of the State.

Be it further enacted,

That all freedmen, free negroes and mulattoes in this State, over the age of eighteen years, found on the second Monday in January, 1866, or thereafter, with no lawful employment or business, or found unlawfully assembling themselves together either in the day or night time, and all white persons so assembling with [them] on terms of equality, or living in adultery or fornication with a freedwoman, free negro, or mulatto, shall be deemed vagrants, and on conviction thereof, shall be fined in the sum of not exceeding, in the case of a freedman, free negro or mulatto, fifty dollars, and a white man two hundred dollars, and imprisoned at the discretion of the court, the free negro not exceeding ten days, and the white man not exceeding six months. . . .

That . . . in case any freedman, free negro or mulatto, shall fail for five days after the imposition of any fine or forfeiture upon him or her for violation of any of the provisions of this act, to pay the same, that it shall be, and is hereby made the duty of the sheriff of the proper county to hire out said freedman, free negro or mulatto, to any person who will, for the shortest period of service, pay said fine or forfeiture and all costs: Provided, a preference shall be given to the employer, if there be one, in which case the employer shall be entitled to deduct and retain the amount so paid from the wages of such freedman, free negro or mulatto, then due or to become due. . . .

AN ACT to punish certain offences. . . .

Be it enacted by the Legislature of the State of Mississippi:

That no freedman, free negro or mulatto . . . shall keep or carry firearms of any kind, or any ammunition, dirk or bowie knife, and on conviction thereof, in the county court, shall be punished by fine, not exceeding ten dollars, and pay the costs of such proceedings, and all such arms or ammunition shall be forfeited to the informer, and it shall be the duty of every civil and military officer to arrest any freedman, free negro or mulatto found with any such arms or ammunition, and cause him or her to be committed for trial in default of bail. . . . *(rude language)*

— That any freedman, free negro or mulatto, committing riots, routs, affrays, trespasses, malicious mischief, cruel treatment of animals, seditious speeches, insulting gestures, language or acts, or assaults on any person, disturbances of the peace, exercising the function of a minister of the Gospel, without a license from some regularly organized church, vending spirituous or intoxicating liquors, or committing any other misdemeanor . . . shall, upon conviction thereof, in the county court, be fined, not less than ten dollars, and not more than one hundred dollars, and may be imprisoned, at the discretion of the court, not exceeding thirty days. . . .

That if any white person shall sell, lend or give to any freedman, free negro or mulatto, any firearms, dirk or bowie-knife, or ammunition, or any spirituous or intoxicating liquors, such person or persons so offending, upon conviction thereof, in the county court of his or her county, shall be fined, not exceeding fifty dollars, and may be imprisoned, at the discretion of the court, not exceeding thirty days. . . .

That all the penal and criminal laws now in force in this State, defining offences and prescribing the mode of punishment for crimes and misdemeanors committed by slaves, free negroes or mulattoes, be and the same are hereby re-enacted, and declared to be in full force and effect, against freedmen, free negroes and mulattoes, except so far as the mode and manner of trial and punishment have been changed or altered by law. . . .

That if any freedman, free negro or mulatto, convicted of any of the misdemeanors provided against in this act, shall fail or refuse, for the space of five days after conviction, to pay the fine and costs imposed, such person shall be hired out by the sheriff or other officer, at public outcry, to any white person who will pay said fine and all costs, and take such convict for the shortest time.

QUESTIONS

What civil rights did these laws confer on freed black men and women? • How did these laws limit the freedom of African Americans in Mississippi? • Were these laws different from the laws governing slaves? • Did former masters have any claims on their former slaves? • Did these laws limit the freedom of white Mississippians?

DOCUMENT 2

A Black Convention in Alabama

Beginning in 1867, state governments throughout the old Confederacy were re-organized under the auspices of Reconstruction legislation passed by Congress, which was controlled by Republicans. Congressional Reconstruction empowered former slaves by granting them the right to vote and permitting their views to be expressed through such traditional political processes as parties, conventions, campaigns, and elections. Across the South, African Americans assembled in conventions and hammered out resolutions that defined their own view of freedom, as revealed in the following address drawn up at a convention in Mobile, Alabama, and published in 1867.

Address of the Colored Convention to the People of Alabama, 1867

As there seems to be considerable difference of opinion concerning the "legal rights of the colored man," it will not be amiss to say that we claim exactly *the same rights, privileges and immunities as are enjoyed by white men*—we ask nothing more and will be content with nothing less. *All legal* distinctions between the races are now abolished. The word white is stricken from our laws, and every privilege which white men were formerly permitted to enjoy, merely because they were white men, now that word is stricken out, we are entitled to on the ground that we are men. *Color can no longer be pleaded for the purpose of curtailing privileges, and every public right, privilege and immunity is enjoyable by every individual member of the public.* This is the touchstone that determines all these points. So long as a park or a street is a public park or street the entire public has the right to use it; so long as a car or a steamboat is a public conveyance, it must carry all who come to it, and serve all alike who pay alike. The law no longer knows white nor black, but simply men, and consequently we are entitled to ride in public conveyances, hold office, sit on juries and do everything else which we have in the past been prevented from doing solely on the ground of our color. . . .

We have said that we intend to claim all our rights, and we submit to our white friends that it is the height of folly on their part to withhold them any longer. One-half of the voters in Alabama are black men, and in a few months there is to be an entire reorganization of the State government. The new officers — legislative, executive and judicial — will owe

---

"Address of the Colored Convention to the People of Alabama," Montgomery *Daily State Sentinel*, May 21, 1867; reprinted in *Reconstruction: The Battle for Democracy 1865–1876,* by James S. Allen (Ann Arbor: Books on Demand, 1963), 236–41.

their election largely, if not mainly to the colored people, and every one must see clearly that the voters will then be certain to require and the officers to compel a cessation of all illegal discriminations. The question which every man now illegally discriminating against us has to decide is whether it is politic to insist upon gratifying prejudices . . . with the certainty by so doing, of incurring the lasting displeasure of one-half of the voting population of the State. We can stand it if they can, but we assure them that they are being watched closely, and that their conduct will be remembered when we have power.

There are some good people who are always preaching patience and procrastination. They would have us wait a few months, years, or generations, until the whites voluntarily give us our rights, but we do not intend to wait one day longer than we are absolutely compelled to. Look at our demands, and then at theirs. We ask of them simply that they surrender unreasonable and unreasoning prejudice; . . . that they consent to allow others as well as themselves to prosper and be happy. But they would have us pay for what we do not get; tramp through the broiling sun or pelting rain, or stand upon a platform, while empty seats mockingly invite us to rest our wearied limbs; our sick must suffer or submit to indignity; we must put up with inconvenience of every kind; and the virtuous aspirations of our children must be continually checked by the knowledge that no matter how upright their conduct, they will be looked on as less worthy of respect than the lowest wretch on earth who wears a white skin. We ask you—only while in public, however—to surrender your prejudices,—nothing but prejudices; and you ask us to sacrifice our personal comfort, health, pecuniary interests, self-respect, and the future prospects of our children. The men who make such requests must suppose us devoid of spirit and of brains, but find themselves mistaken. Solemnly and distinctly, we again say to you, men of Alabama, that we will not submit voluntarily to such infamous discrimination, and if you will insist upon tramping on the rights and outraging the feelings of those who are so soon to pass judgment upon you, then upon your own heads will rest the responsibility for the effect of your course.

All over the state of Alabama—all over the South indeed—the colored people have with singular unanimity, arrayed themselves under the Republican banner, upon the Republican platform, and it is confidently predicted that nine-tenths of them will vote the Republican ticket. Do you ask, why is this? We answer, because:

1. The Republican Party opposed and prohibited the extension of slavery.
2. It repealed the fugitive slave law.
3. It abolished slavery in the District of Columbia.
4. It abolished slavery in the rebellious states.
5. It abolished slavery throughout the rest of the Union.

6. It put down rebellion against the Union.
7. It passed the Freedmen's Bureau Bill and the Civil Rights Bill.
8. It enfranchised the colored people of the District of Columbia.
9. It enfranchised the colored people of the nine territories.
10. It enfranchised the colored people of the ten rebel states.
11. It provided for the formation of new constitutions and state governments in those ten states.
12. It passed new homestead laws, enabling the poor to obtain land.

In short, it has gone on, step by step, doing first one thing for us and then another, and it now proposes to enfranchise our people all over the Union. It is the only party which has ever attempted to extend our privileges, and as it has in the past always been trying to do this, it is but natural that we should trust it for the future.

While this has been the course of the Republican Party, the opposition has unitedly opposed every one of these measures, and it also now opposes the enfranchisement of our people in the North. Everywhere it has been against us in the past, and the great majority of its voters hate us as cordially now as ever before. It is sometimes alleged that the Republicans of the North have not been actuated by love for us in what they have done, and therefore that we should not join them; we answer that even if that were true they certainly never professed to hate us and the opposition party has always been denouncing the "d——n nigger and abolitionist" with equal fervor. When we had no votes to give, the opposition placed us and the Republicans in the same boat, and now we reckon we'll stay in it. It may be and probably is true that some men acting with the Republican Party have cared nothing for the principles of that party; but it is also certainly true that ninety-nine-hundredths of all those who were conscientiously in favor of our rights were and are in the Republican Party, and that the great mass of those who hated, slandered and abused us were and are in the opposition party.

The memories of the opposition must be short indeed, to have forgotten their language of the past twenty years but we have *not* forgotten it.

But, say some of the members of the opposition party, "We intend to turn over a new leaf, and will hereafter give you all your rights." Perhaps they would, but we prefer not to put the new wine of political equality into the old bottles of "sectional animosity" and "caste feeling." We are somewhat fearful that those who have always opposed the extensions of rights are not sincere in their professions. . . .

Another fact should be borne in mind. While a few conservatives are making guarded promises to us the masses of that party are cursing us, and doing all they can to "make the d——d niggers stay in their place." If we were, therefore, to join that party, it would be simply as servants, and not as equals. Some leaders, who needed our votes might treat us decently, but the great majority would expect us to stay at home until election day, and then vote as our employers dictated. This we respectfully decline doing. It seems to us safest to have as little as possible to do with those members of the community who delight to abuse us, and they are nearly, if not quite, all to be found in the ranks of the opposition party. . . .

It cannot be disguised, however, that many men calling themselves conservatives are disposed to use unfair means to carry their points. The press . . . contain numerous threats that those colored people who do not vote as their employers command, will be discharged; that the property-holders will combine, import white laborers, and discharge their colored hands, etc. Numerous instances have come to our knowledge of persons who have already been discharged because they attended Republican meetings, and great numbers more have been threatened. "Vote as we command, or starve," is the argument these men propose to make [use] of, and with it they expect to succeed.

In this expectation they will be mistaken, and we warn them before it is prosecuted any further, that their game is a dangerous one for them-selves. The property which they hold was nearly all earned by the sweat of our brows — not theirs. It has been forfeited to the Government by the treason of its owners, and is liable to be confiscated whenever the Repub-lican Party demands it. The great majority of that party is now opposed to confiscation, but if the owners of property use the power which it gives them to make political slaves of the poor, a cry will go up to Congress which will make the party a unit for confiscation.

Conservatives of Alabama, do you propose to rush upon certain de-struction? Are you mad, that you threaten to pursue a policy which could only result in causing thousands of men to cry out to their leaders, "Our wives and little ones are starving because we stood by you; because we would not be slaves!" When the nation abolished slavery, you used your local governments to neutralize and defeat its action, and the nation an-swered by abolishing your governments and enfranchising us. If you now use your property to neutralize or defeat this, its last act, it will answer by taking away the property you are only allowed to retain through its unparalleled mercy and which you have proved yourselves so unworthy of retaining. . . .

So complete, indeed, will be our victory, that our opponents will be-come disheartened unless they can divide us. This is the great danger which we have to guard against. . . . In nominations for office we expect that there will be no discriminations on account of color by either wing, but that the most capable and honest men will always be put in nomina-tion. We understand full well that our people are too deficient in educa-tion to be generally qualified to fill the higher offices, but when qualified men are found, they must not be rejected for being black.

This lack of education, which is the consequence of our long servitude, and which so diminishes our powers for good, should not be allowed to characterize our children when they come upon the stage of action, and we therefore earnestly call upon every member of the Republican Party to demand the establishment of a thorough system of common schools throughout the State. It will benefit every citizen of the State, and, indeed, of the Union, for the well-being of each enures to the advantage of all. In a Republic, education is especially necessary, as the ignorant are always liable to be led astray by the arts of the demagogue.

With education secured to all; with the old and helpless properly cared for; with justice everywhere impartially administered, Alabama will commence a career of which she will have just cause to be proud. We shall all be prosperous and happy. The sad memories of the past will be forgotten amid the joys of the present and the prospect of the future.

QUESTIONS

How did the Alabama Colored Convention define the "legal rights of the colored man"? • What did they oppose? • Why did they favor the Republican party? • What did they think about the Democratic party? • What did they expect would happen to black voters? • What did their references to "confiscation" mean? • Why did they favor education?

DOCUMENT 3

Klan Violence against Blacks

White vigilantes often terrorized African Americans after emancipation. The violent campaign of terror intensified with congressional Reconstruction and the mobilization of black voters in the Republican party. The violence attracted the attention of Congress, which held committee hearings throughout the South in 1871 to hear testimony about the Ku Klux Klan. The following testimony of Elias Hill—a black preacher and teacher who lived in York County, South Carolina—illustrates the tactics and purposes of white vigilantes.

Elias Hill

Testimony before Congressional Committee Investigating the Ku Klux Klan, 1871

[The committee included a brief description of Hill.] Elias Hill is a remarkable character. He is crippled in both legs and arms, which are shriveled by rheumatism; he cannot walk, cannot help himself, has to be fed and cared for personally by others; was in early life a slave, whose freedom was purchased, his father buying his mother and getting Elias along with her, as a burden of which his master was glad to be rid. Stricken at seven years old with disease, he never was afterward able to

---

U.S. Congress, *Report of the Joint Select Committee to Inquire into the Condition of Affairs in the Late Insurrectionary States* (Washington, D.C., 1872), I, 44–46.

walk, and he presents the appearance of a dwarf with the limbs of a child, the body of a man, and a finely developed intellectual head. He learned his letters and to read by calling the school children into the cabin as they passed, and also learned to write. He became a Baptist preacher, and after the war engaged in teaching colored children, and conducted the business correspondence of many of his colored neighbors. He is a man of blameless character, of unusual intelligence, speaks good English, and we put the story of his wrongs in his own language:

On the night of the 5th of last May, after I had heard a great deal of what they had done in that neighborhood, they came. It was between 12 and 1 o'clock at night when I was awakened and heard the dogs barking, and something walking, very much like horses. As I had often laid awake listening for such persons, for they had been all through the neighborhood, and disturbed all men and many women, I supposed that it was them. They came in a very rapid manner, and I could hardly tell whether it was the sound of horses or men. At last they came to my brother's door, which is in the same yard, and broke open the door and attacked his wife, and I heard her screaming and mourning. I could not understand what they said, for they were talking in an outlandish and unnatural tone, which I had heard they generally used at a negro's house. I heard them knocking around in her house. I was lying in my little cabin in the yard. At last I heard them have her in the yard. She was crying and the Ku-Klux were whipping her to make her tell where I lived. I heard her say, "Yon is his house." She has told me since that they first asked who had taken me out of her house. They said, "Where's Elias?" She said, "He doesn't stay here; yon is his house." They were then in the yard, and I had heard them strike her five or six licks when I heard her say this. Some one then hit my door. It flew open. One ran in the house, and stopping about the middle of the house, which is a small cabin, he turned around, as it seemed to me as I lay there awake, and said, "Who's here?" Then I knew they would take me, and I answered, "I am here." He shouted for joy, as it seemed, "Here he is! Here he is! We have found him!" and he threw the bedclothes off of me and caught me by one arm, while another man took me by the other and they carried me into the yard between the houses, my brother's and mine, and put me on the ground beside a boy. The first thing they asked me was, "Who did that burning? Who burned our houses?" — gin-houses, dwelling houses and such. Some had been burned in the neighborhood. I told them it was not me; I could not burn houses; it was unreasonable to ask me. Then they hit me with their fists, and said I did it, I ordered it. They went on asking me didn't I tell the black men to ravish all the white women. No, I answered them, They struck me again with their fists on my breast, and then they went on, "When did you hold a night-meeting of the Union League[1], and who were

---

[1]**Union League:** Union Leagues were Republican organizations that helped mobilize the African American vote.

the officers? Who was the president?" I told them I had been the president, but that there had been no Union League meeting held at that place where they were formerly held since away in the fall. This was the 5th of May. They said that Jim Raney, that was hung, had been at my house since the time I had said the League was last held, and that he had made a speech. I told them that he had not, because I did not know the man. I said, "Upon honor." They said I had no honor, and hit me again. They went on asking me hadn't I been writing to Mr. A. S. Wallace, in Congress, to get letters from him. I told them I had. They asked what I had been writing about? I told them, "Only tidings." They said, with an oath, "I know the tidings were d——d good, and you were writing something about the Ku-Klux, and haven't you been preaching and praying about the Ku-Klux?" One asked, "Haven't you been preaching political sermons?" Generally, one asked me all the questions, but the rest were squatting over me—some six men I counted as I lay there, Said one, "Didn't you preach against the Ku-Klux," and wasn't that what Mr. Wallace was writing to me about? "Not at all," I said. "Let me see the letter,"said he; "what was it about?" I said it was on the times. They wanted the letter. I told them if they would take me back into the house, and lay me in the bed, which was close adjoining my books and papers, I would try and get it. They said I would never go back to that bed, for they were going to kill me. "Never expect to go back; tell us where the letters are." I told them they were on the shelf somewhere, and I hoped they would not kill me. Two of them went into the house. . . . They staid in there a good while hunting about and then came out and asked me for a lamp. I told them there was a lamp somewhere. They said "Where?" I was so confused I said I could not tell exactly. They caught my leg—you see what it is— and pulled me over the yard, and then left me there, knowing I could not walk nor crawl, and all six went into the house. I was chilled with the cold lying in the yard at that time of night, for it was near 1 o'clock, and they had talked and beat me and so on until half an hour had passed since they first approached. After they had staid in the house for a considerable time, they came back to where I lay and asked if I wasn't afraid at all. They pointed pistols at me all around my head once or twice, as if they were going to shoot me, telling me they were going to kill me; wasn't I ready to die, and willing to die? Didn't I preach? That they came to kill me—all the time pointing pistols at me. This second time they came out of the house, after plundering the house, searching for letters, they came at me with these pistols, and asked if I was ready to die. I told them that I was not exactly ready; that I would rather live; that I hoped they would not kill me that time. They said they would; I had better prepare. One caught me by the leg and hurt me, for my leg for forty years has been drawn each year, more and more year by year, and I made moan when it hurt so. One said "G—d d——n it, hush!" He had a horsewhip, and he told me to pull up my shirt, and he hit me. He told me at every lick, "Hold up your shirt."I made a moan every time he cut with the horsewhip. I reckon he struck me eight cuts right on the hip bone; it was almost the only place he could hit my body, my legs are so short—all my limbs drawn up and withered away with pain. I saw one of them standing over me or by me motion to them to quit. They all had disguises on. I then thought they would not kill me. One of them then took a strap, and buckled it around my neck and said, "Let's take him to the river and drown him.". . . After pulling the strap around my neck, he took it off and gave me a lick on my hip where he had struck me with the horsewhip. One of them said, "Now, you see, I've burned up the d——d letter of Wallace's and all," and he brought out a little book and says, "What's this for?" I told him I did not know; to let me see with a light and I could read it. They brought a lamp and I read it. It was a book in which I had keep an account of the school. I had been licensed to keep a school. I read them some of the names. He said that would do, and asked if I had been paid for those scholars I had put down. I said no. He said I would now have to die. I was somewhat afraid, but one said not to kill me. They said "Look here! Will you put a card in the paper next week like June Moore and Sol Hill?" They had been prevailed on to put a card in the paper to renounce all republicanism and never vote. I said, "If I had the money to pay the expense, I could." They said I could borrow, and gave me another lick. They asked me, "Will you quit preaching?" I told them I did not know. I said that to save my life. They said I must stop that republican paper that was coming to Clay Hill. It has been only a few weeks since it stopped. The republican weekly paper was then coming to me from Charleston. It came to my name. They said I must stop it, quit preaching, and put a card in the newspaper renouncing republicanism, and they would not kill me; but if I did not they would come back the next week and kill me. With that one of them went into the house where my brother and my sister-in-law lived, and brought her to pick me up. As she stooped down to pick me up one of them struck her, and as she was carrying me into the house another struck her with a strap. She carried me into the house and laid me on the bed. Then they gathered around and told me to pray for them. I tried to pray. They said, "Don't you pray against Ku-Klux, but pray that God may forgive Ku-Klux. Don't pray against us. Pray that God may bless and save us." I was so chilled with cold lying out of doors so long and in such pain I could not speak to pray, but I tried to, and they said that would do very well, and all went out of the house.

QUESTIONS

What did the Klan want from Elias Hill? • Why did they ask about the Union League? • Why did they want him to put an announcement (a "card") in the newspaper? • Why were they concerned about his preaching? • What did they force him to do?

DOCUMENT 4

A Northern Republican's Report on Reconstruction

By 1875, many Republican leaders in the North concluded that Reconstruction had done enough for former slaves. Concerned about the political consequences throughout the nation of federal support for southern, mostly black, Republicans, they concluded that the best way to achieve order and stability in the South, as in the North, was to permit home rule. The thinking of many northern Republicans was illustrated in the observations — excerpted here — of Charles Nordhoff, a northern journalist, who spent five months travelling across the South in 1875.

Charles Nordhoff

The Cotton States, 1875

To make clear my point of view, it is proper to say that I am a Republican, and have never voted any other Federal ticket than the Republican; I have been opposed to slavery as long as I have had an opinion on any subject . . . ; and I am a thorough believer in the capacity of the people to rule themselves, even if they are very ignorant, better than any body else can rule them.

The following, then, are the conclusions I draw from my observations in the Cotton States:

There is not, in any of the States of which I speak, any desire for a new war; any hostility to the Union; any even remote wish to re-enslave the blacks; any hope or expectation of repealing any constitutional amendment, or in any way curtailing the rights of the blacks as citizens. The former slave-holders understand perfectly that the blacks can not be re-enslaved. . . .

That the Southern whites should rejoice over their defeat, now, is impossible. That their grandchildren will, I hope and believe. What we have a right to require is, that they shall accept the situation; and that they do. What they have a right to ask of us is, that we shall give them a fair chance under the new order of things; and that we have so far too greatly failed to do. . . .

The Southern Republicans seem to me unfair and unreasonable in another way. They complain constantly that the Southern whites still admire and are faithful to their own leaders; and that they like to talk about the bravery of the South during the war, and about the great qualities of their leading men. There seems to me something childish, and even cowardly, in this complaint. . . .

Charles Nordhoff, *The Cotton States in the Spring and Summer of 1875* (1876); reprinted in *Reconstruction in the South,* by Edwin C. Rozwenc (Lexington, MA: D.C. Heath and Co., 1973), 436–43.

In all the States I have seen, the Republican reconstructors did shamefully rob the people. In several of them they continue to do so. . . .

As to "intimidation," it is a serious mistake to imagine this exclusively a Democratic proceeding in the South. It has been practiced in the last three years quite as much, and even more rigorously, by the Republicans. The negroes are the most savage intimidators of all. In many localities which I visited, it was as much as a negro's life was worth to vote the Democratic ticket. . . . That there has also been Democratic intimidation is undeniable; but it does not belong to the Southern Republicans to complain of it.

Wherever one of these States has fallen under the control of Democrats, this has been followed by important financial reforms; economy of administration; and . . . by the restoration of peace and good-will. . . .

The misconduct of the Republican rulers in all these States has driven out of their party the great mass of the white people, the property-owners, tax-payers, and persons of intelligence and honesty. At first a considerable proportion of these were ranged on the Republican side. Now . . . the Republican party consists almost exclusively of the negroes and the Federal office-holders. . . .

Thus has been perpetuated what is called the "color-line" in politics, the Democratic party being composed of the great mass of the whites, including almost the entire body of those who own property, pay taxes, or have intelligence; while the Republican party is composed almost altogether of the negroes, who are, as a body, illiterate, without property, and easily misled by appeals to their fears, and to their gratitude to "General Grant," who is to them the embodiment of the Federal power.

This division of political parties on the race or color-line has been a great calamity to the Southern States.

It had its origin in the refusal of the Southern whites, after the war, to recognize the equal political rights of the blacks; and their attempts, in State legislatures, to pass laws hostile to them. This folly has been bitterly regretted by the wiser men in the South. . . .

The color-line is maintained mostly by Republican politicians, but they are helped by a part of the Democratic politicians, who see their advantage in having the white vote massed upon their side. . . .

Inevitably in such cases there must be a feeling of hostility by the whites toward the blacks, and it is an evidence of the good nature of the mass of whites that, in the main, they conduct themselves toward the blacks kindly and justly. They concentrate their dislike upon the men who have misled and now misuse the black vote, and this I can not call unjust. It is commonly said, "The negroes are not to blame; they do not know any better."

On the other hand, as the feeling is intense, it is often undiscriminating, and includes the just with the unjust among the Republicans. . . . [It] will last just as long as the color-line is maintained, and as long as Republicans maintain themselves in power by the help of the black vote, and by Federal influence. . . .

There was, in those Southern States which I have visited, for some years after the war and up to the year 1868, or in some cases 1870, much disorder, and a condition of lawlessness toward the blacks—a disposition . . . to trample them underfoot, to deny their equal rights, and to injure or kill them on slight or no provocations. The tremendous change in the social arrangements of the Southern States required time as well as laws and force to be accepted. The Southern whites had suffered a defeat which was sore to bear, and on top of this they saw their slaves—their most valuable and cherished property—taken away and made free, and not only free, but their political equals. One needs to go into the far South to know what this really meant, and what deep resentment and irritation it inevitably bred. . . .

I believe that there was, during some years, a necessity for the interference of the Federal power to repress disorders and crimes which would otherwise have spread, and inflicted, perhaps, irretrievable blows on society itself. But, after all, I am persuaded time was the great and real healer of disorders, as well as differences. We of the North do not always remember that even in the farthest South there were large property interests, important industries, many elements of civilization which can not bear long-continued disorders; and, moreover, that the men of the South are Americans, like ourselves, having, by nature or long training a love of order and permanence, and certain, therefore, to reconstitute society upon the new basis prescribed to them, and to do it by their own efforts, so soon as they were made to feel that the new order of things was inevitable. . . .

No thoughtful man can examine the history of the last ten years in the South, as he may hear it on the spot and from both parties, without being convinced that it was absolutely necessary to the security of the blacks, and the permanent peace of the Southern communities, to give the negro, ignorant, poor, and helpless as he was, every political right and privilege which any other citizen enjoys. That he should vote and that he should be capable of holding office was necessary, I am persuaded, to make him personally secure, and, what is of more importance, to convert him from a *freedman* into a *free man*.

That he has not always conducted himself well in the exercise of his political rights is perfectly and lamentably true; but this is less his fault than that of the bad white men who introduced him to political life. But, on the other hand, the vote has given him what nothing else could give —a substantive existence; it has made him a part of the State. . . .

General manhood suffrage is undoubtedly a danger to a community where, as in these States, the entire body of ignorance and poverty has been massed by adroit politicians upon one side. . . .

But the moment the color-line is broken, the conditions of the problem are essentially changed. Brains and honesty have once more a chance to come to the top. The negro, whose vote will be important to both parties, will find security in that fact. No politician will be so silly as to encroach upon his rights, or allow his opponents to do so; and the black man appears to me to have a sense of respectability which will prevent him, unencouraged by demagogues, from trying to force himself into positions for which he is unfit. He will have his fair chance, and he has no right to more.

Whenever the Federal interference in all its shapes ceases, it will be found, I believe, that the negroes will not at first cast a full vote; take away petty Federal "organizers," and the negro, left face to face with the white man, hearing both sides for the first time; knowing by experience, as he will presently, that the Democrat is not a monster, and that a Democratic victory does not mean his reenslavement, will lose much of his interest in elections. . . .

Of course, as soon as parties are re-arranged on a sound and natural basis, the negro vote will re-appear; for the leaders of each party, the Whig or Republican and the Democrat, will do their utmost to get his vote, and therein will be the absolute security of the black man. I believe, however, that for many years to come, until a new generation arrives at manhood perhaps, and, at any rate, until the black man becomes generally an independent farmer, he will be largely influenced in his political affiliations by the white. He will vote as his employer, or the planter from whom he rents land, or the white man whom he most trusts, and with whom, perhaps, he deposits his savings, tells him is best for his own interest. . . . But, at any rate, he will vote or not, as he pleases. And it is far better for him that he should act under such influences than that his vote should be massed against the property and intelligence of the white people to achieve the purposes of unscrupulous demagogues. . . .

These are my conclusions concerning those Southern States which I have seen. If they are unfavorable to the Republican rule there, I am sorry for it.

QUESTIONS

What conclusions did Nordhoff draw about southern whites? • What political party represented them? • What were the consequence of Republican rule in the South? • How did the color line develop, according to Nordhoff? • How did he believe it would be undermined? • How did he believe order could be established in the South? • In his opinion, what would happen to black voters when home rule was established in the South?

COMPARATIVE QUESTIONS

How do the views of former slaves expressed by white Mississippians in the Mississippi Black Code compare with the views expressed by the Black Convention in Alabama? How does Elias Hill's experience compare with the Mississippi Black Code and the aspirations of the Black Convention? How do Charles Nordhoff's opinions about the South differ from those of black and white southerners described in the other documents?

CHAPTER 17

AMERICANS ON THE MOVE: THE SETTLEMENT OF THE WEST AND THE RISE OF THE CITY
1860–1900

Old expectations encountered new realities as people moved from farm to farm, from farm to city, from Europe to America. The uprooting that accompanied this restless movement strengthened some ties while weakening or breaking others. The struggles of farmers, Native Americans, urban immigrants, and political bosses to come to terms with the consequences of movement are disclosed in the following documents.

DOCUMENT 1
Swedish Immigrants on the Kansas Prairie

Settlers raced to western farms after the Civil War. Some pulled up stakes in an eastern state and moved on. Others immigrated from Europe, lured by the prospects of a better life. Gustaf Lindgren, his wife, Ida, and their five children left Sweden for Lake Sibley, a small settlement in Kansas. Ida's brother, Magnus, his wife, Johanna, and other Swedes accompanied the Lindgrens. Ida's letters to her mother and sister in Sweden described experiences shared by many rural families on the move. Ida wrote in Swedish, of course; English translations from her letters follow.

Ida Lindgren

Letters

15 May 1870

What shall I say? Why has the Lord brought us here? Oh, I feel so op-pressed, so unhappy! Two whole days it took us to get here and they were not the least trying part of our travels. We sat on boards in the work-wagon, packed in so tightly that we could not move a foot, and we drove across endless, endless prairies, on narrow roads; no, not roads, tracks like those in the fields at home when they harvested grain. No forest but only a few trees which grow along the rivers and creeks. And then here and there you see a homestead and pass a little settlement. The closer we came to Lake Sibley the more desolate the country seemed and the roads were altogether frightful, almost trackless. When we finally saw Lake Sibley, at twelve o'clock at night, it consisted of four houses, two larger ones and two small, very small, as well as two under construction. The rooms Albinson had written he wished to rent us were not available but we were quartered here in Albinson's attic. The attic is divided into three rooms but with no doors; I have hung up a sheet in front of our "door." When I immediately asked, after we arrived, to go up with the children and put them to bed, there was no table, no chair, no bed, nothing, and there we were to stay! I set the candle on the floor, sat down beside it, took the children in my lap and burst into tears. I feel about to do so now too, I cannot really pull myself together and the Albinsons appear quite uncomfortable every time they see me. The Indians are not so far away from here, I can understand, and all the men you see coming by, riding or driving wagons, are armed with revolvers and long carbines, and look like highway robbers. . . .

Gustaf is out with Magnus and Albinson to look at the land he bought and to see if there is any that Magnus would like to have. . . .

5 January 1871

. . . I must tell you about our Christmas! On "Little Christmas Eve," Sylvan (he had been in Chicago but came here to celebrate Christmas with us) and Tekla Littorin (she is employed four miles on the other side of Manhattan) arrived, then we all went over to Magnus and his family for Christmas Eve. They had everything so fine and cozy, three rooms downstairs and the attic all in order, and a Christmas tree of green cedar with candles and bonbons and apples on it, and the coffee table set, so it was really Christmas-like, and because of that I could not tear my thoughts away from you and from my old home and the tears kept

---

H. Arnold Barton, ed., *Letters from the Promised Land: Swedes in America, 1840–1914* (Minneapolis: University of Minnesota Press, 1975), 143–55.

welling up! . . . Then we had a few Christmas presents, the finest was a rocking chair which Magnus and his family gave us. From Gustaf I got two serving dishes, since we had none before, from Olga a rolling pin for cookies and three dozen clothespins to hang up wet clothes with when you do laundry, from Hugo a pair of woolen mittens, from Littorin a knitting bag, from Hedenskog material for a little sofa which we have made for the children to sleep on, from Carlson a pair of fire tongs.

I gave Magnus and the family a sofa cover, which I sewed last summer to exhibit, and a couple of pictures of Gustaf Vasa which we had with us. Hugo gave them a pair of drinking glasses and Olga gave Magnus a pipe pouch and Johanna clothespins like those I got. Helge had himself sewn a little lamp mat for them. I gave Gustaf a pair of real coarse, strong gloves for working, and Olga, Hugo, and Helge had gotten together to buy him a hat. Olga and Hugo had earned the money themselves that they used for Christmas presents.

After we had eaten our rice pudding and Christmas cookies, we sang a few hymns and "Hosianna," and then we broke up, though we all slept there, all the bachelors in the attic, Magnus and family in the kitchen, Gustaf, the younger children, and myself in the bedroom, and Olga, Tekla, and their hired girl in the parlor.

We stayed until the morning after the second day of Christmas and then we went home. Tekla, Ida, and Anna stayed on there, and so instead we took their hired girl and their hired man to help us slaughter our pig, which we were to have for New Year's, when Magnus and his family were to come to us. After we had finished with the slaughtering, I got started with laundry while we had Johanna's hired girl here, for it had been so cold that we had not been able to do any washing for some weeks, so now we had so much laundry. *Washing* is the worst work I have to do, for my hands can't take it and they have been so miserable, swollen and raw, that all the knuckles bled, but now it is better. . . .

All my menfolk are out in the woods today to cut fence rails, they took lunch with them so I don't know how long they will be away. . . . Now, dear Mamma, I will end for today, for I must tidy up a little here in the room before they come back from the woods, since it is Twelfth Night, and then I must skin two small hares for this evening. . . .

9 February 1871

. . . Magnus was here for a while this morning, so I can send greetings from them. They are well, but their hired girl has left so that Johanna now has to do everything herself, as I do. With the difference, however, that they are only two plus their hired man, while we are ten to bake and cook and wash up for every day, and worst of all, to wash clothes for. There is not much time for me to sit and do any handwork. America may be good in many respects, but certainly not for having servants. For no matter how good they may be in Sweden, as soon as they reach America's free soil they become far from good and want instead to be gentlemen and ladies themselves, and would rather be waited on than wait on others. It is hard to get used to this and therefore I think it is better to be one's own maid, though one gets awfully tired sometimes in both the back and legs. And my hands will not really accustom themselves to these tasks; they are sometimes roses, sometimes burrs, but never lilies smooth as satin. . . .

18 October 1871

. . . I was alone at home with the younger children, for Hugo had ridden over to Lindesfrid in the morning to help with the corn picking there, and around noon there was such a smell and smoke from burnt grass that I immediately suspected there was a prairie fire somewhere. Suddenly the smoke was so thick and ashes flew around (it was blowing up a real storm and the wind lay this way), that I couldn't see the nearest hills. I believed then that the fire was right upon us, so I ran in and gathered up the silver and Gustaf's watch and a little money all in a bundle, and put Anna on my arm and took Ida by the hand and ran through the woods down to the river. Oh, Mamma, how my heart pounded! I felt I could do nothing else, alone as I was with my little ones, for I believed that with the force with which the fire was moving today, it would go across the cornfield and set off all six haystacks and then there would be no saving the house. And then the woods were close by and there are now so many dry leaves that I felt there was no safety there. No, only in the river, there must I fly; if the fire should come so close to us I would take both children in my arms and go as far out into the water as I could: that was what I thought.

But first we sat down on the bank; Anna did not understand the danger, but Ida cried so bitterly that I had to try to calm her, fearful as I was myself. I told them, "We should pray to the Lord that He protect us." And so I prayed as well as I could, and the children repeated after me, and last of all we prayed for rain—for it had now been dry for several months and everything was so dried out that the fire could range freely, and no autumn grain could be sowed either until rain came. We sat there a couple of hours; once I took water in a spoon to drink but could not for it was black with ash that had flown here. When I thought the smoke had become less, I had the children sit where they were and I went up onto a rise to look.

Behold, there stood our house and home and the six haystacks unharmed, but a few that were out in the field and were intended for the owner were burned up, and the fire flamed on the other side on the hills and dales. We then went home and when we came in we fell on our knees and thanked the Lord who had protected us and our house and home. A little while later Hugo came: they had seen the fire coming toward us and Gustaf had sent him to help me, and a half hour or hour later Lindgren came himself, for all danger was far from past. I now felt so calm and glad, but they had to be out with water and rags with others to fight the fire until late at night, when all danger was over here. How far the fire later continued, we don't know, but many, many people had their hay burned up and we also had two small stacks at Lindesfrid that were lost. At Magnus's no hay burned but a section of fence. . . .

25 August 1874

. . . We have not had rain since the beginning of June, and then with this heat and often strong winds as well, you can imagine how every-thing has dried out. There has also been a general lamentation and fear for the coming year. We have gotten a fair amount of wheat, rye, and oats, for they are ready so early, but no one here will get corn or potatoes. We have a few summer potatoes but many don't even have that, and we thought and hoped we would get a good crop of other potatoes, but will evidently get none. Instead of selling the oats and part of the rye as we had expected, we must now use them for the livestock, since there was no corn. We are glad we have the oats (for many don't have any and must feed wheat to the stock) and had hoped to have the corn leaves to add to the fodder. But then one fine day there came millions, trillions of grasshoppers in great clouds, hiding the sun, and coming down onto the fields, eating up *everything* that was still there, the leaves on the trees, peaches, grapes, cucumbers, onions, cabbage, everything, everything. Only the peach stones still hung on the trees, showing what had once been there.

They are not the kind of grasshoppers we see in Sweden but are large, grayish ones. Now most of them have moved southward, to devastate other areas since there was nothing more to consume here. Certainly it is sad and distressing and depressing for body and soul to find that no matter how hard one drudges and works, one still has nothing, less than nothing.

Don't you think, Mamma, that I could bear a little bit of *success?* I think myself that I could well manage a little, but the Lord sees best what we need and therefore He daily strikes and humiliates us, now in one way, now in another. But still He has not crushed our stubborn hearts. As burdened as I feel, my heart is still not weighed down, it still rises up from time to time.

QUESTIONS

What did Ida Lindgren think about Lake Sibley when she arrived? • Where did the Lindgrens stay? • Who came to the Christmas celebration? • What kinds of gifts did they exchange? • What do the gifts suggest about their other belongings? • What chores did Ida describe? • How were servants different in America? • What dangers did she encounter? • Can you tell if the Lindgrens owned land?

DOCUMENT 2

In-mut-too-yah-lat-lat
Describes White Encroachment

The steady encroachment of white settlers on Native American lands reached a crescendo after 1870. Soldiers who had fought in the Civil War now tried to corral tribes into reservations. In 1877, the chief of the Chute-pa-lu, or Nez Percés, resisted the U.S. government's demands that his tribe relinquish their land. In-mut-too-yah-lat-lat, or Chief Joseph as he was called by the whites, fought against overwhelming odds, was defeated, and with his tribe was moved to Fort Leavenworth, then to Baxter Springs, Kansas, and finally to Indian Territory. In 1879, In-mut-too-yah-lat-lat explained to a white audience why he fought. His explanation, excerpted here, described experiences shared by countless other Native Americans.

Chief Joseph

Speech to a White Audience, 1879

My friends, I have been asked to show you my heart. I am glad to have a chance to do so. I want the white people to understand my people. Some of you think an Indian is like a wild animal. This is a great mistake. I will tell you all about our people, and then you can judge whether an Indian is a man or not. I believe much trouble and blood would be saved if we opened our hearts more. I will tell you in my way how the Indian sees things. . . .

My name is In-mut-too-yah-lat-lat (Thunder traveling over the Mountains). I am chief of the Wal-lam-wat-kin band of Chute-pa-lu, or Nez Percés (nose-pierced Indians). I was born in eastern Oregon, thirty-eight winters ago. My father was chief before me. When a young man, he was called Joseph by Mr. Spaulding, a missionary. He died a few years ago. There was no stain on his hands of the blood of a white man. He left a good name on the earth. He advised me well for my people.

Our fathers gave us many laws, which they had learned from their fathers. These laws were good. They told us to treat all men as they treated us; that we should never be the first to break a bargain; that it was a disgrace to tell a lie; that we should speak only the truth; that it was a shame for one man to take from another his wife, or his property without paying for it. We were taught to believe that the Great Spirit sees and hears everything, and that he never forgets; that hereafter he will give every man a spirit-home according to his deserts: if he has been a good

North American Review (1879); reprinted in *Captive Nations*, 237–51.

man, he will have a good home; if he has been a bad man, he will have a bad home. This I believe, and all my people believe the same.]

We did not know there were other people besides the Indian until about one hundred winters ago, when some men with white faces came to our country. They brought many things with them to trade for furs and skins. They brought tobacco, which was new to us. They brought guns with flint stones on them, which frightened our women and children. Our people could not talk with these white-faced men, but they used signs which all people understand. These men were Frenchmen, and they called our people "Nez Percés," because they wore rings in their noses for ornaments. Although very few of our people wear them now, we are still called by the same name. . . . The first white men of your people who came to our country were named Lewis and Clark. They also brought many things that our people had never seen. They talked straight, and our people gave them a great feast, as a proof that their hearts were friendly. These men were very kind. They made presents to our chiefs and our people made presents to them. We had a great many horses, of which we gave them what they needed, and they gave us guns and to-bacco in return. All the Nez Percés made friends with Lewis and Clark, and agreed to let them pass through their country, and never to make war on white men. This promise the Nez Percés have never broken. No white man can accuse them of bad faith, and speak with a straight tongue. It has always been the pride of the Nez Percés that they were the friends of the white men. When my father was a young man there came to our country a white man [Mr. Spaulding] who talked spirit law. He won the affections of our people because he spoke good things to them. At first he did not say anything about white men wanting to settle on our lands. Nothing was said about that until about twenty winters ago, when a number of white people came into our country and built houses and made farms. At first our people made no complaint. They thought there was room enough for all to live in peace, and they were learning many things from the white men that seemed to be good. But we soon found that the white men were growing rich very fast, and were greedy to possess every-thing the Indian had. My father was the first to see through the schemes of the white men, and he warned his tribe to be careful about trading with them. He had suspicion of men who seemed so anxious to make money. I was a boy then, but I remember well my father's caution. He had sharper eyes than the rest of our people.

Next there came a white officer [Governor Stevens], who invited all the Nez Percés to a treaty council. After the council was opened he made known his heart. He said there were a great many white people in the country, and many more would come; that he wanted the land marked out so that the Indians and white men could be separated. If they were to live in peace it was necessary, he said, that the Indians should have a country set apart for them, and in that country they must stay. My father, who represented his band, refused to have anything to do with the council, because he wished to be a free man. He claimed that no man owned any part of the earth, and a man could not sell what he did not own.

Mr. Spaulding took hold of my father's arm and said, "Come and sign the treaty." My father pushed him away, and said: "Why do you ask me to sign away my country? It is your business to talk to us about spirit matters, and not to talk to us about parting with our land." Governor Stevens urged my father to sign his treaty, but he refused. "I will not sign your paper," he said; "you go where you please, so do I; you are not a child, I am no child; I can think for myself. No man can think for me. I have no other home than this. I will not give it up to any man. My people would have no home. Take away your paper. I will not touch it with my hand."

My father left the council. Some of the chiefs of the other bands of the Nez Percés signed the treaty, and then Governor Stevens gave them presents of blankets. My father cautioned his people to take no presents, for "after a while," he said, "they will claim that you have accepted pay for your country." Since that time four bands of the Nez Percés have received annuities from the United States. My father was invited to many councils, and they tried hard to make him sign the treaty, but he was firm as the rock, and would not sign away his home. His refusal caused a difference among the Nez Percés.

Eight years later [1863] was the next treaty council. A chief called Lawyer, because he was a great talker, took the lead in this council, and sold nearly all the Nez Percés country. . . . In this treaty Lawyer acted without authority from our band. He had no right to sell the Wallowa . . . country. That had always belonged to my father's own people, and the other bands had never disputed our right to it. . . .

In order to have all people understand how much land we owned, my father planted poles around it and said: "Inside is the home of my people—the white man may take the land outside. Inside this boundary all our people were born. It circles around the graves of our fathers, and we will never give up these graves to any man."

The United States claimed they had bought all the Nez Percés country outside of Lapwai Reservation, from Lawyer and other chiefs, but we continued to live in this land in peace until eight years ago, when white men began to come inside the bounds my father had set. We warned them against this great wrong, but they would not leave our land, and some bad blood was raised. The white men represented that we were going upon the war-path. They reported many things that were false.

The United States Government again asked for a treaty council. . . . It was then that I took my father's place as chief. In this council I made my first speech to white men. I said to the agent who held the council:

"I did not want to come to this council, but I came hoping that we could save blood. The white man has no right to come here and take our country.

We have never accepted any presents from the Government. Neither Lawyer nor any other chief had authority to sell this land. It has always belonged to my people. It came unclouded to them from our fathers, and we will defend this land as long as a drop of Indian blood warms the hearts of our men."

The agent said he had orders, from the Great White Chief at Washington, for us to go upon the Lapwai Reservation, and that if we obeyed he would help us in many ways. "You must move to the agency," he said. I answered him: "I will not. I do not need your help; we have plenty and we are contented and happy if the white man will let us alone. The reservation is too small for so many people with all their stock. You can keep your presents; we can go to your towns and pay for all we need; we have plenty of horses and cattle to sell, and we won't have any help from you; we are free now; we can go where we please, Our fathers were born here. Here they lived, here they died, here are their graves. We will never leave them." The agent went away, and we had peace for a little while. . . .

Year after year we have been threatened, but no war was made upon my people until General Howard came to our country two years ago [1877] and told us that he was the white war-chief of all that country. He said: "I have a great many soldiers at my back. . . . The country belongs to the Government, and I intend to make you go upon the reservation." . . .

I said to General Howard: ". . . I do not believe that the Great Spirit Chief gave one kind of men the right to tell another kind of men what they must do."

QUESTIONS

When did the Chute-pa-lu first encounter whites? • How did they deal with whites? • Were their laws similar to white laws? • What did In-mut-too-yat-lat-lat's father think about whites? • What did he do? • How did whites gain control of some Chute-pa-lu land? • Why did In-mut-too-yat-lat-lat refuse General Howard's order to go to a reservation?

DOCUMENT 3

A Romanian Jew Immigrates to America

European immigrants flooded into American cities in the late nineteenth century, each with a story and a hope. Michael Gold, the son of one of these immigrants, recalled his father Herman's story about why he came to America. Gold's recounting of his father's journey to New York City described the mixed motives, misleading information, and unexpected experiences encountered by most immigrants.

Michael Gold

Jews without Money

My father, a house painter, was a tall lively man with Slavic cheek bones and a red mustache. . . . He was born near Yassy, Roumania. . . .

"I was always in trouble in Roumania" said my father. ". . . I was always fighting and drinking, and my father did not know what to do with me. . . .

"Why did I choose to come to America?" asked my father of himself gravely. . . . "I will tell you why: it was because of envy of my dirty thief of a cousin, that Sam Kravitz, may his nose be eaten by the pox.

"All this time, while I was disgracing my family, Sam had gone to America, and was making his fortune. Letters came from him, and were read throughout our village. Sam, in two short years, already owned his own factory for making suspenders. He sent us his picture. It was marveled at by every one. Our Sam no longer wore a fur cap, a long Jewish coat and peasant boots. No. He wore a fine gentleman's suit, a white collar like a doctor, store shoes and a beautiful round fun-hat called a derby.

"He suddenly looked so fat and rich, this beggarly cobbler's son! I tell you, my liver burned with envy when I heard my father and mother praise my cousin Sam. I knew I was better than him in every way, and it hurt me. I said to my father, 'Give me money. Let me go at once to America to redeem myself. I will make more money than Sam, I am smarter than he is. You will see!'

"My mother did not want me to go. But my father was weary of my many misfortunes, and he gave me the money for the trip. So I came to America. It was the greatest mistake in my life. . . .

"[T]hen I was still a foolish boy, and though I left Roumania with great plans in my head, in my heart a foolish voice was saying: 'America is a land of fun.'

"How full I was of all the . . . stories that were told in my village about America! In America, we believed, people dug under the streets and found gold anywhere. In America, the poorest ragpicker lived better than a Roumanian millionaire. In America, people did little work, but had fun all day.

"I had seen two pictures of America. They were shown in the window of a store that sold Singer Sewing Machines in our village. One picture had in it the tallest building I had ever seen. It was called a skyscraper. At the bottom of it walked the proud Americans. The men wore derby hats and had fine mustaches and gold watch chains. The women wore silks and satins, and had proud faces like queens. Not a single poor man or woman was there; every one was rich.

Michael Gold, *Jews without Money* (1930), 81–110.

"The other picture was of Niagara Falls. You have seen the picture on postcards; with Indians and cowboys on horses, who look at a rainbow shining over the water.

"I tell you, I wanted to get to America as fast as I could, so that I might look at the skyscrapers and at the Niagara Falls rainbow, and wear a derby hat.

"In my family were about seventy-five relatives. All came to see me leave Roumania. There was much crying. But I was happy, because I thought I was going to a land of fun.

"The last thing my mother did, was to give me my cousin's address in New York, and say: 'Go to Sam. He will help you in the strange land.'

"But I made up my mind I would die first rather than ask Sam for help.

"Well, for eleven days our boat rocked on the ocean. I was sick, but I wrote out a play . . . and dreamed of America.

"They gave us dry herring and potatoes to eat. The food was like dung and the boat stank like a big water closet. But I was happy.

"I joked all the way. One night all of us young immigrants held a singing party. One young Roumanian had an accordion. We became good friends, because both of us were the happiest people on the boat.

"He was coming to a rich uncle, a cigarmaker who owned a big business, he said. When he learned I had no relatives in America, he asked me to live at his uncle's with him. I agreed, because I liked this boy.

"*Nu,* how shall I tell how glad we were when after eleven days on the empty ocean we saw the buildings of New York?

"It looked so nice and happy, this city standing on end like a child's toys and blocks. It looked like a land of fun, a game waiting for me to play.

"And in Ellis Island, where they kept us overnight, I slept on a spring bed that had no mattress, pillow or blankets. I was such a greenhorn that I had never seen a spring before. I thought it was wonderful, and bounced up and down on it for fun.

"Some one there taught me my first American words. All night my friend Yossel and I bounced up and down on the springs and repeated the new funny words to each other.

"Potato! he would yell at me. Tomato! I would answer, and laugh. Match! he would say. All right! I would answer. Match! all right! go to hell! potato! until every one was angry at us, the way we kept them awake with our laughing and yelling.

"In the morning his uncle came for us and took us home in a horse-car.

"I tell you my eyes were busy on that ride through the streets. I was looking for the American fun.

"*Nu,* I will not mention how bad I felt when I saw the cigarmaker uncle's home. It was just a big dirty dark room in the back of the cigar store where he made and sold cigars. He, his wife and four children lived in that one room.

"He was not glad to have me there, but he spread newspapers on the floor, and Yossel and I slept on them.

"What does it matter, I thought, this is not America. To-morrow morning I will go out in the streets, and see the real American fun.

"The next morning Yossel and I took a long walk. That we might not be lost, we fixed in our minds the big gold tooth of a dentist that hung near the cigar shop.

"We walked and walked. I will not tell you what we saw, because you see it every day. We saw the East Side. To me it was a strange sight. I could not help wondering, where are all the people running? What is happening? And why are they so serious? When does the fun start?

"We came to Allen Street, under the elevated. To show you what a greenhorn I was, I fell in love with the elevated train. I had never seen anything like it in Roumania.

"I was such a greenhorn I believed the elevated train traveled all over America, to Niagara Falls and other places. We rode up and down on it all day. I paid the fare.

"I had some money left. I also bought two fine derby hats from a pushcart; one for Yossel, and one for me. They were a little big, but how proud we felt in these American fun-hats.

"No one wears such hats in Roumania. Both of us had pictures taken in the American fun-hats to send to our parents.

"This foolishness went on for two weeks. Then all my money was gone. So the cigarmaker told me I should find a job and move out from his home. So I found a job for seven dollars a month in a grocery store. I lived over the store, I rose at five o'clock, and went to bed at twelve in the night. My feet became large and red with standing all day. The grocerman, may the worms find him, gave me nothing to eat but dry bread, old cheese, pickles and other stale groceries. I soon became sick and left that job.

"For a week I sat in Hester Park without a bite of food. And I looked around me, but was not unhappy. Because I tell you, I was such a greenhorn, that I still thought fun would start and I was waiting for it.

"One night, after sleeping on the bench, I was very hungry in the morning and decided to look up my rich cousin, Sam Kravitz. I hated to do this, but was weak with fasting. So I came into my cousin's shop. To hide my shame I laughed out loud.

"'Look, Sam, I am here,' I laughed. 'I have just come off the boat, and am ready to make my fortune.'

"So my cousin Sam gave me a job in his factory. He paid me twenty-five cents a day.

"He had three other men working for him. He worked himself. He looked sick and sharp and poor and not at all like the picture of him in the fun-hat he had sent to Roumania.

"*Nu,* so your father worked. I got over my greenhorn idea that there was nothing but fun in America. I learned to work like every one else. I grew thin as my cousin.

"Soon I came to understand it was not a land of fun. It was a Land of Hurry-Up. There was no gold to be dug in the streets here. Derbies were not funhats for holidays. They were work-hats. Nu, so I worked! With my hands, my liver and sides! I worked!

"My cousin Sam had fallen into a good trade. With his machines he manufactured the cotton ends of suspenders. These ends are made of cotton, and are very important to a suspender. It is these ends that fasten to the buttons, and hold up the pants. This is important to the pants, as you know.

"Yes, it was a good trade, and a necessary one.

There was much money to be made, I saw that at once.

"But my cousin Sam was not a good business man. He had no head for figures and his face was like vinegar. None of his customers liked him.

"Gradually, he let me go out and find business for him. I was very good for this. Most of the big suspender shops were owned by Roumanians who had known my father. They greeted me like a relative. I drank wine with them, and passed jokes. So they gave me their orders for suspender ends.

"So one day, seeing how I built up the business, Sam said: 'You shall be my partner. We are making a great deal of money. Leave the machine, Herman. I will take care of the inside shop work. You go out every day, and joke with our customers and bring in the orders.'

"So I was partners with my cousin Sam. So I was very happy. I earned as much as thirty dollars a week; I was at last a success.

"So a matchmaker came, and said I ought to marry. So he brought me to your momma and I saw at once that she was a kind and hard-working woman. So I decided to marry her and have children.

"So this was done.

"It was then I made the greatest mistake of my life.

"Always I had wanted to see that big water with the rainbow and Indians called Niagara Falls.

"So I took your momma there when we married. I spent a month's wages on the trip. I showed America to your momma. We enjoyed ourselves.

"In a week we came back. I went to the shop the next morning to work again. I could not find the shop. It had vanished. I could not find Sam. He had stolen the shop.

"I searched and searched for Sam and the shop. My heart was swollen like a sponge with hate. I was ready to kill my cousin Sam.

"So one day I found him and the shop. I shouted at him, 'Thief, what have you done?' He laughed. He showed me a paper from a lawyer proving that the shop was his. All my work had been for nothing. It had only made Sam rich.

"What could I do? So in my hate I hit him with my fist, and made his nose bleed. He ran into the street yelling for a policeman. I ran after him with a stick, and beat him some more. But what good could it do? The shop was really his, and I was left a pauper.

"So now I work as a house painter. I work for another man, I am not my own master now. I am a man in a trap.

"But I am not defeated. I am a man with a strong will. . . . I am certain to be rich!"

QUESTIONS

Why did Herman Gold decide to go to America? • What did he expect to find there? • How did New York City appear to him in the first few weeks after he arrived? • How did his impressions change? • How did he become a success? • How did he celebrate his success? • How did he respond to his cousin's betrayal?

DOCUMENT 4

George Washington Plunkitt Explains Politics

Political machines ruled big cities, and none was more successful—or notorious— than New York's Tammany Hall. George Washington Plunkitt, a loyal Tammany boss, liked to hold court at the county courthouse shoeshine stand, explaining how things really worked to anyone willing to listen. In 1897, a freelance journalist, William L. Riordon, began recording Plunkitt's remarks and followed him for a day to see what he did. Riordan's account appeared in the New York Evening Post *and was later published in the volume* Plunkitt of Tammany Hall *in 1905. Plunkitt's statements are excerpted here, followed by Riordon's diary of one day in the life of a big-city boss.*

William L. Riordon
Plunkitt of Tammany Hall, 1905

Everybody is talkin' these days about Tammany men growin' rich on graft, but nobody thinks of drawin' the distinction between honest graft and dishonest graft. There's all the difference in the world between the two. Yes, many of our men have grown rich in politics. I have myself. I've

---

William L. Riordon, *Plunkitt of Tammany Hall* (1905; 1948 ed.).

made a big fortune out of the game, and I'm gettin' richer every day, but I've not gone in for dishonest graft—blackmailin' gamblers, saloon-keepers, disorderly people, etc.—and neither has any of the men who have made big fortunes in politics.

There's an honest graft, and I'm an example of how it works. I might sum up the whole thing by sayin': "I seen my opportunities and I took 'em."

Just let me explain by examples. My party's in power in the city, and it's goin' to undertake a lot of public improvements. Well, I'm tipped off, say, that they're going to lay out a new park at a certain place.

I see my opportunity and I take it. I go to that place and I buy up all the land I can in the neighborhood. Then the board of this or that makes its plan public, and there is a rush to get my land, which nobody cared particular for before.

Ain't it perfectly honest to charge a good price and make a profit on my investment and foresight? Of course, it is. Well, that's honest graft. . . .

It's just like lookin' ahead in Wall Street or in the coffee or cotton market. It's honest graft, and I'm lookin' for it every day in the year. I will tell you frankly that I've got a good lot of it, too. . . .

I seen my opportunity and I took it. I haven't confined myself to land; anything that pays is in my line. . . .

I've told you how I got rich by honest graft. Now, let me tell you that most politicians who are accused of robbin' the city get rich the same way.

They didn't steal a dollar from the city treasury. They just seen their opportunities and took them. That is why, when a reform administration comes in and spends a half million dollars in tryin' to find the public robberies they talked about in the campaign, they don't find them.

The books are always all right. The money in the city treasury is all right. Everything is all right. All they can show is that the Tammany heads of departments looked after their friends, within the law, and gave them what opportunities they could to make honest graft. Now, let me tell you that's never going to hurt Tammany with the people. Every good man looks after his friends, and any man who doesn't isn't likely to be popular. If I have a good thing to hand out in private life, I give it to a friend. Why shouldn't I do the same in public life? . . .

There's the biggest kind of a difference between political looters and politicians who make a fortune out of politics by keepin' their eyes wide open. The looter goes in for himself alone without considerin' his organization or his city. The politician looks after his own interests, the organization's interests, and the city's interests all at the same time. See the distinction? . . .

The Irish was born to rule, and they're the honestest people in the world. Show me the Irishman who would steal a roof off an almshouse! He don't exist. Of course, if an Irishman had the political pull and the roof was much worn, he might get the city authorities to put on a new one and get the contract for it himmself, and buy the old roof at a bargain-but that's honest graft. . . .

One reason why the Irishman is more honest in politics than many Sons of the Revolution is that he is grateful to the country and the city that gave him protection and prosperity when he was driven by oppression from the Emerald Isle. . . .His one thought is to serve the city which gave him a home. He has this thought even before he lands in New York, for his friends here often have a good place in one of the city departments picked out for him while he is still in the old country. Is it any wonder that he has a tender spot in his heart for old New York when he is on its salary list the mornin' after he lands?. . .

[H]ave you ever thought what would become of the country if the bosses were put out of business, and their places were taken by a lot of cart-tail orators and college graduates? It would mean chaos. . . .

This is a record of a day's work by Plunkitt:

2 A.M.   Aroused from sleep by the ringing of his door bell; went to the door and found a bartender, who asked him to go to the police station and bail out a saloon-keeper who had been arrested for violating the excise law. Furnished bail and returned to bed at three o'clock.

6 A.M.   Awakened by fire engines passing his house. Hastened to the scene of the fire, according to the custom of the Tammany district leaders, to give assistance to the fire sufferers, if needed. Met several of his election district captains who are always under orders to look out for fires, which are considered great vote-getters. Found several tenants who had been burned out, took them to a hotel, supplied them with clothes, fed them, and arranged temporary quarters for them until they could rent and furnish new apartments.

8:30 A.M.   Went to the police court to look after his constituents. Found six "drunks." Secured the discharge of four by a timely word with the judge, and paid the fines of two.

9 A.M.   Appeared in the Municipal District Court. Directed one of his district captains to act as counsel for a widow against whom dispossess proceedings had been instituted and obtained an extension of time. Paid the rent of a poor family about to be dispossessed and gave them a dollar for food.

11 A.M.   At home again. Found four men waiting for him. One had been discharged by the Metropolitan Railway Company for neglect of duty, and wanted the district leader to fix things. Another wanted a job on the road. The third sought a place on the Subway and the fourth, a

plumber, was looking for work with the Consolidated Gas Company. The district leader spent nearly three hours fixing things for the four men, and succeeded in each case.

3 P.M.   Attended the funeral of an Italian as far as the ferry. Hurried back to make his appearance at the funeral of a Hebrew constituent. Went conspicuously to the front both in the Catholic church and the synagogue, and later attended the Hebrew confirmation ceremonies in the synagogue.

7 P.M.   Went to district headquarters and presided over a meeting of election district captains. Each captain submitted a list of all the voters in his district, reported on their attitude toward Tammany, suggested who might be won over and how they could be won, told who were in need, and who were in trouble of any kind and the best way to reach them. District leader took notes and gave orders.

8 P.M.   Went to a church fair. Took chances on everything, bought ice-cream for the young girls and the children. Kissed the little ones, flattered their mothers and took their fathers out for something down at the corner.

9 P.M.   At the club-house again. Spent $10 on tickets for a church excursion and promised a subscription for a new church-bell. Bought tickets for a base-ball game to be played by two nines from his district. Listened to the complaints of a dozen pushcart peddlers who said they were persecuted by the police and assured them he would go to Police Headquarters in the morning and see about it.

10:30 P.M.   Attended a Hebrew wedding reception and dance. Had previously sent a handsome wedding present to the bride.

12 P.M.   In bed.

That is the actual record of one day in the life of Plunkitt.

QUESTIONS

According to Plunkitt, what was "honest graft"? • What was dishonest graft? • How did Tammany win the loyalty of voters? • Why did Plunkitt believe the Irish were born to rule? • Why did he think chaos would result if the bosses were put out of business? • To Plunkitt, what was politics?

COMPARATIVE QUESTIONS

How do Ida Lindgren's experiences compare with those of In-mut-too-yah-lat-lat? Did they have differing concepts of land and owner-ship? How do Lindgren's experiences as an immigrant differ from Herman Gold's? How were Plunkitt's notions of politics influenced by the experiences of immigrants like Gold? How were Gold's experiences influenced by politics as practiced by Plunkitt?

CHAPTER 18

BUSINESS AND POLITICS IN THE GILDED AGE
1877–1895

The growth of huge corporations during the Gilded Age concentrated great power in the hands of wealthy industrialists and financiers. Their power to hire and fire employees, to make or break the fortunes of many, to shape the economic fate of the nation raised the question of how the principles of democracy should apply to corporations. Should the government attempt to regulate the relations between labor and capital? Should lawmakers set rates for public services such as railroads or telegraphs? What should be done about the growing disparity between rich and poor? Did wealthy capitalists have special social obligations? Captains of industry and their supporters answered these questions by declaring that things were as they should be, as illustrated in the first three selections that follow. Critics pointed out that the actual relations between government and industry were very different from the laissez-faire claims of business leaders, as the fourth selection documents.

DOCUMENT 1
Jay Gould on Capital and Labor

Concerned about numerous strikes in industry after industry, the U.S. Senate initiated a broad investigation of the relations between labor and capital in 1882. Senators traveled throughout the nation and took testimony from workers and bosses, the unemployed and employers. In 1883, Senator Henry W. Blair of New Hampshire questioned Jay Gould, a multimillionaire railroad tycoon and stock speculator. At the time of the testimony excerpted here, Gould's holdings included the Union Pacific Railroad, the Western Union Telegraph Company, and many other enterprises.

37

Testimony before the U.S. Senate, 1883

Senator Blair: We have had a man six feet high, who has driven a truck team, and who has more intellectual capacity than half, or perhaps any, of the members of Congress, offering here before this committee to agree under contract to work diligently and faithfully for the next twenty years for anybody who would give him employment and agree to maintain himself and his family. That man said he had been unable to get anything ahead, and could not find a chance to work; that he was hungry, and his family were hungry, and that he didn't know what to do; and it was represented to us here that he was one of a large class. He said that folks told him to go West; but such a man cannot go West, if he tells the truth about his situation, and even if he were to adopt the plan you suggest, his family certainly could not accompany him, driving a mule on the canal tow-path. . . .

Jay Gould: Well, I know there are a great many cases of actual suffering in a large city like this, and in all large cities. It is a very difficult thing to say exactly how you are to everybody's condition. I have noticed, though, that generally if men are temperate and industrious they are pretty sure of success. In cases such as the one you describe I could almost always go back behind the scenes and find a cause for such a person's "misfortunes."

Blair: There has been testimony before us that the feeling generally between employers and employees throughout the country is one of hostility, especially on the part of the employees toward those whom they designate as monopolists. From your observation, what do you think is really the feeling as a general rule between those two classes?

Gould: I think that if left alone they would mutually regulate their relations. I think there is no disagreement between the great mass of the employees and their employers. These societies that are gotten up magnify these things and create evils which do not exist — create trouble which ought not to exist.

Blair: Of the men who conduct business enterprises and wield the power of capital in this country today, what proportion do you think are what are called "self-made men"?

Gould: I think they are all "self-made men"; I do not say self-made exactly, for the country has grown and they have grown up with it. In this country we have no system of heirlooms or of handing down estates. Every man has to stand here on his own individual merit.

Blair: What is the proportion of those men who have made their own fortunes pecuniarily, such as they are?

U.S. Congress, Senate, *Report of the Senate Committee upon the Relations between Labor and Capital* (1885), 47–133.

Gould: I think they are nearly all of that class. I think, that according to my observation in the field that I have been in, nearly every one that occupies a prominent position has come up from the ranks, worked his own way along up. . . .

Blair: . . . Won't you please give us, . . . as fully as you see fit . . . your idea in regard to the establishment of a postal telegraph for the purpose of supplanting or rivaling the existing telegraphic systems of the country now controlled by private ownership?

Gould: Well, I think that control by the government in such things is contrary to our institutions. A telegraph system, of all businesses in the world, wants to be managed by skilled experts. Our government is founded on a political idea; that is, that the party in power shall control the patronage; and if the government controlled the telegraph, the heads of the general managers and the superintendents would come off every four years, if there was a change in politics—at least as often as that— and you would not have any such efficient service as you have now. The very dividend of the Western Union depends upon the company doing the business well, keeping her customers, and developing the business. But if the government controlled it—why if the Democrats were in power it would be a Democratic telegraph, and if the Republicans came into power it would be a Republican telegraph, and if the great Reformers came in I don't know what they would do with it. I think they would—

Blair: [Interposing.] It will not be very important to decide that until they come in.

Gould: No, sir. . . .

Blair: Would you regard a corporate property like that of the Western Union, which is based upon a franchise to which the public are a party, as standing upon the same ground with reference to its right to create an increase of earning power that a piece of private property stands upon where there is no franchise obtained from the public?

Gould: I look upon corporate property in this way. I make a great difference between corporate property and private property. Corporate property is clothed with public rights and has duties to the public, and I regard those duties as paramount, really, to the rights of the stockholders. A corporation has first to perform its public obligations and the business that it was created to do; but when you have gone to that extent, then beyond that, I put it upon the same ground as private property. I judge of its value by its net earning power, the same as I judge of any private property; because I have faith in the government—I have faith in the republican institutions under which we live.

Blair: Right upon that point, is one of those public rights of which you speak—the right to exercise the power of reducing, regulating, or controlling the charges which the corporation may make for the services which it renders to the public and for which the public pays.

Gould: They can regulate those charges within the limits of legislative direction. For instance, if the legislature should come in and fix a limit, that becomes the law of the corporation. The legislature can regulate the rates to be imposed. That is the great hold of the public upon corporations. If unreasonable rates are established or unreasonable regulations made by a corporation, the legislature can come in and control them, and its directions are paramount. For instance, if there was a great clamor that the Western Union Company was charging unreasonable rates, it would be perfectly fair for the legislature to come in and examine into that question, and if they found the rates or regulations unreasonable, to control them by legislative action. Their control is paramount to every other control. But that would be a very different thing from the government going into the business of telegraphing and destroying the property of her own citizens. . . .

Blair: Do you think there would be any opposition made to a general national law regulating the fares and freight charges upon interstate commerce?

Gould: Well, I don't know about that. I think the freer you allow things to be the better. They regulate themselves. The laws of supply and demand, production and consumption, enter into and settle those matters. . . . I know that some years ago, when I was connected with the Chicago and Northwestern road, the states of Wisconsin and some of the other states passed what were called the "Granger laws"; but they repealed them afterwards, because they found on practical investigation that that legislation was tending to frighten capital away from those states, and to retard their development. Finding that to be so, in order to bring back confidence they repealed the laws and left the roads free to work out their own success. . . .

A corporation is only another name for the means which we have discovered of allowing a poor man to invest his income in a great enterprise. In other words, instead of one man owning any of these great properties in bulk, they are divided into small shares, so that the man who has got only $200 or $500 or $5,000, or whatever it may be, can own an interest in proportion to his capital. That is what a corporation means.

Blair: Then, in your opinion, the natural operation of the laws of descent as they exist in this country is to guard the community against any danger from the perpetuation of associated corporate wealth, or of great individual fortunes in the future?

Gould: Yes, sir; I do not think there is any need to be afraid of capital; capital is scary. What you have got to fear is large, ignorant masses of population; I don't think the liberties of the people have anything to fear from capital. Capital is conservative and scary; but what you have to fear in a republican government like ours, where there is no military control, is large masses of uneducated, ignorant people.

Blair: Do you think there is any danger to this country in that direction?

Gould: I think we are accumulating great masses of such people from abroad. Whether we have a system that will educate them up rapidly enough I do not know.

Blair: If there was to be any legislation in any direction on this general question, don't you think that it might as well be in the direction of educating the people as in any other?

Gould: I think that is what we should do—educate the masses, elevate their moral standards. I think that is the only protection we can have for a long period in the future. When the people are educated and intelligent you have nothing to fear from them.

Blair: Do you think that to do that would accomplish more for labor than anything else we could do?

Gould: Yes, sir; because education fits a man so that if be does not like one field of labor he can go to another. Business is constantly changing, and where there is an excess of one class of labor there is very likely to be a lack of another class, and if a man is properly educated he can turn his hand to a great many different things. . . .

Blair: Do you think that the large employers of labor, the manufacturing corporations, the transportation companies, the telegraph companies, and so on, and also individuals who employ help in large masses and who necessarily classify their help, paying them different rates of wages, according to classes rather than according to their individual merits do you think that they might profitably ingraft upon their business some system of assurance, or some method by which a portion of the earnings of the laborers should be contributed to a fund, and perhaps a proportion of the profit of capital also, to secure the working people against want in seasons of nonemployment, and against the disabilities resulting from accident, sickness, or old age? Could something of that kind be introduced which would be of benefit to the laboring people?

Gould: The trouble about that is that the drones would get control of the money and spend it, in nine cases out of ten. It is a good thing in theory, but I fear it would not work well in practice.

QUESTIONS

According to Gould, why did some people fail to achieve success? • How did he account for his own success? • Why did he oppose government ownership of Western Union? • What responsibilities did he believe corporations to have? • Did he favor government regulation of corporations? • What dangers did he foresee for the nation?

DOCUMENT 2

William Graham Sumner on Social Obligations

Many Americans wondered what to do about those who suffered more than they benefitted from the phenomenal economic development of the Gilded Age. Should one give spare change to a beggar? Should one donate money to a home for un-wed mothers? Should the government somehow help those who needed it? William Graham Sumner, a Yale professor whose ideas attracted a large national audience, answered these questions in his 1883 book, What Social Classes Owe to Each Other, *excerpted here.*

What Social Classes Owe to Each Other, 1883

There is no possible definition of "a poor man." A pauper is a person who cannot earn his living; whose producing powers have fallen positively below his necessary consumption; who cannot, therefore, pay his way. A human society needs the active co-operation and productive energy of every person in it. A man who is present as a consumer, yet who does not contribute either by land, labor, or capital to the work of society, is a burden. On no sound political theory ought such a person to share in the political power of the State. He drops out of the ranks of workers and producers. Society must support him. It accepts the burden, but he must be cancelled from the ranks of the rulers likewise. So much for the pauper. About him no more need be said. But he is not the "poor man.". . .

Neither is there any possible definition of "the weak." Some are weak in one way, and some in another; and those who are weak in one sense are strong in another. In general, however, it may be said that those whom humanitarians and philanthropists call the weak are the ones through whom the productive and conservative forces of society are wasted. They constantly neutralize and destroy the finest efforts of the wise and industrious, and are a dead-weight on the society in all its struggles to realize any better things. . . .

Under the names of the poor and the weak, the negligent, shiftless, inefficient, silly, and imprudent are fastened upon the industrious and prudent as a responsibility and a duty. On the one side, the terms are extended to cover the idle, intemperate, and vicious, who, by the combination, gain credit which they do not deserve, and which they could not get if they stood alone. On the other hand, the terms are extended to include wage-receivers of the humblest rank, who are degraded by the combination. . . .

The humanitarians, philanthropists, and reformers, looking at the facts of life as they present themselves, find enough which is sad and un-

William Graham Sumner, *What Social Classes Owe to Each Other* (1883), 84–90.

promising in the condition of many members of society. They see wealth and poverty side by side. They note great inequality of social position and social chances. They eagerly set about the attempt to account for what they see, and to devise schemes for remedying what they do not like. In their eagerness to recommend the less fortunate classes to pity and consideration they forget all about the rights of other classes; they gloss over all the faults of the classes in question, and they exaggerate their misfortunes and their virtues. They invent new theories of property, distorting rights and perpetrating injustice, as any one is sure to do who sets about the re-adjustment of social relations with the interests of one group distinctly before his mind, and the interests of all other groups thrown into the background. When I have read certain of these discussions I have thought that it must be quite disreputable to be respectable, quite dishonest to own property, quite unjust to go one's own way and earn one's own living, and that the only really admirable person was the good-for-nothing. The man who by his own effort raises himself above poverty appears, in these discussions, to be of no account. The man who has done nothing to raise himself above poverty finds that the social doctors flock about him, bringing the capital which they have collected from the other class, and promising him the aid of the State to give him what the other had to work for. In all these schemes and projects the organized intervention of society through the State is either planned or hoped for, and the State is thus made to become the protector and guardian of certain classes. The agents who are to direct the State action are, of course, the reformers and philanthropists. . . . [O]n the theories of the social philosophers to whom I have referred, we should get a new maxim of judicious living: Poverty is the best policy. If you get wealth, you will have to support other people; if you do not get wealth, it will be the duty of other people to support you.

No doubt one chief reason for the unclear and contradictory theories of class relations lies in the fact that our society, largely controlled in all its organization by one set of doctrines, still contains survivals of old social theories which are totally inconsistent with the former. In the Middle Ages men were united by custom and prescription into associations, ranks, guilds, and communities of various kinds. These ties endured as long as life lasted. Consequently society was dependent, throughout all its details, on status, and the tie, or bond, was sentimental. In our modern state, and in the United States more than anywhere else, the social structure is based on contract, and status is of the least importance. Contract, however, is rational—even rationalistic. It is also realistic, cold, and matter-of-fact. A contract relation is based on a sufficient reason, not on custom or prescription. It is not permanent. It endures only so long as the reason for it endures. In a state based on contract sentiment is out of place in any public or common affairs. It is relegated to the sphere of private and personal relations. . . .

A society based on contract is a society of free and independent men, who form ties without favor or obligation, and cooperate without cringing or intrigue. A society based on contract, therefore, gives the utmost room and chance for individual development, and for all the self-reliance and dignity of a free man. That a society of free men, co-operating under contract, is by far the strongest society which has ever yet existed; that no such society has ever yet developed the full measure of strength of which it is capable; and that the only social improvements which are now conceivable lie in the direction of more complete realization of a society of free men united by contract, are points which cannot be controverted. It follows, however, that one man, in a free state, cannot claim help from, and cannot be charged to give help to, another. . . .

Every honest citizen of a free state owes it to himself, to the community, and especially to those who are at once weak and wronged, to go to their assistance and to help redress their wrongs. Whenever a law or social arrangement acts so as to injure any one, and that one the humblest, then there is a duty on those who are stronger, or who know better, to demand and fight for redress and correction. . . .

We each owe it to the other to guarantee rights. Rights do not pertain to *results*, but only to *chances*. They pertain to the *conditions* of the struggle for existence, not to any of the results of it; to the *pursuit of* happiness, not to the possession of happiness. It cannot be said that each one has a right to have some property, because if one man had such a right some other man or men would be under a corresponding obligation to provide him with some property. Each has a right to acquire and possess property if he can. . . . If we take rights to pertain to results, and then say that rights must be equal, we come to say that men have a right to be equally happy, and so on in all the details. Rights should be equal, because they pertain to chances, and all ought to have equal chances so far as chances are provided or limited by the action of society. This, however, will not produce equal results, but it is right just because it will produce unequal results — that is, results which shall be proportioned to the merits of individuals. We each owe it to the other to guarantee mutually the chance to earn, to possess, to learn, to marry, etc., etc., against any interference which would prevent the exercise of those rights by a person who wishes to prosecute and enjoy them in peace for the pursuit of happiness. If we generalize this, it means that All-of-us ought to guarantee rights to each of us. . . .

The only help which is generally expedient, even within the limits of the private and personal relations of two persons to each other, is that which consists in helping a man to help himself. This always consists in opening the chances. . . .

Now, the aid which helps a man to help himself is not in the least akin to the aid which is given in charity. If alms are given, or if we "make work" for a man, or "give him employment," or "protect" him, we simply take a product from one and give it to another. If we help a man to help himself, by opening the chances around him, we put him in a position to add to the wealth of the community by putting new powers in operation to produce. . . .

The men who have not done their duty in this world never can be equal to those who have done their duty more or less well. If words like wise and foolish, thrifty and extravagant, prudent and negligent, have any meaning in language, then it must make some difference how people behave in this world, and the difference will appear in the position they acquire in the body of society, and in relation to the chances of life. They may, then, be classified in reference to these facts. Such classes always will exist; no other social distinctions can endure. If, then, we look to the origin and definition of these classes, we shall find it impossible to deduce any obligations which one of them bears to the other. The class distinctions simply result from the different degrees of success with which men have availed themselves of the chances which were presented to them. Instead of endeavoring to redistribute the acquisitions which have been made between the existing classes, our aim should be to *increase, multiply,* and *extend the chances.* Such is the work of civilization. Every old error or abuse which is removed opens new chances of development to all the new energy of society. Every improvement in education, science, art, or government expands the chances of man on earth. Such expansion is no guarantee of equality. On the contrary, if there be liberty, some will profit by the chances eagerly and some will neglect them altogether. Therefore, the greater the chances, the more unequal will be the fortune of these two sets of men. So it ought to be, in all justice and right reason.

QUESTIONS

According to Sumner, what was the source of poverty? • What did he believe that humanitarians and philanthropists failed to understand? • What characterized a social structure based on contract? • What did one class owe to another? • Why did increasing chances create greater inequality?

Steel monopoli

DOCUMENT 3

Andrew Carnegie Explains the Gospel of Wealth

Gilded Age critics argued that the concentration of wealth in the bank accounts of the rich robbed workers of just compensation and gave the few too much power. Andrew Carnegie, one of the nation's leading industrialists and among the richest

Americans of the era, defended the concentration of wealth. In an article published in 1889 — the source of the following selection — Carnegie declared that the wealthy knew best how to use their riches for the public welfare.

"Wealth," 1889

The problem of our age is the proper administration of wealth, that the ties of brotherhood may still bind together the rich and poor in harmonious relationship. The conditions of human life have not only been changed, but revolutionized, within the past few hundred years. In former days there was little difference between the dwelling, dress, food, and environment of the chief and those of his retainers. The Indians are today where civilized man then was. . . .The contrast between the palace of the millionaire and the cottage of the laborer with us to-day measures the change which has come with civilization. This change, however, is not to be deplored, but welcomed as highly beneficial. It is well, nay, essential, for the progress of the race that the houses of some should be homes for all that is highest and best in literature and the arts, — and for all the refinements of civilization, rather than that none should be so. Much better this great irregularity than universal squalor. . . . The "good old times" were not good old times. Neither master nor servant was as well situated then as to-day. A relapse to old conditions would be disastrous to both — not the least so to him who serves — and would sweep away civilization with it. But whether the change be for good or ill, it is upon us, beyond our power to alter, and, therefore, to be accepted and made the best of. It is a waste of time to criticize the inevitable.

It is easy to see how the change has come. . . . In the manufacture of products we have the whole story. . . . Formerly, articles were manufactured at the domestic hearth, or in small shops which formed part of the household. The master and his apprentices worked side by side, the latter living with the master, and therefore subject to the same conditions. When these apprentices rose to be masters, there was little or no change in their mode of life, and they, in turn, educated succeeding apprentices in the same routine. There was, substantially, social equality, and even political equality, for those engaged in industrial pursuits had then little or no voice in the State.

The inevitable result of such a mode of manufacture was crude articles at high prices. To-day the world obtains commodities of excellent quality at prices which even the preceding generation would have deemed incredible. . . . The poor enjoy what the rich could not before afford. What were the luxuries have become the necessaries of life. The laborer has

Andrew Carnegie, "Wealth," *North American Review* (1889); reprinted in *Industrialism and Opportunity*, 212–22.

now more comforts than the farmer had a few generations ago. The farmer has more luxuries than the landlord had, and is more richly clad and better housed. The landlord has books and pictures rarer and appointments more artistic than the king could then obtain.

The price we pay for this salutary change is, no doubt, great. We assemble thousands of operatives in the factory, and in the mine, of whom the employer can know little or nothing, and to whom he is little better than a myth. All intercourse between them is at an end. Rigid castes are formed, and, as usual, mutual ignorance breeds mutual distrust. Each caste is without sympathy with the other, and ready to credit anything disparaging in regard to it. Under the law of competition, the employer of thousands is forced into the strictest economies, among which the rates paid to labor figure prominently, and often there is friction between the employer and the employed, between capital and labor, between rich and poor. Human society loses homogeneity.

The price which society pays for the law of competition, like the price it pays for cheap comforts and luxuries, is also great; but the advantages of this law are also greater still than its cost—for it is to this law that we owe our wonderful material development, which brings improved conditions in its train. But, whether the law be benign or not, we must say of it, as we say of the change in the conditions of men to which we have referred: It is here; we cannot evade it; no substitutes for it have been found; and while the law may be sometimes hard for the individual, it is best for the race, because it insures the survival of the fittest in every department. We accept and welcome, therefore, as conditions to which we must accommodate ourselves, great inequality of environments; the concentration of business, industrial and commercial, in the hands of a few; and the law of competition between these, as being not only beneficial, but essential to the future progress of the race. . . .

What is the proper mode of administering wealth after the laws upon which civilization is founded have thrown it into the hands of the few? And it is of this great question that I believe I offer the true solution. It will be understood that fortunes are here spoken of, not moderate sums saved by many years of effort, the returns from which are required for the comfortable maintenance and education of families. This is not wealth, but only competence, which it should be the aim of all to acquire, and which it is for the best interests of society should be acquired. . . .

There remains . . . only one mode of using great fortunes; . . . in this we have the true antidote for the temporary unequal distribution of wealth, the reconciliation of the rich and the poor—a reign of harmony. . . . It is founded upon the present most intense Individualism, and the race is prepared to put it in practice by degrees whenever it pleases. Under its sway we shall have an ideal State, in which the surplus wealth of the few will become, in the best sense, the property of the many, because administered for the common good; and this wealth, passing through the hands of the few, can be made a much more potent force for the elevation of our race than if distributed in small sums to the people themselves. Even the poorest can be made to see this, and to agree that great sums gathered by some of their fellow-citizens and spent for public purposes, from which the masses reap the principal benefit, are more valuable to them than if scattered among themselves in trifling amounts through the course of many years. . . .

Poor and restricted are our opportunities in this life, narrow our horizon, our best work most imperfect; but rich men should be thankful for one inestimable boon. They have it in their power during their lives to busy themselves in organizing benefactions from which the masses of their fellows will derive lasting advantage, and thus dignify their own lives. The highest life is probably to be reached, not by such imitation of the life of Christ as Count Tolstoi gives us, but, while animated by Christ's spirit, by recognizing the changed conditions of this age, and adopting modes of expressing this spirit suitable to the changed conditions under which we live, still laboring for the good of our fellows, which was the essence of his life and teaching, but laboring in a different manner.

This, then, is held to be the duty of the man of wealth: To set an example of modest, unostentatious living, shunning display or extravagance; to provide moderately for the legitimate wants of those dependent upon him; and, after doing so, to consider all surplus revenues which come to him simply as trust funds, which he is called upon to administer, and strictly bound as a matter of duty to administer in the manner which, in his judgment, is best calculated to produce the most beneficial results for the community — the man of wealth thus becoming the mere trustee and agent for his poorer brethren, bringing to their service his superior wisdom, experience, and ability to administer, doing for them better than they would or could do for themselves. . . . *a dream*.

[O]ne of the serious obstacles to the improvement of our race is indiscriminate charity. It were better for mankind that the millions of the rich were thrown into the sea than so spent as to encourage the slothful, the drunken, the unworthy. Of every thousand dollars spent in so-called charity to-day, it is probable that nine hundred and fifty dollars is unwisely spent — so spent, indeed, as to produce the very evils which it hopes to mitigate or cure. . . .

¶[T]he best means of benefiting the community is to place within its reach the ladders upon which the aspiring can rise — free libraries, parks, and means of recreation, by which men are helped in body and mind; works of art, certain to give pleasure and improve the public taste; and public institutions of various kinds, which will improve the general condition of the people; in this manner returning their surplus wealth to the mass of their fellows in the forms best calculated to do them lasting good.

Thus is the problem of rich and poor to be solved. The laws of accumulation will be left free, the laws of distribution free. Individualism will continue, but the millionaire will be but a trustee for the poor, intrusted for a season with a great part of the increased wealth of the community, but administering it for the community far better than it could or would have done for itself. . . .

Such, in my opinion, is the true gospel concerning wealth, obedience to which is destined some day to solve the problem of the rich and the poor, and to bring "Peace on earth, among men good will."

QUESTIONS

According to Carnegie, what were the revolutionary changes in the conditions of life? • Why did those changes occur? • Did Carnegie believe the changes were all good? • What should the truly wealthy do with their riches? • Why were the wealthy especially suited to contribute to public welfare? • How could their wealth bring about peace and harmony?

DOCUMENT 4

Henry Demarest Lloyd Describes How Jay Gould Got Rich

Muckraking journalists attacked the pompous rhetoric of free markets and self-made men. They argued that the realities of the Gilded Age had more to do with favoritism, buying votes, shady deals, dishonesty, and exploitation than with hard work, competition, and perseverance. In 1882, a year before Jay Gould's testimony to the Senate Committee on the Relations between Labor and Capital (see Document 1), muckraker Henry Demarest Lloyd described how Gould accumulated his wealth of $73 million.

"The Political Economy of Seventy-three Million Dollars," 1882

There is not . . . any purely industrial human being. But occasionally there flourish, outside the jails, persons who are almost ideal exemplifications of the principles of the competitive political economy. America has produced the most successful of these practical political economists. His career illustrates what may be accomplished by a scientific devotion

---

Henry Demarest Lloyd, "The Political Economy of Seventy-three Million Dollars," *Atlantic Monthly* (1882); reprinted in *The Businessman: For and Against*, 141–8.

to the principles of competition, laissez-faire, desire of wealth, and self-interest, if not the harmony of interests.

While the Crystal Palace exhibition of 1853 was open in New York, there came to seek his fortune in the city a slender, black-eyed, black-haired boy, from the interior of the State. He brought with him a very handsome mahogany box. In the box was an invention: "a little thing," he once said, "I had brought from my country home, and thought was going to make my fortune and revolutionize the world. It was a mouse-trap." The unsophisticated boy left his treasure on the seat of a Sixth Avenue car, while he stood on the platform to stare at the crowd, and it was stolen. But he pursued and caught the thief, who was an old offender, for whom the police of New York were looking at that moment. The *Herald* of the next day, under the heading "How a Mouse-Trap caught a Thief," gave his first taste of publicity to the youth who for the next thirty years was to be continually before the public, and, by a singular coincidence, always in connection with some kind of trap. The genius that had divined from afar that the great city was full of mice, and had contrived a trap to catch them, could not be stolen. Its first impulse grew to be a passion. Brains and strict attention to the laws of supply and demand have made the country boy the greatest mouse-catcher of America, and his traps have become the envy of every man of feline aspirations.

Four of his inventions were masterpieces. In the first of them he gained the confidence of his simple prey by assuming a position of trust as director, and afterwards as president, of the largest railroad but one in his native State. At once there began to turn before the eyes of the stock-holders and the public a kaleidoscope of ruin: shower after shower of stocks and bonds issued to run the road, while the trustee and his pals . . . drank dry the stream of earnings; a devil's dance of lawyers, judges, legislators, governors, and Tammany politicians, flinging themselves into every attitude of betrayal of trust, an orgy of fiduciary harlotry, led by a great law reformer; a tangled web of injunctions and counter-injunctions, and more injunctions, contradictory orders of courts, perjured affidavits — every thread spun by its poisonous spinner around and around a trust; a phantasmagoria of prosperity of busy trains and steamers, crowded ferries, marble opera-houses, bursting warehouses, glowing mills, precious franchises, and rich contracts — a fair but hollow scene, where all the expenses go to the owner, and all the receipts to the trustee.

Our economist, having been charged with a fraud upon his road, at once procured from one of his courts the place of receiver, with a fund of $8,000,000, to protect his trust against himself. In one of his stock-exchange campaigns he locked up $12,500,000 of money—other people's money. . . .

When this [man] . . . became trustee, his trust was in debt $51,065,943. Under his administration of the laws of competition, this became $115,449,211, while the [railroad] mileage increased but 186 miles. In four months the increase was $23,500,000. The moral bankruptcy that festooned this ruin could not be expressed in figures. These surprising achievements in the pursuit of wealth led the New York legislature to order an investigation. The political economist of the mousetrap was charmingly frank in his answers to the committee:

"I was first elected president of the Erie Railroad in 1868, and I was president in 1869, 1870, and 1871. I do not remember whether I approved payment to William M. Tweed of money for legal services, while he was senator. I do not know whether he is a lawyer. He was a director of Erie and member of its executive committee. I would not have allowed pecuniary transactions with Mr. Tweed to be put in the shape of legal services, if my attention had been called to them. . . . I should say that paper was in my handwriting. The name William M. Tweed is in my handwriting. The words in my handwriting are, William M. Tweed, legal disbursements as per order J. G., $35,000, April 25, 1871. The approval of voucher, April 5, 1869, name of William M. Tweed, legal expenses, $15,000, looks like my handwriting. Mr. Tweed's name at the top is my handwriting, and I should say his name at the foot of the receipt is my handwriting. He was senator in 1869; also in 1871 and 1872. . . . I gave large amounts for elections in 1869, 1870, 1871, and 1872 in the senatorial and assembly districts. It was what they said would be necessary to carry the day in addition to the amount forwarded by the committee. I contributed more or less to all the districts along the line of the [rail]road. We had to look after four States, New York, New Jersey, Pennsylvania, and Ohio. It was the custom, when men received nominations, to come to me for contributions, and I made them, and considered them good paying investments for the company. In a republican district, I was a strong republican; in a democratic district, I was democratic; and in doubtful districts, I was doubtful. In politics, I was an Erie railroad man, every time. We had friends who were on both sides, friends in a business way. The amounts contributed for the elections were large, but I could not give any definite estimate. No names occur to me at the moment. I am a poor hand to remember names. I had relations in several States. I did not keep separate what I paid out in New Jersey from what I paid out in New York. We had the same ground to go over there, *and there has been so much of it.* It has been so extensive that I have no details now to refresh my mind. You might as well go back and ask me how many cars of freight were moved on a particular day. . . ."

It was no ordinary trap in which Wall Street and the whole country were caught on that darkest day of all our financial history—Black Friday, September 21, 1869. . . . There are to-day men proud to tell you that in that moment of frenzy and horror they hunted, rope in hand, for this disciple of self-interest, and if they could have caught him would have hanged the maker of the mouse-trap that caught a thief only sixteen years before. But the president of the Erie road fled to his arsenal on Twenty-

Third Street, and was secure. He saved his millions. . . . He was promoted from investigation by a committee of the New York legislature to investigation by a committee of Congress. He told them, "I had my own views about the market, and my own fish to fry.". . . In December, 1880, what may be accomplished by steadfast faithfulness to the principles of competition was shown by a statement, made by the most trustworthy financial paper in the United States, that our political economist was in control of ten thousand miles of railroad, or more than one ninth the entire mileage of the country.

It was during the same month that the conflict between the Western Union and American Union telegraph companies was raging at its worst. The American Union had been started in 1879, by our hero, with an investment of less than five million dollars. . . . February 5, 1881, Western Union and the American Union and the Atlantic and Pacific telegraph companies were consolidated, and . . . the public found that the ex-trustee of Erie, the ally of the Tammany ring, the corrupter of justice, and the artificer of panic was master of the rapid transit of news and confidence within the United States, and between them and the rest of the world.

Hardly had the details of the telegraph consolidation been announced, February, 1881, when a flutter in the New York Stock Exchange followed the publication of a letter from the president of the Manhattan Elevated Railroad Company, begging the State to remit the taxes due from the company. . . . Suddenly what had seemed a mass of ruin crystallized into the symmetrical structure of a monopoly, and on its peak, but a few days after he had sworn that Manhattan was hopelessly and irretrievably insolvent, sat the manufacturer of mouse-traps, master of the rapid transit of the greatest city of America. . . . He bought his law in the courts where it was cheapest, and sold it in the Stock Exchange where it was dearest. . . . When a property owner of New York remonstrated . . . about some encroachments by the elevated roads, he received this reply, which embodied the whole of one of the latter-day theories of wealth: "We have the legislature on our side, the courts on our side, and we hire our law by the year."

A man who braves the heart-broken rage of fifty millions of men, and in daylight shoots their President, we call an assassin. George Washington hanged as a spy a man who traveled the high-road as an instrument in Benedict Arnold's treachery. We teach our children to execrate as traitors the men who stood up in a fair fight to divide the Union. What shall we call the man and the men who seduce, but do not assassinate—Guiteaus of political economy who would overcome, not one, but all departments of our government; who travel by night and under-ground to betray trusts they have invited; who, living among us as fellow-men and neighbors, loyal to the covenants of society, are traitors to all the ties of honor, justice, and mercy that make the American community possible . . . ?

By what title do these men hold their acquisitions? Private property is sacred, but plunder must not be private. A philosopher of the [Paris] commune said, "Property is theft." American self-government must have a philosophy to say, Theft shall not be property.

It is March 13, 1882. The boy who brought his mahogany box and his mouse-trap to New York in 1853 sits in an office rich with plate-glass and precious woods. He opens his box, which like him has grown, and shows a group of friends twenty-three million dollars of Western Union stock, twelve millions of Missouri Pacific stock, eight millions of elevated railroad stocks and bonds, ten millions of Wabash common and preferred, and other stock. . . . This . . . was a "partial list." Seventy-three millions, and more, accumulated by an enthusiast in competition in twenty-nine years of office work! Never before in the history of the desire of wealth had such a sight been seen. The mouse-trap man's wires told the news to the people of two continents, and the world held its breath.

On the same day, while the president of the Wabash road, which had appropriated for dividends to stockholders the wages due its men, was thus spreading out his millions, a day laborer, in the employ of the Wabash at St. Louis, said to a reporter:—

The delay in the payment of my wages has reduced me almost to beggary. Had not the grocer helped me with credit in January and February, my children would have starved.

An engineer said:

My family were sick in January. They had no doctor and no medicines. I could not get the money due me from the Wabash road.

An old man, who watched a crossing, an infirm old man, with a family, said:

My rent is six dollars a month; my groceries are eighteen dollars. This leaves us one dollar a month for clothing, medicine, and other necessaries. My pay is twenty-five dollars a month, and I have to wait two months for that. We are on the edge of starvation.

It is a solemn truth . . . that every man has to choose in this world whether he will be a laborer or an assassin. There are men who murder for money, but there must be no science of assassination.

QUESTIONS

According to Lloyd, why was Jay Gould an ideal example of "competitive political economy"? • Why did Lloyd consider a mousetrap a metaphor for Gould's success? • What did Gould say about the finances and politics of the Erie Railroad? • How did Gould get away with his manipulations? • According to Lloyd, who was the assassin? • Why?

COMPARATIVE QUESTIONS

How do the views that Jay Gould held about the obligations of wealthy people compare with those of William Graham Sumner? How do Gould's and Sumner's views compare with Andrew Carnegie's? How do Lloyd's ideas about wealth differ from those of Gould, Sumner, and Carnegie? What did the individuals described in these documents believe about the proper role of government?

CHAPTER 19

AMERICA THROUGH THE EYES OF THE WORKERS
1870–1890

The economic achievements of the Gilded Age did not appear to be miraculous to working people. Factory workers knew that profits often meant low wages, long hours, and frequent unemployment. Domestic servants knew how much work it took to supply their employers with the comforts of home. Union members knew that strikes could win them a share of gains in productivity. As the following documents illustrate, the Gilded Age looked different when viewed from the shop floor rather than corner office.

DOCUMENT 1

A Textile Worker Explains the Labor Market

Wage workers had jobs as long as they could be hired. Employers laid off workers during business slumps or replaced those whose jobs could be done cheaper by a machine or a worker with a lower wage. In 1883, Thomas O'Donnell, who had worked as a mule spinner for eleven years in textile mills in Fall River, Massachusetts, testified before the U.S. Senate Committee on Relations between Capital and Labor. O'Donnell explained to Senator Henry W. Blair of New Hampshire what is was like to be a working man in the 1880s.

Thomas O'Donnell

Testimony before a U.S. Senate Committee, 1885

Senator Blair: Are you a married man?

O'Donnell: Yes, sir; I am a married man; have a wife and two children. I am not very well educated. I went to work when I was young, and have been working ever since in the cotton business; went to work when I was

U.S. Congress, Senate, *Report of the Senate Committee upon the Relations between Labor and Capital* (1885).

about eight or nine years old. I was going to state how I live. My children get along very well in summer time, on account of not having to buy fuel or shoes or one thing and another. I earn $1.50 a day and can't afford to pay a very big house rent. I pay $1.50 a week for rent, which comes to about $6.00 a month.

Blair: That is, you pay this where you are at Fall River?

O'Donnell: Yes, Sir.

Blair: Do you have work right along?

O'Donnell: No, sir; since that strike we had down in Fall River about three years ago I have not worked much more than half the time, and that has brought my circumstances down very much.

Blair: Why have you not worked more than half the time since then?

O'Donnell: Well, at Fall River if a man has not got a boy to act as "back-boy" it is very hard for him to get along. In a great many cases they discharge men in that work and put in men who have boys.

Blair: Men who have boys of their own?

O'Donnell: Men who have boys of their own capable enough to work in a mill, to earn $.30 or $.40 a day.

Blair: Is the object of that to enable the boy to earn something for himself?

O'Donnell: Well, no; the object is this: They are doing away with a great deal of mule-spinning there and putting in ring-spinning, and for that reason it takes a good deal of small help to run this ring work, and it throws the men out of work. . . . For that reason they get all the small help they can to run these ring-frames. There are so many men in the city to work, and whoever has a boy can have work, and whoever has no boy stands no chance. Probably he may have a few months of work in the summer time, but will be discharged in the fall. That is what leaves me in poor circumstances. Our children, of course, are very often sickly from one cause or another, on account of not having sufficient clothes, or shoes, or food, or something. And also my woman; she never did work in a mill; she was a housekeeper, and for that reason she can't help me to anything at present, as many women do help their husbands down there, by working, like themselves. My wife never did work in a mill, and that leaves me to provide for the whole family. I have two children. . . .

Blair: How much [work] have you had within a year?

O'Donnell: Since Thanksgiving I happened to get work in the Crescent Mill, and worked there exactly thirteen weeks. I got just $1.50 a day, with the exception of a few days that I lost because in following up mule-spinning you are obliged to lose a day once in a while; you can't follow it up regularly.

Blair: Thirteen weeks would be seventy-eight days, and, at $1.50 a day, that would make $117, less whatever time you lost?

O'Donnell: Yes. I worked thirteen weeks there and ten days in another place, and then there was a dollar I got this week, Wednesday.

Blair: Taking a full year back can you tell how much you have had?

O'Donnell: That would be about fifteen weeks' work. . . .

Blair: That would be somewhere about $133, if you had not lost any time?

O'Donnell: Yes, sir.

Blair: That is all you have had?

O'Donnell: Yes, sir.

Blair: To support yourself and wife and two children?

O'Donnell: Yes, sir.

Blair: Have you had any help from outside?

O'Donnell: No, sir.

Blair: Do you mean that yourself and wife and two children have had nothing but that for all this time?

O'Donnell: That is all. I got a couple dollars' worth of coal last winter, and the wood I picked up myself. I goes around with a shovel and picks up clams and wood.

Blair: What do you do with the clams?

O'Donnell: We eat them. I don't get them to sell, but just to eat, for the family. That is the way my brother lives, too, mostly. He lives close by us.

Blair: How many live in that way down there?

O'Donnell: I could not count them, they are so numerous. I suppose there are one thousand down there.

Blair: A thousand that live on $150 a year?

O'Donnell: They live on less.

Blair: Less than that?

O'Donnell: Yes; they live on less than I do.

Blair: How long has that been so?

O'Donnell: Mostly so since I have been married.

Blair: How long is that?

O'Donnell: Six years this month.

Blair: Why do you not go West on a farm?

O'Donnell: How could I go, walk it?

Blair: Well, I want to know why you do not go out West on a $2,000 farm, or take up a homestead and break it and work it up, and then have it for yourself and family?

O'Donnell: I can't see how I could get out West. I have got nothing to go with.

Blair: It would not cost you over $1,500.

O'Donnell: Well, I never saw over a $20 bill, and that is when I have been getting a month's pay at once. If someone would give me $1,500 I will go. . . .

Blair: Are you a good workman?

O'Donnell: Yes, sir.

Blair: Were you ever turned off because of misconduct or incapacity or unfitness for work?

O'Donnell: No, sir.

Blair: Or because you did bad work?

O'Donnell: No, sir.

Blair: Or because you made trouble among the help?

O'Donnell: No, sir.

Blair: Did you ever have any personal trouble with an employer?

O'Donnell: No, sir.

Blair: You have not anything now you say?

O'Donnell: No, sir.

Blair: How old are you?

O'Donnell: About thirty.

Blair: Is your health good?

O'Donnell: Yes, sir.

Blair: What would you work for if you could get work right along; if you could be sure to have it for five years, staying right where you are?

O'Donnell: Well, if I was where my family could be with me, and I could have work every day I would take $1.50, and be glad to. . . .

Blair: You spoke of fuel—what do you have for fuel?

O'Donnell: Wood and coal.

Blair: Where does the wood come from?

O'Donnell: I pick it up around the shore —any old pieces I see around that are not good for anything. There are many more that do the same thing.

Blair: Do you get meat to live on much?

O'Donnell: Very seldom.

Blair: What kinds of meat do you get for your family?

O'Donnell: Well, once in a while we get a piece of pork and some clams and make a clam chowder. That makes a very good meal. We sometimes get a piece of corn beef or something like that. . . .

Blair: What have you eaten?

O'Donnell: Well, bread mostly, when we could get it; we sometimes couldn't make out to get that, and have had to go without a meal.

Blair: Has there been any day in the year that you have had to go without anything to eat?

O'Donnell: Yes, sir, several days.

Blair: More than one day at a time?

O'Donnell: No. . . .

Blair: What have the children got on in the way of clothing?

O'Donnell: They have got along very nicely all summer, but now they are beginning to feel quite sickly. One has one shoe on, a very poor one, and a slipper, that was picked up somewhere. The other has two odd shoes on, with the heel out. He has got cold and is sickly now.

Blair: Have they any stockings?

O'Donnell: He had got stockings, but his feet comes through them, for there is a hole in the bottom of the shoe.

Blair: What have they got on the rest of their person?

O'Donnell: Well, they have a little calico shirt—what should be a shirt; it is sewed up in some shape—and one little petticoat, and a kind of little dress.

Blair: How many dresses has your wife got?

O'Donnell: She has got one since she was married, and she hasn't worn that more than half a dozen times; she has worn it just going to church and coming back. She is very good in going to church, but when she comes back she takes it off, and it is pretty near as good now as when she bought it.

Blair: She keeps that dress to go to church in?

O'Donnell: Yes, sir.

Blair: How many dresses aside from that has she?

O'Donnell: Well, she got one here three months ago.

Blair: What did it cost?

O'Donnell: It cost $1.00 to make it and I guess about a dollar for the stuff, as near as I can tell.

Blair: The dress cost $2.00?

O'Donnell: Yes.

Blair: What else has she?

O'Donnell: Well, she has an undershirt that she got given to her, and she has an old wrapper, which is about a mile too big for her; somebody gave it to her.

Blair: She did not buy it?

O'Donnell: No. That is all that I know that she has. . . .

Blair: Do you see any way out of your troubles—what are you going to do for a living—or do you expect to have to stay right there?

O'Donnell: Yes. I can't run around with my family.

Blair: You have nowhere to go to, and no way of getting there if there was any place to go to?

O'Donnell: No, sir; I have no means nor anything, so I am obliged to remain there and try to pick up something as I can.

Blair: Do the children go to school?

O'Donnell: No, sir; they are not old enough; the oldest child is only three and a half; the youngest one is one and a half years old.

Blair: Is there anything else you wanted to say?

O'Donnell: Nothing further, except that I would like some remedy to be got to help us poor people down there in some way. Excepting the government decides to do something with us we have a poor show. We are all, or mostly all, in good health; that is, as far as the men who are at work go.

Blair: You do not know anything but mule-spinning, I suppose?

O'Donnell: That is what I have been doing, but I sometimes do something with pick and shovel. I have worked for a man at that, because I am so put on. I am looking for work in a mill. The way they do there is this: There are about twelve or thirteen men that go into a mill every morning, and they have to stand their chance, looking for work. The man who has a boy with him he stands the best chance, and then, if it is my turn or a neighbor's turn who has no boy, if another man comes in who has a boy he is taken right in, and we are left out. I said to the boss once it was my turn to go in, and now you have taken on that man; what am I to do; I have got two little boys at home, one of them three years and a half and the other one year and a half old, and how am I to find something for them to eat; I can't get my turn when I come here. He said he could not do anything for me. I says, "Have I got to starve; ain't I to have any work?" They are forcing these young boys into the mills that should not be in mills at all; forcing them in because they are throwing the mules out and putting on ring-frames. They are doing everything of that kind that they possibly can to crush down the poor people—the poor operatives there.

QUESTIONS

What wages did O'Donnell earn? • How much did he work and why didn't he work more? • Why didn't he leave Fall River? • How did he support his family? • What kinds of food and clothing did the family have? • What did he want? • What kind of future could his children look forward to?

DOCUMENT 2

Domestic Servants on Household Work

Millions of women worked in factories and shops during the Gilded Age. Millions more worked as domestic servants for people who could afford to pay somebody else to do the household chores. Many women preferred to become factory laborers or shop clerks rather than domestic servants. In the 1880s, journalist Helen Campbell interviewed a number of former servants to try to find out why. A selection of Campbell's interviews follows.

Interviews with Journalist Helen Campbell, 1880s

First on the list stands Margaret M——, an American, twenty-three years old, and for five years in a paper-box factory. Seven others nodded their assent, or added a word here and there as she gave her view, two of them Irish-Americans who had had some years in the public schools.

Helen Campbell, *Prisoners of Poverty* (1900); reprinted in *Root of Bitterness: Documents in the Social History of American Women,* ed. Nancy F. Cott (Boston: Northeastern University Press, 1996), 322–26.

"It's freedom that we want when the day's work is done. I know, some nice girls, Bridget's cousins, that make more money and dress better and everything for being in service. They're waitresses, and have Thursday afternoon out and part of every other Sunday. But they're never sure of one minute that's their own when they're in the house. Our day is ten hours long, but when it's done it's done, and we can do what we like with the evenings. That's what I've heard from every nice girl that ever tried service. You're never sure that your soul's your own except when you are out of the house, and I couldn't stand that a day. Women care just as much for freedom as men do. Of course they don't get so much, but I know I'd fight for mine."

"Women are always harder on women than men are," said a fur sewer, an intelligent American about thirty. "I got tired of always sitting, and took a place as chambermaid. The work was all right and the wages good, but I'll tell you what I couldn't stand. The cook and the waitress were just common, uneducated Irish, and I had to room with one and stand the personal habits of both, and the way they did at table took all my appetite. I couldn't eat, and began to run down; and at last I gave notice, and told the truth when I was asked why. The lady just looked at me astonished: 'If you take a servant's place, you can't expect to be one of the family,' she said. 'I never asked it,' I said; 'all I ask is a chance at common decency.' 'It will be difficult to find an easier place than this,' she said, and I knew it; but ease one way was hardness another, and she couldn't see that I had any right to complain. That's one trouble in the way. It's the mixing up of things, and mistresses don't think how they would feel in the same place."

Third came an Irish-American whose mother had been cook for years in one family, but who had, after a few months of service, gone into a jute-mill, followed gradually by five sisters.

"I hate the very words 'service' and 'servant,'" she said. "We came to this country to better ourselves, and it's not bettering to have anybody ordering you round."

"But you are ordered in the mill."

"That's different. A man knows what he wants, and doesn't go beyond it; but a woman never knows what she wants, and sort of bosses you everlastingly. If there was such a thing as fixed hours it might be different, but I tell every girl I know, 'Whatever you do, don't go into service. You'll always be prisoners and always looked down on.' You can do things at home for them as belongs to you that somehow it seems different to do for strangers. Anyway, I hate it, and there's plenty like me."

"What I minded," said a gentle, quiet girl, who worked at a stationer's, and who had tried household service for a year,—"what I minded was the awful lonesomeness. I went for general housework, because I knew all about it, and there were only three in the family. I never minded being alone evenings in my own room, for I'm always reading or something, and I don't go out hardly at all, but then I always know I can, and that there is somebody to talk to if I like. But there, except to give orders, they had nothing to do with me. It got to feel sort of crushing at last. I cried myself sick, and at last I gave it up, though I don't mind the work at all. I know there are good places, but the two I tried happened to be about alike, and I shan't try again. There are a good many would feel just the same."

"Oh, nobody need to tell me about poor servants," said an energetic woman of forty, Irish-American, and for years in a shirt factory. "Don't I know the way the hussies'll do, comin' out of a bog maybe, an' not knowing the names even, let alone the use, of half the things in the kitchen, and asking their twelve and fourteen dollars a month? Don't I know it well, an' the shame it is to 'em! but I know plenty o' decent, hard-workin' girls too, that give good satisfaction, an' this is what they say. They say the main trouble is, the mistresses don't know, no more than babies, what a day's work really is. A smart girl keeps on her feet all the time to prove she isn't lazy, for if the mistress finds her sitting down, she thinks there can't be much to do and that she doesn't earn her wages. Then if a girl tries to save herself or is deliberate, they call her slow. They want girls on tap from six in the morning till ten and eleven at night. 'Tisn't fair. And then, if there's a let-up in the work, maybe they give you the baby to see to. I like a nice baby, but I don't like having one turned over to me when I'm fit to drop scrabbling to get through and sit down a bit. I've naught to say for the girls that's breaking things and half doing the work. They're a shameful set, and ought to be put down somehow; but it's a fact that the most I've known in service have been another sort that stayed long in places and hated change. There's many a good place too, but the bad ones outnumber 'em. Women make hard mistresses, and I say again, I'd rather be under a man, that knows what he wants. That's the way with most."

"I don't see why people are surprised that we don't rush into places," said a shop-girl. "Our world may be a very narrow world, and I know it is; but for all that, it's the only one we've got, and right or wrong, we're out of it if we go into service. A teacher or cashier or anybody in a store, no matter if they have got common-sense, doesn't want to associate with servants. Somehow you get a sort of smooch. Young men think and say, for I have heard lots of them, 'Oh, she can't amount to much if she hasn't brains enough to make a living outside of a kitchen!' You're just down once for all if you go into one."

"I don't agree with you at all," said a young teacher who had come with her. "The people that hire you go into kitchens and are not disgraced. What I felt was, for you see I tried it, that they oughtn't to make me go into livery. I was worn out with teaching, and so I concluded to try being a nurse for a while. I found two hard things: one, that I was never free for an hour from the children, for I took meals and all with them, and any mother knows what a rest it is to go quite away from them, even for an hour; and the other was that she wanted me to wear the nurse's cap and apron. She was real good and kind; but when I said, 'Would you like your sister, Miss Louise, to put on cap and apron when she goes out with them?' she got very red, and straightened up. 'It's a very different matter,' she said; 'you must not forget that in accepting a servant's place you accept a servant's limitations.' That finished me. I loved the children, but I said, 'If you have no other thought of what I am to the children than that, I had better go.' I went, and she put a common, uneducated Irish girl in my place. I know a good many who would take nurse's places, and who are sensible enough not to want to push into the family life. But the trouble is that almost every one wants to make a show, and it is more stylish to have the nurse in a cap and apron and so she is ordered into them."

"I've tried it," said one who had been a dressmaker and found her health going from long sitting. "My trouble was, no conscience as to hours; and I believe you'll find that is, at the bottom, one of the chief objections. My first employer was a smart, energetic woman, who had done her own work when she was first married and knew what it meant, or you'd think she might have known. But she had no more thought for me than if I had been a machine. She'd sit in her sitting room on the second floor and ring for me twenty times a day to do little things, and she wanted me up till eleven to answer the bell, for she had a great deal of company. I had a good room and everything nice, and she gave me a great many things, but I'd have spared them all if only I could have had a little time to myself. I was all worn out, and at last I had to go. There was another reason. I had no place but the kitchen to see my friends. I was thirty years old and as well born and well educated as she, and it didn't seem right. The mistresses think it's all the girls' fault, but I've seen enough to know that women haven't found out what justice means, and that a girl knows it, many a time, better than her employer. Anyway, you couldn't make me try it again."

"My trouble was," said another, who had been in a cotton-mill and gone into the home of one of the mill-owners as chambermaid, "I hadn't any place that I could be alone a minute. We were poor at home, and four of us worked in the mill, but I had a little room all my own, even if it didn't hold much. In that splendid big house the servants' room was over the kitchen, hot and close in summer, and cold in winter, and four beds in it. We five had to live there together, with only two bureaus and a bit of a closet, and one washstand for all. There was no chance to keep clean or your things in nice order, or anything by yourself, and I gave up. Then I went into a little family and tried general housework, and the mistress taught me a great deal, and was good and kind, only there the kitchen was a dark little place and my room like it, and I hadn't an hour in anything that was pleasant and warm. A mistress might see, you'd think, when a girl was quiet and fond of her home, and treat her different from the kind that destroy everything; but I suppose the truth is, they're worn out with that kind and don't make any difference. It's hard to give up your whole life to somebody else's orders, and always feel as if you was looked at over a wall like; but so it is, and you won't get girls to try it, till somehow or other things are different."

QUESTIONS

Why did these women object to domestic service? • What did they think of their employers? • Why did they find it preferable to work in a factory or shop? • Why did some of them complain about Irish servants? • What were the differences between domestic service and factory work?

DOCUMENT 3

Samuel Gompers Explains Why Strikes Are Necessary

Strikes were one of the most important weapons of working people in the labor conflicts of the Gilded Age. Samuel Gompers, who joined the Cigarmakers Union in New York City when he was thirteen, explained the purposes and goals of strikes to a U.S. Senate Committee in 1899. Gompers was a well-qualified witness. He served as president of the American Federation of Labor every year except one from its founding in 1886 until he died in 1924.

Testimony before a U.S. Senate Committee, 1899

The working people find that improvements in the methods of production and distribution are constantly being made, and unless they occasionally strike, or have the power to enter upon a strike, the improvements will all go to the employer and all the injuries to the employees. A strike is an effort on the part of the workers to obtain some of the improvements that have occurred resultant from bygone and present genius of our intelligence, of our mental progress. We are producing wealth today at a greater ratio than ever in the history of mankind, and a strike on the part of workers is, first, against deterioration in their condition, and, second, to be participants in some of the improvements. Strikes are caused from various reasons. The employer desires to reduce wages and lengthen hours of labor, while the desire on the part of employees is to

U.S. Congress, House, *Report of the Industrial Commission on the Relations and Conditions of Capital and Labor Employed in Manufactures and General Business* (1901).

obtain shorter hours of labor and better wages, and better surroundings. Strikes establish or maintain the rights of unionism; that is, to establish and maintain the organization by which the rights of the workers can be the better protected and advanced against the little forms of oppression, sometimes economical, sometimes political—the effort on the part of employers to influence and intimidate workmen's political preferences; strikes against victimization; activity in the cause of the workers against the blacklist. . . .

It required 40,000 people in the city of New York in my own trade [of cigarmaking] in 1877 to demonstrate to the employers that we had a right to be heard in our own defense of our trade, and an opportunity to be heard in our own interests. . . . It cost the railroad brotherhoods long months of suffering, many of them sacrificing their positions, in the railroad strike of 1877, and in the Chicago, Burlington, and Quincy strike, of the same year, to secure from the employers the right to be heard through committees, their representatives—that is, their committees of the organization to secure these rights. Workmen have had to stand the brunt of the suffering. The American Republic was not established without some suffering, without some sacrifice, and no tangible right has yet been achieved in the interest of the people unless it has been secured by sacrifices and persistency. After a while we become a little more tolerant to each other and recognize all have rights; get around the table and chaff each other; all recognize that they were not so reasonable in the beginning. Now we propose to meet and discuss our interests, and if we can not agree we propose in a more reasonable way to conduct our contests, each to decide how to hold out and bring the other one to terms. . . . A strike on the part of workmen is to close production and compel better terms and more rights to be acceded to the producers. The economic results of strikes to workers have been advantageous. Without strikes their rights would not have been considered. It is not that workmen or organized labor desires the strike, but it will tenaciously hold to the right to strike. We recognize that peaceful industry is necessary to successful civilized life, but the right to strike and the preparation to strike is the greatest preventive to strikes. If the workmen were to make up their minds tomorrow that they would under no circumstances strike, the employers would do all the striking for them in the way of lesser wages and longer hours of labor.

QUESTIONS

According to Gompers, what was the purpose of a strike? • What would happen if workers did not strike? • What did Gompers mean by "little forms of oppression"? • Why did he believe workers had a right to strike? • Did he believe strikes only helped workers?

DOCUMENT 4

Chicago Workers Satirize Their Bosses

Working people often resented the ways their bosses treated them. Sometimes they expressed their resentment by making fun of bosses' petty tyrannies and blind refusals to recognize their own interests. German-language newspapers in Chicago published satires of the Ten Commandments as if they were written by bosses and of a capitalist's diary of a strike. The satires expressed many workers' views of the people who employed them. They also disclosed much about the workers' views of themselves. English translations of the satires follow.

very sarcastic.

"Ten Commandments for Workers," September 25, 1885

1. Thou shalt have no other Bosses before Me.

2. Thou shalt make unto thee no comfort, or any likeness of anything which is advantageous to thee in heaven above or which is in the earth beneath. Thou shalt bow down to Me, and idolize Me and serve Me, for I am the Lord, thy Boss, and am an angry and jealous Boss and will have no mercy with thee, but rather will force thee to honor My commandments.

3. Thou shalt not use the name of thy Boss in vain, or I thy Boss will give you the sack for having done so.

4. Remember that thou shalt labor from sunrise to sundown, eleven hours each day, six days a week, with all thy spirit, and that thou shalt do all that I, thy Boss, demand of thee; but on the seventh thou shalt remain within thy gates, and shalt not amuse thyself in any way, so that thou canst rest and gain strength, courage and force, and serve Me again on Monday.

5. Honor thy Boss and thy Foreman, that thy days may be few and evil; for I will vomit thee out of My mouth and will cast thee from My view, when thou becomest old and fragile and thou shalt then spend the rest of thy days in the house which is called the poorhouse.

6. Thou shalt not walk on the paths of evil, midst heathens and sinners which are called labor unions; for they are an outrage before the Lord, thy Boss.

7. Thou shalt not bear false witness against Me or Mine, though I may cut thy wages from ten to fifteen percent. Be content that I, in My grace and in My endless mercy, allow thee to work for Me, though I pay thee 90 cents a day and advise thee the half of it to save.

Möbel-Arbeiter-Journal, September 25, 1885, and *Chicagoer Arbeiter-Zeitung,* February 1, 1889; both in Hartmut Keil and John B. Jentz, eds., *German Workers in Chicago: A Documentary History of Working-Class Culture from 1850 to World War I* (Champaign, IL: University of Illinois Press, 1988), 305–10.

8. Thou shalt go hungry and thirsty, naked and cold, if it so pleases the Lord thy Boss. Thou shalt receive thy wages so that I may earn golden shekels and silver shekels, and that I may build My house, clothe Myself in purple and fine cloth, and fill My stables with fiery horses.

9. Thou shalt not come into contact with others or hold meetings. Thou shalt not confer with others as to thy own well-being, or grumble about cuts in thy pay. Thou shalt also not read newspapers, that I may keep thee in ignorance and stupidity all the days of thy life.

10. Thou shalt not covet thy Boss's money, nor His ease, nor His conveniences, nor anything which is His. Thou shalt not covet thy Foreman's wages, though he earn 3 dollars each day to thy one. Thou shalt object to nothing, for I shall rule over thee and order thee, and I shall keep thee in servitude all the days of thy life till thy death, and then, for all I care, thou canst go to Sheol.

"The Strike: from a Capitalist's Diary," February 1, 1899

January 2   The pack of workers is getting greedier with each passing week. Just last week I had to equip the machines with new protective gear because some stupid oaf had three fingers chewed off his right hand. Today the pack demanded another pay raise and discontinuance of the piecework system. I wouldn't even mind granting the former request, but absolutely not the latter! No, never! I'd sooner close the whole shop! Thank God the government finally came up with the prison bill! If it only wouldn't take so damned long! A few years behind bars on bread and water would serve that red incendiary right! That rabble-rousing Social Democratic agitator, going around seducing all the others, I'll have to can him first. But I will absolutely not give in to anything!

January 3   Today they sent their so-called "commission" to my office again; they trampled all over my good carpets from Brussels with their filthy boots. But I immediately told them that there was no way I was going to negotiate with a commission; whoever didn't like it at my place could see where the carpenter had left a hole in the wall. To which they replied that if this was my last word concerning their just requests, they would pass it on to their colleagues. I told them to do just that; but inside I was boiling over with anger and rage at the fact that I had to lower myself to deal with these creatures at all; these creatures whose salutations I ignored as, leaning back in my landau, I slipped by them while they slowly and drunkenly skulked along the street with swaying stride! . . . All right then! Let's put it to a test of strength, my good workers! . . .

January 4   Save a few apprentices, nobody showed up to work today! So the union dares spite me! Let's just see who's the strongest! . . .

January 5 These damned apprentices are good for absolutely nothing! They can't even work a lathe. A purely mechanical operation. I tried to insert the support myself, but got all jammed up in it. Go ahead and strike! Don't worry, I'll find workers all right! The new workers will get a pay raise, but not you—I don't let anyone tell me what to do! My agents are already looking around in lots of industrial cities. Free beer and cigarettes at the recruitment headquarters should do the trick. In two days my shop will be running as though nothing had ever happened.

January 6 Now of all times Bonily and Co. have to have their joiners benches. They want to remind me that they were supposed to have been delivered yesterday, and let me know of the fine stipulated in the contract.

January 7 What am I supposed to do now? Another telegram. The joiners benches have to be finished by the day after tomorrow at the latest. Where am I supposed to get workers? The other factories have declined the offer to make the joiners benches, because they're afraid of an uprising in their shops, too. I didn't get a wink of sleep all night.

January 8 If only I had granted their requests. I'm going to try to renegotiate with the commission. I'll grant everything, put everyone back to work, everyone except those damned rabble-rousing reds!

January 9 Today the negotiations were resumed. I had to grin and bear it, though I had to bite my tongue when, for the sake of propriety, I not only had to offer these plebs a chair but also my good cigars. But this pack is proud! My cigars were curtly, though politely declined, and it was clear that they didn't want any gifts from me. With a distinguished smile and a shrug of the shoulders, I snapped the case shut and placed it back on top of my iron strongbox. We didn't reach an agreement today. These workers' skulls are thick. Would anyone fifty years ago have thought that the factory owner would have to negotiate with the people who are dependent on him for their bread and wages? Times are changing at an unbelievable rate!

January 10 Thank God! Eleven "nonstrikers" arrived today from the country. That puts an end to my humiliation, I can cut off the hateful negotiations and will be able to deliver the machines in three to four days!

January 11 This pack of country workers that I've picked up off the street and that's now filled up my factory—new ones also came—are simply too stupid and lazy! They haven't the vaguest idea how to mount the files or forge a length of steel. Today they ruined more tools and wrecked more material than the others did in half a year. I wish the others were here in my shop, those men whose honest faces I know. This shady mob, slithering around with bowed backs, gives me the creeps, makes me nervous! I've already warned my gatekeeper to keep an eye out that nobody walks off the grounds with a tool or something. This sort of security measure wasn't necessary when my old people were there. If only the prison bill were already law, it would end these strikes once and for all! With the people I have here now, my shop may as well be empty!

January 12   Today something happened which really gratified me and relieved my burdened and irritated heart. The main rabble-rousers were sentenced to 2 and 3 months in prison for violating paragraph 153 of the penal code. They have to start serving time immediately. Recently they tried to prevent the "nonstrikers" I've brought in from coming to work for me. But ours is a constitutional system, where the police do their duty. Maybe the others will knuckle under now that the main ringleaders are behind bars.

January 13   I'd pull my hair out if any grew on my polished skull. The machines aren't ready. They're barely half done, and now I'm going to have to pay the 2,000 Mark fine stipulated in the contract. These sluggards, these bunglers, loafers—and all here in my shop. Today I'm going to throw the whole lot out. If this goes on for another fourteen days, I'm ruined, bankrupt. I wrote the "commission" again. I'm ready to throw myself at their mercy and disgrace myself. I have no choice, otherwise I may as well pack everything up and join the beggars.

January 14   How small I felt today vis-a-vis my workers. My face must have shown plainly how desperate I was. I listened again to all their demands, which now also include the immediate release of all the recently hired nonstrikers; I asked them to make a few notes for me, as I'd need two days to think it over.

January 15   I wracked my brain over this affair all day and all night. The conditions they've given me are pretty tough, considering how working conditions used to be, when I could manage things as I pleased. But as they say, any port in a storm. I'll just have to drink my cup of bile. Not counting future pay raises, the strike has cost me some 10,000 Marks. I'll have to work awfully hard to make it up. Tomorrow I'll dismiss the provisional personnel. It'll be my only satisfaction in this whole affair, finally getting rid of this rabble; somehow I didn't feel like master in my own shop anymore. Tomorrow I'll have to air my defeat publicly.

January 16   The commission has left. I granted all their demands and signed a statement saying that I would honor the conditions. Midst much grumping and coarse remarks, I also cleared the shop of the "nonstrikers." At their insistence, I had to pay them their wages—right down to the last penny through the end of the week, as had been agreed to. A quick tour of the factory was more than enough to show what enormous amounts of materials had been wasted in the past few days. Big piles of burnt steel and broken pieces of cast iron had been stacked up in the corners behind tin plates. That's what you get when you hire unskilled labor. But oh what a shameful feeling to be pressured by the very people who are dependent on you for their living. This foul plague. Whoever wants to fight against the epidemic should first have the antidote. This mob's red fury should be beaten out of them with a whip. Like they say, if you're not just parrying, always give the whip free rein.

January 17   Today they came back to work. The files and wheels took up their old, industrious melody again, the big flywheels and hammers clanking and humming. I was too embarrassed to go down and exchange a friendly word with the people who had forced my hand. From the window of my apartment, I watched them arrive, clothed in their thin jackets and shirts; a few of them looked up to the window where, hidden behind the curtains, I was watching them; I almost had the feeling that the set of their pale lips indicated a sense of pride and victory. . . . But maybe I just imagined it, and it was just the reflection from the two big lanterns at the factory entrance.

QUESTIONS

In these satires, what motivated bosses? • What did bosses think of workers? • Why did the capitalist initially refuse to negotiate with his workers? • What did he do when they went on strike? • What changed his mind about negotiation? • What happened to the strike leaders? • Were the strikers replaced by new workers? • Why did the capitalist fail to break the strike? • What did the satires suggest about workers' view of themselves?

COMPARATIVE QUESTIONS

What portrait of bosses emerges from the descriptions in these documents? How do Thomas O'Donnell's experiences with factory work compare with the experiences of women domestic servants? How does Samuel Gompers's view of the need for strikes compare with the boss's view of strikes in the Chicago workers' satire? How did the individuals described in these documents define economic justice and injustice?

CHAPTER 20

FIGHTING FOR CHANGE IN THE TURBULENT NINETIES

1890–1900

Profound moral conflict lay beneath the strife of the 1890s. Many Americans believed the basic principles of order in the economy, in society, and in politics were immoral and unjust. Many others believed the opposite. The Populists voiced many of the moral doubts while their opponents reaffirmed their faith in the conventional virtues. This conflict was more than a debate, as African Americans, striking workers, and Filipino nationalists knew. The following documents disclose the contours of the moral conflict and some of its many consequences in the 1890s and beyond.

DOCUMENT 1

The Populists' Omaha Platform

Hard times in agriculture pushed farmers in the Midwest and South to organize a wide variety of local reform movements. Selling their crops in distant markets for prices that often seemed to be rigged against them, shipping their produce on railroads that manipulated rates to their disadvantage, borrowing money for land and supplies at what seemed extravagant interest rates—these and other common experiences bred a sense of helplessness that many farmers came to believe could only be overcome by cooperation and organization. The Omaha Platform of the People's party, adopted at the first national convention in 1892, expressed many rural Americans' sense of crisis. The preamble preceding the platform, which follows, was written by Ignatius Donnelly, a Minnesota reform politician and one of the party's founders.

Populist Party Platform, July 4, 1892

PREAMBLE

Assembled upon the 116th anniversary of the Declaration of Independence, the People's Party of America, in their first national convention, invoking upon their action the blessing of Almighty God, puts forth, in the name and on behalf of the people of this country, the following preamble and declaration of principles:

The conditions which surround us best justify our cooperation: we meet in the midst of a nation brought to the verge of moral, political, and material ruin. Corruption dominates the ballot-box, the legislatures, the Congress, and touches even the ermine of the bench. The people are demoralized; most of the States have been compelled to isolate the voters at the polling-places to prevent universal intimidation or bribery. The newspapers are largely subsidized or muzzled; public opinion silenced; business prostrated; our homes covered with mortgages; labor impoverished; and the land concentrating in the hands of the capitalists. The urban workmen are denied the right of organization for self-protection; imported pauperized labor beats down their wages; a hireling standing army, unrecognized by our laws, is established to shoot them down, and they are rapidly degenerating into European conditions. The fruits of the toil of millions are boldly stolen to build up colossal fortunes for a few, unprecedented in the history of mankind; and the possessors of these, in turn, despise the republic and endanger liberty. From the same prolific womb of governmental injustice we breed the two great classes—tramps and millionaires.

The national power to create money is appropriated to enrich bond-holders; a vast public debt, payable in legal tender currency, has been funded into gold-bearing bonds, thereby adding millions to the burdens of the people. Silver, which has been accepted as coin since the dawn of history, has been demonetized to add to the purchasing power of gold by decreasing the value of all forms of property as well as human labor; and the supply of currency is purposely abridged to fatten usurers, bankrupt enterprise, and enslave industry. A vast conspiracy against mankind has been organized on two continents, and it is rapidly taking possession of the world. If not met and overthrown at once, it forebodes terrible social convulsions, the destruction of civilization, or the establishment of an absolute despotism.

We have witnessed for more than a quarter of a century the struggles of the two great political parties for power and plunder, while grievous wrongs have been inflicted upon the suffering people. We charge that the controlling influences dominating both these parties have permitted the

The People's Party Paper (July 1892); reprinted in *The Populist Mind,* by Norman Pollack (Old Tappan, NJ: Macmillan, 1967), 60–66.

existing dreadful conditions to develop without serious effort to prevent or restrain them. Neither do they now promise us any substantial reform. They have agreed together to ignore in the coming campaign every issue but one. They propose to drown the outcries of a plundered people with the uproar of a sham battle over the tariff, so that capitalists, corporations, national banks, rings, trusts, watered stock, the demonetization of silver, and the oppressions of the usurers may all be lost sight of. They propose to sacrifice our homes, lives and children on the altar of mammon; to destroy the multitude in order to secure corruption funds from the millionaires.

Assembled on the anniversary of the birthday of the nation, and filled with the spirit of the grand general and chieftain who established our independence, we seek to restore the government of the Republic to the hands of "the plain people," with whose class it originated. We assert our purposes to be identical with the purposes of the National Constitution, "to form a more perfect union and establish justice, insure domestic tranquillity, provide for the common defence, promote the general welfare, and secure the blessings of liberty for ourselves and our posterity." We declare that this republic can only endure as a free government while built upon the love of the whole people for each other and for the nation; that it cannot be pinned together by bayonets; that the civil war is over, and that every passion and resentment which grew out of it must die with it; and that we must be in fact, as we are in name, one united brotherhood of freemen.

Our country finds itself confronted by conditions for which there is no precedent in the history of the world; our annual agricultural productions amount to billions of dollars in value, which must, within a few weeks or months, be exchanged for billions of dollars of commodities consumed in their production; the existing currency supply is wholly inadequate to make this exchange; the results are falling prices, the formation of combines and rings, the impoverishment of the producing class. We pledge ourselves, if given power, we will labor to correct these evils by wise and reasonable legislation, in accordance with the terms of our platform. We believe that the powers of government—in other words, of the people should be expanded (as in the case of the postal service) as rapidly and as far as the good sense of an intelligent people and the teachings of experience shall justify, to the end that oppression, injustice, and poverty shall eventually cease in the land.

While our sympathies as a party of reform are naturally upon the side of every proposition which will tend to make men intelligent, virtuous, and temperate, we nevertheless regard these questions—important as they are—as secondary to the great issues now pressing for solution, and upon which not only our individual prosperity but the very existence of free institutions depends; and we ask all men to first help us to determine whether we are to have a republic to administer before we differ as to the conditions upon which it is to be administered; believing that the forces of reform this day organized will never cease to move forward until every wrong is remedied, and equal rights and equal privileges securely established for all the men and women of this country.

PLATFORM

We declare, therefore,

First. That the union of the labor forces of the United States this day consummated shall be permanent and perpetual; may its spirit enter all hearts for the salvation of the republic and the uplifting of mankind!

Second. Wealth belongs to him who creates it, and every dollar taken from industry without an equivalent is robbery. "If any will not work, neither shall he eat." The interests of rural and civic labor are the same; their enemies are identical.

Third. We believe that the time has come when the railroad corporations will either own the people or the people must own the railroads; and, should the government enter upon the work of owning and managing all railroads, we should favor an amendment to the Constitution by which all persons engaged in the government service shall be placed under a civil service regulation of the most rigid character, so as to prevent the increase of the power of the national administration by the use of such additional government employees.

First, *Money.* We demand a national currency, safe, sound, and flexible, issued by the general government only, a full legal tender for all debts, public and private, and that, without the use of banking corporations, a just, equitable, and efficient means of distribution direct to the people, at a tax not to exceed two per cent per annum, to be provided as set forth in the sub-treasury plan of the Farmers' Alliance, or a better system; also, by payments in discharge of its obligations for public improvements.

(a) We demand free and unlimited coinage of silver and gold at the present legal ratio of sixteen to one.

(b) We demand that the amount of circulating medium be speedily increased to not less than fifty dollars per capita.

(c) We demand a graduated income tax.

(d) We believe that the money of the country should be kept as much as possible in the hands of the people, and hence we demand that all state and national revenues shall be limited to the necessary expenses of the government economically and honestly administered.

(e) We demand that postal savings banks be established by the government for the safe deposit of the earnings of the people and to facilitate exchange.

Second, *Transportation.* Transportation being a means of exchange and a public necessity, the government should own and operate the railroads in the interest of the people.

(a) The telegraph and telephone, like the post-office system, being a necessity for the transmission of news, should be owned and operated by the government in the interest of the people.

Third, *Land*. The land, including all the natural sources of wealth, is the heritage of the people, and should not be monopolized for speculative purposes, and alien ownership of land should be prohibited. All land now held by railroads and other corporations in excess of their actual needs, and all lands now owned by aliens, should be reclaimed by the government and held for actual settlers only.

RESOLUTIONS

Whereas, Other questions have been presented for our consideration, we hereby submit the following, not as a part of the platform of the People's party, but as resolutions expressive of the sentiment of this convention.

1. *Resolved,* That we demand a free ballot and a fair count in all elections, and pledge ourselves to secure it to every legal voter without federal intervention, through the adoption by the States of the unperverted Australian or secret ballot system.

2. *Resolved,* That the revenue derived from a graduated income tax should be applied to the reduction of the burden of taxation now resting upon the domestic industries of this country.

3. *Resolved,* That we pledge our support to fair and liberal pensions to ex-Union soldiers and sailors.

4. *Resolved,* That we condemn the fallacy of protecting American labor under the present system, which opens our ports to the pauper and criminal classes of the world, and crowds out our wage-earners; and we denounce the present ineffective laws against contract labor, and demand the further restriction of undesirable immigration.

5. *Resolved,* That we cordially sympathize with the efforts of organized workingmen to shorten the hours of labor, and demand a rigid enforcement of the existing eight-hour law on government work, and ask that a penalty clause be added to the said law.

6. *Resolved,* That we regard the maintenance of a large standing army of mercenaries, known as the Pinkerton system, as a menace to our liberties, and we demand its abolition; and we condemn the recent invasion of the Territory of Wyoming by the hired assassins of plutocracy, assisted by federal officials.

7. *Resolved,* That we commend to the favorable consideration of the people and the reform press the legislative system known as the initiative and referendum.

8. *Resolved,* That we favor a constitutional provision limiting the office of President and Vice-President to one term, and providing for the election of senators of the United States by a direct vote of the people.

9. *Resolved,* That we oppose any subsidy or national aid to any private corporation for any purpose.

10. *Resolved,* That this convention sympathizes with the Knights of Labor and their righteous contest with the tyrannical combine of clothing manufacturers of Rochester, [Minnesota] and declares it to be the duty of all who hate tyranny and oppression to refuse to purchase the goods made by said manufacturers, or to patronize any merchants who sell such goods.

QUESTIONS

According to the Populist platform, what ills plagued America? • What had the two major parties done about those problems? • What was the proper role of government? • What general principles did the Populists support and what specific remedies did they propose? • Who did they regard as their potential allies and who did they believe were likely to be their opponents? • What was their attitude toward immigrants and immigration? • What methods did they think would be effective in bringing about desirable change?

DOCUMENT 2

White Supremacy in Wilmington, North Carolina

Black southerners affiliated with the Republican party often cooperated with Populists to defeat Democrats. Such a fusion of Republicans and Populists carried North Carolina in 1894 and 1896, resulting in the election and appointment of a number of black officeholders, including the mayor and aldermen of Wilmington. In 1898, Democrats struck back with a campaign of terror and intimidation that culminated two days after their victory at the polls by what Gunner Jesse Blake called a "rebellion" that established white supremacy by killing at least twenty blacks. Blake, a Confederate veteran who participated in the "rebellion," recalled the event for a sympathetic white writer in the 1930s. Blake's narrative, excerpted here, illustrates the explosive racism that confronted southern blacks every day and ultimately undermined the Populist revolt in the South.

Gunner Jesse Blake

Narrative of the Wilmington "Rebellion" of 1898

"So, I am going to give you the inside story of this insurrection," he proceeded, "wherein the white people of Wilmington overthrew the constituted municipal authority overnight and substituted a reform rule, doing all this legally and with some needless bloodshed, to be sure, but at the

Harry Hayden, *The Wilmington Rebellion* (1936), 231–36.

same time they eliminated the Negroes from the political life of the city and the state. This Rebellion was the very beginning of Negro disfranchisement in the South and an important step in the establishment of 'White Supremacy' in the Southland. . . .

"The Rebellion was an organized resistance," Mr. Blake said, "on the part of the white citizens of this community to the established government, which had long irked them because it was dominated by 'Carpet Baggers' and Negroes, and also because the better element here wished to establish 'White Supremacy' in the city, the state and throughout the South, and thereby remove the then stupid and ignorant Negroes from their numerically dominating position in the government. . . .

"The older generation of Southern born men were at their wits' end. They had passed through the rigors of the North-South war and through the tyrannies of Reconstruction when Confiscation . . . of properties without due process of law, was the rule rather than the exception. They had seen 'Forty Acres and a Mule' buy many a Negro's vote.

"Black rapists were attacking Southern girls and women, those pure and lovely creatures who graced the homes in Dixie Land, and the brutes were committing this dastardly crime with more frequency while the majority of them were escaping punishment through the influence of the powers that be.

"These old Southern gentlemen had calculated that time and time only would remove the terrors of Reconstruction, a condition that was imposed upon the conquered Southerners by the victorious Northerners, but they were not willing to sit supinely by and see their girls and women assaulted by beastly brutes.

"The better element among the Northerners in the North could not want them and their little friends to grow up amid such conditions. . . .

"A group of nine citizens met at the home of Mr. Hugh MacRae and there decided that the attitude and actions of the Negroes made it necessary for them to take some steps towards protecting their families and homes in their immediate neighborhood, Seventh and Market Streets. . . .

"This group of citizens, . . . referred to as the 'Secret Nine,' divided the city into sections, placing a responsible citizen as captain in charge of each area. . . .

"The better element planned to gain relief from Negro impudence and domination, from grafting and from immoral conditions; the 'Secret Nine' and the white leaders marked time, hoping something would happen to arouse the citizenry to concerted action.

"But the 'watch-and-wait policy' of the 'Secret Nine' did not obtain for long, as during the latter part of October [1898] there appeared in the columns of [t]he *Wilmington* (Negro) *Daily Record* an editorial, written by the Negro editor, Alex Manly, which aroused a state-wide revulsion to the city and state administrations then in the hands of the Republicans and Fusionists. The editorial attempted to justify the Negro rape fiends at the expense of the virtue of Southern womanhood."

Mr. Blake . . . read the following . . . editorial from [t]he *Wilmington Record:*

> Poor whites are careless in the matter of protecting their women, especially on the farm. They are careless of their conduct towards them, and our experience among the poor white people in the county teaches us that women of that race are not more particular in the matter of clandestine meetings with colored men, than are the white man and colored women.
>
> Meetings of this kind go on for some time until the woman's infatuation, or the man's boldness, bring attention to them, and the man is lynched for rape.
>
> Every Negro lynched is called a "big, burly, black brute," when in fact, many of those who have been thus dealt with had white men for their fathers, and were not only not "black" and "burly," but were sufficiently attractive for white girls of culture and refinement to fall in love with them, as is very well known to all.

"That editorial," Mr. Blake declared . . . , "is the straw that broke Mister Nigger's political back in the Southland.". . .

"Excitement reigned supreme on election day and the day following," Mr. Blake said, adding that "the tension between the races was at the breaking point, as two Pinkerton detectives, Negroes, had reported to their white employers that the Negro women, servants in the homes of white citizens, had agreed to set fire to the dwellings of their employers, and the Negro men had openly threatened to 'burn the town down' if the 'White Supremacy' issue was carried in the political contest. The very atmosphere was surcharged with tinder, and only a spark, a misstep by individuals of either race, was needed to set the whites and the blacks at each other's throats.

"When Mr. Hugh MacRae was sitting on his porch on Market Street on the afternoon of the election, he saw a band of 'Red Shirts,' fifty in number, with blood in their eyes; mounted upon fiery and well caparisoned steeds and led by Mike Dowling, an Irishman, who had organized this band of vigilantes. The hot headed 'Red Shirts' paused in front of Mr. MacRae's home and the level headed Scotsman walked toward the group to learn what was amiss.

"Dowling told Mr. MacRae that they were headed for 'The Record' building to lynch Editor Manly and burn the structure. Mr. MacRae pleaded with Dowling and his 'Red Shirts' to desist in their plans. Messrs. MacRae, Dowling and other leaders of the 'Red Shirts' repaired across the street to Sasser's Drug store and there he, Mr. MacRae, showed them a 'Declaration of White Independence' that he had drawn up for presentation at a mass meeting of white citizens the next day.

"The 'Red Shirts' were finally persuaded by Mr. MacRae to abandon their plans for the lynching, but only after Mr. MacRae had called up the newspapers on the telephone and dictated a call for a mass meeting of the citizens for the next morning. . . .

"A thousand or more white citizens, representative of all walks of life . . . attended the mass meeting in the New Hanover county court house the next morning, November 10, at 11 o'clock.

"Colonel Alfred Moore Waddell, a mild mannered Southern gentleman, noted for his extremely conservative tendencies, was called upon to preside over the gathering. In addressing this meeting, Colonel Waddell said: . . . 'We will not live under these intolerable conditions. No society can stand it. We intend to change it, if we have to choke the current of Cape Fear River with (Negro) carcasses!'"

"*That* declaration," Mr. Blake said, "brought forth tremendous applause from the large gathering of white men at the mass meeting. . . .

"Colonel Waddell . . . announced that he heartily approved the set of resolutions which had been prepared by Mr. Hugh MacRae and which included the latter's 'Declaration of White Independence.'

"These resolutions were unanimously approved by the meeting, followed by a wonderful demonstration, the assemblage rising to its feet and cheering: 'Right! Right! Right!' and there were cries of 'Fumigate' the city with 'The Record' and 'Lynch Manly.'"

Blake then read the resolutions from the scrap book, as follows:

Believing that the Constitution of the United States contemplated a government to be carried on by an enlightened people; believing that its framers did not anticipate the enfranchisement of an ignorant population of African origin, and believing that those men of the state of North Carolina, who joined in framing the union, did not contemplate for their descendants subjection to an inferior race.

We, the undersigned citizens of the city of Wilmington and county of New Hanover, do hereby declare that we will no longer be ruled and will never again be ruled, by men of African origin.

This condition we have in part endured because we felt that the consequences of the war of secession were such as to deprive us of the fair consideration of many of our countrymen. . . .

"Armed with a Winchester rifle, Colonel Waddell ordered the citizens to form in front of the Armory for an orderly procession out to 'The Record' plant. . . .

"As this band of silent yet determined men marched up Market Street it passed the beautiful colonial columned mansion, the Bellamy home. From the balcony of this mansion, a Chief justice of the United States Supreme Court, Salmon P. Chase, delivered an address shortly after Lincoln's tragic assassination, advocating Negro suffrage and thereby sowing the seeds that were now blossoming forth into a white rebellion.

"The printing press of 'The Record' was wrecked by the maddened white men, who also destroyed other equipment, and the type that had been used in producing the editorial that had reflected upon the virtue and character of Southern womanhood was scattered to the four winds by these men, who stood four-square for the virtue of their women and for the supremacy of the white race over the African.

"Some lamps that had been hanging from the ceiling of the plant were torn down and thrown upon the floor, which then became saturated with kerosene oil; and then a member of the band struck a match, with the result that the two-story frame building was soon in flames.

"The leaders and most of the citizens had designed only to destroy the press," Mr. Blake averred, adding . . ."all of which proves that a mob, no matter how well disciplined, is no stronger than its weakest link.

"The crowd of armed men, which had destroyed the plant and building of the nefarious *Wilmington* (Negro) *Daily Record,* dispersed, repairing peacefully to their respective homes," Mr. Blake said. . . .

"But in about an hour the tension between the two races broke with the shooting of William H. (Bill) Mayo, a white citizen, who was wounded by the first shot that was fired in the Wilmington Rebellion as he was standing on the sidewalk near his home. . . . Mayo's assailant, Dan Wright, was captured by members of the Wilmington Light Infantry and the Naval Reserves after he had been riddled by 13 bullets. Wright died next day in a hospital.

"Then the 'Red Shirts' began to ride and the Negroes began to run. . . . The Africans, or at least those Negroes who had foolishly believed in the remote possibility of social equality with the former masters of their parents, began to slink before the Caucasians. They, the Negroes, appeared to turn primal, slinking away like tigers at bay, snarling as they retreated before the bristling bayonets, barking guns and flaming 'Red Shirts.'

"Six Negroes were shot down near the corner of Fourth and Brunswick Streets, the Negro casualties for the day—November 11, 1898—totaling nine. One of these, who had fired at the whites from a Negro dance hall, 'Manhattan,' over in 'Brooklyn,' was shot 15 or 20 times. . . .

"One 'Red Shirt' said he had seen six Negroes shot down near the Cape Fear Lumber Company's plant and that their bodies were buried in a ditch. . . . Another 'Red Shirt' described the killing of nine Negroes by a lone white man, who killed them one at a time with his Winchester rifle as they filed out of a shanty door in 'Brooklyn' and after they had fired on him. . . . Another told of how a Negro had been killed and his body thrown in Cape Fear River after he had approached two white men on the wharf. . . .

"Other military units came to Wilmington to assist the white citizens in establishing 'White Supremacy' here. . . . Military organizations from as far South as New Orleans telegraphed offering to come here if their services were needed in the contest.

"When the Rebellion was in full blast 'The Committee of Twenty-five' appointed . . . a committee to call upon Mayor Silas P. Wright and the

Board of Aldermen and demand that these officials resign. The mayor had expressed a willingness to quit, but not during the crisis. He changed his mind, however, when he saw white citizens walking the streets with revolvers in their hands. The Negroes, too, had suddenly turned submissive, they were carrying their hats in their hands. . . .

"African continued to cringe before Caucasian as the troops paraded the streets, as the guns barked and the bayonets flared, for a new municipal administration of the 'White Supremacy' persuasion had been established in a day! The old order of Negro domination over the white citizenry had ended."

QUESTIONS

According to Blake, why did the "better element" want to establish white supremacy? • What steps did they take to further their goals? • What did Blake claim precipitated the violence? • Did the "better element" take a leading role? • What did the Declaration of White Independence assert? • What did the Red Shirts do? • How do you think events like this might have influenced the prospects of Republicans and Populists in the South?

DOCUMENT 3

Pinkertons Defeated at Homestead

Corporations sometimes used private armies to defeat strikes. When strikers seized the Homestead steel mill in 1892, Henry Clay Frick hired 300 Pinkerton men, loaded them on barges, and ordered them to launch an amphibious attack on the mill. One of the Pinkerton guards later recalled his experience as an industrial mercenary at Homestead for a Congressional inquiry.

Testimony of a Pinkerton Guard to the U.S. Senate, 1892

We started out [in Chicago] . . . [and] we went into the three rear cars of the train very quickly. . . . [M]en who seemed to be detectives and not patrolmen, stationed themselves at the doors, and they prevented our exit, and they prevented the entrance of any outside parties who might wish to enter. . . .

U.S. Congress, Senate, Report No. 1280, 53d Cong., 2d sess., 68–72.

We ran rather slowly — it was not a scheduled train — on to Cleveland. . . . There we waited for an hour and our three cars were joined to seven other cars of men from the east. We then, the whole train, went rapidly on. . . . During our trip we were not allowed to leave the cars at all, we were kind of prisoners. We did not have any rights. That might have been because they were afraid of union men, perhaps spies, who would telegraph ahead to Homestead. They wanted to get inside the works without bloodshed, but we had no rights whatever. Then we entered the boats, some 300 of us. There was two covered barges, like these Mississippi covered boats. . . .

We were told to fall in, and the roll of our names was called, and we were told to secure our uniforms, which consisted of coat, hat, vest, and pair of trowsers. When we had secured our uniforms we were some distance down the river, and we were told to keep quiet, and the lights were turned out, and everything kept very quiet until we were given orders softly to arise. I was lying down about an hour when the order was sent around the boat for all the men to get ready to land. Then the captain called out for men who could handle rifles. I did not want to handle a rifle, and then he said we want two or three men here to guard the door with clubs, so I said I would do that, and I got over the table and got a club like a policeman's club to guard the side door — that was to prevent men from coming in boats and jumping on to our barge from the river. I stayed there while the men who could handle rifles were marched down to the open end of the boat, and I did not see anything more of them until the firing commenced. . . .

I had a curiosity to see what was going on on the bank. . . . I saw what appeared to be a lot of young men and boys on the bank, swearing and cursing and having large sticks. I did not see a gun or anything. They were swearing at our men. I did not see any more. . . . I heard a sharp pistol shot, and then there were 30, 40, or 100 of them, and our men came running and stampeding back as fast as they could and they got in the shelter of the door, and then they turned around and blazed away. It was so dark I could see the flames from the rifles easily. They fired about 50 shots — I was surprised to see them stand up, because the strikers were shooting also but they did not seem to be afraid of being hit. They had some shelter from the door. They fired in rather a professional manner I thought. The men inside the Chicago boat were rather afraid at hearing the rifles, and we all jumped for rifles that were laying on a table ready, and someone . . . opened a box of revolvers, and said, "all get revolvers," so I had now a Winchester rifle and a revolver. I called out to see if anybody had been hurt, and I saw a man there apparently strangling. He had been shot through the head and he died sometime afterwards, I think. . . . Of course it rather made us incensed to be shot at that way, but I kept out of danger as much as possible.

I was standing there when Nordrum came up, and he said to follow him, and I crossed over to the New York boat, where there were 40 men with rifles standing on the edge of the boat watching what was going on on shore. Nordrum spoke to the men on shore. He spoke in rather a loud manner — say a commanding manner. He said: "We are coming up that hill anyway, and we don't want any more trouble from you men." The men were in the mill windows. The mill is iron-clad. There were a few boys in sight, but the men were under shelter, all of them. I supposed I should have to go up the hill, and I didn't like the idea very well, because it was pretty nearly certain death, as I supposed. I thought it over in what little time I had, and I thought I would have to go anyway. While I was standing there, waiting for Nordrum to charge up the hill and we follow him, he went away, and he was gone quite a few minutes. I took advantage of that to look around the New York men's boat to see what was going on, and I saw about 150 of the New York men hiding in the aisle furthest from the shore. It was divided into bunks. They were hiding in the bunks — they were hiding under the mattresses; they didn't want to be told to shoulder a rifle and charge up the hill; they were naturally afraid of it. They were watchmen, and not detectives. Now the men who had the rifles were mostly detectives. There were 40 of the detectives, who I afterwards learned were regular employees of Pinkerton, but these other men were simply watchmen, and hired as watchmen, and told so, and nothing else. Seeing these men so afraid and cowering rather dispirited the rest of us, and those who had rifles — I noticed there seemed to be a fear among them all. I went to the end of the boat, and there I saw crowds on the bank, waving their hands, and all looking at the boat and appearing to be very frantic.

I judged we were going to have trouble and went back to the end where I had been placed and waited for Nordrum to come, but he did not turn up, and after I stood there about half an hour I concluded, as there was no one there to order us to do anything and as it was stated that the steam tug had pulled out, taking all those who had charge of us — I concluded I would look out for my life, and if anything was said about my leaving and not staying there I would say I did not intend to work for them any more; so I returned to the door I was told to guard, and in that place I stayed for the remainder of the day, during all the shooting and firing. I concluded if the boat was burned — we expected a thousand men would charge down the embankment and put us to massacre; that was what we expected all throughout the day — I concluded if the boat was burned I would defend my life with the other men. . . . During this firing there was a second battle. I was out of sight, but there were cracks of rifles, and our men replied with a regular fusilade. It kept up for ten minutes, bullets flying around as thick as hail, and men coming in shot and covered with blood. . . .

A good many of the men were thoroughly demoralized. They put on life-preservers and jumped under the tables and had no control over themselves whatever. Through the rest of the day there was this second battle when the strikers started the firing. There seemed to be sharp-shooters picking us off. . . . [A]bout 12 o'clock barrels of burning oil were floating around the bank to burn us up, to compel us to go on the wharf and there shoot us down, but they didn't succeed because the oil was taken up by the water, and at about 1 o'clock a cannon was fired by the strikers. . . . At about 3 o'clock we heard something; we thought was a cannon, but it was dynamite. . . . It partially wrecked the other boat. A stick of it fell near me. It broke open the door of the aisles, and it smashed open the door, and the sharpshooters were firing directly at any man in sight. . . . Most of the men were for surrender at this time, but the old detectives held out and said, "If you surrender you will be shot down like dogs; the best thing to do is to stay here." We could not cut our barges loose because there was a fall below, where we would be sunk. We were deserted by our captains and by our tug, and left there to be shot. We felt as though we had been betrayed and we did not understand it, and we did not know why the tug had pulled off and didn't know it had come back. About 4 o'clock some one or other authorized a surrender. . . . [T]he strikers held that we should depart by way of the depot.

That surrender was effected, and I started up the embankment with the men who went out, and we were glad to get away and did not expect trouble; but I looked up the hill and there were our men being struck as they went up, and it looked rather disheartening. . . . I supposed there was not going to be any more crowds, but in front of the miners' cottages there were crowds of miners, women, etc., and as we all went by they commenced to strike at us again, and a man picked up a stone and hit me upon the ear. . . . I got on further toward the depot and there were tremendous crowds on both sides and the men were just hauling and striking our men, and you would see them stumble as they passed by. I tried to get away from the crowd . . . , so I put my hat on and walked out of the line of Pinkerton men, but some one noticed me, and I started to run and about 100 got after me. I ran down a side street and ran through a yard. I ran about half a mile I suppose, but was rather weak and had had nothing to eat or drink and my legs gave out, could not run any further, and some man got hold of me by the back of my coat, and about 20 or 30 men came up and kicked me and pounded me with stones. I had no control of myself then. I thought I was about going and commenced to scream, and there were 2 or 3 strikers with rifles rushed up then and kept off the crowd and rushed me forward to a theater, and I was put in the theater and found about 150 of the Pinkerton men there, and that was the last violence offered me.

QUESTIONS

Why did the Pinkerton men travel in secrecy? • Why do you think this man took a job as a Pinkerton guard? • What did he mean by saying he had no rights? • Once he was on the barge, what did he see on shore? • What was his opinion of the strikers? • What was his view of the Pinkerton detectives? • Why did he feel betrayed? • What was his principal goal? • What happened to him after the Pinkerton men surrendered?

Document 4

Mark Twain on the Blessings-of-Civilization Trust

Many Americans welcomed the war against Spain in 1898. The notion of American soldiers liberating colonists from a decaying monarchy had wide appeal. But the temptation to start an American overseas empire in the Philippines proved irresistible. Mark Twain wrote a bitter satire that ridiculed American policy as a betrayal of fundamental national values. Selections from Twain's essay "To the Person Sitting in Darkness" follow.

"To the Person Sitting in Darkness," February 1901

[S]hall we go on conferring our Civilization upon the peoples that sit in darkness, or shall we give those poor things a rest? Shall we bang right ahead in our old-time, loud, pious way, and commit the new century to the game; or shall we sober up and sit down and think it over first? Would it not be prudent to get our Civilization-tools together, and see how much stock is left on hand in the way of Glass Beads and Theology, and Maxim Guns and Hymn Books, and Trade-Gin and Torches of Progress and En-lightenment (patent adjustable ones, good to fire villages with, upon occasion), and balance the books, and arrive at the profit and loss, so that we may intelligently decide whether to continue the business or sell out the property and start a new Civilization Scheme on the proceeds?

Extending the Blessings of Civilization to our Brother who Sits in Darkness has been a good trade and has paid well, on the whole; and there is money in it yet, if carefully worked but not enough, in my judgment, to make any considerable risk advisable. The People that Sit in Darkness are getting to be too scarce—too scarce and too shy. And such

Mark Twain, "To the Person Sitting in Darkness," *North American Review* (February 1901), 461–73.

darkness as is now left is really of but an indifferent quality, and not dark enough for the game. The most of those People that Sit in Darkness have been furnished with more light than was good for them or profitable for us. We have been injudicious.

The Blessings-of-Civilization Trust, wisely and cautiously administered, is a Daisy. There is more money in it, more territory, more sovereignty, and other kinds of emolument, than there is in any other game that is played. But Christendom has been playing it badly of late years, and must certainly suffer by it, in my opinion. She has been so eager to get every stake that appeared on the green cloth, that the People who Sit in Darkness have noticed it — they have noticed it, and have begun to show alarm. They have become suspicious of the Blessings of Civilization. More — they have begun to examine them. This is not well. The Blessings of Civilization are all right, and a good commercial property; there could not be a better, in a dim light. In the right kind of a light, and at a proper distance, with the goods a little out of focus, they furnish this desirable exhibit to the Gentlemen who Sit in Darkness:

LOVE, LAW AND ORDER, JUSTICE, LIBERTY, GENTLENESS, EQUALITY, CHRISTIANITY, HONORABLE DEALING, PROTECTION TO THE WEAK, MERCY, TEMPERANCE, EDUCATION, and so on.

There. Is it good? Sir, it is pie. It will bring into camp any idiot that sits in darkness anywhere. But not if we adulterate it. It is proper to be emphatic upon that point. This brand is strictly for Export — apparently. *Apparently.* Privately and confidentially, it is nothing of the kind. Privately and confidentially, it is merely an outside cover, gay and pretty and attractive, displaying the special patterns of our Civilization which we reserve for Home Consumption, while *inside* the bale is the Actual Thing that the Customer Sitting in Darkness buys with his blood and tears and land and liberty. That Actual Thing is, indeed, Civilization, but it is only for Export. . . .

We all know that the Business is being ruined. The reason is not far to seek. It is because our Mr. McKinley . . . [has] been exporting the Actual Thing *with the outside cover left off.* This is bad for the Game. . . .

Now, my plan is . . . let us audaciously present the whole of the facts, shirking none. . . . This daring truthfulness will astonish and dazzle the Person Sitting in Darkness. . . . Let us say to him:

"Our case is simple. On the 1st of May, Dewey destroyed the Spanish fleet. This left the [Philippine] Archipelago in the hands of its proper and rightful owners, the Filipino nation. Their army numbered 30,000 men, and they were competent to whip out or starve out the little Spanish garrison; then the people could set up a government of their own devising. Our traditions required that Dewey should now set up his warning sign, and go away. But the Master of the Game happened to think of another plan—the European plan. He acted upon it. This was, to send out an army—ostensibly to help the native patriots put the finishing touch upon their long and plucky struggle for independence, but really to take their land away from them and keep it. That is, in the interest of Progress and Civilization. The plan developed, stage by stage, and quite satisfactorily. We entered into a military alliance with the trusting Filipinos, and they hemmed in Manila on the land side, and by their valuable help the place, with its garrison of 8,000 or 10,000 Spaniards, was captured—a thing which we could not have accomplished unaided at that time. We got their help by ingenuity. We knew they were fighting for their independence, and that they had been at it for two years. We knew they supposed that we also were fighting in their worthy cause—just as we had helped the Cubans fight for Cuban independence—and we allowed them to go on thinking so. *Until Manila was ours and we could get along without them.* Then we showed our hand. Of course, they were surprised—that was natural; surprised and disappointed; disappointed and grieved. To them it looked un-American; uncharacteristic; foreign to our established traditions. And this was natural, too; for we were only playing the American Game in public—in private it was the European. It was neatly done, very neatly, and it bewildered them. They could not understand it; for we had been so friendly—so affectionate. . . .

"We and the patriots having captured Manila, Spain's ownership of the Archipelago and her sovereignty over it were at an end—obliterated —annihilated—not a rag or shred of either remaining behind. It was then that we conceived the divinely humorous idea of *buying* both of these spectres from Spain! (It is quite safe to confess this to the Person Sitting in Darkness, since neither he nor any other sane person will believe it.) In buying those ghosts for twenty millions, we also contracted to take care of the friars and their accumulations. I think we also agreed to propagate leprosy and smallpox, but as to this there is doubt. But it is not important; persons afflicted with the friars do not mind other diseases.

"With our Treaty ratified, Manila subdued, and our Ghosts secured, we had no further use for Aguinaldo and the owners of the Archipelago. We forced a war, and we have been hunting America's guest and ally through the woods and swamps ever since.". . .

Having now laid all the historical facts before the Person Sitting in Darkness, we should bring him to again, and explain them to him. We should say to him:

"They look doubtful, but in reality they are not. There have been lies; yes, but they were told in a good cause. We have been treacherous; but that was only in order that real good might come out of apparent evil. True, we have crushed a deceived and confiding people; we have turned against the weak and the friendless who trusted us; we have stamped out a just and intelligent and well-ordered republic; we have stabbed an ally in the back and slapped the face of a guest; we have bought a Shadow from an enemy that hadn't it to sell; we have robbed a trusting friend of his land and his liberty; we have invited our clean young men to shoulder a discredited musket and do bandit's work under a flag which bandits have been accustomed to fear, not to follow; we have debauched America's honor and blackened her face before the world; but each detail was for the best. We know this. The Head of every State and Sovereignty in Christendom and ninety per cent. of every legislative body in Christendom, including our Congress and our fifty State Legislatures, are members not only of the church, but also of the Blessings-of-Civilization Trust. This world-girdling accumulation of trained morals, high principles, and justice, cannot do an unright thing, an unfair thing, an ungenerous thing, an unclean thing. It knows what it is about. Give yourself no uneasiness; it is all right."

Now then, that will convince the Person. You will see. It will restore the Business. . . .

And as for a flag for the Philippine Province, it is easily managed. We can have a special one. . . : we can have just our usual flag, with the white stripes painted black and the stars replaced by the skull and crossbones.

QUESTIONS

What was the Blessings-of-Civilization Trust? • Who were "the People that Sit in Darkness"? • What was the "Civilization . . . only for Export"? • Why did American involvement in the Philippines threaten to ruin the Trust? • How was that different from America's policy toward Cuba? • What did Aguinaldo and other Filipinos think about American policy? • Why should they think American policy was "all right"?

COMPARATIVE QUESTIONS

How do the Populists' concepts of justice, freedom, and equality differ from those of the leading white citizens in Wilmington, North Carolina? How do they differ from those of the Blessings-of-Civilization Trust? How do the experiences of the Pinkerton guard compare with those of the Red Shirts in Wilmington? How do the experiences of Filipinos compare with those of black Republicans in Wilmington?

CHAPTER 21

PROGRESSIVE REFORM FROM THE GRASSROOTS TO THE WHITE HOUSE

1890–1916

Progressives sought to reunite Americans, to overcome the many bitter divisions that separated rich and poor, employers and employees, native citizens and immigrants, adherents of one faith and those of all others. The settlement house movement reflected the desire to bridge divisions by bringing the ideas and energies of middle-class Americans to poor immigrant neighborhoods. Many grassroots Americans did not share the Progressives' desire to find some middle ground between conflicting groups. Members of labor unions and black Americans feared that the middle ground would be nothing more than the continuation of a status quo they found unacceptable. The following documents illustrate the attitudes and experiences that drew some people toward progressive reforms and that caused others to seek change by insisting on the recognition of fundamental differences among Americans.

DOCUMENT 1

Jane Addams on the Necessity for Social Settlements

Progressives engaged in many reform activities besides electoral politics. Settlement houses were among the most important centers of progressive reform. Jane Addams, founder of Chicago's Hull House, explained her motives in a paper she presented in 1892 to a group of women considering settlement work. In her paper, "The Subjective Necessity for Social Settlements," Addams revealed attitudes and perceptions that motivated many other progressive reformers.

"The Subjective Necessity for Social Settlements," 1892

This paper is an attempt to analyze the motives which underlie a movement based, not only upon conviction, but upon genuine emotion, wherever educated young people are seeking an outlet for that sentiment of universal brotherhood, which the best spirit of our times is forcing from an emotion into a motive. These young people accomplish little toward the solution of this social problem, and bear the brunt of being cultivated into unnourished, oversensitive lives. They have been shut off from the common labor by which they live which is a great source of moral and physical health. They feel a fatal want of harmony between their theory and their lives, a lack of coordination between thought and action. I think it is hard for us to realize how seriously many of them are taking to the notion of human brotherhood, how eagerly they long to give tangible expression to the democratic ideal. These young men and women, longing to socialize their democracy, are animated by certain hopes which may be thus loosely formulated; that if in a democratic country nothing can be permanently achieved save through the masses of the people, it will be impossible to establish a higher political life than the people themselves crave; that it is difficult to see how the notion of a higher civic life can be fostered save through common intercourse; that the blessings which we associate with a life of refinement and cultivation can be made universal and must be made universal if they are to be permanent; that the good we secure for ourselves is precarious and uncertain, is floating in mid-air, until it is secured for all of us and incorporated into our common life. It is easier to state these hopes than to formulate the line of motives, which I believe to constitute the trend of the subjective pressure toward the Settlement. . . .

You may remember the forlorn feeling which occasionally seizes you when you arrive early in the morning a stranger in a great city: the stream of laboring people goes past you as you gaze through the plate-glass window of your hotel; you see hard workingmen lifting great burdens; you hear the driving and jostling of huge carts and your heart sinks with a sudden sense of futility. The door opens behind you and you turn to the man who brings you in your breakfast with a quick sense of human fellowship. You find yourself praying that you may never lose your hold on it all. . . . You turn helplessly to the waiter and feel that it would be almost grotesque to claim from him the sympathy you crave because civilization has placed you apart, but you resent your position with a sudden sense of snobbery. . . .

I have seen young girls suffer and grow sensibly lowered in vitality in the first years after they leave school. In our attempt . . . to give a girl

Jane Addams, *Twenty Years at Hull-House* (1910; reprint, New York: Penguin USA, 1981), 91–100.

pleasure and freedom from care we succeed, for the most part, in making her pitifully miserable. She finds "life" so different from what she expected it to be. She is besotted with innocent little ambitions, and does not understand this apparent waste of herself, this elaborate preparation, if no work is provided for her. There is a heritage of noble obligation which young people accept and long to perpetuate. The desire for action, the wish to right wrong and alleviate suffering haunts them daily. Society smiles at it indulgently instead of making it of value to itself. . . .

[F]rom babyhood the altruistic tendencies of these daughters are persistently cultivated. They are taught to be self-forgetting and self-sacrificing, to consider the good of the whole before the good of the ego. But when all this information and culture show results, when the daughter comes back from college and begins to recognize her social claim to the "submerged tenth," and to evince a disposition to fulfill it, the family claim is strenuously asserted; she is told that she is unjustified, ill-advised in her efforts. . . .

We have in America a fast-growing number of cultivated young people who have no recognized outlet for their active faculties. They hear constantly of the great social maladjustment, but no way is provided for them to change it, and their uselessness hangs about them heavily. . . . These young people have had advantages of college, of European travel, and of economic study, but they are sustaining this shock of inaction. They have pet phrases , and they tell you that the things that make us all alike are stronger than the things that make us different. They say that all men are united by needs and sympathies far more permanent and radical than anything that temporarily divides them and sets them in opposition to each other. . . .

This young life, so sincere in its emotion and good phrase and yet so undirected, seems to me as pitiful as the other great mass of destitute lives. One is supplementary to the other, and some method of communication can surely be devised. . . . Our young people feel nervously the need of putting theory into action, and respond quickly to the Settlement form of activity.

Other motives which I believe make toward the Settlement are the result of a certain renaissance going forward in Christianity. The impulse to share the lives of the poor, the desire to make social service, irrespective of propaganda, express the spirit of Christ, is as old as Christianity itself. . . .

I believe that there is a distinct turning among many young men and women toward this simple acceptance of Christ's message. They resent the assumption that Christianity is a set of ideas which belong to the religious consciousness, whatever that may be. They insist that it cannot be proclaimed and instituted apart from the social life of the community and that it must seek a simple and natural expression in the social organism itself. The Settlement movement is only one manifestation of that wider humanitarian movement which throughout Christendom . . . is endeavoring to embody itself, not in a sect, but in society itself.

I believe that this turning, this renaissance of the early Christian humanitarianism, is going on in America, in Chicago, if you please, without leaders who write or philosophize, without much speaking, but with a bent to express in social service and in terms of action the spirit of Christ. Certain it is that spiritual force is found in the Settlement movement, and it is also true that this force must be evoked and must be called into play before the success of any Settlement is assured. There must be the overmastering belief that all that is noblest in life is common to men as men, in order to accentuate the likenesses and ignore the differences which are found among the people whom the Settlement constantly brings into juxtaposition. . . .

In a thousand voices singing the Hallelujah Chorus in Handel's *Messiah*, it is possible to distinguish the leading voices, but the differences of training and cultivation between them and the voices of the chorus, are lost in the unity of purpose and in the fact that they are all human voices lifted by a high motive. This is a weak illustration of what a Settlement attempts to do. It aims, in a measure, to develop whatever of social life its neighborhood may afford, to focus and give form to that life, to bring to bear upon it the results of cultivation and training; but it receives in exchange for the music of isolated voices the volume and strength of the chorus. It is quite impossible for me to say in what proportion or degree the subjective necessity which led to the opening of Hull-House combined the three trends: first, the desire to interpret democracy in social terms; secondly, the impulse beating at the very source of our lives, urging us to aid in the race progress; and, thirdly, the Christian movement toward humanitarianism. It is difficult to analyze a living thing; the analysis is at best imperfect. Many more motives may blend with the three trends, possibly the desire for a new form of social success due to the nicety of imagination, which refuses worldly pleasures unmixed with the joys of self-sacrifice; possibly a love of approbation, so vast that it is not content with the treble clapping of delicate hands, but wishes also to hear the brass notes from toughened palms may mingle with these.

The Settlement, then, is an experimental effort to aid in the solution of the social and industrial problems which are engendered by the modern conditions of life in a great city. It insists that these problems are not confined to any one portion of a city. It is an attempt to relieve, at the same time, the overaccumulation at one end of society and the destitution at the other; but it assumes that this overaccumulation and destitution is most sorely felt in the things that pertain to social and educational privileges. From its very nature it can stand for no political or social propaganda. . . . The one thing to be dreaded in the Settlement is that it lose its flexibility, its power of quick adaptation, its readiness to change its methods as its environment may demand. It must be open to conviction and must have a deep and abiding sense of tolerance. It must be hospitable and ready for experiment. It should demand from its residents a scientific patience in the accumulation of facts and the steady holding of their sympathies as one of the best instruments for that accumulation. It must be grounded in a philosophy whose foundation is on the solidarity of the human race, a philosophy which will not waver when the race happens to be represented by a drunken woman or an idiot boy. Its residents must be emptied of all conceit of opinion and all self-assertion, and ready to arouse and interpret the public opinion of their neighborhood. They must be content to live quietly side by side with their neighbors, until they grow into a sense of relationship and mutual interests. Their neighbors are held apart by differences of race and language which the residents can more easily overcome. They are bound to see the needs of their neighborhood as a whole, to furnish data for legislation, and to use their influence to secure it. In short, residents are pledged to devote themselves to the duties of good citizenship and to the arousing of the social energies which too largely lie dormant in every neighborhood given over to industrialism. . . .

I may be forgiven the reminder that the best speculative philosophy sets forth the solidarity of the human race; that the highest moralists have taught that without the advance and improvement of the whole, no man ran hope for any lasting improvement in his own moral or material individual condition; and that the subjective necessity for Social Settlements is therefore identical with that necessity, which urges us on toward social and individual salvation.

QUESTIONS

According to Addams, what was subjective about the necessity for social settlements? • What meaning did she associate with the term "to socialize democracy"? • What did she see as major problems of her society? • What was her own perspective on society? • What differences did she notice among people and what did she identify as the unity underlying all those differences? • How did Christianity motivate her? • Did she acknowledge other motives? • How would settlement houses aid in the solution of social and industrial problems?

Document 2

Mother Jones on the Futility of Class Harmony

Progressive impulses to reconcile differences, to find common ground, and to reduce conflict rang false to labor union activists. Struggling to defend working people from industrial abuses, union organizers often viewed progressive reforms as dangerous compromises that defeated the goals of working people. Mother

Jones, a tireless organizer for the United Mine Workers, expressed in a public letter her opinion of the efforts of a Chicago socialite to reduce the strife between labor and capital. Born in 1830, Mother Jones began to attend meetings of the Knights of Labor in 1871 and participated in many of the most important labor conflicts of the next half-century.

Letter to Mrs. Potter Palmer, January 12, 1907

43 Welton Place, Chicago, Ill.
January 12, 1907.

Mrs. Potter Palmer
100 Lake Shore Drive
Chicago, Ill.

Dear Madam:

By the announcement of the daily press I learn that you are to entertain a number of persons who are to be present as representatives of two recognized classes of American citizens—the working class and the capitalist class, and that the purpose of this gathering is to choose a common ground on which the conflicting interests of these two classes may be harmonized and the present strife between the organized forces of these two classes may be brought to a peaceful and satisfactory end.

I credit you with perfect sincerity in this matter, but being fully aware that your environment and whole life has prevented you from seeing and understanding the true relationship of these two classes in this republic and the nature of the conflict which you think can be ended by such means as you are so prominently associated with, and with a desire that you may see and understand it in all its grim reality, I respectfully submit these few personal experiences for your kind consideration.

I am a workman's daughter, by occupation a dress-maker and school teacher, and during this last twenty-five years an active worker in the organized labor movement. During the past seventy years of my life I have been subject to the authority of the capitalist class and for the last thirty-five years I have been conscious of this fact. With the years' personal experience—the roughest kind best of all teachers—I have learned that there is an irrepressible conflict that will never end between the working-class and the capitalist-class, until these two classes disappear and the worker alone remains the producer and owner of the capital produced.

In this fight I wept at the grave of nineteen workers shot on the highways of Latterman, Pennsylvania in 1897. In the same place I marched with 5,000 women eighteen miles in the night seeking bread for their children, and halted with the bayonets of the Coal and Iron police who had orders to shoot to kill.

I was at Stanford Mountain, W.Va., in 1903 where seven of my brother workers were shot dead while asleep in their little shanties by the same forces.

I was in Colorado at the bull pens in which men, women and children were enclosed by the same forces, directed by that instrument of the capitalist class recently promoted by President Roosevelt, General Bell, who achieved some fame for his declaration that "in place of Habeas Corpus" he would give them "Post Mortems."

The same forces put me, an inoffensive old woman, in jail in West Virginia in 1902. They dragged me out of bed in Colorado in March, 1904, and marched me at the point of fixed bayonets to the border line of Kansas in the night-time. The same force took me from the streets of Price, Utah, in 1904, and put me in jail. They did this to me in my old age, though I have never violated the law of the land, never been tried by a court on any charge but once, and that was for speaking to my fellow workers, and then I was discharged by the federal court whose injunction I was charged with violating.

The capitalist class, whose representatives you will entertain, did this to me, and these other lawless acts have and are being committed every hour by this same class all over this land, and this they will continue to do till the working-class send their representatives into the legislative halls of this nation and by law take away the power of this capitalist class to rob and oppress the workers.

The workers are coming to understand this and the intelligent part of that class while respecting you, understand the uselessness of such conferences as will assemble in your mansion.

Permit me to quote from [Oliver] Goldsmith's "Deserted Village," where he says:

Ill fares the land, to hast'ning ills a prey,
Where wealth accumulates and men decay.

Quite appropriate to this fair land to-day.

Sincerely yours, for justice,
Mother Jones

QUESTIONS

According to Mother Jones, why was Mrs. Palmer's meeting misguided? • Why did Mrs. Palmer's life and environment prevent her from understanding class relationships? • How did Mother Jones describe the relationship between workers and capitalists? • What was the source of her belief? • What remedy did she propose? • Would meetings such as Mrs. Palmer's contribute to such a remedy?

An Anonymous Man Explains Why He Is a Wobbly

Progressive reformers concentrated their attention on large cities, and most labor unions focused on big factories. Many working people moved from job to job in small towns, in western mining and logging camps, or from farm to farm as migratory laborers in fields of wheat, sugar beets, grapes, or vegetables. The Industrial Workers of the World (IWW), formed in Chicago in 1905, tried to organize these scattered workers under the tent of One Big Union dedicated to overthrowing capitalism. The IWW—or Wobblies, as they were called—attracted many working people throughout the west. One of them wrote an anonymous account of why he became a Wobbly—an account that illustrates the appeal of revolutionary doctrines anathema to Progressives.

"Why I Am a Member of the I.W.W.," 1922

I come from a part of Europe which furnishes a very large percentage of the loggers in the northwest.

As to my past I might say that life has offered me a very varied bill of fare. From my seventh to my fourteenth year I generally put in from seven to eight months a year at the "point of production." We kids in the sugar beet fields of southern Sweden began our day at 6 A.M. and were kept busy until 8 P.M., with three rests a day, totaling altogether two hours, making a twelve-hour day. You can easily imagine how much time we had for play or study and how physically fit we were for either.

So my childhood was lost and I was an old man at 14, when I struck a job in a grocery store, and at the age of 23 I found myself manager for quite a large business enterprise in my native country—a co-operative association composed of several thousand members. . . .

At the age of 25 I emigrated to the United States. To me it was not a question of journeying to some place where I hoped to gain fortune and fame. It was merely the satisfying of a desire for adventure and for knowledge of the world, a desire long suppressed for reasons of entirely personal nature. My first job in this country was in a packing plant at South St. Paul, Minn. There I received a splendid illustration of Upton Sinclair's book, "The Jungle," perhaps the most read book in Sweden at the time of my departure. It was a ten-hour day, with lots of overtime at regular pay, 16 1/2 cents per hour. Never do I see a sign advertising a certain brand

---

"Why Am I a Member of the I.W.W.," *Four L. Bulletin* (1922); reprinted in Joyce L. Kornbluh, ed., *Rebel Voices: An IWW Anthology* (Ann Arbor: University of Michigan Press, 1964), 286–89.

of ham and bacon without thinking of the terrible high premium in sweat and blood, in misery and starvation, in ignorance and degeneration, the workers in those establishments have to pay before these products reach your table.

I turned down offers to again enter the commercial field back in Minnesota in order to be able to study another class of men, the man of the "wild west," as well as the wild west itself, and early in March, 1910, I headed for this coast.

I'll never forget my first experience in camp. It was a railroad camp up in the Rockies. I was tired after the hike with my bundle on my back, and attempted to sit down on a bed, the only furniture I could see that would furnish me a rest. Before I could accomplish the deed I was told in a very sharp voice in my mother tongue not to do so. I moved a little and tried another bed, when another Swede gave a similar command. After a third experiment which ended in a similar way, I got kind of peeved and began to lecture my countrymen a little as to civilized manners, when one of the boys explained: "We only warn you so as not to get lousy."

Suffice it to say that I made no more attempts to rest in that camp, but took a freight train that very evening and stayed two nights and one day in a box car before I, nearly froze to death, was dumped off at Hillyard, Wash., penniless, with no one I knew, and unable to speak a word in English.

Shortly after this incident I found myself in a logging camp in Idaho, across from the city of Coeur d'Alene. It was double beds two stories high, sleep on straw, work eleven to twelve hours per day, but the board was fairly good. I stayed there for several months, mostly because I wanted to stay away from my countrymen in order to learn the language. From there I went to British Columbia. Put in one year in a logging camp in the Frazer Valley and then one year and a half in a railroad camp on the Kettle Valley railroad. It was here I aligned myself with the I.W.W., and may I state that there was no delegate in that camp, and, to the best of my knowledge, not one member, I went over a hundred miles into Vancouver, B.C., to get that "little red card."

Why did I do it?

The reasons were many. While young I had associated myself with the prohibitionists, joining the Independent Order of Good Templars. I soon came to the conclusion that the liquor traffic itself is but a natural outgrowth of our existing social system, and that I could not abolish it without a fundamental change in society itself.

When working on the Kettle Valley road I observed quite a few interesting facts in this connection. Of over three thousand workers employed for a couple of years I doubt if there were two dozen men who left that job with sufficient funds to carry them for two months. The general routine was to work for a month, draw your check, go down to a little town named Hope (the most hopeless city I've seen) composed of two very large saloons, a couple of dirty rooming houses, a couple of stores and half a dozen houses of prostitution, and to spend, in a day or two, your every nickel in either the saloons or the brothels, usually in both. . . .

The I.W.W. seemed to me then and seems to me now the only group offering me any sensible program under which I could operate with a view to gaining these good things in life, and such changes in society as I desired. The I.W.W. declared that our real ruler is our boss. He decides our wages and thereby our standard of living, our pleasure or our misery, our education as well as the education of our children, our health and our comfort in life; in fact, he almost decides if we shall be allowed to live. The I.W.W. also told me that by uniting with my fellow-workers in the industry and all industries combined into One Big Union of all the workers, we could successfully combat our masters' One Big Union and gain the good things in life. We did not need to live in misery, we did not need to be ignorant for lack of time and access to study. And furthermore, we would become trained and organized for our final task, the control and management of industries. And as this program met my demands I naturally joined the I.W.W.

Some particular influences caused me to devote my whole life to the organization, and I am sure that perhaps thousands of others have been similarly influenced and simply forced to align themselves with the movement.

I knew a young fellow-worker in Seattle, by name Gust Johnson. He was only a little more than 20 years of age, a very quiet and very studious fellow. He surely had the courage of his convictions and he practiced what he preached to the limit of his ability. He was refined in manners, exceedingly clean, neat and orderly. He had been in the United States for about two years, when the Everett free-speech fight took place. He went on board the Verona to go with the bunch to Everett on the fifth of November, 1916, to assist in enforcing the constitutional right of free speech and free assemblage. In the shooting that followed Gust Johnson was the first one who fell with a bullet through his heart. Gust Johnson, who would hesitate even to kill a fly, Gust Johnson, to whom violence and disorder were an abhorrence.

I did what every one of you would have done for a true friend on whom such a cruel outrage had been committed. I threw myself into the harness and faithfully worked for the defense of the seventy-two victims, unjustly arrested, until the day of their release, and until the memory of Gust Johnson and the other four victims of the Everett tragedy stood shining bright before their relatives and their class.

During this defense work I got acquainted with another countryman of mine who toured the country in behalf of the I.W.W. His name is Ragnar Johanson. Ragnar has all the advantages in life which I lack. He is well educated, well built, handsome, a gifted orator and accomplished writer. Now, there is no intelligent human being who thinks that any question can be solved by violence. So Ragnar's theme has always been: "Violence signifies weakness; reason, strength." In hundreds of lectures I have heard this man urge his fellow-workers to educate themselves, to study and organize, but never have I heard him utter one word about using brutal force or violence to accomplish their ends. On the contrary he has always argued against all such teachings as being harmful and detrimental to the workers as a class or as individuals. Where is Ragnar Johanson now? He is serving ten years in the Leavenworth, Kan., federal prison, together with about seventy other fellow-workers who are my personal acquaintances or friends.

And lastly, although I am a foreigner, it is only because I am in America that I am an I.W.W. For, contrary to the belief of many, the I.W.W. is an outgrowth of advanced economic developments in America, and the Italian, the Russian or the Swede that you may find in the organization here would not have been "wobblies" had they remained in their native countries.

The economic law which says "that commodities shall be produced by that method which allows for the least expenditure of human labor" is the real ruler of society. This law cannot be abrogated by any combinations, trusts, monopolies, parties or organizations of any kind. . . . At present time production on large scale affords the greatest conformity to this law, hence the success of the trusts and the great industrial combinations. United States, with its immensely large natural resources and its shortage of labor power in years gone by has offered the best opportunity for the development of machine production on a large scale, while at the same time the aforesaid shortage of labor power has served as a spur to progress in this direction. The result is that no country in the world is so far advanced, industrially, as the U. S., particularly in leading industries, such as agriculture, mining, lumbering and manufacturing of machinery and means of locomotion.

The saving of labor power appears through a thorough-going specialization of the work, through elimination of competition by means of amalgamations into large trusts whereby unnecessary labor in management in advertising, in salesmanship, and in distribution are avoided, and at the same time over-production with its loss of values in perishable goods, etc., is limited to a minimum. The trust is the bosses' One Big Union whereby they not only control the price on labor power, but also safeguard themselves against waste of labor power.

The I.W.W. is the result of the trust, the bosses' One Big Union. As the trust becomes universal, succeeds in organizing the industries internationally, so will the I.W.W. expand. As the trust is the logical outcome of technical progress in our mode of production, is a means by which commodities can be produced with a smaller expenditure of human labor than under a competitive system, so is the I.W.W. [an] outcome of the same forces whose object is to counteract the power of the trust and ultimately take full control of the trusts and the means of production for the benefit of mankind as a whole. Neither of them can be talked, written or legislated away. Let's make an effort to understand them and the underlying causes for their existence, and much suffering and much hatred will be avoided.

QUESTIONS

What kinds of work did this man do? • How did temperance influence his decision to become a Wobbly? • What did the IWW offer? • What were the differences between the two "One Big Unions" he described? • What tactics did he support? • What were his goals? • Why did he believe the IWW was an outgrowth of American economic conditions?

DOCUMENT 4

Booker T. Washington on Racial Accommodation

Most Progressives showed little interest in changing race relations; many in fact actively supported white supremacy. Beset by the dilemmas of sharecropping, Jim Crow laws, disfranchisement, poverty, illiteracy, and the constant threat of violence, black southerners had few champions among Progressives. Booker T. Washington, perhaps the era's most celebrated black leader, spelled out a plan of racial accommodation as a path toward progress. In an address to white business leaders gathered at the Cotton States and International Exposition in Atlanta in 1895, Washington outlined ideas that remained at the center of debate among black Americans for decades.

The Atlanta Exposition Address, 1895

Mr. President and Gentlemen of the Board of Directors and Citizens,

One-third of the population of the South is of the Negro race. No enterprise seeking the material, civil, or moral welfare of this section can disregard this element of our population and reach the highest success. I but convey to you . . . the sentiment of the masses of my race when I say that in no way have the value and manhood of the American Negro been more

---

Booker T. Washington, *Up from Slavery* (1901); reprinted in *Black Protest Thought in the Twentieth Century,* ed. August Meier, Elliott Rudwick, and Frances L. Broderick (Indianapolis: Bobbs-Merrill, 1971), 4–8.

fittingly and generously recognized than by the managers of this magnificent Exposition at every stage of its progress. It is a recognition that will do more to cement the friendship of the two races than any occurrence since the dawn of our freedom.

Not only this, but the opportunity here afforded will awaken among us a new era of industrial progress. Ignorant and inexperienced, it is not strange that in the first years of our new life we began at the top instead of at the bottom; that a seat in Congress or the state legislature was more sought than real estate or industrial skill; that the political convention or stump speaking had more attractions than starting a dairy farm or truck garden.

A ship lost at sea for many days suddenly sighted a friendly vessel. From the mast of the unfortunate vessel was seen a signal, "Water, water; we die of thirst!" The answer from the friendly vessel at once came back, "Cast down your bucket where you are.". . .The captain of the distressed vessel, at last heeding the injunction, cast down his bucket, and it came up full of fresh, sparkling water from the mouth of the Amazon River. To those of my race who depend on bettering their condition in a foreign land or who underestimate the importance of cultivating friendly relations with the Southern white man, who is their next-door neighbor, I would say: "Cast down your bucket where you are" — cast it down in making friends in every manly way of the people of all races by whom we are surrounded.

Cast it down in agriculture, mechanics, in commerce, in domestic service, and in the professions. And in this connection it is well to bear in mind that whatever other sins the South may be called to bear, when it comes to business, pure and simple, it is in the South that the Negro is given a man's chance in the commercial world, and in nothing is this Exposition more eloquent than in emphasizing this chance. Our greatest danger is that in the great leap from slavery to freedom we may overlook the fact that the masses of us are to live by the productions of our hands, and fail to keep in mind that we shall prosper in proportion as we learn to dignify and glorify common labour and put brains and skill into the common occupations of life; shall prosper in proportion as we learn to draw the line between the superficial and the substantial, the ornamental gewgaws of life and the useful. No race can prosper till it learns that there is as much dignity in tilling a field as in writing a poem. It is at the bottom of life we must begin, and not at the top. Nor should we permit our grievances to overshadow our opportunities.

To those of the white race who look to the incoming of those of foreign birth and strange tongue and habits for the prosperity of the South, were I permitted I would repeat what I say to my own race, "Cast down your bucket where you are." Cast it down among the eight millions of Negroes whose habits you know, whose fidelity and love you have tested in days when to have proved treacherous meant the ruins of your firesides. Cast down your bucket among these people who have, without strikes and labour wars, tilled your fields, cleared your forests, builded your railroads and cities, and brought forth treasures from the bowels of the earth, and helped make possible this magnificent representation of the progress of the South. Casting down your bucket among my people, helping and encouraging them as you are doing on these grounds, and to education of head, hand, and heart, you will find that they will buy your surplus land, make blossom the waste places in your fields, and run your factories. While doing this, you can be sure in the future, as in the past, that you and your families will be surrounded by the most patient, faithful, law-abiding, and unresentful people that the world has seen As we have proved our loyalty to you in the past, in nursing your children, watching by the sick-bed of your mothers and fathers, and often following them with tear-dimmed eyes to their graves, so in the future, in our humble way, we shall stand by you with a devotion that no foreigner can approach, ready to lay down our lives, if need be, in defence of yours, interlacing our industrial, commercial, civil, and religious life with yours in a way that shall make the interests of both races one. In all things that are purely social we can be as separate as the fingers, yet one as the hand in all things essential to mutual progress. . . .

Nearly sixteen millions of hands will aid you in pulling the load upward, or they will pull against you the load downward. We shall constitute one-third and more of the ignorance and crime of the South, or one-third its intelligence and progress; we shall contribute one-third to the business and industrial prosperity of the South, or we shall prove a veritable body of death, stagnating, depressing, retarding every effort to advance the body politic. . . .

The wisest among my race understand that the agitation of questions of social equality is the extremest folly, and that progress in the enjoyment of all the privileges that will come to us must be the result of severe and constant struggle rather than of artificial forcing. No race that has anything to contribute to the markets of the world is long in any degree ostracized. It is important and right that all privileges of the law be ours, but it is vastly more important that we be prepared for the exercises of these privileges. The opportunity to earn a dollar in a factory just now is worth infinitely more than the opportunity to spend a dollar in an opera-house.

QUESTIONS

What was Washington's view of southern whites? • What did he mean by "Cast down your bucket where you are"? • How did he believe blacks should contribute to the South? • What were his goals? • How did he define equality? • What was his view of politics? • How did he measure progress? • Would Washington's speech have been different if he were addressing a black audience? • How?

DOCUMENT 5

W. E. B. Du Bois on Racial Equality

Many educated African Americans, especially in the North, objected to Booker T. Washington's policy of racial accommodation. In 1903, W. E. B. Du Bois attacked Washington's ideas and proposed alternatives that made sense to many black Americans, then and since. One of the organizers of the Niagara Movement and of the National Association for the Advancement of Colored People, Du Bois had earned a doctorate in history from Harvard and was a professor at Atlanta University when he published his criticisms of Washington, excerpted from his work The Souls of Black Folk.

"Booker T. Washington and Others," from **The Souls of Black Folk**, *1903*

Easily the most striking thing in the history of the American Negro since 1876 is the ascendancy of Mr. Booker T. Washington. It began at the time when war memories and ideals were rapidly passing; a day of astonishing commercial development was dawning; a sense of doubt and hesitation overtook the freedmen's sons, — then it was that his leading began. Mr. Washington came, with a simple definite programme, at the psychological moment when the nation was a little ashamed of having bestowed so much sentiment on Negroes, and was concentrating its energies on Dollars. His programme of industrial education, conciliation of the South, and submission and silence as to civil and political rights, was not wholly original. . . . But Mr. Washington first indissolubly linked these things; he put enthusiasm, unlimited energy, and perfect faith into this programme, and changed it from a by-path into a veritable Way of Life. . . .

It startled the nation to hear a Negro advocating such a programme after many decades of bitter complaint; it startled and won the applause of the South, it interested and won the admiration of the North; and after a confused murmur of protest, it silenced if it did not convert the Negroes themselves.

To gain the sympathy and cooperation of the various elements comprising the white South was Mr. Washington's first task; and [it]. . . seemed, for a black man, well-nigh impossible. And yet ten years later it was done in the word spoken at Atlanta: "In all things purely social we can be as separate as five fingers, and yet one as the hand in all things essential to mutual progress." This "Atlanta Compromise" is by all odds

W. E. B. Du Bois, *The Souls of Black Folk* (1903); reprinted in *Black Protest Thought in the Twentieth Century,* ed. August Meier, Elliott Rudwick, and Frances L. Broderick (Indianapolis: Bobbs-Merrill, 1971), 37–47.

the most notable thing in Mr. Washington's career. The South interpreted it in different ways: the radicals received it as a complete surrender of the demand for civil and political equality; the conservatives, as a generously conceived working basis for mutual understanding. . . .

So Mr. Washington's cult has gained unquestioning followers, his work has wonderfully prospered, his friends are legion, and his enemies are confounded. To-day he stands as the one recognized spokesman of his ten million fellows, and one of the most notable figures in a nation of seventy millions. . . .

But Booker T. Washington arose as essentially the leader not of one race but of two,—a compromiser between the South, the North, and the Negro. Naturally the Negroes resented, at first bitterly, signs of compromise which surrendered their civil and political rights, even though this was to be exchanged for larger chances of economic development. The rich and dominating North, however, was not only weary of the race problem, but was investing largely in Southern enterprises, and welcomed any method of peaceful cooperation. Thus, by national opinion, the Negroes began to recognize Mr. Washington's leadership; and the voice of criticism was hushed.

Mr. Washington represents in Negro thought the old attitude of adjustment and submission; but adjustment at such a peculiar time as to make his programme unique. This is an age of unusual economic development, and Mr. Washington's programme naturally takes an economic cast, becoming a gospel of Work and Money to such an extent as apparently almost completely to overshadow the higher aims of life. Moreover, this is an age when the more advanced races are coming in closer contact with the less developed races, and the race-feeling is therefore intensified; and Mr. Washington's programme practically accepts the alleged inferiority of the Negro races. Again, in our own land, the reaction from the sentiment of war time has given impetus to race-prejudice against Negroes, and Mr. Washington withdraws many of the high demands of Negroes as men and American citizens. . . .

In answer to this, it has been claimed that the Negro can survive only through submission. Mr. Washington distinctly asks that black people give up, at least for the present, three things,

First, political power,
Second, insistence on civil rights,
Third, higher education of Negro youth,—

and concentrate all their energies on industrial education, the accumulation of wealth, and the conciliation of the South. This policy has been courageously and insistently advocated for over fifteen years, and has been triumphant for perhaps ten years. As a result of this tender of the palm-branch, what has been the return? In these years there have occurred:

1. The disfranchisement of the Negro.
2. The legal creation of a distinct status of civil inferiority for the Negro.
3. The steady withdrawal of aid from institutions for the higher training of the Negro.

These movements are not, to be sure, direct results of Mr. Washington's teachings; but his propaganda has, without a shadow of doubt, helped their speedier accomplishment. The question then comes: Is it possible, and probable, that nine millions of men can make effective progress in economic lines if they are deprived of political rights, made a servile caste, and allowed only the most meagre chance for developing their exceptional men? If history and reason give any distinct answer to these questions, it is an, emphatic *No.* And Mr. Washington thus faces the triple paradox of his career:

1. He is striving nobly to make Negro artisans business men and property-owners; but it is utterly impossible, under modern competitive methods, for workingmen and property-owners to defend their rights and exist without the right of suffrage.
2. He insists on thrift and self-respect, but at the same time counsels a silent submission to civic inferiority such as is bound to sap the manhood of any race in the long run.
3. He advocates common-school and industrial training, and depreciates institutions of higher learning. . . .

This triple paradox in Mr. Washington's position is the object of criticism by two classes of colored Americans. One class is spiritually descended from Toussaint the Savior, through Gabriel, Vesey, and Turner[1], and they represent the attitude of revolt and revenge; they hate the white South blindly and distrust the white race generally, and so far as they agree on definite action, think that the Negro's only hope lies in emigration beyond the borders of the United States. And yet, by the irony of fate, nothing has more effectively made this programme seem hopeless than the recent course of the United States toward weaker and darker peoples in the West Indies, Hawaii, and the Philippines,—for where in the world may we go and be safe from lying and brute force?

The other class of Negroes who cannot agree with Mr. Washington has hitherto said little aloud. . . . Such men feel in conscience bound to ask of this nation three things:

1. The right to vote.
2. Civic equality.
3. The education of youth according to ability.

---

[1] **Toussaint the Savior . . . Gabriel, Vesey, and Turner:** Toussaint L'Ouverture was a former slave who led the Revolution of Haiti in 1798; African Americans Gabriel, Denmark Vesey, and Nat Turner all attempted to lead slave rebellions in the first half of the nineteenth century.

They acknowledge Mr. Washington's invaluable service in counselling patience and courtesy in such demands; they do not ask that ignorant black men vote when ignorant whites are debarred, or that any reasonable restrictions in the suffrage should not be applied; they know that the low social level of the mass of the race is responsible for much discrimination against it, but they also know, and the nation knows, that relentless color prejudice is more often a cause than a result of the Negro's degradation; they seek the abatement of this relic of barbarism, and not its systematic encouragement and pampering by all agencies of social power. . . . They advocate, with Mr. Washington, a broad system of Negro common schools supplemented by thorough industrial training; but they are surprised that a man of Mr. Washington's insight cannot see that no educational system ever has rested or can rest on any other basis than that of the well equipped college and university, and they insist that there is a demand for a few such institutions throughout the South to train the best of the Negro youth as teachers, professional men, and leaders. . . .

They do not expect that the free right to vote, to enjoy civic rights, and to be educated, will come in a moment; they do not expect to see the bias and prejudices of years disappear at the blast of a trumpet; but they are absolutely certain that the way for a people to gain their reasonable rights is not by voluntarily throwing them away and insisting that they do not want them; that the way for a people to gain respect is not by continually belittling and ridiculing themselves; that, on the contrary, Negroes must insist continually, in season and out of season, that voting is necessary to modern manhood, that color discrimination is barbarism, and that black boys need education as well as white boys. . . .

. . . [T]he distinct impression left by Mr. Washington's propaganda is, first, that the South is justified in its present attitude toward the Negro because of the Negro's degradation; secondly, that the prime cause of the Negro's failure to rise more quickly is his wrong education in the past; and, thirdly, that his future rise depends primarily on his own efforts. Each of these propositions is a dangerous half-truth. The supplementary truths must never be lost sight of: first, slavery and race-prejudice are potent if not sufficient causes of the Negro's position; second, industrial and common-school training were necessarily slow in planting because they had to await the black teachers trained by higher institutions . . . ; and, third, while it is a great truth to say that the Negro must strive and strive mightily to help himself, it is equally true that unless his striving be not simply seconded, but rather aroused and encouraged, by the initiative of the richer and wiser environing group, he cannot hope for great success.

In his failure to realize and impress this last point, Mr. Washington is especially to be criticised. His doctrine has tended to make the whites, North and South, shift the burden of the Negro problem to the Negro's shoulders and stand aside as critical and rather pessimistic spectators; when in fact the burden belongs to the nation, and the hands of none of us are clean if we bend not our energies to righting these great wrongs.

QUESTIONS

According to Du Bois, why did Washington become recognized as a leader? • Why was the Atlanta Compromise attractive to many whites? • What did Washington ask of black people? • What did Du Bois believe were the shortcomings of Washington's strategy? • What did Du Bois identify as the triple paradox of Washington's career? • What alternatives did Du Bois propose? • Who would have been most receptive to Du Bois's criticism of Washington, and why?

COMPARATIVE QUESTIONS

How do Mother Jones's ideas about the possibility of harmony between classes compare with those of Jane Addams? How do Booker T. Washington's ideas about progress for black Americans compare with the Wobbly's concept of One Big Union? Compare W. E. B. Du Bois's ideas about the necessity of equality and political conflict with Addams's notions about the role of settlement houses.

CHAPTER 22

THE UNITED STATES AND THE "GREAT WAR"
1914–1920

With the declaration of war against Germany in 1917, the United States unmistakably asserted its status as a major power in world affairs. European nations had admired American economic might for decades and watched the politics of the nation's constitutional democracy with interest for more than a century. Now, by entering the war and claiming a decisive voice in the peace, the United States took its place as one of the powerful industrial nations that would shape global history in the twentieth century. The following documents illustrate the idealism of President Woodrow Wilson, the patriotism of war posters, the excitement of the war in the skies over Europe, and the bitter criticism of the war by American Socialists.

DOCUMENT 1
President Wilson Asks Congress for a Declaration of War

For more than two years after the beginning of war in Europe in 1914, the United States maintained a policy of neutrality. In the spring of 1917, President Woodrow Wilson called an emergency session of Congress to ask for a declaration of war against Germany. Wilson's speech to Congress, excerpted here, outlined the reasons for America's entry into the war, explained what actions would be necessary to mobilize for warfare, and declared the noble motives for which the nation would fight.

Speech to Congress, April 2, 1917

I have called the Congress into extraordinary session because there are serious, very serious, choices of policy to be made, and made immediately, which it was neither right nor constitutionally permissible that I should assume the responsibility of making.

On the third of February . . . I officially laid before you the extraordinary announcement of the Imperial German Government that on and after the first day of February it was its purpose to put aside all restraints of law or of humanity and use its submarines to sink every vessel that sought to approach either the ports of Great Britain and Ireland or the western coasts of Europe or any of the ports controlled by the enemies of Germany within the Mediterranean. That had seemed to be the object of the German submarine warfare earlier in the war, but since April of last year the Imperial Government had somewhat restrained the commanders of its undersea craft in conformity with its promise then given to us that passenger boats should not be sunk and that due warning would be given to all other vessels which its submarines might seek to destroy, when no resistance was offered or escape attempted. . . . The new policy has swept every restriction aside. Vessels of every kind, whatever their flag, their character, their cargo, their destination, their errand, have been ruthlessly sent to the bottom without warning and without thought of help or mercy for those on board, the vessels of friendly neutrals along with those of belligerents. . . .

I was for a little while unable to believe that such things would in fact be done by any government that had hitherto subscribed to the humane practices of civilized nations. . . . [T]he German Government has swept aside . . . all scruples of humanity or of respect for the understandings that were supposed to underlie the intercourse of the world. I am not now thinking of the loss of property involved, immense and serious as that is, but only of the wanton and wholesale destruction of the lives of non-combatants, men, women, and children, engaged in pursuits which have always, even in the darkest periods of modern history, been deemed innocent and legitimate. Property can be paid for; the lives of peaceful and innocent people cannot be. The present German submarine warfare against commerce is a warfare against mankind.

It is a war against all nations. American ships have been sunk, American lives taken, in ways which it has stirred us very deeply to learn of, but the ships and people of other neutral and friendly nations have been sunk and overwhelmed in the waters in the same, way. There has been no discrimination. The challenge is to all mankind. Each nation must decide for itself how it will meet it. . . . Our motive will not be revenge or the

the U.S is the only nation that practices human rights. (p ☺)

victorious assertion of the physical might of the nation, but only the vindi-
cation of right, of human right, of which we are only a single champion. . . .

[A]rmed neutrality, it now appears, is impracticable. Because submarines are in effect outlaws when used as the German submarines have
been used against merchant shipping. . . . There is one choice we cannot
make, we are incapable of making: we will not choose the path of submission and suffer the most sacred rights of our nation and our people to
be ignored or violated. The wrongs against which we now array ourselves are no common wrongs; they cut to the very roots of human life.

With a profound sense of the solemn and even tragical character of
the step I am taking and of the grave responsibilities which it involves,
but in unhesitating obedience to what I deem my constitutional duty, I
advise that the Congress declare the recent course of the Imperial German Government to be in fact nothing less than war against the government and people of the United States; that it formally accept the status of
belligerent which has thus been thrust upon it; and that it take immediate steps not only to put the country in a more thorough state of defense
but also to exert all its power and employ all its resources to bring the
Government of the German Empire to terms and end the war.

What this will involve is clear. It will involve the utmost practicable
cooperation in counsel and action with the governments now at war with
Germany, and, as incident to that, the extension to those governments of
the most liberal financial credits, in order that our resources may so far
as possible be added to theirs. It will involve the organization and mobilization of all the material resources of the country to supply the materials of war and serve the incidental needs of the nation in the most
abundant and yet the most economical and efficient way possible. It will
involve the immediate full equipment of the navy in all respects but particularly in supplying it with the best means of dealing with the enemy's
submarines. It will involve the immediate addition to the armed forces of
the United States already provided for by law in case of war at least five
hundred thousand men, who should, in my opinion, be chosen upon the
principle of universal liability to service, and also the authorization of
subsequent additional increments of equal force so soon as they may be
needed and can be handled in training. It will involve also, of course, the
granting of adequate credits to the Government, sustained, I hope, so far
as they can equitably be sustained by the present generation, by well conceived taxation. . . .

While we do these things, these deeply momentous things, let us be
very clear, and make very clear to all the world what our motives and
our objects are. . . . Our object now, as then, is to vindicate the principles of
peace and justice in the life of the world as against selfish and autocratic
power and to set up amongst the really free and self-governed peoples of
the world such a concert of purpose and of action as will henceforth ensure the observance of those principles. Neutrality is no longer feasible

or desirable where the peace of the world is involved and the freedom of its peoples, and the menace to that peace and freedom lies in the existence of autocratic governments backed by organized force which is controlled wholly by their will, not by the will of their people. We have seen the last of neutrality in such circumstances. We are at the beginning of an age in which it will be insisted that the same standards of conduct and of responsibility for wrong done shall be observed among nations and their governments that are observed among the individual citizens of civilized states.

We have no quarrel with the German people. We have no feeling towards them but one of sympathy and friendship. It was not upon their impulse that their government acted in entering this war. It was not with their previous knowledge or approval. It was a war determined upon as wars used to be determined upon in the old, unhappy days when peoples were nowhere consulted by their rulers and wars were provoked and waged in the interest of dynasties or of little groups of ambitious men who were accustomed to use their fellow men as pawns and tools. . . .

A steadfast concert for peace can never be maintained except by a partnership of democratic nations. . . . It must be a league of honour, a partnership of opinion. . . . Only free peoples can hold their purpose and their honour steady to a common end and prefer the interests of mankind to any narrow interest of their own.

Does not every American feel that assurance has been added to our hope for the future peace of the world by the wonderful and heartening things that have been happening within the last few weeks in Russia? Russia was known by those who knew it best to have been always in fact democratic at heart, in all the vital habits of her thought, in all the intimate relationships of her people that spoke their natural instinct, their habitual attitude towards life. The autocracy that crowned the summit of her political structure, long as it had stood and terrible as was the reality of its power, was not in fact Russian in origin, character, or purpose; and now it has been shaken off and the great, generous Russian people have been added in all their naive majesty and might to the forces that are fighting for freedom in the world, for justice, and for peace. Here is a fit partner for a League of Honour.

One of the things that has served to convince us that the Prussian autocracy was not and could never be our friend is that from the very outset of the present war it has filled our unsuspecting communities and even our offices of government with spies and set criminal intrigues everywhere afoot against our national unity of counsel, our peace within and without, our industries and our commerce. Indeed it is now evident that its spies were here even before the war began; and it is unhappily not a matter of conjecture but a fact proved in our courts of justice that the intrigues which have more than once come perilously near to disturbing the peace and dislocating the industries of the country have been carried on at the instigation, with the support, and even under the personal direction of official agents of the Imperial Government accredited to the Government of the United States. . . .

We are now about to accept gauge of battle with this natural foe to liberty and shall, if necessary, spend the whole force of the nation to check and nullify its pretensions and its power. We are glad, now that we see the facts with no veil of false pretense about them, to fight thus for the ultimate peace of the world and for the liberation of its peoples, the German peoples included: for the rights of nations great and small and the privilege of men everywhere to choose their way of life and of obedience. The world must be made safe for democracy. Its peace must be planted upon the tested foundations of political liberty. We have no selfish ends to serve. We desire no conquest, no dominion. We seek no indemnities for ourselves, no material compensation for the sacrifices we shall freely make. We are but one of the champions of the rights of mankind. We shall be satisfied when those rights have been made as secure as the faith and the freedom of nations can make them. . . .

It is a distressing and oppressive duty, Gentlemen of the Congress, which I have performed in thus addressing you. There are, it may be, many months of fiery trial and sacrifice ahead of us. It is a fearful thing to lead this great peaceful people into war, into the most terrible and disastrous of all wars, civilization itself seeming to be in the balance. But the right is more precious than peace, and we shall fight for the things which we have always carried nearest our hearts,—for democracy, for the right of those who submit to authority to have a voice in their own governments, for the rights and liberties of small nations, for a universal dominion of right by such a concert of free peoples as shall bring peace and safety to all nations and make the world itself at last free. To such a task we can dedicate our lives and our fortunes, everything that we are and everything that we have, with the pride of those who know that the day has come when America is privileged to spend her blood and her might for the principles that gave her birth and happiness and the peace which she has treasured, God helping her, she can do no other.

QUESTIONS

How had the German government changed its policy on submarine warfare? • According to President Wilson, what did the new policy mean? • What should the United States do and what actions did Wilson recommend? • What were the motives for a declaration of war? • Why was Wilson encouraged about events in Russia? • How, according to the president, would war make the world safe for democracy?

DOCUMENT 2

Patriotism and World War I Posters

America's entry into World War I required rapid mobilization. Factories had to start making bullets, bombs, and even airplanes. Soldiers had to be recruited, trained, and armed for battle. In addition, the American people had to be mobilized to support the war. Posters were an important part of the massive campaign to rally Americans at home behind the soldiers in the field. Slogans from World War I posters, which follow, illustrate the ideals employed to portray the American war effort. (Of course, in the original posters each slogan was accompanied by a powerful visual image that dramatized the central idea.)

"AMMUNITION!"
AND REMEMBER
BONDS BUY BULLETS!

ARE YOU 100% AMERICAN?
PROVE IT!
BUY U.S. GOVERNMENT BONDS . . .

BEAT BACK THE HUN
WITH LIBERTY BONDS.

BLOOD OR BREAD
OTHERS ARE GIVING THEIR BLOOD
YOU WILL SHORTEN THE WAR
SAVE LIFE
IF YOU EAT ONLY WHAT YOU NEED,
AND WASTE NOTHING.
UNITED STATES FOOD ADMINISTRATION.

BUY LIBERTY BONDS
"THAT GOVERNMENT OF THE PEOPLE,
BY THE PEOPLE, FOR THE PEOPLE SHALL NOT
PERISH FROM THE EARTH"
A. LINCOLN.

BUY UNITED STATES GOVERNMENT
WAR SAVINGS STAMPS
YOUR MONEY BACK WITH INTEREST FROM THE
UNITED STATES TREASURY.

Posters of World War I and World War II in the George C. Marshall Research Foundation, ed. Anthony R. Crawford (1979).

CAN VEGETABLES FRUIT AND
THE KAISER TOO
WRITE FOR FREE BOOK TO
NATIONAL WAR GARDEN COMMISSION
WASHINGTON, D.C.

CANTIGNY
CHATEAU THIERRY
ST. MIHIEL
ARGONNE
MARNE
"PUT FIGHTING BLOOD IN YOUR BUSINESS
HERE'S HIS RECORD!
DOES HE GET A JOB?"
ARTHUR WOODS, ASSISTANT TO THE SECRETARY OF WAR
LIST YOUR EMPLOYMENT NEEDS WITH THE U. S. EMPLOY-
    MENT SERVICE

COLORED MAN IS NO SLACKER.
COLUMBIA CALLS
ENLIST NOW
FOR U. S. ARMY
NEAREST RECRUITING STATION

CRUSH THE PRUSSIAN
BUY A BOND . . .

ENLIST IN THE NAVY
AMERICANS!
STAND BY UNCLE SAM
FOR LIBERTY
AGAINST TYRANNY! . . .

FIGHT
OR BUY BONDS . . .

FOLLOW THE BOYS IN BLUE
FOR HOME AND COUNTRY
ENLIST IN THE NAVY.

FOOD IS AMMUNITION
DON'T WASTE IT.

FOR HOME AND COUNTRY
VICTORY LIBERTY LOAN.

"GOOD BYE, DAD, I'M OFF
TO FIGHT FOR OLD GLORY,
YOU BUY U. S. GOV'T BONDS". . .

HALT THE HUN
BUY U. S. GOVERNMENT BONDS

HAY
ENRIGHT
GRESHAM
"THE FIRST THREE!"
GIVE TILL IT HURTS
THEY GAVE TILL THEY DIED
WAR FUND WEEK ONE HUNDRED MILLION DOLLARS.

HELP CRUSH THE MENACE OF THE SEAS
BUY LIBERTY BONDS
BUY QUICKLY BUY FREELY . . .

HOLD UP YOUR END!
WAR FUND WEEK
ONE HUNDRED MILLION DOLLARS

I AM TELLING YOU
ON JUNE 28TH I EXPECT YOU
TO ENLIST IN THE ARMY OF WAR SAVERS
TO BACK UP MY ARMY OF FIGHTERS . . .

INVITATIONS TO HOMES
AND ENTERTAINMENTS
THE SPIRIT OF WAR CAMP
COMMUNITY SERVICE
UNITED WAR WORK CAMPAIGN.

JOAN OF ARC SAVED FRANCE
WOMEN OF AMERICA
SAVE YOUR COUNTRY
BUY WAR SAVINGS STAMPS.

JOIN THE AIR SERVICE
AND SERVE IN FRANCE
DO IT NOW.

KEEP 'EM SMILING!
HELP WAR CAMP COMMUNITY SERVICE
"MORALE IS WINNING THE WAR"
UNITED WAR WORK CAMPAIGN.

KEEP IT COMING
"WE MUST NOT ONLY FEED OUR SOLDIERS
AT THE FRONT BUT THE MILLIONS OF
WOMEN & CHILDREN BEHIND OUR LINES"
GEN. JOHN J. PERSHING
WASTE NOTHING.

MUST CHILDREN DIE
AND MOTHERS PLEAD IN VAIN ?
BUY MORE LIBERTY BONDS.

MY DADDY BOUGHT ME A GOVERNMENT BOND
OF THE THIRD LIBERTY LOAN
DID YOURS?

MY SOLDIER
NOW I LAY ME DOWN TO SLEEP
I PRAY THE LORD MY SOUL TO KEEP.
GOD BLESS MY BROTHER GONE TO WAR
ACROSS THE SEAS, IN FRANCE, SO FAR.
OH, MAY HIS FIGHT FOR LIBERTY,
SAVE MILLIONS MORE THAN LITTLE ME
FROM CRUEL FATES OR RUTHLESS BLAST,
AND BRING HIM SAFELY HOME AT LAST.
BUY UNITED STATES GOVERNMENT BONDS . . .

OH BOY!
THAT'S THE GIRL!
THE SALVATION ARMY LASSIE
KEEP HER ON THE JOB . . .
UNITED WAR WORK CAMPAIGN.

OUR DADDY IS FIGHTING
AT THE FRONT FOR YOU BACK HIM UP
BUY A UNITED STATES GOV'T BOND . . .

PVT. TREPTOW'S PLEDGE
HE HAD ALMOST REACHED HIS GOAL
WHEN A MACHINE GUN DROPPED HIM.
IN A POCKET OF HIS BLOUSE
THEY FOUND HIS PLEDGE
"I WILL FIGHT CHEERFULLY
AND DO MY UTMOST
AS IF THE WHOLE ISSUE OF THE STRUGGLE DEPENDED
  ON ME ALONE."

YOU WHO ARE NOT CALLED UPON TO DIE
SUBSCRIBE TO THE FOURTH LIBERTY LOAN.

PROVIDE THE SINEWS OF WAR
BUY LIBERTY BONDS.

REMEMBER ARGONNE
AND INVEST VICTORY LIBERTY LOAN
WOMAN'S LIBERTY LOAN COMMITTEE.

SAVE YOUR CHILD
FROM AUTOCRACY
AND POVERTY
BUY WAR SAVINGS STAMPS

STRAIGHT FROM THE TRENCHES.
ORIGINATED AND PRODUCED FOR
THE LIBERTY LOAN COMMITTEE
ENTIRELY BY MEMBERS OF THE
AMERICAN EXPEDITIONARY FORCE
THE A.E.F. TO THE PRESIDENT:
"IF THE FOLKS BACK HOME FALL SHORT
ON THE BILLIONS YOU NEED, MR. PRESIDENT,
CALL ON US FOR THE BALANCE.
WE LIKE OUR PAY—BUT IF WE HAVE TO
WE CAN GO WITHOUT IT.
YOURS FOR VICTORY,
A.E.F. FRANCE, SEPT. 7, 1918
4TH LIBERTY LOAN.

TEAM WORK WINS!
YOUR WORK HERE
MAKES THEIR WORK OVER THERE POSSIBLE
WITH YOUR HELP THEY ARE INVINCIBLE
WITHOUT IT THEY ARE HELPLESS
WHATEVER YOU MAKE,
MACHINE GUN OR HARNESS,
CARTRIDGES OR HELMET,
THEY ARE WAITING FOR IT.

THE NAVY NEEDS YOU!
DON'T READ AMERICAN HISTORY
MAKE IT! . . .

WOMEN!
HELP AMERICA'S SONS
WIN THE WAR
BUY U. S. GOVERNMENT BONDS.

QUESTIONS

Which Americans were the posters designed to address? • What arguments did the posters make to appeal for support for the war? • According to the posters, what was at stake in the war? • What portrait of America emerges from the slogans of the posters?

DOCUMENT 3

An American Pilot Describes the Air War

Airplanes became important military weapons for the first time during World War I. When the United States entered the war, the military possessed only fifty-five airplanes and very few pilots. Kenneth MacLeish, a junior at Yale University, enlisted in the Naval Reserve along with other Yale undergraduates. The Yale group paid for their own flight training, using equipment supplied by rich businessmen. MacLeish, who had grown up in a prominent family in Illinois, was soon sent to England to train and then to France to fight. MacLeish wrote numerous letters home, the source of the following selections. His letters illustrate the high spirits, new experiences, and deadly risks encountered by thousands of Americans "over there."

Kenneth MacLeish

World War I Letters

London, 16 December 1917

. . . I met several boys in Paris who had just come from the States, and one of them . . . had a package for me . . . and it surely was welcome. If you can possibly work it, please send me some sweet milk chocolate — like Hershey's, or something of the sort. Also, all the large, heavy woolen socks in the world would be more than welcome, and one of those woolen helmets that fits my head, and is large enough, yet very warm, wouldn't go amiss if sent my way. . . .

Geoffrey L. Rossano, ed., *The Price of Honor: The World War One Letters of Naval Aviator Kenneth MacLeish* (Annapolis: Naval Institute Press, 1991), 67–232.

I haven't had any American cigarettes for so long that I really don't remember what they taste like. You can't really appreciate the difference between a good smoke and one of these French smokes till you've coughed yourself blue in the face over the latter. . . .

The war news is getting gloomier every day, isn't it? It surely looks bad at present. I wonder if the Americans really will wake up and send over the promised ten thousand aviators and machines. I'm almost certain that there won't be over five hundred trained aviators out of ten thousand unless they have a finishing school in the States. . . .

London, 25 December 1917

. . . I had a funny time at Gosport the day I left. I went up alone, and after doing a few loops, tailspins, and sideslips I got up enough nerve to "roll" the Avro. Well, I got around once beautifully, but I didn't know they would only roll once. The result was that I got into a spin with my motor full on, and before I could cut it, it went "dud." I was 2,500 feet up and quite a distance from the aerodrome with a stiff breeze in my face. I nearly had a fever before I got down. I just skimmed over some telegraph poles and wires and fell into the field. Gee, it was fun for a while!

You know at Gosport they expel you from the school if you limit yourself to straight flying, you must do stunts all the time. It's seventh heaven. Poor Shorty gets airsick all the time. When his instructor rolls him around, he gets seasick and has to come down. My instructor was shot twice through the chest, crashed in no-man's-land, and crawled in at night. His machine burned up right on top of him, and it didn't hurt him. He was under shellfire for six hours while it was light. . . .

Gosport, 29 December 1917

. . .This winter flying is not so very much fun. I went up this morning and flew for about an hour, and I've never been so cold. I had lots of fun, though. The clouds were only 2,000 feet up today and I amused myself by getting up as much speed as possible, just below them, and then pulling back and looping into them, or diving in and letting go of the controls, and then I'd come crashing and spinning out of them. I got one fine old thrill. I came down, made a landing, and was just getting off again, turning as I climbed. All at once my motor began to sputter and I started to sideslip into a large brick house. I just pulled out in time to avoid the chimneys. It was only oil pressure and I was able to fix it without having to land. My old heart was pumping at an awful rate for a second or two. Lord, there's no game like this in all the world. You're always taking such wonderful chances, and it's a grand feeling to get away with them, because you gain such self-confidence. . . . I wish this war would end. I want to get home. You don't appreciate America till you are forced to stay away from the place against your wishes. . . . I don't believe that there are more than two furnaces and heating systems in Europe, and I haven't had the good luck to see either of them yet. . . .

Gosport, 3 January 1918

Today was quite an eventful day for me. . . . I went out to the aero-drome expecting to fly an Avro. I did. I went up with my instructor and we did some forced landings in little fields by sideslipping into them. Then we did some cross-wind landings, which are fairly hard as you have to be banked way up on one side and land on one wheel and your tail skid. I was simply rotten at the sideslipping. I lost my eye for distance and altitude altogether. I was fairly disappointed and thoroughly dis-couraged when we landed, and guess my surprise when he said, "Well, you're ready to go up in a Sopwith Camel." I almost fell over backwards. A Camel is quite a step from an Avro because a Camel is the hardest scout to fly. He was either doing his damndest to kill me, or he had an exalted opinion of my flying ability. He gave me a few pointers and I started. He told me that it climbed best at 60 mph. I pulled it up into what I thought was a good climb and looked at my airspeed meter. I received shock num-ber two—I was going 95 mph. I pulled the nose up into what looked worse than a stall before she read 60. Then I looked down at the carbure-tor adjustment and set it. When I looked up only a moment or two later I was at 3,200 feet. Then I fixed my glove which was flapping around, and when I looked again I was at 6,000 feet. By that time I wouldn't have been the least bit surprised if the machine had started talking to me.

Nothing, I thought, could surprise me after all this. I was ready for anything. I nosed down a bit to what I thought was flying level and throt-tled my motor a bit. I was thoroughly enjoying life when I noticed I was over Southampton. That's about thirty miles away. I looked at the air-speed indicator and it said 110 mph.

My instructor had told me not to try any tricks under any circum-stance, because the machine went into a tailspin so easily and because it spun so fast that very few men can stand more than six revolutions with-out losing their head. . . . I tried a left-hand turn, banking the little bus up vertically, and everything went beautifully. Then I banked up to turn to the right, but she wouldn't turn, so I thought I would start with a little right rudder and then give her full left. Just about the time I made up my mind to push the right rudder I had been around twice. I never went so fast in my life. . . . I was scared pea green. Then I decided to spin the thing if it wanted to spin so much, and just about the time I decided on this momentous action, I realized that I was already in one of those bloody things. Honestly, those Camels will do a thing so darn quickly that you barely have time to decide upon it. How or when I came out of that spin will always be a mystery to me. I'm still a bit woozy. I gave up the idea of tricks and started to come down. It occurred to me it would be a good idea to fool with my motor and get used to it, so I throttled down from 1,200 to 800 revolutions. Then I decided to see how fast I would be going when my motor was turning up to 1,200 again, so I nosed down. When I saw the needle at 1,200 I looked at the airspeed indicator and guess what I saw? The darn thing said 205 mph. I soon stopped that. I made a perfect landing. . . . I had two more rides in the bus this afternoon, and each time I got away with it. . . .

One of these Camels would fit into your library in the house at Peacock Point without any difficulty. You can touch the tail planes from the pilot's seat, and the motor is practically in your lap. . . . It's called a Camel because there is a funny hump between the pilot and the propeller which covers the machine guns and makes them streamlined. They are tremendously overengined, and as a result are so tricky that they're the hardest fighting machine to fly. . . .

Dunkirk, 7 April 1918

Just a word or two which will shatter all your illusions about this flying game. It may be great sport some of the time, but when it isn't sport it's positively torture. Yesterday, for instance, we were ordered up into the rain. The clouds were low and the visibility almost impossible. All we did was get wet, cold, and mad, also frightfully "Archied" as we were low and beautifully silhouetted against the clouds. Today was worse torture than any I have ever read about. In the first place we went 4,000 feet higher than I've ever been before in my life. I had on a pair of silk gloves next to my hands, a pair of rubber gloves over that, and then a pair of fur-lined, fur-covered flying gloves. To my mind that combination is the warmest possible, yet I froze two fingers absolutely solid, and my thumb and one other finger were frostbitten. The altitude gave me the worst headache I've ever had. Of course, there was practically no pressure up there, because it is halved at only 7,000 or 8,000 feet. It affected me strangely. At first it was nauseating, then I felt weak and dizzy. Finally, after about half an hour, I got used to it, and the only effect was a splitting headache and a funny noise in my ears. The veins around my ears expanded enormously at every heartbeat, and cut off my hearing entirely, so that when my heart throbbed I couldn't even hear the terrific roar of my motor or the tat-tat-tat of my machine guns which were firing about eight or ten inches in front of my face. I was in this condition for about an hour, under some really enterprising "Archie" fire. But, by George, I wouldn't give it up for all the love, money, and marbles on earth.

If you want to do me a favor, get me some very heavily knitted silk gloves. They are the warmest things on earth. Ishbel's helmet is in use every moment; when I'm not wearing it, someone else is. It went through two flights today alone, for instance, and kept three aviators warm where it seems impossible that anything could.

Dunkirk, 11 April 1918

. . . They rigged our scouts with bomb-carrying devices for little bombs. The idea was a bombing raid in broad daylight. For a good time give me one of those things anytime. Wow! I don't think I'll ever get over it. The clouds were only 1,000 feet up, and we were to get near to our objective, climb into the clouds, and when we thought we were directly over, to dive down to about 300 or 400 feet and let go our "pills." The first man over had a wonderful time—they didn't even shoot at him. The second had a little hot weather, the third some real hot weather, the fourth had a—of a time, the fifth had to turn back and try it again, the sixth wasn't much more successful. Then I came! In my wildest dreams of all hell turned loose, I never pictured anything like that. There must have been a thousand machine guns working on a twenty-four-hour day schedule. The tracer bullets were doing loops and split turns around my neck. I got dizzy watching them. I put my fingers on both triggers and had my two guns going full blast while I dove. It was no use. I saw in a second that I never in the world could get there. The rapid fire pom-poms were putting up a barrage in front of me, and it was getting closer and closer as I dove. There were so many bursts of smoke that I lost sight of the target. I thought of home and Mother and zoomed back into the clouds and waited for it to quiet down. When I came back out again I was completely lost—I couldn't even see land. I flew by compass until I came to the coast, and, thinking I was east of my objective, began working my way west along the coast, "Archied" to blazes every foot of the way, first on one ear, and then on the other, and once in a while on my back. I came to a town I'd never seen before and thought I was in Holland. I kept on and finally came to a town I knew, but it was twenty miles west of my objective. I didn't like the idea of going back, so as this town was an excellent objective, I at once decided to drop my pill there instead. I looked around for my target, found it, and went into the clouds. After flying for a second or two, to my horror, I popped out of the clouds into a patch of perfectly blue sky, only 1,200 feet up and directly over the hottest "Archie" battery the Huns have. I thought I was sure gone, but I guess the Huns were as surprised as I was, and about as scared, because I dove on them, both guns doing their ——est. I dove right for the Archie battery first, and you should have seen them drop their work and find that they had a date miles away and were late already. Lord! Did they run! Then I leveled off, dropped my pill, and absorbed myself in the business of getting back to the clouds, without flying straight for a second. Do you know, they never even fired a single shot at me, not one.

When I got back I expected to find the bus had been riddled with bullet holes, but to my surprise there wasn't one. I was disappointed and tickled to death at the same time—this combination causes one to itch violently.

I learn something every day. Today I learned never to be the last machine in a daylight, low bombing stunt. I may know enough to keep out of trouble one of these days. One never knows, does one?

Eastleigh, 15 September 1918

With this new draft law in effect, things must be pretty lonely at home. I've never seen so many Americans in my life, not even in America, as I've seen recently. It seems as though there must be an awfully big bunch over here, or else I'm a poor judge of numbers. If the old kaiser could see some of the sights I've seen, he'd pull in his neck and ask who got America sore at him. There are doughboys of every possible kind. Bunches of splendid young men, many of them college men, crowds of men who were "boys" in every city and town at home. Big, awkward, gawky, yet powerful farmers from the backwoods. And here and there a "weak sister" with watery blue eyes, glasses a foot thick, but with an expression that never passed over his face before. . . .

Report of Lt. John Menzies, 2 February 1919

I have interviewed Mr. Alfred Rouse, solicitor and landowner at Ghiselles, Belgium, on the 28th of January 1919 concerning the finding and disposal of the body of Lieut. MacLeish who was killed in an air battle near Schoore, Belgium, on the 14th of October 1918.

Mr. Rouse is the owner of the farm upon which the body of Lieut. MacLeish was found and upon which his body is now buried.

Lieut. MacLeish's body was found in the location indicated on the accompanying sketch, laying face down on a pile of debris at the side of a small outbuilding. His flying helmet was still strapped, his coat was buttoned, and his flying gloves were still on his hands. Nothing had been removed from the body in the lines of valuables or papers. These papers and valuables have since been removed by Mr. Rouse and forwarded through proper channels.

I questioned Mr. Rouse concerning the condition of the body when found. The body had been lying on the ground from the 14th of October 1918 until the 26th of December 1918, and was in an advanced stage of decomposition, but the flying helmet was unpierced by bullets as was his flying coat, and upon opening the coat no trace of blood was found upon the white shirt which he wore, thus indicating that he had received no body or head wounds.

No trace of Lieut. MacLeish's airplane could be found within a radius of one mile from the spot on which his body was found. . . . [I]t is my opinion that either Lieut. MacLeish had traveled some distance from the spot where he was brought down or else the Germans removed the plane from the spot.

Lieut. MacLeish, at the time of his death, was flying a Camel scout machine belonging to #213 Squadron, Royal Air Force. . . .

Considering the condition of the body as it was found, and the terrain surrounding the spot, my opinion is that Lieut. MacLeish died after reaching the ground. The spot on which the body was found was in the active battle area at that time, and he may have run into gas while attempting to get to cover or to escape.

QUESTIONS

How did Kenneth MacLeish feel about flying? • What risks did he take? • What conditions did he encounter in the airplanes he flew? • What was his attitude toward the war?

political prisoner for ~ 20 yrs.

DOCUMENT 4

Eugene V. Debs Attacks Capitalist War Mongers

The Socialist party opposed American entry into World War I, calling it "a crime against the people of the United States." In June 1918, Eugene V. Debs, the party's perennial presidential candidate, spoke at Canton, Ohio, to a group of working people. In his speech, excerpted here, Debs explained that Socialists opposed the war not because they were pro-German but because they were anticapitalist. This speech precipitated Debs's arrest for violating the Espionage Act; he was convicted and sentenced to ten years in prison. In 1920 he campaigned for president from his prison cell.

Speech at Canton, Ohio, June 16, 1918

Reference of 1917 Russian Revolution

Why should a Socialist be discouraged on the eve of the greatest triumph in all the history of the Socialist movement? It is true that these are anxious, trying days for us all—testing days for the women and men who are upholding the banner of labor in the struggle of the working class of all the world against the exploiters of all the world. . . .

Reference to WWI

Are we opposed to Prussian militarism? Why, we have been fighting it since the day the Socialist movement was born; and we are going to continue to fight it, day and night, until it is wiped from the face of the

---

Eugene V. Debs, Speech at Canton, Ohio, June 16, 1918, 66–78.

Demo / Rep.   Socialist
    ↑   ↑
Exploiters ⇔ Exploited
(Capitalists)   (labors)
(Militarist)

ruling elite

earth. Between us there is no truce—no compromise. . . . Multiplied thousands of Socialists have languished in the jails of Germany because of their heroic warfare upon the despotic ruling class of that country. . . .

I hate, I loathe, I despise Junkers and junkerdom.[1] I have no earthly use for the Junkers of Germany, and not one particle more use for the Junkers in the United States.

Junkers They tell us that we live in a great free republic; that our institutions are democratic; that we are a free and self-governing people. This is too much, even for a joke. But it is not a subject for levity; it is an exceedingly serious matter.   *lightness*

To whom do the Wall Street Junkers in our country marry their daughters? After they have wrung their countless millions from your sweat, your agony and your life's blood, in a time of war as in a time of peace, they invest these untold millions in the purchase of titles of broken-down aristocrats, such as princes, dukes, counts, and other parasites and no-accounts. Would they be satisfied to wed their daughters to honest workingmen? To real democrats? Oh, no! . . .   *The rich intermarry each other*

These are the gentry who are today wrapped up in the American flag, who shout their claim from the housetops that they are the only patriots, and who have their magnifying glasses in hand, scanning the country for evidence of disloyalty, eager to apply the brand of treason to the men who dare to even whisper their opposition to junker rule in the United States. No wonder Sam Johnson declared that "patriotism is the last refuge of the scoundrel." He must have had this Wall Street gentry in mind, or at least their prototypes, for in every age it has been the tyrant, the oppressor, and the exploiter who has wrapped himself in the cloak of patriotism, or religion, or both to deceive and overawe the people. . . .

Socialism is a growing idea, an expanding philosophy. It is spreading over the entire face of the earth. It is as vain to resist it as it would be to arrest the sunrise on the morrow. It is coming, coming, coming all along the line. . . . It is the mightiest movement in the history of mankind. . . . It has enabled me . . . to feel life truly worth while; . . . to be class-conscious, and to realize that, regardless of nationality, race, creed, color, or sex, every man, every woman who toils, who renders useful service, every member of the working class without an exception, is my comrade, my brother and sister—and that to serve them and their cause is the highest duty of my life. . . .

[O]ur hearts are with the Bolsheviki of Russia. Those heroic men and women, those unconquerable comrades have by their incomparable valor and sacrifice added fresh lustre to the fame of the international movement. . . . The very first act of the triumphant Russian revolution was to

---

[1]**Junkers:** Members of the Prussian aristocracy, an especially militaristic and politically reactionary class of German society at the time.

proclaim a state of peace with all mankind, coupled with a fervent moral appeal, not to kings, not to emperors, rulers or diplomats, but to the people of all nations. . . .

Wars throughout history have been waged for conquest and plunder. . . . The feudal barons of the Middle Ages, the economic predecessors of the capitalists of our day, declared all wars. And their miserable serfs fought all the battles. The poor, ignorant serfs had been taught to revere their masters; to believe that when their masters declared war upon one another, it was their patriotic duty to fall upon one another and to cut one another's throats for the profit and glory of the lords and barons who held them in contempt. And that is war in a nutshell. The master class has always declared the wars; the subject class has always fought the battles. The master class has had all to gain and nothing to lose, while the subject class has had nothing to gain and all to lose—especially their lives. . . .

And here let me emphasize the fact—and it cannot be repeated, too often—that the working class who fight all the battles, the working class who make the supreme sacrifices, the working class, who freely shed their blood and furnish the corpses, have never yet had a voice in either declaring war or making peace. It is the ruling class that invariably does both. They alone declare war and they alone make peace. . . .

What a compliment it is to the Socialist movement to be persecuted for the sake of the truth! The truth alone will make the people free. And for this reason the truth must not be permitted to reach the people. The truth has always been dangerous to the rule of the rogue, the exploiter, the robber. So the truth must be ruthlessly suppressed. That is why they are trying to destroy the Socialist movement. . . .

We do not attack individuals. We do not seek to avenge ourselves upon those opposed to our faith. . . . There is no room in our hearts for hate, except for the system, the social system in which it is possible for one man to amass a stupendous fortune doing nothing, while millions of others suffer and struggle and agonize and die for the bare necessities of existence. . . .

To turn your back on the corrupt Republican party and the corrupt Democratic party—the gold-dust lackeys of the ruling class counts for something. It counts for still more after you have stepped out of those popular and corrupt capitalist parties to join a minority party that has an ideal, that stands for a principle, and fights for a cause. This will be the most important change you have ever made. . . .

Give me a hundred capitalists and let me ask them a dozen simple questions about the history of their own country and I will prove to you that they are as ignorant and unlettered as any you may find in the so-called lower class. They know little of history; they are strangers to science; they are ignorant of sociology and blind to art but they know how to exploit, how to gouge, how to rob, and do it with legal sanction. They always proceed legally for the reason that the class which has the power to rob upon a large scale has also the power to control the government and legalize their robbery. . . .

They are continually talking about your patriotic duty. It is not their but your patriotic duty that they are concerned about. There is a decided difference. Their patriotic duty never takes them to the firing line or chucks them into the trenches.

And now among other things they are urging you to "cultivate" war gardens, while at the same time a government war report just issued shows that practically 52 percent of the arable, tillable soil is held out of use by the landlords, speculators, and profiteers. They themselves do not cultivate the soil. They could not if they would. Nor do they allow others to cultivate it. They keep it idle to enrich themselves, to pocket the millions of dollars of unearned increment. Who is it that makes this land valuable while it is fenced in and kept out of use? It is the people. Who pockets this tremendous accumulation of value? The landlords. And these landlords who toil not and spin not are supreme among American "patriots." . . .

This lord who practically owns the earth tells you that we are fighting this war to make the world safe for democracy—he, who shuts out all humanity from his private domain; he, who profiteers at the expense of the people who have been slain and mutilated by multiplied thousands, under pretense of being the great Americans patriot. It is he, this identical patriot who is in fact the arch-enemy of the people; it is he that you need to wipe from power. It is he who is a far greater menace to your liberty and your well-being than the Prussian junkers on the other side of the Atlantic Ocean. Fifty-two percent of the land kept out of use, according to their own figures! They tell you that there is an alarming shortage of flour and that you need to produce more. They tell you further that you have got to save wheat so that more can be exported for the soldiers who are fighting on the other side, while half of your tillable soil is held out of use by the landlords and profiteers. What do you think of that? . . .

[W]ar comes in spite of the people. When Wall Street says war the press says war and the pulpit promptly follows with its Amen. In every age the pulpit has been on the side of the rulers and not on the side of the people. . . .

Political action and industrial action must supplement and sustain each other. You will never vote the Socialist republic into existence. You will have to lay its foundations in industrial organization. The industrial union is the forerunner of industrial democracy. In the shop where the workers are associated is where industrial democracy has its beginning. Organize according to your industries! . . .

Then unite in the Socialist party. Vote as you strike and strike as you vote. . . .

When we unite and act together on the industrial field and when we vote together on election day we shall develop the supreme power of the one class that can and will bring permanent peace to the world. . . . We shall conquer the public power. We shall then transfer the title deeds of the railroads, the telegraph lines, the mines, mills, and great industries to the people in their collective capacity; we shall take possession of all these social utilities in the name of the people. We shall then have industrial democracy. We shall be a free nation whose government is of and by and for the people.

And now for all of us to do our duty! The clarion call is ringing in our ears and we cannot falter without being convicted of treason to ourselves and to our great cause.

Do not worry over the charge of treason to your masters, but be concerned about the treason that involves yourselves. Be true to yourself and you cannot be a traitor to any good cause on earth.

QUESTIONS

According to Debs, why were "these . . . anxious, trying days"? • What did Debs mean by comparing the Junkers of Germany and the Junkers of the United States? • Who were the patriots? • Who declared war? • Who fought, and why? • What did Debs think about war gardens? • What did he think of the view that the war would make the world safe for democracy? • How could peace be achieved? • From Debs's viewpoint, what was treason? • Do you think Debs should have had the right to take a stand against the war, even though U.S. troops were fighting in it?

COMPARATIVE QUESTIONS

How do Woodrow Wilson's arguments about American war aims differ from Eugene Debs's views? If Debs were writing poster slogans, how might they have differed from the ones in Document 2? How do MacLeish's views of the war compare with those of Wilson and Debs?

CHAPTER 23

FROM "NORMALCY" TO THE GREAT DEPRESSION

1920–1932

Satisfaction

During the 1920s, complacency became an article of faith among many comfortable Americans. Things were as they should be, business was good, America was strong, and God was in his heaven. Republican presidents explained the logic of complacency that appealed to many voters. Beneath the gaze of the complacent, however, other Americans inhabited a world of work that made complacency impossible for them. When the stock market crashed in 1929, many Americans began to question their faith that they had nothing to worry about.

DOCUMENT 1

President Calvin Coolidge on Government and Business

The success of the Bolshevik Revolution frightened most American leaders and strengthened the appeal of the argument that government should not interfere with business. As governor of Massachusetts, Calvin Coolidge won national recognition in 1919 for using the state militia to break the Boston police strike, which he declared was an intolerable threat to public order. As president, Coolidge explained his concept of the proper relation between government and business in an address, excerpted here, to the New York Chamber of Commerce in 1925.

Address before the New York Chamber of Commerce, November 19, 1925

This time and place naturally suggest some consideration of commerce in its relation to Government and society. We are finishing a year which can justly be said to surpass all others in the overwhelming success of general business. We are met not only in the greatest American metropolis, but in the greatest center of population and business that the world has ever known. . . .

The foundation of this enormous development rests upon commerce. New York is an imperial city, but it is not a seat of government. The empire over which it rules is not political, but commercial. The great cities of the ancient world were the seats of both government and industrial power. . . . In the modern world government is inclined to be merely a tenant of the city. Political life and industrial life flow on side by side, but practically separated from each other. When we contemplate the enormous power, autocratic and uncontrolled, which would have been created by joining the authority of government with the influence of business, we can better appreciate the wisdom of the fathers in their wise dispensation which made Washington the political center of the country and left New York to develop into its business center. They wrought mightily for freedom. . . .

I should put an even stronger emphasis on the desirability of the largest possible independence between government and business. Each ought to be sovereign in its own sphere. When government comes unduly under the influence of business, the tendency is to develop an administration which closes the door of opportunity; becomes narrow and selfish in its outlook, and results in an oligarchy. When government enters the field of business with its great resources, it has a tendency to extravagance and inefficiency, but, having the power to crush all competitors, likewise closes the door of opportunity and results in monopoly. It is always a problem in a republic to maintain on the one side that efficiency which comes only from trained and skillful management without running into fossilization and autocracy, and to maintain on the other that equality of opportunity which is the result of political and economic liberty without running into dissolution and anarchy. The general results in our country, our freedom and prosperity, warrant the assertion that our system of institutions has been advancing in the right direction in the attempt to solve these problems. We have order, opportunity, wealth, and progress.

Calvin Coolidge, "Government and Business," in *Foundations of the Republic: Speeches and Addresses* (1926); reprinted in *The Plastic Age,* by Robert Sklar (New York: George Braziller, 1970), 272–82.

While there has been in the past and will be in the future a considerable effort in this country of different business interests to attempt to run the Government in such a way as to set up a system of privilege, and while there have been and will be those who are constantly seeking to commit the Government to a policy of infringing upon the domain of private business, both of these efforts have been very largely discredited, and with reasonable vigilance on the part of the people to preserve their freedom do not now appear to be dangerous.

When I have been referring to business, I have used the word in its all-inclusive sense to denote alike the employer and employee, the production of agriculture and industry, the distribution of transportation and commerce, and the service of finance and banking. It is the work of the world. In modern life, with all its intricacies, business has come to hold a very dominant position in the thoughts of all enlightened peoples. Rightly understood, this is not a criticism, but a compliment. In its great economic organization it does not represent, as some have hastily concluded, a mere desire to minister to selfishness. The New York Chamber of Commerce is not made up of men merely animated with a purpose to get the better of each other. It is something far more important than a sordid desire for gain. It could not successively succeed on that basis. It is dominated by a more worthy impulse; its rests on a higher law. True business represents the mutual organized effort of society to minister to the economic requirements of civilization. It is an effort by which men provide for the material needs of each other. While it is not an end in itself, it is the important means for the attainment of a supreme end. It rests squarely on the law of service. It has for its main reliance truth and faith and justice. In its larger sense it is one of the greatest contributing forces to the moral and spiritual advancement of the race.

It is the important and righteous position that business holds in relation to life which gives warrant to the great interest which the National Government constantly exercises for the promotion of its success. This is not exercised as has been the autocratic practice abroad of directly supporting and financing different business projects, except in case of great emergency; but we have rather held to a democratic policy of cherishing the general structure of business while holding its avenues open to the widest competition, in order that its opportunities and its benefits might be given the broadest possible participation. . . . Those who are so engaged, instead of regarding the Government as their opponent and enemy, ought to regard it as their vigilant supporter and friend. . . .

Except for the requirements of safety, health and taxation, the law enters very little into the work of production. It is mostly when we come to the problems of distribution that we meet the more rigid exactions of legislation. The main reason why certain practices in this direction have been denounced is because they are a species of unfair competition on the one hand or tend to monopoly and restraint of trade on the other. The whole policy of the Government in its system of opposition to monopoly, and its public regulation of transportation and trade, has been animated by a desire to have business remain business. We are politically free people and must be an economically free people.

It is my belief that the whole material development of our country has been enormously stimulated by reason of the general insistence on the part of the public authorities that economic effort ought not to partake of privilege, and that business should be unhampered and free. This could never have been done under a system of freight-rate discriminations or monopolistic trade associations. These might have enriched a few for a limited period, but they never would have enriched the country, while on the firmer foundation of justice we have achieved even more ample individual fortunes and a perfectly unprecedented era of general prosperity. This has resulted in no small part from the general acceptance on the part of those who own and control the wealth of the Nation, that it is to be used not to oppress but to serve. It is that policy, sometimes perhaps imperfectly expressed and clumsily administered, that has animated the National Government. In its observance there is unlimited opportunity for progress and prosperity.

It would be difficult, if not impossible, to estimate the contribution which government makes to business. It is notorious that where the government is bad, business is bad. The mere fundamental precepts of the administration of justice, the providing of order and security, are priceless, The prime element in the value of all property is the knowledge that its peaceful enjoyment will be publicly defended. . . . It is really the extension of these fundamental rights that the Government is constantly attempting to apply to modern business. It wants its rightful possessors to rest in security, it wants any wrongs that they may suffer to have a legal remedy, and it is all the time striving through administrative machinery to prevent in advance the infliction of injustice.

These undoubtedly represent policies which are wise and sound and necessary. That they have often been misapplied and many times run into excesses, nobody can deny. Regulation has often become restriction, and inspection has too frequently been little less than obstruction. This was the natural result of those times in the past when there were practices in business which warranted severe disapprobation. It was only natural that when these abuses were reformed by an aroused public opinion a great deal of prejudice which ought to have been discriminating and directed only at certain evil practices came to include almost the whole domain of business, especially where it had been gathered into large units. After the abuses had been discontinued the prejudice remained to produce a large amount of legislation, which, however well meant in its application to trade, undoubtedly hampered but did not improve. It is this misconception and misapplication, disturbing and wasteful in their results, which the National Government is attempting to avoid. Proper regulation and control are disagreeable and expensive. They represent the suffering that the just must endure because of the unjust. They are a part of the price which must be paid to promote the cause of economic justice.

Undoubtedly if public vigilance were relaxed, the generation to come might suffer a relapse. But the present generation of business almost universally throughout its responsible organization and management has shown every disposition to correct its own abuses with as little intervention of the Government as possible. This position is recognized by the public, and due to the appreciation of the needs which the country has for great units of production in time of war, and to the better understanding of the service which they perform in time of peace, . . . a new attitude of the public mind is distinctly discernible toward great aggregations of capital. Their prosperity goes very far to insure the prosperity of all the country. The contending elements have each learned a most profitable lesson.

This development has left the Government free to advance from the problems of reform and repression to those of economy and construction. A very large progress is being made in these directions. Our country is in a state of unexampled and apparently sound and well distributed prosperity. . . .

. . . [N]o positive and constructive accomplishment of the past five years compares with the support which America has contributed to the financial stability of the world. It clearly marks a new epoch.

This holds a distinctly higher rank than a mere barter and sale. It reaches above the ordinary business transaction into a broader realm. America has disbanded her huge armies and reduced her powerful fleet, but in attempting to deal justly through the sharing of our financial resources we have done more for peace than we could have done with all our military power. Peace, we know, rests to a great extent upon justice, but it is very difficult for the public mind to divorce justice from economic opportunity. The problem for which we have been attempting a solution is in the first instance to place the people of the earth back into avenues of profitable employment. It was necessary to restore hope, to renew courage. A great contribution to this end has been made with American money. The work is not all done yet. No doubt it will develop that this has not been accomplished without some mistakes, but the important fact remains that when the world needed to be revived we did respond. As nations see their way to a safer economic existence, they will see their way to a more peaceful existence. Possessed of the means to meet personal and public obligations, people are reestablishing their self respect. The financial strength of America has contributed to the spiritual restoration of the world. It has risen into the domain of true business.

QUESTIONS

According to President Coolidge, why should government and business have "the largest possible independence"? • What were the dangers of failing to observe that principle? • Were there also dangers of absolutely no connection between government and business? • What was the purpose of business? • What purpose did government have? • How had businesses changed since the imposition of government regulations and inspections? • What future did Coolidge envision?

DOCUMENT 2

Reinhold Niebuhr on Christianity in Detroit

What meaning did Christianity have in an industrial society? Many Americans answered that question by affirming that Christianity and industrial capitalism were perfectly compatible. Businessmen went to church and ministers preached the gospel of business. Reinhold Niebuhr, a young minister in Detroit, criticized the comfortable equation of Christianity with industrialization in a diary he kept between 1915 and 1928. In his diary, excerpted here, Niebuhr noted the frequent conflict between Christian ideals and the industrial realities he encountered in Detroit.

Diary Entries, 1925–1928

1925   We went through one of the big automobile factories today. So artificial is life that these factories are like a strange world to me though I have lived close to them for many years. The foundry interested me particularly. The heat was terrific. The men seemed weary. Here manual labor is a drudgery and toil is slavery. The men cannot possibly find any satisfaction in their work. They simply work to make a living. Their sweat and their dull pain are part of the price paid for the fine cars we all run. And most of us run the cars without knowing what price is being paid for them. . . .

We are all responsible. We all want the things which the factory produces and none of us is sensitive enough to care how much in human values the efficiency of the modern factory costs. Beside the brutal facts of modern industrial life, how futile are all our homiletical spoutings! The church is undoubtedly cultivating graces and preserving spiritual amenities in the more protected areas of society. But it isn't changing the

---

Reinhold Niebuhr, *Leaves from the Notebook of a Tamed Cynic* (1929); reprinted in *The Plastic Age,* by Robert Sklar (New York: George Braziller, 1970), 318–29.

essential facts of modern industrial civilization by a hair's breadth. It isn't even thinking about them.

The morality of the church is anachronistic. Will it ever develop a moral insight and courage sufficient to cope with the real problems of modern society?. . . We ministers maintain our pride and self-respect and our sense of importance only through a vast and inclusive ignorance. If we knew the world in which we live a little better we would perish in shame or be overcome by a sense of futility. . . .

1926   Several ministers have been commended for "courage" because they permitted labor leaders to speak in their churches who represented pretty much their own convictions and said pretty much what they had been saying for years.

It does seem pretty bad to have the churches lined up so solidly against labor and for the open shop policy of the town. The ministers are hardly to blame, except if they are to be condemned for not bringing out the meaning of Christianity for industrial relations more clearly in their ministry previous to the moment of crisis. As it was, few of the churches were sufficiently liberal to be able to risk an heretical voice in their pulpits. The idea that these A. F. of L. leaders are dangerous heretics is itself a rather illuminating clue to the mind of Detroit. I attended several sessions of the [labor] convention and the men impressed me as having about the same amount of daring and imagination as a group of village bankers. . . .

There are few cities in which wealth, suddenly acquired and proud of the mechanical efficiency which produced it, is so little mellowed by social intelligence. Detroit produces automobiles and is not yet willing to admit that the poor automata who are geared in on the production lines have any human problems.

Yet we differ only in degree from the rest of the country. The churches of America are on the whole thoroughly committed to the interests and prejudices of the middle classes. I think it is a bit of unwarranted optimism to expect them to make any serious contribution to the reorganization of society. I still have hopes that they will become sufficiently intelligent and heroic to develop some qualifying considerations in the great industrial struggle, but I can no longer envisage them as really determining factors in the struggle. . . .

If religion is to contribute anything to the solution of the industrial problem, a more heroic type of religion than flourishes in the average church must be set to the task. . . .

That resolution we passed in our pastors' meeting, calling upon the police to be more rigorous in the enforcement of law, is a nice admission of defeat upon the part of the church. Every one of our cities has a crime problem, not so much because the police are not vigilant as because great masses of men in an urban community are undisciplined and chaotic souls, emancipated from the traditions which guided their fathers and incapable of forming new and equally potent cultural and moral restraints. . . .

Perhaps the real reason that we live such chaotic lives in urban communities is because a city is not a society at all, and moral standards are formed only in societies and through the sense of mutual obligation which neighbors feel for one another. A big city is not a society held together by human bonds. It is a mass of individuals, held together by a productive process. Its people are spiritually isolated even though they are mechanically dependent upon one another. In such a situation it is difficult to create and preserve the moral and cultural traditions which each individual needs to save his life from anarchy.

All of us do not live in moral chaos. But in so far as we escape it, it is due to our loyalty to religious, moral and cultural traditions which have come out of other ages and other circumstances. That is why churches, Protestant, Catholic and Jewish, however irrelevant their ethical idealism may be to the main facts of an industrial civilization, are nevertheless indispensable. . . .

There is something very pathetic about the efforts of almost every one of our large cities to restore by police coercion what has been lost by the decay of moral and cultural traditions. But of course we do have to save ourselves from anarchy, even if it must be done by force. Only I think the church would do well to leave the police problem alone. If violence must be used temporarily, let the state do so without undue encouragement from the church. The church must work in another field and if it has failed in that field, it cannot recoup its failures by giving advice to the police department. The priest as a sublimated policeman is a sorry spectacle. . . .

1927   Our city race commission has finally made its report after months of investigation and further months of deliberation on our findings. It has been a rare experience to meet with these white and colored leaders and talk over our race problems. The situation which the colored people of the city face is really a desperate one, and no one who does not spend real time in gathering the facts can have any idea of the misery and pain which exists among these people, recently migrated from the south and unadjusted to our industrial civilization. Hampered both by their own inadequacies and the hostility of a white world they have a desperate fight to keep body and soul together, to say nothing of developing those amenities which raise life above the brute level.

I wish that some of our romanticists and sentimentalists could sit through a series of meetings where the real social problems of a city are discussed. They would be cured of their optimism. A city which is built around a productive process and which gives only casual thought and incidental attention to its human problems is really a kind of hell. Thousands in this town are really living in torment while the rest of us eat, drink and make merry. What a civilization! . . .

Mother and I visited at the home of —— today where the husband is sick and was out of employment before he became sick. The folks have few connections in the city. They belong to no church. What a miserable existence it is to be friendless in a large city. And to be dependent upon a heartless industry. The man is about 55 or 57 I should judge, and he is going to have a desperate time securing employment after he gets well. These modern factories are not meant for old men. They want young men and they use them up pretty quickly. Your modern worker, with no skill but what is in the machine, is a sorry individual, After he loses the stamina of youth, he has nothing to sell.

I promised —— I would try to find him a job. I did it to relieve the despair of that family, but I will have a hard time making good on my promise. According to the ethics of our modern industrialism men over fifty, without special training, are so much junk. It is a pleasure to see how such an ethic is qualified as soon as the industrial unit is smaller and the owner has a personal interest in his men. I could mention quite a few such instances. But unfortunately the units are getting larger and larger and more inhuman. . . .

The new Ford car is out. The town is full of talk about it. Newspaper reports reveal that it is the topic of the day in all world centers. Crowds storm every exhibit to get the first glimpse of this new creation. Mr. Ford has given out an interview saying that the car has cost him about a hundred million dollars and that after finishing it he still has about a quarter of a billion dollars in the bank.

I have been doing a little arithmetic and have come to the conclusion that the car cost Ford workers at least fifty million in lost wages during the past year. No one knows how many hundreds lost their homes in the period of unemployment, and how many children were taken out of school to help fill the depleted family exchequer, and how many more children lived on short rations during this period. Mr. Ford refuses to concede that he made a mistake in bringing the car out so late. He has a way of impressing the public even with his mistakes. We are now asked to believe that the whole idea of waiting a year after the old car stopped selling before bringing out a new one was a great advertising scheme which reveals the perspicacity of this industrial genius. But no one asks about the toll in human lives.

What a civilization this is! Naïve gentlemen with a genius for mechanics suddenly become the arbiters over the lives and fortunes of hundreds of thousands. Their moral pretentions are credulously accepted at full value. No one bothers to ask whether an industry which can maintain a cash reserve of a quarter of a billion ought not make some provision for its unemployed. It is enough that the new car is a good one. . . . The cry of the hungry is drowned in the song, "Henry has made a lady out of Lizzy.". . .

1928   It is almost impossible to be sane and Christian at the same time, and on the whole I have been more sane than Christian. . . . The church can really be a community of love and can give one new confidence in the efficacy of the principles of brotherhood outside of the family relation. The questions and qualms of conscience arise when one measures the church in its relationships to society, particularly to the facts of modern industry. It is at this point where it seems to me that we had better admit failure than to claim any victory. . . .

Modern industry, particularly American industry, is not Christian. The economic forces which move it are hardly qualified at a single point by really ethical considerations. If, while it is in the flush of its early triumphs, it may seem impossible to bring it under the restraint of moral law, it may strengthen faith to know that life without law destroys itself. If the church can do nothing else, it can bear witness to the truth until such a day as bitter experience will force a recalcitrant civilization to a humility which it does not now possess.

QUESTIONS

What did Niebuhr notice in his visit to the auto factory? • In his view, who was responsible for working conditions there? • What did Niebuhr consider to be the proper role of the church in industrial society? • What did he think about labor leaders? • What was his opinion of the support of Detroit churches for the open-shop policy? • Why, according to Niebuhr, were police important in cities? • What did he think about Henry Ford's new car? • What did he identify as the moral basis of business?

DOCUMENT 3

A Southern Textile Worker Describes a Strike

Wage workers did not share the prosperity of the 1920s. Long hours, low pay, and poor working conditions often meant better profits for employers, but they also often meant strikes by employees. The U.S. Senate investigated strikes that swept through the southern textile industry in 1929. Margaret Bowen, who worked in a textile mill in Elizabethton, Tennessee, explained to the senators the conditions that precipitated a strike. Bowen's testimony, excerpted here, illustrates experiences faced by many working people during the 1920s.

Margaret Bowen
Testimony before U.S. Senate Committee, 1929

Senator Wheeler: Just tell the committee what the situation is and what the conditions are there. First, are you a native of Tennessee?

Miss Bowen: Yes, sir.

Senator Wheeler: You were born and raised there?

Miss Bowen: Yes; but not in Elizabethton. The reason I went to Elizabethton was to go to work; the plants were misrepresented to me. I had worked in a silk mill at Old Hickory, Tenn., and they wrote to me that they would give me $16 a week to begin with, and a raise. I went to Elizabethton on the 31st of October this past year and went to work on the lst day of November. I did not ask at the time what my salary would be because I knew they knew I was an experienced hand. My first check was $10.08.

Senator Wheeler: For how long?

Miss Bowen: For 56 hours' work. My board was $5 a week. and the taxi $1, and my laundry bill $1. So you can readily see how much I had left. Yet my foreman insisted that I should have a savings account on that. I may say also that my insurance was 60 cents a month.

I worked for two weeks in the instruction department to get used to this silk; it is usually called yarn, but it is nothing but silk. Then they put me over into the final inspection department and in the inspection room. My work consisted of the best quality of silk that is produced in the plant to be reinspected, and then the orders are filled through my girls; I have 52 girls.

I worked on. I had been sick, and told Mr. Burnett—he was my foreman—that I had to have more money and I thought I deserved a raise. He said, "You do not deserve a raise," and I worked on until the first week of February, the first pay week of February, and got a 1-cent raise to $10.64 a week, and on Friday before the girls came out I decided to ask for another raise, and he refused me. Now, I asked for a raise for my girls—they were only getting $10.08 a week—and he also refused that. . . .

U.S. Congress, Senate, Committee on Manufactures, *Hearings on S. Res. 49. Working Conditions of the Textile Industry in North Carolina, South Carolina, and Tennessee.* 71st Cong., lst sess., 1929.

Senator Wheeler: How old are the girls working under you?

Miss Bowen: I had one girl who is 16 years old, my girls though usually run from 16 to 20 years of age. On Tuesday morning of the strike my girls were taken away from me for the simple reason that I had asked for a raise for them and had asked for a raise for myself.

The Chairman: What do you mean when you say they were taken away from you? Do you mean that they were discharged?

Miss Bowen: No, sir; nothing, only they gave me another section of girls and took the reinspection department entirely away from me and gave me another section in the house.

Senator Tyson: Did you get a raise then?

Miss Bowen: No; I did not. They took the reinspectors away from me and gave them a raise to $11.20 a week and the section girl they put over them, they gave her $12.32. The girls said to me, "Why don't you walk out and we will walk out with you?" That was before 8 o'clock in the morning on Tuesday, March 12.

Senator Wheeler: How much were they getting?

Miss Bowen: $10.08. I said, "No, I will not walk out, but if enough will walk out, I will go out." The assistant general forelady of the plant worked this strike up. She said, "If the other departments can walk out and get a raise, we can, too. We are more important than any other department of the plant." So she insisted that we walk out, and I was watched all that day. We knew that something was up, and they watched me entirely all day long. I did not even have a chance to go to the washroom. One of the section girls sent me word that there were eight sections in the room going to walk out by 10 o'clock and 14 sections in the inspection department. She said, "Will you walk out?" And I said, "Yes, at 1 o'clock"; we had lunch at 11:30. We had 30 minutes for lunch. So this girl that was put over on the section went and told the general forelady that we were planning the strike at 1 o'clock. She refused to walk out, she was getting enough. She was getting $12.32 a week. So the girl said if she did not walk out they would take her out. This general forelady told the superintendent, Mr. Gill, that we were planning the strike, and he called the section girls together and told us he would give us 20 cents an hour if we would fight the strike.

Senator Wheeler: That is, give you?

Miss Bowen: Give the section girls; he did not include the inspectors. So I did not say anything to my girls about it, and none of the rest of the section girls said anything.

At 12:30, that is when he got through talking with us, the inspection room got up and walked out, except 17. There are 550 girls in the inspection room . . . , and they walked out. We could not get outside the gate—we were locked in. We worked under lock and key altogether. We got on the outside and asked Mr. Gill to come and talk with us, which he refused. We stayed there all the afternoon up to 6:30, and he still refused.

At 3 o'clock the spinners who went on that afternoon told us if they did not hear from us in the afternoon they would be with us in the morning. We stayed until 6:30 that night. . . .

Senator Tyson: What time is the regular working time?

Miss Bowen: Seven o'clock in the morning until 5:30 at night. We have a 30-minute lunch period. In the morning we were joined by several of the men in town—the men and boys in the town who did not work at the plant. The 3 o'clock shift of spinners was also out. The other girls, the reelers and lacers, had left word on the outside that at 9 o'clock, if they did not talk with us, they would come out. The rest of the spinners in the plant—they run three shifts of spinners—also said they would come out and did about 10 o'clock that day.

At 10 minutes of 9 the girls decided that nobody intended to come out and talk with us, so we climbed the fence and went in. They had all the doors locked except the lower spinning-room door, and we went through there and, of course, took everything as we went—

The Chairman: What do you mean by "taking everything"?

Miss Bowen: The workers. All the people followed us. We did not damage any machinery at all. The 17 who were left in the inspection room were put in elevators going back and forth to keep the inspectors from getting to talk with them.

Of course, at that time we did not know anything about the union, none of us knew anything about organized labor at all. All we wanted was higher wages. One of the taxi drivers came down about 11 o'clock and said "Crawl in here and we will take you to the tabernacle and you can there join the union and get started." Nothing had happened; everybody was just boisterous, that is all; they had not hurt anybody. A policeman struck a girl over the head with his billy—of course, that was not very nice—and the boys beat him up. . . .

Senator Wheeler: What proportion of the help in this mill are women?

Miss Bowen: Seventy-five per cent are women.

Senator Wheeler: And that is the reason they got out the militia, to keep you women going on right, is that it?

Miss Bowen: I guess that is right.

Senator Hatfield: What would be the average age of those women?

Miss Bowen: I do not know as to that. I could not give you the exact average. Some of the girls are 10 years old, as I said awhile ago—10 to 14, then there are some from 16 to 20, a very few over 25 years of age, the girls that I am speaking about, that are working in the plant.

Senator Tyson: Where do they largely come from?

Miss Bowen: Out in the mountains of North Carolina, Tennessee, and Virginia.

Senator Wheeler: They are all American and native born?

Miss Bowen: Yes, sir. . . . These companies would have paid more and they started out paying more at the beginning, but the Chamber of

Commerce of Elizabethton said, "What is the need; you can get cheap labor for $8 and $10 a week," and so therefore they decided if they could get it they would not pay any more than what they really had to pay. . . .

Senator Wheeler: You do not mean to tell me that the Chamber of Commerce down there urged the factory owners not to pay their help as much money as they were paying?

Miss Bowen: Yes, sir.

The CHairman: How do you know that?

Miss Bowen: Through their own statements.

Senator Wheeler: You mean the statements of the members of the Chamber of Commerce?

Miss Bowen: Yes, sir.

Senator Hatfield: Were they printed statements?

Miss Bowen: No; they were verbal. . . .

Senator Metcalf: Did you say you worked 10 hours a day?

Miss Bowen: Yes, sir; the girls work 10 hours a day, and then on Saturday you can not eat a bite of lunch from the time you get in the plant until you get out Saturday, and when you think about working until 11:30 through the week and getting a lunch at 11:30 and then have to work until 1 o'clock on Saturday before you get anything to eat, you are exhausted.

Senator Metcalf: That is on Saturdays you have to go right through to 1 o'clock?

Miss Bowen: Yes, sir. If they catch you eating anything you are discharged, for the simple reason that they claim you are liable to drop a crumb on the silk and that damages it, of course; and they also stopped the girls from using cosmetics in the plant for the simple reason of ruining silk.

Senator Tyson: How do they manage with the men's shifts on Sundays?

Miss Bowen: Just the same as they do at other times.

Senator Tyson: They do not work on Sundays, do they?

Miss Bowen: Yes, sir.

Senator Tyson: They shift all day Sunday?

Miss Bowen: Yes, sir.

Senator Wheeler: I thought they were very religious down in Tennessee.

Miss Bowen: Not where work is concerned. . . .

Senator Wheeler: The reason they do not work the men longer than eight hours is because of these chemicals they use; they claim that the men do not live very long who work with those chemicals?

Miss Bowen: Yes, sir. They have what they call a death house at Elizabethton, and a man's average life is six months there. That is where they make all the chemicals. . . .

Senator Wheeler: What has become of the southern chivalry that we have heard so much about?

Miss Bowen: I do not know.

QUESTIONS

What wages did Margaret Bowen earn? • What hours did she work? • How many other workers did she supervise? • Why did the strike occur? • Who were the strikers? • How was it organized? • What was the attitude of the strikers toward unions? • Why did the Chamber of Commerce recommend lowering wages? • Why did men work on Sundays?

DOCUMENT 4

The Crash:
A Journalist Investigates Who Lost and Why

The collapse of the stock market in October 1929 revealed a dark side of Americans' infatuation with business. Edwin Lefevre, a journalist who visited Wall Street the day of the crash, later interviewed brokers and industrialists to try to discover who lost and why. In an article in the Saturday Evening Post, *excerpted here, Lefevre reported the consequences of the crash for millions of Americans.*

Edwin Lefevre

"The Little Fellow in Wall Street,"
January 4, 1930

On October 24, 1929, millions of Americans recalled poignantly the hundreds of blithe prophecies that our feelings never again would be harrowed by absurd exhibitions of mob hysteria or mass emotionalism in the stock market. We were living in a new era. Everybody told you this, the week before, whether he was carrying ten shares or 10,000. . . .

Well, . . . we had a panic in the stock market, which makes it proper to answer three questions: Who lost? Why? And how? . . .

The head of a bond house . . . told me:

"I shouldn't be at all surprised if 10,000,000 Americans lost money directly by the crash in the stock market. You must not forget that the bull market lasted more than six years, even though the public did not come in in hordes until 1928. Of course, there was plenty of justification for a bull market. There always is. But don't forget that this time we had factors that made it the greatest of all bull markets: Increased population,

---

Edwin Lefevre, "The Little Fellow in Wall Street," *Saturday Evening Post,* January 4, 1930.

greater wealth, more widespread prosperity, and marvelous machinery for the distribution of bull tips on a scale unprecedented in the world's history. You know that stocks do not go up; they are put up. . . . The best way to bull a stock is by advertising through the ticker. No ticker, no free quotations. No free quotations, no dreams. No dreams, no speculators. No speculators, no buyers. No buyers, no losers! This time the stock-market manipulators could reach practically everybody in the United States; and this time, also, the manipulators were not old market plungers but high-class bankers and financiers and industrial leaders of fine repute. It wasn't necessary to go to your broker's offices to get the gambling dope. You got it by radio in your own home, as well as by long-distance ticker, by telegraph, by telephone, by wireless, by daily newspapers, by statistical agencies and by neighbors.

"One of my recreations is antiquing. I regularly . . . motor through the Atlantic States and New England in the hope of finding bargains in the country shops. Last August, when the danger signals in the stock market were beginning to make themselves plain . . . , I stopped at an antique shop in a small town in Southern New Jersey.

"I caught the owner as he was about to leave. . . .

"'You close early,' I said.

"'Yes, unless someone telephones they are on the way. Looking for anything in particular?'

"'Glass,' I said.

"'Haven't any that's any good. I haven't got around as much as usual, this year.'

"'Don't let me keep you from going home,' I said politely.

"'That's all right. I live upstairs, but I got to get to the drug store.'

"'You don't look sick.'

"'Oh, no. We just meet there every night at seven, to get the close.'

"'What close?'

" 'The stock market,' he said. I understood then why he didn't have any glass. But all I asked was: 'Who else, besides you, goes?' 'Oh,' he answered, 'the gang! Everybody!'

"I am no Sherlock Holmes, but I knew those Jerseymen, representing the best element in the village, met not merely to get the closing prices, which they could have at home from their own radios, but to talk about the market. You know that nine out of ten people who talk about the market really talk about their profits. They crave applause for their cleverness. . . .

A rather intelligent commercial traveler who covers a wide territory told me:

"I firmly believe that there isn't a town of 10,000 inhabitants or over in the United States, North, South, East and West, that hasn't at least one night club. In the past year and a half I have been in a hundred or more of them, and I'll swear that nine-tenths of the people I saw there were having the time of their lives spending their uncashed stock-market profits. It struck me that these people had acquired the worst habits of the idle rich, without the riches.". . .

Never before did so many people make so much money, or spend it so lavishly, as during the late bull market. Prolonged prosperity makes the new-rich seek new ways of spending; and spending for new luxuries gives to money a pleasure-giving power that it did not have in the less affluent days. But as expenses rise, there develops the need of increasing the income to keep pace with the new living standard.

From hardship to comfort, the gap is a million miles wide. From comfort to luxury, the step is only four inches long. Ask any man who has made easy money.

Stock speculation always has seemed the cleanest way of making easy money. It is legalized gambling masquerading as a legitimate business. . . .

For at least two years, wherever one went one met people who told of their stock-market winnings. At dinner tables, at bridge, on golf links, on trolley cars, in country post offices, in barber shops, in factories and shops of all kinds. If I went into a hospital, within five minutes after hearing that the patient I called to see was . . . getting well, I learned that the nurses, the internes, the doorkeeper, the elevator man, the other patients, and every doctor on the staff, were making fortunes. A few had cashed in. The rest were all waiting for a stake big enough to retire on, and all told me how moderate they were! It was the same thing in hotels, in clubs, in your friends' offices, even in the vestry rooms of churches.

The ticker's advertising was successful beyond expectations. Never before had such sensational advances been scored by so many stocks, and, naturally, never such fortunes made overnight by so many people. . . .

The case of the individual plungers of great wealth is not so amazing as that of no end of business men who enjoyed a reputation for shrewdness and ability as heads of manufacturing enterprises or of mercantile concerns. Here were men long familiar with financial, industrial and commercial methods, as the prosperity of their companies amply proved. Nevertheless, they personally lost more in one week than they made in two years of boom. . . .

While the panic was on, you could not go into the main office of any corporation whose shares had been actively traded in without becoming aware that the ticker had played the dickens in that office. From the keeper at the gate to the president in conference, everybody showed the strain.

Never before in the history of stock speculation in these United States did so many executives of corporations not only encourage but even advise their subordinates to buy all the stock they could carry. The same fever burned in the souls of all. The honored heads of departments and their underlings alike spent half their time reading the financial pages or talking about their market operations.

Men high in the employ of great corporations have lost or will lose their jobs, just as they lost their fortunes. But of course it is the losses of the humbler employees that are often most distressing. . . .

The vice president of one of the largest utilities corporations, the stock of which showed highly sensational advances all through the boom, told me . . . :

"I was abroad on a big job for several months. Of course I knew that our stock had gone up beyond all rime or reason. . . .

"When I got back to New York, I found everybody in our office was loaded up. They had quintupled . . . their original holdings. Every vice president, every head of department, every clerk, male and female—in short, every employee had pleasing paper profits. They told me all about it. Not only was this true of our office but of the building as well. The elevator men, the barbers, the bootblack, the engineers, the porters, the news-stand man and the help in the drug store were long of our stock. Being in the same building with our company made them insiders, in the estimation of their admiring friends. I gather that hundreds of people got these inside buying tips from the building, and they in turn passed it on, so that thousands were properly advised from our office, and the real inside dope was that we were earning less than two dollars a share on the stock and the price was more than 200. Everybody knew it, but nobody cared about earnings. Their concern was with a further rise.

"Well, I am no philanthropist and I did not feel called upon to come out with an interview telling the public our stock was too high. . . .

"Well, many of my own subordinates sold out, but others didn't. Then came the panic. In their anxiety to stave off a worse crash, newspapers and bankers, business men and political leaders all over the United States emitted optimism through a megaphone. Every loud-speaker in the land told the public that the worst was over—always just before a fresh break.

"I can tell you that I don't want to go through again what I did in November. Girls that I had known for years—hard-working, respectable women; many of them middle-aged, and older—came out of the panic flat broke; some of them in debt; all of them wrecks. Do you know where I have just come from? From a visit to my secretary, who told me that she had sold when she hadn't. She is in a hospital uptown, suffering from a nervous breakdown. We are paying the bills and she gets her salary, but I doubt if she'll ever get over the blow.

"I was talking to the doctor at the hospital. He told me that there were thousands of cases of nervous collapse among men and women who lost everything in the stock market—not only well-to-do people but school-teachers, bookkeepers, wage earners of all degrees.

QUESTIONS

According to Lefevre, why had the crash occurred? • Who lost? • Why had so many people invested in the stock market? • Why were the losses so severe? • What were the human consequences of the crash?

COMPARATIVE QUESTIONS

How does Reinhold Niebuhr's view of industrial society differ from President Coolidge's view? How does Margaret Bowen's view of factories compare with Niebuhr's and with Coolidge's? What do the documents suggest about Americans' religious faith? In his speech, Coolidge stated that "the present generation of business has shown every disposition to correct its own abuses with as little intervention of the government as possible." Consider this statement in light of the events described in Lefevre's **Saturday Evening Post** *article.*

CHAPTER 24

THE NEW DEAL ERA
1932–1939

T he New Deal initiated an unprecedented array of government reforms in response to the unprecedented crisis of the Great Depression. Franklin D. Roosevelt had few specific plans other than to
constantly improvise and experiment until something worked. The New
Deal's willingness to identify problems and to try to solve them represented a departure from the laissez-faire policies of Roosevelt's Republican predecessors. Working people appreciated the New Dealers' efforts
to help, but by the end of the 1930s many remained mired in hard times.
The following documents illustrate Roosevelt's concept of what government could and should do and the hopes many working people had
about what government would do.

DOCUMENT 1
Franklin D. Roosevelt Proposes
an Activist Government

*The severity of the Great Depression made it almost certain that the Democratic
presidential candidate, Franklin D. Roosevelt, would be elected in 1932. The
severity of the depression also made it profoundly uncertain what Roosevelt
should or would do as president. On the campaign trail, Roosevelt delivered an
ambitious speech to the Commonwealth Club in San Francisco that outlined his
ideas about fundamental historical changes that required new relations between
government, citizens, and the economy. Roosevelt's speech, excerpted here, proposed principles that lie behind many New Deal initiatives.*

Speech to the Commonwealth Club,
San Francisco, 1932

Sometimes, my friends, particularly in years such as these, the hand of discouragement falls upon us. It seems that things are in a rut, fixed, settled, that the world has grown old and tired and very much out of joint. This is the mood of depression, of dire and weary depression.

But then we look around us in America, and everything tells us that we are wrong. America is new. It is in the process of change and development. It has the great potentialities of youth, and particularly is this true of the great West, and of this coast, and of California. . . .

The issue of Government has always been whether individual men and women will have to serve some system of Government or economics, or whether a system of Government and economics exists to serve individual men and women. . . .

There were those who because they had seen the confusion which attended the years of war for American independence surrendered to the belief that popular Government was essentially dangerous and essentially unworkable. They were honest people, my friends, and we cannot deny that their experience had warranted some measure of fear. The most brilliant, honest and able exponent of this point of view was Hamilton. . . . Fundamentally he believed that the safety of the republic lay in the autocratic strength of its Government, that the destiny of individuals was to serve that Government, and that fundamentally a great and strong group of central institutions, guided by a small group of able and public spirited citizens, could best direct all Government.

But Mr. Jefferson, in the summer of 1776, after drafting the Declaration of Independence turned his mind to the same problem and took a different view. . . . [A] Government must so order its functions as not to interfere with the individual. But . . . Jefferson realized that the exercise of the property rights might so interfere with the rights of the individual that the Government, without whose assistance the property rights could not exist, must intervene, not to destroy individualism, but to protect it.

You are familiar with the great political duel which followed; and how Hamilton, and his friends, building toward a dominant centralized power were at length defeated in the great election of 1800, by Mr. Jefferson's party. Out of that duel came the two parties, Republican and Democratic, as we know them today.

So began, in American political life, the new day, the day of the individual against the system, the day in which individualism was made the

Samuel Rosenman, ed., *The Public Papers and Addresses of Franklin D. Roosevelt, vol. 1, The Genesis of the New Deal, 1928–1932* (1938).

great watchword of American life. The happiest of economic conditions made that day long and splendid. . . .

It was in the middle of the nineteenth century that a new force was released and a new dream created. The force was what is called the industrial revolution, the advance of steam and machinery and the rise of the forerunners of the modern industrial plant. The dream was the dream of an economic machine, able to raise the standard of living for everyone; to bring luxury within the reach of the humblest; to annihilate distance by steam power and later by electricity, and to release everyone from the drudgery of the heaviest manual toil. It was to be expected that this would necessarily affect Government. Heretofore, Government had merely been called upon to produce conditions within which people could live happily, labor peacefully, and rest secure. Now it was called upon to aid in the consummation of this new dream. There was, however, a shadow over the dream. To be made real, it required use of the talents of men of tremendous will and tremendous ambition, since by no other force could the problems of financing and engineering and new developments be brought to a consummation.

So manifest were the advantages of the machine age, however, that the United States fearlessly, cheerfully, and, I think, rightly, accepted the bitter with the sweet. It was thought that no price was too high to pay for the advantages which we could draw from a finished industrial system. The history of the last half century is accordingly in large measure a history of a group of financial Titans, whose methods were not scrutinized with too much care, and who were honored in proportion as they produced the results, irrespective of the means they used. The financiers who pushed the railroads to the Pacific were always ruthless, often wasteful, and frequently corrupt; but they did build railroads, and we have them today. . . . As long as we had free land; as long as population was growing by leaps and bounds; as long as our industrial plants were insufficient to supply our own needs, society chose to give the ambitious man free play and unlimited reward provided only that he produced the economic plant so much desired.

During this period of expansion, there was equal opportunity for all and the business of Government was not to interfere but to assist in the development of industry. This was done at the request of business men themselves. The tariff was originally imposed for the purpose of "fostering our infant industry.". . . The railroads were subsidized, sometimes by grants of money, oftener by grants of land. . . . Some of my friends tell me that they do not want the Government in business. With this I agree; but I wonder whether they realize the implications of the past. For while it has been American doctrine that the Government must not go into business in competition with private enterprises, still it has been traditional, particularly in Republican administrations, for business urgently to ask the Government to put at private disposal all kinds of Government assistance. The same man who tells you that he does not want to see the Government interfere in business—and he means it, and has plenty of good reasons for saying so—is the first to go to Washington and ask the Government for a prohibitory tariff on his product. . . . Each group has sought protection from the Government for its own special interests, without realizing that the function of Government must be to favor no small group at the expense of its duty to protect the rights of personal freedom and of private property of all its citizens.

In retrospect we can now see that the turn of the tide came with the turn of the century. We were reaching our last frontier; there was no more free land and our industrial combinations had become great uncontrolled and irresponsible units of power within the State. Clear-sighted men saw with fear the danger that opportunity would no longer be equal; that the growing corporation, like the feudal baron of old, might threaten the economic freedom of individuals to earn a living. . . .

A glance at the situation today only too clearly indicates that equality of opportunity as we have known it no longer exists. Our industrial plant is built; the problem just now is whether under existing conditions it is not overbuilt. Our last frontier has long since been reached, and there is practically no more free land. More than half of our people do not live on the farms or on lands and cannot derive a living by cultivating their own property. There is no safety valve in the form of a Western prairie to which those thrown out of work by the Eastern economic machines can go for a new start. We are not able to invite the immigration from Europe to share our endless plenty. We are now providing a drab living for our own people. . . .

Just as freedom to farm has ceased, so also the opportunity in business has narrowed. It still is true that men can start small enterprises, trusting to native shrewdness and ability to keep abreast of competitors; but area after area has been preempted altogether by the great corporations, and even in the fields which still have no great concerns, the small man starts under a handicap. The unfeeling statistics of the past three decades show that the independent business man is running a losing race. Perhaps he is forced to the wall; perhaps he cannot command credit; perhaps he is "squeezed out". . . by highly organized corporate competitors, as your corner grocery man can tell you. Recently a careful study was made of the concentration of business in the United States. It showed that our economic life was dominated by some six hundred odd corporations who controlled two-thirds of American industry. Ten million small business men divided the other third. . . . Put plainly, we are steering a steady course toward economic oligarchy, if we are not there already.

Clearly, all this calls for a re-appraisal of values. A mere builder of more industrial plants, a creator of more railroad systems, an organizer of more corporations, is as likely to be a danger as a help. The day of the great promoter or the financial Titan, to whom we granted anything if only he would build, or develop, is over. Our task now is not discovery or exploitation of natural resources, or necessarily producing more goods. It is the soberer, less dramatic business of administering resources and plants already in hand, of seeking to reestablish foreign markets for our surplus production, of meeting the problem of underconsumption, of adjusting production to consumption, of distributing wealth and products more equitably, of adapting existing economic organizations to the service of the people. The day of enlightened administration has come. . . .

As I see it, the task of Government in its relation to business is to assist the development of an economic declaration of rights, an economic constitutional order. This is the common task of statesman and business man. It is the minimum requirement of a more permanently safe order of things.

Happily, the times indicate that to create such an order not only is the proper policy of Government, but it is the only line of safety for our economic structures as well. We know, now, that these economic units cannot exist unless prosperity is uniform, that is, unless purchasing power is well distributed throughout every group in the Nation. That is why even the most selfish of corporations for its own interest would be glad to see wages restored and unemployment ended and to bring the Western farmer back to his accustomed level of prosperity and to assure a permanent safety to both groups. That is why some enlightened industries themselves endeavor to limit the freedom of action of each man and business group within the industry in the common interest of all; why business men everywhere are asking a form of organization which will bring the scheme of things into balance, even though it may in some measure qualify the freedom of action of individual units within the business. . . .

I feel that we are coming to a view through the drift of our legislation and our public thinking in the past quarter century that private economic power is, to enlarge an old phrase, a public trust as well. I hold that continued enjoyment of that power by an individual or group must depend upon the fulfillment of that trust. The men who have reached the summit of American business life know this best; happily, many of these urge the binding quality of this greater social contract.

The terms of that contract are as old as the Republic, and as new as the new economic order.

Every man has a right to life; and this means that he has also a right to make a comfortable living. He may by sloth or crime decline to exercise that right; but it may not be denied him. We have no actual famine or dearth; our industrial and agricultural mechanism can produce enough and to spare. Our Government formal and informal, political and economic, owes to everyone an avenue to possess himself of a portion of that plenty sufficient for his needs, through his own work.

Every man has a right to his own property; which means a right to be assured, to the fullest extent attainable, in the safety of his savings. By no other means can men carry the burdens of those parts of life which, in the nature of things, afford no chance of labor; childhood, sickness, old age. In all thought of property, this right is paramount; all other property rights must yield to it. If, in accord with this principle, we must restrict the operations of the speculator, the manipulator, even the financier, I believe we must accept the restriction as needful, not to hamper individualism but to protect it.

These two requirements must be satisfied, in the main, by the individuals who claim and hold control of the great industrial and financial combinations which dominate so large a part of our industrial life. They have undertaken to be, not business men, but princes of property. I am not prepared to say that the system which produces them is wrong. I am very clear that they must fearlessly and competently assume the responsibility which goes with the power. So many enlightened business men know this that the statement would be little more than a platitude, were it not for an added implication.

This implication is, briefly, that the responsible heads of finance and industry instead of acting each for himself, must work together to achieve the common end. They must, where necessary, sacrifice this or that private advantage; and in reciprocal self-denial must seek a general advantage. It is here that formal Government—political Government, if you choose—comes in. Whenever in the pursuit of this objective the lone wolf, the unethical competitor, the reckless promoter . . . whose hand is against every man's, declines to join in achieving an end recognized as being for the public welfare, and threatens to drag the industry back to a state of anarchy, the Government may properly be asked to apply restraint. Likewise, should the group ever use its collective power contrary to the public welfare, the Government must be swift to enter and protect the public interest.

The Government should assume the function of economic regulation only as a last resort, to be tried only when private initiative, inspired by high responsibility, with such assistance and balance as Government can give, has finally failed. As yet there has been no final failure, because there has been no attempt; and I decline to assume that this Nation is unable to meet the situation.

The final term of the high contract was for liberty and the pursuit of happiness. We have learned a great deal of both in the past century. We know that individual liberty and individual happiness mean nothing unless both are ordered in the sense that one man's meat is not another man's poison. We know that the old "rights of personal competency," the right to read, to think, to speak, to choose and live a mode of life, must be respected at all hazards. We know that liberty to do anything which deprives others of those elemental rights is outside the protection of any compact; and that Government in this regard is the maintenance of a balance, within which every individual may have a place if he will take it; in which every individual may find safety if he wishes it; in which every individual may attain such power as his ability permits, consistent with his assuming the accompanying responsibility. . . .

Faith in America, faith in our tradition of personal responsibility, faith in our institutions, faith in ourselves demand that we recognize the new terms of the old social contract. We shall fulfill them. . . . We must do so, lest a rising tide of misery, engendered by our common failure, engulf us all. But failure is not an American habit; and in the strength of great hope we must all shoulder our common load.

QUESTIONS

According to Roosevelt, what were the differences between the Republican and Democratic parties? • How did industrialization change the role of government in the nineteenth century? • By 1932, what changes in the economy required a new role for government? • What did Roosevelt believe was the government's proper function in the economy? • What were the terms of what he called the "social contract"? • Who was responsible to see that the contract was fulfilled?

DOCUMENT 2

Working People's Letters to New Dealers

President Roosevelt expressed sympathy for the plight of working people during the depression. That sympathy, heard by millions in Roosevelt's fireside chats and frequent press conferences, helped to shape efforts to provide relief, to restore employment, and to regulate wages, hours, and working conditions. Feeling they had a friend in the White House, thousands of American working people wrote the president and other New Dealers, especially Secretary of Labor Frances Perkins. Those letters, excerpted here, illustrated the hard times many Americans continued to face long after the New Deal was under way.

Letter to Frances Perkins

Winston-Salem, North Carolina, January 27, 1935

Dear Miss Perkins:

Please allow me to state some of the facts concerning our wages paid in the Tobacco factories first I want to call your attention to the firm I am working for. The Brown & Williamson Co; We make 40 hours a week and we don't average $10.00 per week for semi skilled labor in my depart-

---

Gerald Markowitz and David Rosner, *"Slaves of the Depression": Workers' Letters about Life on the Job* (Ithaca, NY: Cornell University Press, 1987), 21–167.

ment where the *plug tobacco is manufactured* we that are doing semi skilled labor make less than those doing common labor. [T]hey make around $12.00 per week while we make from $7.00 to $10.00 and maybe some few of us might make $13.00 once and a while. Now how can we be considered in the Presidents spending program when we don't make enough to live on and pay our just and honest debts. Please take notice Meat advanced from 6 cents to 16 cents sugar from 5 to 6 cents flour has almost doubled and house rent and every thing but our wages the idea of men young and middle age making less than $2.00 while we are piling up millions for the firms we work and the sad part of it is the majority are afraid to make an out cry about conditions. Now I think our great trouble lies in the fact that no[body] ever investigates our working conditions and the greatest portion of us are colored people and I think every body hates a colored man. How can we support a family of 7 or 8 send our children to school and teach them citizen ship when capitalist choke us and make criminals out of some of us that might be a bit weak. Now Miss Perkins just think about our condition how hard it is to come up to the American Standard of living on less than $10.00 for 40 hours work and 7 or 8 in family or it seems that my race of people are not considered in the American Standard of living. Now most of my people are afraid to complain because some few years ago the R. J. Reynolds Tobacco Co. discharged every one that joined a union they were trying to organize here and for reason you can't find any union workers in the R. J. Reynolds firm among the colored people. . . . It seems that some investigations should be made. Now how can we pay our debts educate our children and if we have to call a doctor we don't have the money to pay him for his visit. . . . How can we get a square deal as our case is continued to be pushed a side. Please consider these facts Miss Perkins We are up against a hard proposition.

O. G.

Letter to Frances Perkins

Brooklyn, New York, March 29, 1935

Dear Miss Perkins:

Reading about you as I do I have come to the understanding, that you are a fair and impartial observer of labor conditions in the United States. Well, I'll have to get a load off my chest, and tell you of the labor conditions in a place which is laughingly called a factory. We work in a Woolstock Concern. We handle discarded rags. We work, ten hours a day for six days. In the grime and dirt of a nation. We go home tired and sick — dirty — disgusted — with the world in general, work — work all day, low pay — average wage sixteen dollars. Tired in the train going home, sitting at the dinner table, too tired to even wash ourselves, what for — to keep body and souls together not to depend on charity. What of N.R.A.? What of everything—? We handle diseased rags all day. Tuberculosis roaming loose, unsanitary conditions—, slaves—slaves of the depression! I'm even tired as I write this letter—, a letter of hope—. What am I? I am young—I am twenty, a high school education—no recreation—no fun—. Pardon ma'am—but I want to live—! Do you deny me that right—? As an American citizen I ask you—, what—what must we do? Please investigate this matter. I sleep now, yes ma'am with a prayer on my lips, hoping against hope—, that you will better our conditions. I'll sign my name, but if my boss finds out—, well—Give us a new deal, Miss Perkins. . . .

Yours hoping,
J. G.

Letter to Franklin D. Roosevelt

Paris, Texas, November 23, 1936

Dear President now that we have had a land Slide and done just what was best for our country & I will Say more done the only thing that could of bin done to Save this Country I do believe you Will Strain a point to help the ones who helped you mostly & that is the Working Class of People I am not smart or I would be in a different line of work & better up in ever way yet I will Know you are the one & only President that ever helped a Working Class of People I have Writen you several letters & have always received a answer from Some of you officials clerks or Some one & I will know you have to much to think about to answer a little man letter like my Self yet I will Say I and thousands of men just like me were in the fight for you & I for one will go down for you any day I am a White Man American age, 47 married wife 2 children in high School am a Finishing room foreman I mean a Working foreman & am in a furniture Factory here in Paris Texas where thaire is 175 to 200 Working & when the NRA came in I was Proud to See my fellow workmen Rec 30 Per hour in Place of 8 cents to 20 cents Per hour yet the NRA did not make any allowance for Skilled labor or foreman unless they rec as much as 35.00 Per Week & very few Furniture Makers rec Such a Price I have bin with this firm for 25 years & they have Surly reaped the harvest. . . . I can't see for my life President why a man must toil & work his life out in Such factories 10 long hours ever day except Sunday for a small sum of 15 cents to 35 cents per hour & pay the high cost of honest & deason living expences is thaire any way in the world to help this one class of Laboring People just a little I admit this class of Working People should form a union but ever time it talked the big boy owners say we will close down then it is more releaf workers to take care of more expence to our Government and more trouble to you what we need is a law passed to shorten our hours at a living & let live scal & take more men off the Government expense & put them in the factories & get things to running normal but if a co cuts hours & then tells Foreman shove & push them & keeps putting out as much with short hours & driving the men like convicts it will never help a bit you have had your load & I well know it but please see if something can be done to help this one Class of Working People the factories are a man killer not venelated or kept up just a bunch of Republickins Grafters 90/100 of them Please help us some way I Pray to God for relief. I am a christian . . . and a truthful man & have not told you wrong & am for you to the end.

Letter to Frances Perkins

Plaquemine, Louisiana, July 27, 1937

Dear Miss Perkins:

I am writing to you because I think you are pretty square to the average laboring man. but I am wondering if anyone has told you of the cruel and terrible condition that exist in this part of the country or the so called sugar cane belt in Louisiana. I am sure that it hasn't made any progress or improvement since slavery days and to many people here that toil the soil or saw mills as laboring men I am sure slavery days were much better for the black slaves had their meals for sure three times a day and medical attention at that. but if an American nowadays had that much he is a communist I am speaking of the labor not the ones that the government give a sugar bounty too but the real forgotten people for the ones the government give the sugar bounty too are the ones that really don't need it for those same people that has drawn the sugar bonus for two years has never gave an extra penny to their white and black slaves labor. I will now make an effort to give you an idea of the terrible inhuman condition.

I will first give you the idea of the sugar cane tenants and plantations poor laboring people. The bell rings at 2 A.M. in the morning when all should really be sleeping at rest. they work in the summer until 9 or 10 A.M. the reason they knock them off from the heat is not because of killing the labor from heat but they are afraid it kills the mule not the slave. Their wages runs from go 90¢ to $1.10 per day. Their average days per week runs from three to four days a week in other words people that are living in so called United States have to live on the about $4.00 per week standing of living in a so called American Community which is way below the Chinese standard of living for the Chinese at least have a cheaper food and clothing living but here one has to pay dear for food and clothing because these sugar cane slave owners not only give inhuman wages but the ones that work for them have to buy to their stores, which sells from 50 per cent to 60 per cent higher than the stores in town still these same people that are worst than the old time slave owners or yelling and hollering for more sugar protection, why should they get more when they don't pay their white and black slaves more. It is true they give the white and black slaves a place to live on. But Miss Perkins if you were to see these places they live on you'd swear that this is not our so call rich America with it high standing of living for I am sure that the lowest places in China or Mexico or Africa has better places to live in. These Southern Senators which are backed by the big shots will tell you it is cheaper to live in the South but have you investigated their living condition. Sometimes I don't wonder why some of these people don't be really communism but they are true Americans only they are living in such a low standing of living that one wouldn't believe they are living in the good old U.S.A.

Now regarding the saw mills of this town and other towns in this section but most particular this town they pay slightly more than the plantation but they get it back by charging more for food & clothing which they have to buy in their stores.

I am writing you this hoping that you will try to read it and understand the situation which if you think is not true you can send an investigator in this section of Louisiana that has American freedom of speech for some hasn't that speech in our so called free America. . . .

Thanking you for humanity sake.
R. J.

Letter to Franklin D. Roosevelt

Denver, Colorado, April 14, 1938

Dear Mr. Roosevelt:

I listened to your address over the radio tonight and want to tell you how much I appreciate what you are trying to do for the people and can see what a fight and struggle you have. Wish it was so you could see and know how things are here in Denver. You can't even buy a job and if you do get one they expect you to work 9 to 10 hrs a day and the most you can get for cooking and such is $10.00 a week. Something should be done with these chain eating houses as they work their boys 12 and 14 hrs and just give them a 14% of earnings charge them for shortages dishes broken, their eats and etc, and when they get their weekly salary sometimes they have from $7.00 to $9.00 coming to them for their long hrs of service and they keep taking in boys to learn and lay off the regular help as the boys they break in has to work a week or so without pay. Its no wonder so many are without work and can't eat half the time. Its no wonder so much crime exists. These chain sandwich shops are the AVB and the owners are out of Wichita Kans. They have seven of these shops here in Denver at this time and are figuring on putting in more. They should be made [to] pay a certain salary as well as every other place of business. Do hope you can get a wage and hour law here that will put more people to work and at least give the head of the family wages that they can at least pay the rent and have enough left to eat a week on. My husband has been out of work since Jan 1st and all we have had is what I can earn at Restaurant work and have a family of five to try to care for. Sure wish could have some good hours and then some one to see that they were enforced. I was sick in the winter and was off of work and the W.P.A. wouldn't give my husband a days work because he had worked out of Denver and out of town 3 months out of year. He works for the Great Western Sugar Co each year during their campaign. I am truly thankful for all you have accomplished so far and hope you may be able to see much more realized.

Mrs. A. F. T.

Letter to Franklin D. Roosevelt

Detroit, Michigan, November 27, 1939

President Roosevelt
Dear Honorable Sir:

I am living in a city that should be one of the prized possessions of these United States of America but it isn't only to a small group of chiseling money mongers.

I and my husband are and have been Americans for three generations and we are proud of what our parents did also our grandparents to help America progress. They were builders of our country not destructers as is now going on to make the rich man richer and the poor man poorer in fact try and starve them in a land of plenty. We have six growing children that are all separated each one pining for each other and our hearts nearly broken because we cannot keep them all together.

We have tried so hard these past seven years we lost our furniture twice lost our car our insurance even my engagement ring and finally the wedding ring to buy groceries pay rent and for illness. Neither one of us are lazy he worked in steel mills auto factories painting dishwashing and anything he could get. I worked at waitress janitress selling to make a few dollars now my health is slowly ebbing. I was a widow when I married my present husband my first husband died shortly after the world war having served as a submarine chaser. I received a check for $1.00 for each day he served he died leaving me two lovely children. Why should descent American people be made suffer in this manner living in an attic room paying $5.00 per week and if its not paid out you go on the streets.

Welfare has never solved these problems as there are far too many inefficient social workers also too much political graft for it to survive or even help survive. We are one family out of 100,000 that are in the same position right here in Detroit where the ones we labor for and help build up vast fortunes and estates do nothing but push us down farther. They cheat the government out of taxes hire foreign labor at lower rates and if we get discouraged and take some groceries to feed our family we must serve time.

They have 40 to 100 room houses with no children to make it even like a home while we are denied a small home and enough wages to provide for them. Barbara Hutton has herself exploited that she pays $650.00 to have one tooth pulled and the girls in her dime stores slave all week for $12 or $14 and must help provide for others out of it. I'll wager to say that the poor class were lucky to have roast pork @ 13¢ per lb on Thanksgiving Day while the rich people in this country probably threw a lot out in there garbage cans. These so called intelligent rich men including the Congressmen and the Senators better wake up and pass some laws that will aid labor to make a living as they would have never accumulated their vast fortunes had it not been from the hard sweat that honest labor men brought them.

We read with horror of the war in Europe and of the blockade to starve the people into submission and right here in Detroit we have the same kind of a blockade. Do the intelligent men of America think we are going to stand for this much longer. I alone hear a lot of viewpoints and it will be very hard to get our men to fight another war to make more wealth for men that never had to labor and never appreciated where the real source of their wealth derived from. This country was founded on Thanksgiving day to get away from the brutal treatment the British gave them and us real true Americans intend keeping it so. We need men of wealth and men of intelligence but we also need to make labor healthy and self supporting or our nation will soon crumble and it is head on to a good start. Even prisoners will balk at an injustice and we are not prisoners. . . .

A true American mother & family
M. Q. L.

QUESTIONS

What did these individuals want the government to do? • How did they describe their working conditions? • What did they complain about? • If they did not like their jobs, why didn't they find another place to work? • Why didn't they ask their employers for better wages, hours, and working conditions? • What fears did they express?

DOCUMENT 3

Woody Guthrie on Hard-Hitting Songs for Hard-Hit People

Most Americans did not write to Washington about their troubles during the depression. They did their best to find work, to put food on the table, and to get by until tomorrow. But many of them hummed a tune or sang a song, and the songs often voiced their fears, hopes, and dreams. During the depression, Woody Guthrie, a troubadour of working people, wrote an introduction to a book of songs he had sung, written, or heard. His introduction, excerpted here, discloses the spirit of many "hard-hit people" in the hard times of the 1930s.

Songbook Introduction

Here's a book of songs that's going to last a mighty long time, because these are the kind of songs that folks make up when they're a-singing about their hard luck, and hard luck is one thing that you sing louder about than you do about boots and saddles, or moons on the river, or cigarettes a shining in the dark.

There's a heap of people in the country that's a having the hardest time of their life right this minute; and songs are just like having babies. You can take either, but you can't fake it, and if you try to fake it, you don't fool anybody except yourself.

For the last eight years I've been a rambling man, from Oklahoma to California and back three times by freight train, highway, and thumb, and I've been stranded, and disbanded, busted, disgusted with people of all sorts, sizes, shapes, and calibers—folks that wandered around over the country looking for work, down and out, and hungry half of the time. I've slept on and with them, with their feet in my face and my feet in theirs—in bed rolls with Canadian Lumberjacks, in greasy rotten shacks and tents with the Okies and Arkies that are grazing today over the states of California and Arizona like a herd of lost buffalo with the hot hoof and empty mouth disease.

Then to New York in the month of February, the thumb route, in the snow that blanketed from Big Springs, Texas, north to New York, and south again into even Florida. . . . Walking down the big road, no job, no money, no home . . . no nothing. Nights I slept in jails, and the cells were piled high with young boys, strong men, and old men; and they talked and they sung, and they told you the story of their life, how it used to be,

Woody Guthrie, "Introduction," *Hard-Hitting Songs for Hard-Hit People* (1967) in Warren Susman, *Culture and Commitment* (New York: George Braziller, 1973).

how it got to be, how the home went to pieces, how the young wife died or left, how the mother died in the insane asylum, how Dad tried twice to kill himself, and lay flat on his back for 18 months—and then crops got to where they wouldn't bring nothing, work in the factories would kill a dog, work on the belt line killed your soul, work in the cement and limestone quarries withered your lungs, work in the cotton mills shot your feet and legs all to hell, work in the steel mills burned your system up like a gnat that lit in the melting pot, and—always, always had to fight and argue and cuss and swear, and shoot and slaughter and wade mud and sling blood—to try to get a nickel more out of the rich bosses. But out of all of this mixing bowl of hell and high waters by George, the hardworking folks have done something that the bosses, his sons, his wives, his whores, and his daughters have failed to do—the working folks have walked bare handed against clubs, gas bombs, billys, blackjacks, saps, knucks, machine guns, and log chains—and they sang their way through the whole dirty mess. And that's why I say the songs in this book will be sung coast to coast acrost the country a hundred years after all nickel phonographs have turned back into dust.

I ain't a writer, I want that understood, I'm just a little one-cylinder guitar picker. But I don't get no kick out of these here songs that are imitation and made up by guys that's paid by the week to write 'em up that reminds me of a crow a settin' on a fence post a singing when some guy is a sawing his leg off at the same time. . . .

This book is . . . a song book that come from the lungs of the workin' folks—and every little song was easy and simple, but mighty pretty, and it caught on like a whirlwind—it didn't need sheet music, it didn't need nickel phonographs, and it didn't take nothing but a little fanning from the bosses, the landlords, the deputies, and the cops, and the big shots, and the bankers, and the business men to flare up like an oil field on fire, and the big cloud of black smoke turn into a cyclone—and cut a swath straight to the door of the man that started the whole thing, the greedy rich people.

You'll find the songs the hungry farmers sing as they bend their backs and drag their sacks, and split their fingers to pieces grabbing your shirts and dresses out of the thorns on a cotton boll. You'll find the blues. The blues are my favorite, because the blues are the saddest and lonesomest, and say the right thing in a way that most preachers ought to pattern after. All honky tonk and dance hall blues had parents, and those parents were the blues that come from the workers in the factories, mills, mines, crops, orchards, and oil fields—but by the time a blues reaches a honky tonk music box, it is changed from chains to kisses, and from a cold prison cell to a warm bed with a hot mama, and from a sunstroke on a chain gang, to a chock house song, or a brand new baby and a bottle of gin.

You'll find a bunch of songs made up by folks back in the hills of old Kentucky. The hills was full of coal. The men was full of pep and wanted to work. But houses wasn't no good, and wages was next to nothing. Kids died like flies. The mothers couldn't pay the doctor, so the doctor didn't come. It was the midwives, the women like old Aunt Molly Jackson, that rolled up her sleeves, spit out the window, grabbed a wash pan in one hand and a armful of old pads and rags, and old newspapers, and dived under the covers and old rotten blankets—to come up with a brand new human being in one hand and a hungry mother in the other. Aunt Molly was just a coal miner's wife, and a coal miner's daughter, but she took the place of the doctor in 850 cases, because the coal miners didn't have the money.

You'll find the songs that were scribbled down on the margins of almanacs with a penny pencil, and sung to the rhythms of splinters and rocks that the Winchester rifles kicked up in your face as you sang them. . . .

Then . . . out pops the New Deal songs—the songs that the people sung when they heard the mighty good sounding promises of a reshuffle, a honest deck, and a brand new deal from the big shots. A Straight flush, the Ace for One Big Union, the King for One Happy Family, the Queen for a happy mother with a full cupboard, the Jack for a hard working young man with money enough in his pockets to show his gal a good time, and the ten spot for the ten commandments that are overlooked too damn much by the big boys.

Next you'll run across some songs called "Songs of the One Big Union"—which is the same Big Union that Abe Lincoln lived for and fought for and died for. Something has happened to that Big Union since Abe Lincoln was here. It has been raped. The Banking men has got their Big Union, and the Land Lords has got their Big Union, and the Merchants has got their Kiwanis and Lions Club, and the Finance Men has got their Big Union, and the Associated Farmers has got their Big Union, but down south and out west, on the cotton farms, and working in the orchards and fruit crops it is a jail house offence for a few common everyday workers to form them a Union, and get together for higher wages and honest pay and fair treatment. It's damn funny how all of the big boys are in Big Unions, but they cuss and raise old billy hell when us poor damn working guys try to get together and make us a Working Man's Union. This Book is full of songs that the working folks made up about the beatings and the sluggings and the cheatings and the killings that they got when they said they was a going to form them a Working Man's Union. It is a jail house crime for a poor damn working man to even hold a meeting with other working men. They call you a red or a radical or something, and throw you and your family off of the farm and let you starve to death. . . . These songs will echo that song of starvation till the world looks level—till the world is level—and there ain't no rich men, and there ain't no poor men, and every man on earth is at work and his family is living as human beings instead of like a nest of rats.

A last section of this book is called Mulligan Stew which are songs that you make up when you're a trying to speak something that's on your mind . . . telling your troubles to the blue sky, or a walkin' down the road with your 2 little kids by the hand, thinking of your wife that's just died with her third one—and you get to speaking your mind—maybe to yourself the first time, then when you get it a little better fixed in your head, and you squeeze out all of the words you don't need, and you boil it down to just a few that tell the whole story of your hard luck. Then you talk it or sing it to somebody you meet in the hobo jungle or stranded high and dry in the skid row section of a big town, or just fresh kicked off a Georgia farm, and a going nowhere, just a walkin' along, and a draggin' your feet along in the deep sand, and—then you hear him sing you his song or tell you his tale, and you think, That's a mighty funny thing. His song is just like mine. And my tale is just like his. And everywhere you ramble, under California R.R. bridges, or the mosquito swamps of Louisiana, or the dustbowl deserts of the Texas plains—it's a different man, a different woman, a different kid a speaking his mind, but it's the same old tale, and the same old song. Maybe different words. Maybe different tune. But it's hard times, and the same hard times. The same big song. This book is that song. . . .

I know how it was with me, there's been a many a time that I set around with my head hanging down, broke, clothes no good, old slouchy shoes, and no place to go to have a good time, and no money to spend on the women, and a sleeping in cattle cars like a whiteface steer, and a starving for days at a time up and down the railroad tracks and then a seeing other people all fixed up with a good high rolling car, and good suits of clothes, and high priced whiskey, and more pretty gals than one. Even had money to blow on damn fool rings and necklaces and bracelets around their necks and arms—and I would just set there by the side of the road and think . . . just one of them diamonds would buy a little farm with a nice little house and a water well and a gourd dipper, and forty acres of good bottom land to raise a crop on, and a good rich garden spot up next to the house, and a couple of jersey cows . . . , and some chickens to wake me up of a morning, and . . . the whole picture of the little house and piece of land would go through my head every time I seen a drunk man with three drunk women a driving a big Lincoln Zephyr down the road—with money to burn, and they didn't even know where the money was coming from. . . .

Now, I might be a little haywired, but I ain't no big hand to like a song because it's pretty, or because it's fancy, or done up with a big smile and a pink ribbon, I'm a man to like songs that ain't sung too good. Big hand to sing songs that ain't really much account. . . . I like songs, by george, that's sung by folks that ain't musicians, and ain't able to read music, don't know one note from another'n, and—say something that amounts to something. That a way you can say what you got to say just singing it and if you use the same dern tune, or change it around twice, and turn it upside down, why that still don't amount to a dern, you have spoke what you had to speak, and if folks don't like the music, well, you can still pass better than some political speakers.

But it just so happens that these songs here, they're pretty, they're easy, they got something to say, and they say it in a way you can understand, and if you go off somewhere and change 'em around a little bit, well, that don't hurt nothin'. Maybe you got a new song. You have, if you said what you really had to say—about how the old world looks to you, or how it ought to be fixed. . . .

It wouldn't have to be fancy words. It wouldn't have to be a fancy tune. The fancier it is the worse it is. The plainer it is the easier it is, and the easier it is, the better it is—and the words don't even have to be spelt right.

You can write it down with the stub of a burnt match, or with an old chewed up penny pencil, on the back of a sack, or on the edge of a almanac, or you could pitch in and write your walls full or your own songs. They don't even have to rhyme to suit me. If they don't rhyme a tall, well, then it's prose, and all of the college boys will study on it for a couple of hundred years, and because they cain't make heads nor tails of it, they'll swear you're a natural born song writer, maybe call you a natural born genius.

QUESTIONS

What had Woody Guthrie seen in his travels during the 1930s? • According to Guthrie, what did the working people do that their bosses failed to do? • What kind of songs did he like? • Why? • How did songs express the experiences of "hard-hit people"?

COMPARATIVE QUESTIONS

Does the view of government in letters from working people differ from the views expressed by Franklin Roosevelt? How do the views of bosses and wealthy Americans expressed by Woody Guthrie and in the letters of working people compare with those of Roosevelt? How do their political goals compare?

CHAPTER 25

THE UNITED STATES AND THE SECOND WORLD WAR
1939–1945

Nothing in the previous history of the world compared with the conflagration of World War II. Literally the entire globe became engulfed by fighting, preparing to fight, or supplying combatants. The high stakes of the conflict were made clear by reports of the aims of Nazi Germany and by the attack on Pearl Harbor. Nearly all Americans enlisted in the war effort, whether or not they wore a uniform. The following documents illustrate ideas and experiences shared by millions of Americans during World War II.

DOCUMENT 1

An American Diplomat Analyzes the Nazis

While the New Deal was under way in the United States, the National Socialist party came to power in Germany under the leadership of Adolf Hitler. The Nazis' fascist program alarmed Douglas Miller, an American diplomat stationed in Vienna. In April 1934, long before the outbreak of war in Europe, Miller sent the United States State Department the following report on the Nazis and their vision of the future.

Douglas Miller

Memorandum to the U.S. Embassy, April 17, 1934

The fundamental purpose [of the Nazis] is to secure a greater share of the world's future for the Germans, the expansion of German territory and growth of the German race until it constitutes the largest and most powerful nation in the world, and ultimately, according to some Nazi leaders, until it dominates the entire globe.

Douglas Miller, "Memorandum to the Embassy, April 17, 1934," *Peace and War.*

The German people suffering from a traditional inferiority complex, smarting from their defeat in the [first world] war and the indignities of the post-war period, disillusioned in their hopes of a speedy return to prosperity along traditional lines, inflamed by irresponsible demagogic slogans and flattered by the statement that their German racial inheritance gives them inherent superior rights over other peoples, have to a large measure adopted the National Socialist point of view for the time being.

Economic Aims

There are two other purposes subsidiary to the main purpose. Germany is to be made the economic center of a self-sustaining territorial block whose dependent nations in Central and Eastern Europe will look to Berlin for leadership. This block is to be so constituted that it can defy wartime blockade and be large enough to give the peoples in it the benefits of free trade now enjoyed by the 48 American States. In accordance with this purpose, an agricultural self-sufficiency program has been adopted, foreign foodstuffs are being rigorously excluded or the imported supply secured in increasing quantities from Central and Southeastern Europe. A hereditary peasantry has been set up, firmly attached to the soil through the prohibition of the sale or mortgaging of the peasants' land or crops. An increasing number of commodities have been placed under Government monopolies with fixed prices to consumers and producers, [and] the principle of . . . [a] fixed number of persons engaged in any occupation has been increasingly adopted. The National Socialist conception of the correct or Government-fixed price instead of the price fixed by supply and demand has been introduced.

Social Aims

The second subsidiary purpose is the welding of all individuals in the present and future Greater Germany into a homogeneous racial family, gladly obedient to the will of its leader, with class and cultural differences inside the country eliminated, but a sharp line drawn between Germans and the foreign world outside. In carrying out this purpose, the Jews are to be entirely eliminated, the Slavic or eastern elements in the population to be minimized and eventually bred out of the race. A national religion is in process of organization; trade unions, political parties and all social, political, cultural, trade or other organizations not affiliated with the National Socialist party, have been abolished, the individual's rights have been largely taken away. In the future the nation is to count for everything, the individual for nothing. Germany is to engage in a gigantic struggle with the rest of the world to grow at the expense of its neighbors. The German population owes the nation the patriotic duty of supporting it and bringing forward all necessary sacrifices to reach the common goal.

Retention of Power

To these long-distance objectives must be added the . . . most important purpose of all, namely to retain control at all costs. The National Socialist party may compromise on distant objectives, if necessary, but cannot compromise on a question of retaining its absolute hold on the German people. This control had been gained by making most irresponsible and extravagant promises; by the studied use of the press, the radio, public meetings, parades, flags, uniforms, and all methods of working on popular psychology and finally by the use of force. This control once lost, could never be regained. It is absolutely necessary for the party to continue to make a show of success and to keep popular enthusiasm and fanaticism alive. There must be no open criticism or grumbling, even discussion of the future form of the State, the form in which industry is to be organized, or the laws regarding the hereditary peasantry is prohibited. Since the German public is politically inept and unusually docile, the Nazi movement has been able to dominate the situation for the past year, but the hard facts of the economic situation are beginning to be felt by the more intelligent Germans, particularly bankers, business men, professional men and persons who have touch with the outside world.

Danger of War

The Nazis are not satisfied with the existing map of Europe. They are at heart belligerent and aggressive. True, they desire nothing more than a period of peace for several years in which they can gradually re-arm and discipline their people. This period may be 5 years, 10 years, or longer, but the more completely their experiments succeed the more certain is a large-scale war in Europe some day.

Nazis Want to Wipe Out 1918

In estimating the aims and purposes of the National Socialist movement, we must not make the mistake of putting too much reliance on public statements designed for consumption abroad which breathe the spirit of good peace and will and assert the intention of the Government to promote the welfare of the German people and good relations with their neighbors. Nor should we imagine that the present Government leaders will feel and act as we would in their circumstances, namely think only of Germany's welfare. The real emotional drive behind the Nazi program is not so much love of their own country as dislike of other countries. The Nazis will never be content in merely promoting the welfare of the German people. They desire to be feared and envied by foreigners and to wipe out the memory of 1918 by inflicting humiliations in particular upon the French, the Poles, the Czechs and anybody else they can get their hands on. A careful examination of Hitler's book and his public speeches reveals the fact that he cannot be considered as absolutely sane and normal on this subject. The same is true of many other Nazi leaders. They have capitalized the wounded inferiority complex of the German people, and magnified their own bitter feelings into a cult of dislike against the foreign world which is past the bounds of ordinary good sense and reason. Let us repeat this fact and let it sink in, the National Socialist movement is building a tremendous military machine, physically very poorly armed, but morally aggressive and belligerent. The control of this machine lies in the hands of narrow, ignorant and unscrupulous adventurers who have been slightly touched with madness from brooding over Germany's real or imagined wrongs, as well as the slights and indignities thrown in their own individual way as they attempted to organize the movement. Power of this kind concentrated in hands like these is dangerous. The Nazis are determined to secure more power and more territory in Europe. If this is voluntarily given to them by peaceful means, well and good, but if not, they will certainly use force. That is the only meaning behind the manifold activities of the movement in Germany today.

QUESTIONS

What did Miller identify as the fundamental purpose of the Nazis? • Why did he think they were successful in appealing to the German people? • What were the Nazis' economic and social aims? • How did they maintain control? • Did Miller believe the Nazis could be trusted? • What was the basis of his belief?

DOCUMENT 2

President Franklin D. Roosevelt Requests Declaration of War on Japan

The Japanese surprise attack on Pearl Harbor catapulted the United States into World War II. The attack erased hesitations many Americans had felt about getting entangled in another foreign war. Although the war in Europe had been under way since 1939 and the United States had aided the Allies, war was not declared on Germany until, after Pearl Harbor, Hitler declared war on the United States. President Roosevelt's speech to Congress on December 8, 1941, communicated the sense of crisis and resolve felt by most Americans on the day after Pearl Harbor.

Speech to Congress, December 8, 1941

Yesterday, December 7, 1941—a date which will live in infamy—the United States of America was suddenly and deliberately attacked by naval and air forces of the Empire of Japan.

The United States was at peace with that Nation and, at the solicitation of Japan, was still in conversation with its Government and its Emperor looking toward the maintenance of peace in the Pacific. Indeed, one hour after Japanese air squadrons had commenced bombing in Oahu, the Japanese Ambassador to the United States and his colleague delivered to the Secretary of State a formal reply to a recent American message. While this reply stated that it seemed useless to continue the existing diplomatic negotiations, it contained no threat or hint of war or armed attack.

It will be recorded that the distance of Hawaii from Japan makes it obvious that the attack was deliberately planned many days or even weeks ago. During the intervening time the Japanese Government has deliberately sought to deceive the United States by false statements and expressions of hope for continued peace.

The attack yesterday on the Hawaiian Islands has caused severe damage to American naval and military forces. Very many American lives have been lost. In addition American ships have been reported torpedoed on the high seas between San Francisco and Honolulu.

Yesterday the Japanese Government also launched an attack against Malaya.

Last night Japanese forces attacked Hong Kong.

Last night Japanese forces attacked Guam.

Last night Japanese forces attacked the Philippine Islands.

Last night the Japanese attacked Wake Island.

This morning the Japanese attacked Midway Island.

Japan has, therefore, undertaken a surprise offensive extending throughout the Pacific area. The facts of yesterday speak for themselves. The people of the United States have already formed their opinions and well understand the implications to the very life and safety of our Nation.

As Commander in Chief of the Army and Navy I have directed that all measures be taken for our defense.

Always will we remember the character of the onslaught against us.

No matter how long it may take us to overcome this premeditated invasion, the American people in their righteous might will win through to absolute victory.

I believe I interpret the will of the Congress and of the people when I assert that we will not only defend ourselves to the uttermost but will make very certain that this form of treachery shall never endanger us again.

Congressional Record, 77th Cong., 1st sess., 1941. Vol. 87, pt. 9, pp. 9519–20.

Hostilities exist. There is no blinking at the fact that our people, our territory, and our interests are in grave danger.

With confidence in our armed force—with the unbounded determination of our people—we will gain the inevitable triumph—so help us God.

I ask that the Congress declare that since the unprovoked and dastardly attack by Japan on Sunday, December 7, a state of war has existed between the United States and the Japanese Empire.

QUESTIONS

Why did President Roosevelt call the attack on Pearl Harbor a "a date that will live in infamy"? • Where else did Japanese forces attack? • Do you think Roosevelt's speech would have been effective in enlisting Americans' support for the war against Japan? • If so, why?

DOCUMENT 3

A Japanese American Woman Recalls Pearl Harbor

The attack on Pearl Harbor inaugurated a wave of anti-Japanese sentiment and activity that culminated in the internment of citizens of Japanese ancestry in camps scattered throughout the West. Monica Sone, a native of Seattle and student at the University of Washington, was first interned along with her family at Camp Harmony in Puyallup, Washington, and later moved to Camp Minidoka in Idaho. Sone's memoir, the source of the following excerpt, reveals the emotions that engulfed her and her family members as the nation mobilized for war against Japan.

Monica Sone
Nisei Daughter

On a peaceful Sunday Morning, December 7, 1941, Henry, Sumi, and I were at choir rehearsal singing ourselves hoarse in preparation for the annual Christmas recital of Handel's "Messiah." Suddenly Chuck Mizuno, a young University of Washington student, burst into the chapel, gasping as if he had sprinted all the way up the stairs.

"Listen, everybody!" he shouted. "Japan just bombed Pearl Harbor . . . in Hawaii It's war!"

Monica Sone, *Nisei Daughter* (Boston: Little, Brown and Company, 1953).

The terrible words hit like a blockbuster, paralyzing us. . . . I felt as if a fist had smashed my pleasant little existence, breaking it into jigsaw puzzle pieces. An old wound opened up again, and I found myself shrinking inwardly from my Japanese blood, the blood of an enemy. I knew instinctively that the fact that I was an American by birthright was not going to help me escape the consequences of this unhappy war.

One girl mumbled over and over again, "It can't be, God, it can't be!" Someone else was saying, "What a spot to be in! Do you think we'll be considered Japanese or Americans?"

A boy replied quietly, "We'll be Japs, same as always. But our parents are enemy aliens now, you know."

A shocked silence followed. Henry came for Sumi and me. "Come on, let's go home," he said. . . .

Mother was sitting limp in the huge armchair as if she had collapsed there, listening dazedly to the turbulent radio. Her face was frozen still, and the only words she could utter were, *"Komatta neh, komatta neh.* How dreadful, how dreadful.". . .

With every fiber of my being I resented this war. I felt as if I were on fire. "Mama, they should never have done it," I cried. "Why did they do it? Why? Why?"

Mother's face turned paper white. "What do you know about it? Right or wrong, the Japanese have been chafing with resentment for years. It was bound to happen, one time or another. You're young, Ka-chan, you know very little about the ways of nations. . . ."

Discussion of politics, especially Japan versus America, had become taboo in our family for it sent tempers skyrocketing. Henry and I used to criticize Japan's aggressions in China and Manchuria while Father and Mother condemned Great Britain and America's superior attitude toward Asiatics and their interference with Japan's economic growth. During these arguments, we had eyed each other like strangers, parents against children. . . .

Just then the shrill peel of the telephone cut off the possibility of a family argument. When I answered, a young girl's voice fluttered through breathily, "Hello, this is Taeko Tanabe. . . ."

The next day we learned that Taeko was trying desperately to locate her mother because FBI agents had swept into their home and arrested Mr. Tanabe, a newspaper editor. The FBI had permitted Taeko to try to locate her mother before they took Mr. Tanabe away while they searched the house for contraband and subversive material, but she was not to let anyone else know what was happening. . . .

We were shocked to read Attorney General Biddle's announcement that 736 Japanese had been picked up in the United States and Hawaii. Then Mrs. Tanabe called Mother about her husband's arrest, and she said at least a hundred others had been taken from our community. Messrs. Okayama, Higashi, Sughira, Mori, Okada — we knew them all.

"But why were they arrested, Papa? They weren't spies, were they?"

Father replied almost curtly, "Of course not! They were probably taken for questioning."

The pressure of war moved in on our little community. The Chinese consul announced that all the Chinese would carry identification cards and wear "China" badges to distinguish them from the Japanese. Then I really felt left standing out in the cold. The government ordered the bank funds of all Japanese nationals frozen. Father could no longer handle financial transactions through his bank accounts, but Henry, fortunately, was of legal age so that business could be negotiated in his name.

In the afternoon President Roosevelt's formal declaration of war against Japan was broadcast throughout the nation. In grave, measured words, he described the attack on Pearl Harbor as shameful, infamous. I writhed involuntarily. I could no more have escaped the stab of self-consciousness than I could have changed my Oriental features. . . .

It made me positively hivey the way the FBI agents continued their raids into Japanese homes and business places and marched the Issei men away into the old red brick immigration building, systematically and efficiently, as if they were stocking a cellarful of choice bottles of wine. At first we noted that the men arrested were those who had been prominent in community affairs, like Mr. Kato, many times president of the Seattle Japanese Chamber of Commerce, and Mr. Ohashi, the principal of our Japanese language school, or individuals whose business was directly connected with firms in Japan; but as time went on, it became less and less apparent why the others were included in these raids.

We wondered when Father's time would come. We expected momentarily to hear strange footsteps on the porch and the sudden demanding ring of the front doorbell. . . . Once when our doorbell rang after curfew hour, I completely lost my Oriental stoicism which I had believed would serve me well under the most trying circumstances. . . .

Gradually we became uncomfortable with our Japanese books, magazines, wall scrolls, and knickknacks. When Father's hotel friends, Messrs. Sakaguchi, Horiuchi, Nishibue, and a few others vanished, and their wives called Mother weeping and warning her again about having too many Japanese objects around the house, we finally decided to get rid of some of ours. We knew it was impossible to destroy everything. The FBI would certainly think it strange if they found us sitting in a bare house, totally purged of things Japanese. But it was as if we could no longer stand the tension of waiting, and we just had to do something against the black day. We worked all night, feverishly combing through bookshelves, closets, drawers, and furtively creeping down to the basement furnace for the burning. I gathered together my well-worn Japanese language schoolbooks which I had been saving over a period of ten years with the thought that they might come in handy when I wanted to teach Japanese to my own children. I threw them into the fire and watched them flame and shrivel into black ashes. . . .

Mrs. Matsui kept assuring us that the FBI would get around to us yet. It was just a matter of time and the least Mother could do for Father was to pack a suitcase for him. . . . So Mother dutifully packed a suitcase for Father with toilet articles, warm flannel pajamas, and extra clothes, and placed it in the front hall by the door. It was a personal affront, the way it stood there so frank and unabashedly. Henry and I said that it was practically a confession that Papa was a spy, "So please help yourself to him, Mr. FBI, and God speed you.". . .

We had a family conference to discuss the possibility of Father and Mother's internment. Henry was in graduate school and I was beginning my second year at the university. We agreed to drop out should they be taken and we would manage the hotel during our parents' absence. Every weekend Henry and I accompanied Father to the hotel and learned how to keep the hotel books, how to open the office safe, and what kind of linen, paper towels, and soap to order.

Then a new menace appeared on the scene. Cries began to sound up and down the coast that everyone of Japanese ancestry should be taken into custody. For years the professional guardians of the Golden West had wanted to rid their land of the Yellow Peril, and the war provided an opportunity for them to push their program through. As the chain of Pacific islands fell to the Japanese, patriots shrieked for protection from us. A Californian sounded the alarm: "The Japanese are dangerous and they must leave. Remember the destruction and the sabotage perpetrated at Pearl Harbor. Notice how they have infiltrated into the harbor towns and taken our best land.". . .

In February, Executive Order No. 9066 came out, authorizing the War Department to remove the Japanese from such military areas as it saw fit, aliens and citizens alike. Even if a person had a fraction of Japanese blood in him, he must leave on demand.

A pall of gloom settled upon our home. We couldn't believe that the government meant that the Japanese-Americans must go, too. We had heard the clamoring of superpatriots who insisted loudly, "Throw the whole kaboodle out. A Jap's a Jap, no matter how you slice him. You can't make an American out of little Jap junior just by handing him an American birth certificate." But we had dismissed these remarks as just hot blasts of air from an overheated patriot. We were quite sure that our rights as American citizens would not be violated, and we would not be marched out of our homes on the same basis as enemy aliens.

In anger, Henry and I read and reread the Executive Order. Henry crumpled the newspaper in his hand and threw it against the wall. "Doesn't my citizenship mean a single blessed thing to anyone? Why doesn't somebody make up my mind for me. First they want me in the army. Now they're going to slap an alien 4-C on me because of my ancestry. What the hell!"

Once more I felt like a despised, pathetic two-headed freak, a Japanese and an American, neither of which seemed to be doing me any good. The

Nisei leaders in the community rose above their personal feelings and stated that they would cooperate and comply with the decision of the government as their sacrifice in keeping with the country's war effort, thus proving themselves loyal American citizens. I was too jealous of my recently acquired voting privilege to be gracious about giving in, and I felt most uncooperative. . . .

Events moved rapidly. General DeWitt marked off western Washington, Oregon, and all of California, and the southern half of Arizona as Military Area No. 1, hallowed ground from which we must remove ourselves as rapidly as possible. Unfortunately we could not simply vanish into thin air, and we had no place to go. We had no relatives in the east we could move in on. All our relatives were sitting with us in the forbidden area, themselves wondering where to go. The neighboring states in the line of exit for the Japanese protested violently at the prospect of any mass invasion. They said, very sensibly, that if the coast didn't want the Japanese hanging around, they didn't either. A few hardy families in the community liquidated their property, tied suitcases all around their cars, and sallied eastward. They were greeted by signs in front of store windows, "Open season for Japs!" and "We kill rats and Japs here.". . .

General DeWitt must have finally realized that if he insisted on voluntary mass evacuation, hundreds and thousands of us would have wandered back and forth, clogging the highways and pitching tents along the roadside, eating and sleeping in colossal disorder. He suddenly called a halt to voluntary movement, although most of the Japanese were not budging an inch. He issued a new order, stating that no Japanese could leave the city, under penalty of arrest. The command had hatched another plan, a better one. The army would move us out as only the army could do it, and march us in neat, orderly fashion into assembly centers. We would stay in these centers only until permanent camps were set up inland to isolate us.

The orders were simple:

> Dispose of your homes and property. Wind up your business. Register the family. One seabag of bedding, two suitcases of clothing allowed per person. People in District #1 must report at 8th and Lane Street, 8 P.M. on April 28.

I wanted no part of this new order. I had read in the paper that the Japanese from the state of Washington would be taken to a camp in Puyallup, on the state fairgrounds. The article apologetically assured the public that the camp would be temporary and that the Japanese would be removed from the fairgrounds and parking lots in time for the opening of the annual State Fair. . . .

One evening Father told us that he would lose the management of the hotel unless he could find someone to operate it for the duration. . . .

Sumi asked, "What happens if we can't find anyone?"

"I lose my business and my livelihood. I'll be saying good-bye to a lifetime of labor and all the hopes and plans I had for the family."

We sagged. . . .

We listened to Father wide-eyed and wistful. It had been a wonderful, wonderful dream.

QUESTIONS

How did Pearl Harbor make Monica Sone feel? • What was the reaction of her parents? • What did the FBI do in Seattle shortly after Pearl Harbor? • How did the Sones respond to the arrests of men of Japanese ancestry? • How did Henry Sone react to the internment order? • What effect did the order have on the Sone family?

DOCUMENT 4

Soldiers Send Messages Home

At home, Americans built a war economy. Thousands of tanks, airplanes, and ships came off American assembly lines. Millions of uniforms, bombs, and bullets funneled from civilian plants into military warehouses. Vital and compelling as all this military production was, probably no domestic activity was more important to Americans on the homefront than the post office. Letters from loved ones in uniform overseas — "V mail" — were treasured. News of the war was always welcome, but news that the soldier was still alive was far better. The following correspondence illustrates what homefront Americans learned when they opened V mail.

Sergeant Irving Strobing

Radio Address from Corregidor, Philippines, May 5 or 6, 1942

They are not yet near. We are waiting for God only knows what. How about a chocolate soda? Not many. Not here yet. Lots of heavy fighting going on. We've only got about one hour, twenty minutes before. . . . We may have to give up by noon. We don't know yet. They are throwing men and shells at us and we may not be able to stand it. They have been shelling us faster than you can count. . . .

Annette Tapert, ed., *Lines of Battle: Letters from American Servicemen, 1941–1945* (New York: Times Books, 1987), 20–286.

We've got about fifty-five minutes and I feel sick at my stomach. I am really low down. They are around us now smashing rifles, They bring in the wounded every minute. We will be waiting for you guys to help. This is the only thing I guess that can be done. General Wainwright is a right guy and we are willing to go on for him, but shells are dropping all night, faster than hell. Damage terrific. Too much for guys to take.

Enemy heavy cross-shelling and bombing. They have got us all around and from skies. From here it looks like firing ceased on both sides. Men here all feeling bad, because of terrific nervous strain of the siege. Corregidor used to be a nice place, but it's haunted now. Withstood a terrific pounding. just made broadcast to Manila to arrange meeting for surrender. Talk made by General Beebe. I can't say much.

I can hardly think. Can't think at all. Say, I have sixty pesos you can have for this weekend. The jig is up. Everyone is bawling like a baby. They are piling dead and wounded in our tunnel. Arms weak from pounding [radio] key long hours, no rest, short rations. Tired. I know now how a mouse feels. Caught in a trap waiting for guys to come along finish it. Got a treat. Can pineapple. Opening it with a Signal Corps knife.

My name Irving Strobing. Get this to my mother. Mrs. Minnie Strobing, 605 Barbey Street, Brooklyn, New York. They are to get along O.K. Get in touch with them soon as possible. Message, My love to Pa, Joe, Sue, Mac, Carrie, Joy and Paul. Also to all family and friends. God bless 'em all, hope they be here when I come home. Tell Joe wherever he is to give 'em hell for us. My love to all. God bless you and keep you. Love.

Sign my name and tell Mother how you heard from me. Stand by. . . . Strobing

John Conroy
Letter, December 24, 1942

Mare Island Naval Hospital, San Francisco
December 24, 1942

Dear Mother and Dad:

. . .You keep asking so I'll tell you. I have been shell-shocked and bomb-shocked. My memory is very dim regarding my civilian days. They feel that sudden shock in action now would affect my sanity. All the boys back here have received the same diagnosis. Injury to my back helps to make further combat service for me impossible. It's so very difficult for me to explain, to say the things I want to, my thoughts are so disconnected.

Of course I'm not insane. But I've been living the life of a savage and haven't quite got used to a world of laws and new responsibilities. So many of my platoon were wiped out, my old Parris Island buddies, that it's hard to sleep without seeing them die all over again. Our living conditions on Guadalcanal had been so bad—little food or hope—fighting and dying each day—four hours sleep out of 72—the medicos here optimistically say I'll pay for it the rest of my life. My bayonet and shrapnel cuts are all healed up, however. Most of us will be fairly well in six months, but none of us will be completely cured for years. My back is in bad condition. I can't stand or walk much. The sudden beat of a drum or any sharp, resonant noise has a nerve-ripping effect on us.

Ah, well, let's not think, but just be happy that we'll all be together soon.

Loads and loads of love,
John

Allen Spach
Letter, February 1943

[February 1943]

Dear Dad,
I think you will find this letter quite different than the others which you've received from me. My health is well as could be expected as most of us boys in the original outfit that left the States together about [CENSORED] of us are still here. The other are replacements. The missing have either been killed, wounded or from other various sources mainly malaria fever.

On May 16 '42 we left New River N.C., and went to the docks at Norfolk. On the 20th at midnight we hit the high seas with 7,000 marines aboard the U.S.S. Wakefield. We went down through the Panama Canal and past Cuba. On the 29th we crossed the international date line. . . . Was continually harassed by submarines as we had no convoy whatsoever.

We landed in New Zealand 28 days later and they were wonderful to us as we were the first Americans to arrive there. We lived aboard ship at the dock for about a month loading equipment on incoming ships getting ready for "The Day." After working day and night we left and went to one of the Fiji Islands for four days. I was aboard the U.S.S. Fuller picked up in New Zealand. In our convoy were about 100 ships including 3 aircraft carriers and the battleship, North Carolina. We also had air protection from Flying Fortresses coming from Australia. On August 6 we had our last dinner aboard ship and they gave us all we wanted with ice cream and a pack of cigarettes. Just like a man doomed for the electric chair he got any kind of food for this last meal. That was our last for a while. Each one of us received a letter from our commanding officer, the last sentence reading Good Luck, God Bless You and to hell with the japs. On the morning of the 7th I went over the side with the first wave of troops as Rifle Grenadier, just another chicken in the infantry. With naval bombardment and supreme control of the air we hit the beach at 9.47. All hell broke loose. Two days later our ships left taking our aircraft with them, never to have any sea and air protection for the next two [CENSORED]. In the meantime the Japanese navy and air force took the advantage and gave us hell from sea and air. I won't say what the ground troops had to offer us yet. I can say we never once retreated but kept rushing forward taking the airport first thing.

Left to do or die we fought hard with one purpose in mind to do, kill every slant eyed bastard within range of rifle fire or the bayonet which was the only thing left to stop their charge. We were on the front lines *110 days* before we could drop back for a shave, wash up. Don't many people know it but we were the first allied troops to be on the lines that long, either in this war or the last. We have had to face artillery both naval and field, mortar bombings sometimes three or four times a day, also at night, flame throwers, hand grenades, tanks, booby traps, land mines, everything I guess except gas. The most common headache caused by machine gun fire, snipers, rifle fire, and facing sabers, bayonet fighting, the last most feared by all. A war in five offensive drives and also in defense of our own lines. I've had buddies shot down on both sides of me, my closest calls being a shot put through the top of my helmet by a sniper. Once I had to swim a river when we were trapped by the enemy.

With no supplies coming in we had to eat coconuts, captured rice, crab meat, fish heads. We also smoked their dopey cigarettes. We also captured a warehouse full of good Saba Beer, made in Tokyo. Didn't shave or have hair cut for nearly four months, looked rather funny too. Wore Jap clothing such as underwear, socks, shoes. Had plenty of thrills watching our boys in the air planes dog fighting after they sent us some planes to go on the newly finished field that they had built. . . . What few of the old fellows here are scarred by various wounds and 90% have malaria. I've been down with it several times but I dose heavy with quinine till I feel drunk. . . . We want to come home for a while before seeing action again which is in the very near future, but they won't do it even though the doctors want us to. We were continually bombed and strafed but took it pretty good. The average age of the boys was 21 and were around 18 to 20. When we were finally relieved by the army who were all larger and older they were surprised to find us kids who had done such a good job. My best buddie at the time was caught in the face by a full blast of machine gun fire and when the hole we were laying in became swamped by flies gathering about him and being already dead, I had to roll him out of the small hole on top of the open ground and the dirty SOBs kept shooting him full of holes. Well anyway God spared my life and I am thankful for it. I know that your and dear Mama's prayers helped bring me safely through the long months of it. I hope that you will forgive me of my misdoings as it had to take this war to bring me to my senses. Only then did I realize how much you both had done for me and Dear God, maybe I can come through the next to see you and my friends again. . . .

God bless the whole world and I'm looking forward to the days when Italy and Germany are licked so that the whole might of the allied nations can be thrown in to crush Japan and the swines that are her sons, fighting to rule the white race. I heard an English speaking Nip say that if he didn't die fighting, that is if he didn't win or if he was captured and later came to Japan, he would be put in prison for 17 years and that all his property would be taken over by the government. That's his point of view. Where ever we go us boys will do our best always till the end when we don't have the strength to press a trigger.

Love always,
Your son,
Allen

James McMahon
Letter, March 10, 1944

March 10, 1944

My Dear Parents:
    This letter will introduce my best buddy Bill Nelson. I was on Captain DeMont's crew with him. . . .

10.18.43.   My first raid was a diversion over the North Sea. We had no fighter escort and got lost and ended up over Holland (Friesian Islands). I saw my first enemy fighters, four ME-109s, and they shot down a B-24. It went into a dive and no one got out. The next raid was Wilhelmshaven on Nov. 3rd (1943). The sky was overcast, but we bombed anyway and did a good job. I only saw one other B-24 go down. My next raid was Bremen on November 13th. About 10 minutes from the target I noticed our waist gunner was unconscious and appeared to be dying (which he was). Immediately Captain DeMont dropped down to 5,000 feet and headed for home. The waist gunner (Erderly) was dying from lack of oxygen and frostbite (57 below). On the way home he came to and when we landed he went into the hospital. That day Freddie's ship and two others from our squadron went down. One of the waist gunners on his crew is safe but we believe all others are dead. It was over the North Sea they went down and you can't live more than 10 minutes in that water.
    Well, my next raid was Kjeller, Norway, November 18th. It was cold as hell and Bill will go more into detail for you. No flack but coming out we were about 50 miles from land and the Jerry fighters jumped us. There was about 25 or 30 (maybe more) twin engine jobs. . . . Well, Bill got the first one, and then things popped. Our tail gunner Ray Russell got the next one and then (I was on the right waist gun) one popped up out of a cloud and tried to draw a bead on us. I shot his left engine off and killed

the pilot and it went down in flames, its wing falling off. Bill in the meantime is having a party for himself. I looks over to see how he's going and he is firing so long at one of the bastards that his bullets are coming out red hot. He kills the pilot of this one and shoots the left wing off, and down goes number four in flames. In the meantime 12 B-24s get shot down, but then the fighters leave us and we pat each other on the back. Boy what a day. Man did we have fun. Well on my next raid, Kiel Dec. 13th, I was engineer riding the top turret. The flack was bad, but again the cloud cover was with us and we didn't get any holes. . . .

Dec. 31st. St. Angeley. Again I went to Kiel. This time as a waist gunner. My ship was in the low element flying in "Coffin Corner." The weather was perfect over the target and we didn't even see any flack till we opened our bomb bay doors. Then all hell broke loose. The sky turned black with flack. Our control cables were shot out on the left hand side, and our 4 engine was also shot out. The top turret got about 20 holes in it, and also the nose turret. The bombardier was hit in the throat (he recovered). All at once I was knocked down as something hit me in the back. A piece of flack was sticking out of my jacket. I was so scared by now that I could hardly stand up and I couldn't see as the sweat was running into my eyes. The temperature was 45 below too. Well, we went into a crazy spin and I was halfway out of the window when he pulled it out and we headed for home. We almost didn't make it. The fighters stayed a way out and didn't attack us. After this raid my nerves were so shot I could hardly write. We were under artillery (flack) fire for 12 minutes that time. It is the most terrible experience you can have. It is just like going "over the top" into an artillery barrage. I saw 2 ships blow up this day, and one go down by fighters. It makes a guy so damned mad and you can't do anything about it.

1.7.44 Well I figured I'd better go on another raid damn quick or I'd never fly again so, 2 days later I went to Ludwigshaven. It was wonderful going in, and we had plenty of fighter protection. Coming out after getting our 4 engine shot out and plenty holes in the ship, we figured we'd go to Switzerland. We decided we'd better stay with the formation (which we now lost) two groups of 24s. Well we headed for home (without our fighters) and ended up at Paris. It is a very pretty city. Well then all hell broke loose. About 150 of the Goering Sqdn . . . hit us with everything they had. I got some pretty good shots at them and am pretty sure I hit a few of them. Well, our right wing man pulls out and blows up. Then our other wing man pulls out and goes down in a spin and blows up on the ground. All around us they were blowing up, going down in a dive and in spins. After an hour of constant attack the fighters leave us and later I find out that we lost two and the other group lost 10. All because of a damned lousey navigator. I hope he goes to hell. This raid was the 7th of January. They picked on our ship because we had one engine shot out. Our bombardier and the other waist gunner got one FW-190 apiece. This raid cured my case of nerves and put me back in the groove.

2.20.44.   Well my next raid was Gotha. It's a wonderful trip. I was in the nose turret and I didn't even see a burst of flack. This raid is a milk run. Too bad they can't all be like that. Well now comes the next one. This one will slay you.

BERLIN! on the 6th March. I was in the tail turret and we were high element and "coffin corner." The sky was perfect, no clouds, which meant the fighters were going to come up and the flack would be accurate. On this raid I should have been as nervous as hell, but I thought of Thom, Henn, Fred, and all the fellows I had seen go down. I figured if I came back, O.K., but if I went down it would be for Thom. Gee I felt glad. Well, all the way in to the target the flack was bad, and the Jerry fighters sure played hell. Our fighters sure gave them hell too. Well I didn't get any more shots at fighters till the target. I saw one FW-190 shoot down one of our planes which went into a dive and went straight down. Then all hell broke loose. The flack was terrible and the fighters everywhere. The group right behind us was catching hell with fighters (FW-190s) and I got in about 10 squirts at them. We kept flying through the flack and made two runs on the target which took about 20 minutes. All this time I can see Berlin, and man there are 24's and 17's all over the place. I see our bombs hit smack on the target and my heart bleeds for those damned Krauts down there. Well after that for 100 miles I can see the fires and smoke. It looks like all Berlin is on fire. Boy do I feel good. I'm laughing like hell for some reason. I guess it is because I am still there. Well after I get back to base (after squirting those Jerry fighters all the way home) I go to sleep and dream of Thom. All the time over the target I was think-ing about him and Dad and Mom and Sis and . . . [e]verything was going through my mind at once. I sure feel good, 'cause we knocked the hell out of them. We didn't even get a scratch on the plane either. And that sure is something for the books. By the time you get this letter, I will prob-ably have 5 or 6 more raids in, but I will explain them to you myself. I want you to promise that you will not tell about anything in this letter. Except maybe that I've been to Berlin. I am sure proud of my record. 9 times over the target and 7 times deep into Germany.

I want you to know that if anything ever happens to me that I think I have the most wonderful and courageous parents in the world, and the most beautiful and wonderful sister on this earth. I am proud of you all and my brother Thom. . . . God Bless you all and keep you safe. I'll come back. I can't say I know I will, but I have as good a chance as anyone. Give my pal Bill the best you've got, 'cause he's the best the E.T.O. [Euro-pean Theater of Operations] has. Let Joe take him down to Eddie's and give him plenty Scotch. He was raised on the stuff. God bless you. I hope this letter gives you an idea of what Bill and I have been through. So long. Hope I see you soon.

Your loving son,
Jimmie

David Mark Olds
Letter, July 12, 1945

Rosenheim
July 12, 1945

Dear family:

. . . Dad, you ask for my opinion and reactions and those of the GI in general about several things, including the San Francisco conference. . . . For one thing everybody is mostly concerned with getting his own skin back to the States and home, regardless of what he leaves here and in what condition it is. I think this is a pretty universal feeling anyway — leave it to the next fellow or the politicians to worry about the world. I wanna go home and get some small measure of happiness out of life. There are many of us who feel that not much good will be done with all these noble efforts. First of all, the death of President Roosevelt was almost a mortal blow. Second the regrowth of national selfishness which we can plainly see in France, where we are no longer the saviors but annoying foreigners who interfere with their life. Thirdly, the turmoil in England, and finally the pathetic shortsightedness of those who keep hinting at and whooping up talk of war with Russia. Everywhere we hear how terrible the occupying Russian forces are, how barbaric, how savage, how primitive, etc. etc., and I blush to say, many who say this are wearing the American uniform, men who should realize that without Russia's help we would have surely been beaten. . . . [S]ooner or later . . . the disarming friendliness and cleverness of the Germans will make us doubt if they are so bad. "After all they are a civilized nation, they have great men, etc. etc." My own solution . . . would have a very liberal policy of passes so that men could get out of this accursed country say once a month or so, to breathe the freer air of the Allied countries. Let them change the occupying personnel every six months or so. Let the German PWs be kept in the Army and used as labor of all kinds, farm, factory, etc., instead of discharging them here while we poor bastards have to sit and sweat in the Army in a foreign hated land. I would crush every vestige of military or industrial might in Germany. Let them be a pauper nation. They deserve it. Let the Russians take over, they have shown how to handle them—be rough with them. Of course some innocent and some helpless will suffer—too bad—in the Army you learn callousness. It is impossible I know, but I would love to personally shoot all young Hitlerites, say between the ages of 10 and 30, and have a rigidly supervised program of education for the young. I don't know if that gives you any better idea of how I feel. . . .

You also asked about the concentration camps and the mass grave victims. It is hard for me to convey all of it to you. You drive through the surrounding towns where there are happy little children at play, and people going about their business, looking like any townspeople the world over, yet within two miles of them, its charged fences harsh against the plains, its chimneys belching smoke from cremating ovens — within two miles is a concentration camp whose very existence is such a horrible thought that a man may doubt that any good can exist in the same world, let alone area, with them. The humans who, though long dead, are yet physically alive with their stick like limbs and vacant faces are so terrible a blasphemy on civilization — yet the German civilians nearby either pretend not to realize them, or what is worse, see no wrong. God, how can people be like that. The concentration camp is even worse when it is empty, and just stands there, a mute testimonial to a brutality beyond comprehension. The gas chambers, as neat and as clean as shower rooms, the cremating ovens where the odor of human flesh is yet ingrained in the bricks, the pitiful barracks and grounds enclosed by the deadly barbed wire and guarded walls. I have seen soldiers get sick standing in the empty desolate chambers, thinking of the horror the walls have seen.

The mass graves and reburials are, for brutality, even worse. Is your stomach strong? Let me tell you about Volarv. The SS troopers and the civilians of the town, including some women, when the Germans were falling back in April, rounded up some 200 Jews with about 50 women in the lot. The men were emasculated, disembowelled and shot. The women were killed very simply. A bayonet was run into their reproductive organs and into their bowels. Pretty, isn't it. When they were being dug up from the ditch where they had been thrown, placed in rude but honorable wooden coffins, and being reburied in plots dug by German civilians and soldiers, American officers and men called all the people out of the town to witness the burial, to see the bodies, to touch the bodies, to have that memory printed on their minds of what a horrible thing they had done, only few of them showed either remorse or sickness. They stood there, hard and sullenfaced, muttering and obstinate. They would turn away and be forced to turn back and look. These same people would have cried in anguish had this been done to their own, to Germans, but what if it happened to inferior people, to Jews, and Russians, and Poles? A shrug of the shoulders, too bad, it had to be done. And yet how quickly these things can be forgotten here. . . . I want to get out of this country while I still hate it. Forgive me if this picture seems too pessimistic — I have been here longer than I want to, and it is all getting on my nerves.

Love,
David

QUESTIONS

How did the war affect these soldiers? • What did they think about the enemy? • What did they think about their fellow soldiers? • What did they think about the folks at home? • What goals did they have?

COMPARATIVE QUESTIONS

How do the servicemen's experiences in war compare with the views of Germany and Japan expressed in the diplomat's report from Vienna and President Roosevelt's request for a declaration of war? How does the experience of the Sone family compare with the policies of the governments against which the United States fought?

CHAPTER 26

COLD WAR POLITICS IN THE TRUMAN YEARS
1945–1953

After World War II, the United States and the Soviet Union—former allies—squared off as antagonists. Their confrontation escalated to a cold war within months after the surrender of Germany and Japan. The cold war shaped American foreign and domestic policy for the remainder of the twentieth century. American policy makers maneuvered to contain Soviet influence in the world while many politicians worried about internal subversion by Communist agents or dupes. GIs returning from Europe or the Pacific found a homefront transformed by American power and prosperity, which the Korean War soon tested. The following documents reveal the crosscurrents of victory and continued warfare, of confidence and anxiety, and of possibilities and threats that characterized the Truman years.

DOCUMENT 1

George F. Kennan Outlines Containment

For American policy makers, no problem loomed larger in the postwar world than relations with the Soviet Union. Soviet armies had been decisive in the defeat of Nazi Germany and currently occupied most of Eastern Europe. Soviet leaders were Communists who professed their hatred of capitalism and the political institutions of the United States and other Western democracies. George F. Kennan, a diplomat in the U.S. Embassy in Moscow, sent a long, secret telegram to the State Department early in 1946 that was the embryo of what became the American policy of containment. Excerpts from that telegram follow.

"The Long Telegram"

February 22, 1946

Secret

. . . BASIC FEATURES OF POST-WAR SOVIET OUTLOOK, AS PUT FORWARD BY OFFICIAL PROPAGANDA MACHINE, ARE AS FOLLOWS:

(A) USSR still lives in antagonistic "capitalist encirclement" with which in the long run there can be no permanent peaceful coexistence. . . .

(B) Capitalist world is beset with internal conflicts, inherent in nature of capitalist society. . . .

(C) Internal conflicts of capitalism inevitably generate wars. . . .

(D) Intervention against USSR, while it would be disastrous to those who undertook it, would cause renewed delay in progress of Soviet socialism and must therefore be forestalled at all costs.

(E) Conflicts between capitalist states, though likewise fraught with danger for USSR, nevertheless hold out great possibilities for advancement of socialist cause, particularly if USSR remains militarily powerful, ideologically monolithic and faithful to its present brilliant leadership. . . .

So much for premises. To what deductions do they lead from standpoint of Soviet policy? To following:

(A) Everything must be done to advance relative strength of USSR as factor in international society. Conversely, no opportunity must be missed to reduce strength and influence, collectively as well as individually, of capitalist powers.

(B) Soviet efforts, and those of Russia's friends abroad, must be directed toward deepening and exploiting of differences and conflicts between capitalist powers. . . .

(C) "Democratic-progressive" elements abroad are to be utilized to maximum to bring pressure to bear on capitalist governments along lines agreeable to Soviet interests. . . .

Before examining ramifications of this party line in practice there are certain aspects of it to which I wish to draw attention.

First, it does not represent natural outlook of Russian people. Latter are, by and large, friendly to outside world, eager for experience of it, eager to measure against it talents they are conscious of possessing, eager above all to live in peace and enjoy fruits of their own labor. Party line only represents thesis which official propaganda machine puts forward with great skill and persistence to a public often remarkably resistant in the stronghold of its innermost thoughts. But party line is binding for outlook and

Foreign Relations of the United States, 1946, vol. 6. Barton J. Bernstein and Allan J. Matusow, *The Truman Administration: A Documentary History,* (New York: Harper Row, 1966).

conduct of people who make up apparatus of power-party, secret police and government—and it is exclusively with these that we have to deal.

Second, please note that premises on which this party line is based are for most part simply not true. Experience has shown that peaceful and mutually profitable coexistence of capitalist and socialist states is entirely possible. Basic internal conflicts in advanced countries are no longer primarily those arising out of capitalist ownership of means of production, but are ones arising from advanced urbanism and industrialism as such, which Russia has thus far been spared not by socialism but only by her own backwardness. . . .

At bottom of Kremlin's neurotic view of world affairs is traditional and instinctive Russian sense of insecurity. Originally, this was insecurity of a peaceful agricultural people trying to live on vast exposed plain in neighborhood of fierce nomadic peoples. To this was added, as Russia came into contact with economically advanced west, fear of more competent, more powerful, more highly organized societies in that area. But this latter type of insecurity was one which afflicted rather Russian rulers than Russian people; for Russian rulers have invariably sensed that their rule was relatively archaic in form, fragile and artificial in its psychological foundation, unable to stand comparison or contact with political systems of western countries. For this reason they have always feared foreign penetration, feared direct contact between western world and their own, feared what would happen if Russians learned truth about world without or if foreigners learned truth about world within. And they have learned to seek security only in patient but deadly struggle for total destruction of rival power, never in compacts and compromises with it. . . .

This thesis provides justification for that increase of military and police power of Russian state, for that isolation of Russian population from outside world, and for that fluid and constant pressure to extend limits of Russian police power which are together the natural and instinctive urges of Russian rulers. Basically this is only the steady advance of uneasy Russian nationalism, a centuries old movement in which conceptions of offense and defense are inextricably confused. But in new guise of international Marxism, with its honeyed promises to a desperate and war torn outside world, it is more dangerous and insidious than ever before. . . .

In summary, we have here a political force committed fanatically to the belief that with US there can be no permanent modus vivendi, that it is desirable and necessary that the internal harmony of our society be disrupted, our traditional way of life be destroyed, the international authority of our state be broken, if Soviet power is to be secure. This political force has complete power of disposition over energies of one of world's greatest peoples and resources of world's richest national territory, and is borne along by deep and powerful currents of Russian nationalism. In addition, it has an elaborate and far flung apparatus for exertion of its influence in other countries, an apparatus of amazing flexibility and versatility, managed by people whose experience and skill in underground methods are presumably without parallel in history. Finally, it is seemingly inaccessible to considerations of reality in its basic reactions. For it, the vast fund of objective fact about human society is not, as with us, the measure against which outlook is constantly being tested and re-formed, but a grab bag from which individual items are selected arbitrarily and tendenciously to bolster an outlook already preconceived. This is admittedly not a pleasant picture. Problem of how to cope with this force is undoubtedly greatest task our diplomacy has ever faced and probably greatest it will ever have to face. . . . It should be approached with same thoroughness and care as solution of major strategic problem in war, and if necessary, with no smaller outlay in planning effort. I cannot attempt to suggest all answers here. But I would like to record my conviction that problem is within our power to solve—and that without recourse to any general military conflict. And in support of this conviction there are certain observations of a more encouraging nature I should like to make:

(One) Soviet power, unlike that of Hitlerite Germany, is neither schematic nor adventuristic. It does not work by fixed plans. It does not take unnecessary risks. Impervious to logic of reason, and it is highly sensitive to logic of force. For this reason it can easily withdraw—and usually does—when strong resistance is encountered at any point. Thus, if the adversary has sufficient force and makes clear his readiness to use it, he rarely has to do so. . . .

(Two) Gauged against western world as a whole, Soviets are still by far the weaker force. Thus, their success will really depend on degree of cohesion, firmness and vigor which western world can muster. And this is factor which it is within our power to influence.

(Three) Success of Soviet system, as form of internal power, is not yet finally proven. It has yet to be demonstrated that it can survive supreme test of successive transfer of power from one individual or group to another. Lenin's death was first such transfer, and its effects wracked Soviet state for 15 years after. Stalin's death or retirement will be second. But even this will not be final test. Soviet internal system will now be subjected, by virtue of recent territorial expansions, to series of additional strains which once proved severe tax on Tsardom. We here are convinced that never since termination of civil war have mass of Russian people, been emotionally farther removed from doctrines of communist party than they are today. In Russia, party has now become a great and—for the moment—highly successful apparatus of dictatorial administration, but it has ceased to be a source of emotional inspiration. Thus, internal soundness and permanence of movement need not yet be regarded as assured.

(Four) All Soviet propaganda beyond Soviet security sphere is basically negative and destructive. It should therefore be relatively easy to combat it by any intelligent and really constructive program.

For these reasons I think we may approach calmly and with good heart problem of how to deal with Russia. As to how this approach should be made, I only wish to advance, by way of conclusion, following comments:

(One) Our first step must be to apprehend, and recognize for what it is, the nature of the movement with which we are dealing. We must study it with same courage, detachment, objectivity, and same determination not to be emotionally provoked or unseated by it, with which doctor studies unruly and unreasonable individual.

(Two) We must see that our public is educated to realities of Russian situation. I cannot over-emphasize importance of this. Press cannot do this alone. It must be done mainly by government, which is necessarily more experienced and better informed on practical problems involved. . . . I am convinced that there would be far less hysterical anti-Sovietism in our country today if realities of this situation were better understood by our people. There is nothing as dangerous or as terrifying as the unknown. It may also be argued that to reveal more information on our difficulties with Russia would reflect unfavorably on Russian American relations. I feel that if there is any real risk here involved, it is one which we should have courage to face, and sooner the better. But I cannot see what we would be risking. Our stake in this country, even coming on heels of tremendous demonstrations of our friendship for Russian people, is remarkably small. We have here no investments to guard, no actual trade to lose, virtually no citizens to protect, few cultural contacts to preserve. Our only stake lies in what we hope rather than what we have; and I am convinced we have better chance of realizing those hopes if our public is enlightened and if our dealings with Russians are placed entirely on realistic and matter of fact basis.

(Three) Much depends on health and vigor of our own society. World communism is like malignant parasite which feeds only on diseased tissue. This is point at which domestic and foreign policies meet. Every courageous and incisive measure to solve internal problems of our own society, to improve self-confidence, discipline, morale and community spirit of our own people, is a diplomatic victory over Moscow worth a thousand diplomatic notes and joint communiqués. If we cannot abandon fatalism and indifference in face of deficiencies of our own society, Moscow will profit. . . .

(Four) We must formulate and put forward for other nations a much more positive and constructive picture of sort of world we would like to see than we have put forward in past. It is not enough to urge people to develop political processes similar to our own. Many foreign peoples, in Europe at least, are tired and frightened by experiences of past, and are less interested in abstract freedom than in security. They are seeking guidance rather than responsibilities. We should be better able than Russians to give them this. And unless we do, Russians certainly will.

(Five) Finally we must have courage and self-confidence to cling to our own methods and conceptions of human society. After all, the greatest danger that can befall us in coping with this problem of Soviet Communism, is that we shall allow ourselves to become like those with whom we are coping.

QUESTIONS

According to Kennan, what was the official Soviet view of the United States? • What policies were the leaders of the Soviet Union likely to follow? • What were the sources of the Soviet leaders' outlook? • Did the Russian people share their leaders' perspectives? • What policies did Kennan recommend that the United States adopt toward the Soviets? • Which U.S. interests were involved? • What did the United States have to fear from the Russians? • How did Kennan recommend that the U.S. government build support for its policy toward the Soviets?

DOCUMENT 2

Senator Joseph McCarthy Hunts Communists

The cold war was fought at home as well as overseas. The notion that Soviet spies had infiltrated the U.S. government as well as labor unions, universities, and the entertainment industry appealed to many Americans. Joseph R. McCarthy, a Republican senator from Wisconsin, intensified the search for secret Communists with his speech in Wheeling, West Virginia, in February 1950. At Wheeling, McCarthy charged that the State Department employed over 200 Communists, but in the version of the speech he entered in the Congressional Record, excerpted here, he reduced the number to 57. McCarthy's speech illustrates the tendency of many politicians during the cold war to label their political opponents Communists or Communist sympathizers.

Speech at Wheeling, West Virginia, February 9, 1950

Today we are engaged in a final, all-out battle between communistic atheism and Christianity. The modern champions of communism have selected this as the time. And, ladies and gentlemen, the chips are down —they are truly down. . . .

Ladies and gentlemen, can there be anyone here tonight who is so blind as to say that the war is not on? Can there be anyone who fails to

---

Congressional Record, Senate, 81st Cong., 2d sess., 1950. Barton J. Bernstein and Allan J. Matusow, *The Truman Administration: A Documentary History,* (New York: Harper & Row, 1966).

realize that the Communist world has said, "The time is now" that this is the time for the show-down between the democratic Christian world and the Communist atheistic world?

Unless we face this fact, we shall pay the price that must be paid by those who wait too long.

Six years ago, at the time of the first conference to map out the peace —Dumbarton Oaks—there was within the Soviet orbit 180,000,000 people. Lined up on the antitotalitarian side there were in the world at that time roughly 1,625,000,000 people. Today, only 6 years later, there are 800,000,000 people under the absolute domination of Soviet Russia—an increase of over 400 percent. On our side, the figure has shrunk to around 500,000,000. In other words, in less than 6 years the odds have changed from 9 to 1 in our favor to 8 to 5 against us. This indicates the swiftness of the tempo of Communist victories and American defeats in the cold war. As one of our outstanding historical figures once said, "When a great democracy is destroyed, it will not be because of enemies from without, but rather because of enemies from within."

The truth of this statement is becoming terrifyingly clear as we see this country each day losing on every front.

At war's end we were physically the strongest nation on earth and, at least potentially, the most powerful intellectually and morally. Ours could have been the honor of being a beacon in the desert of destruction, a shining living proof that civilization was not yet ready to destroy itself. Unfortunately, we have failed miserably and tragically to arise to the opportunity.

The reason why we find ourselves in a position of impotency is not because our only powerful potential enemy has sent men to invade our shores, but rather because of the traitorous actions of those who have been treated so well by this Nation. It has not been the less fortunate or members of minority groups who have been selling this Nation out, but rather those who have had all the benefits that the wealthiest nation on earth has had to offer—the finest homes, the finest college education, and the finest jobs in Government we can give.

This is glaringly true in the State Department. There the bright young men who are born with silver spoons in their mouths are the ones who have been worst.

Now I know it is very easy for anyone to condemn a particular bureau or department in general terms. Therefore, I would like to cite one rather unusual case—the case of a man who has done much to shape our foreign policy.

When Chiang Kai-shek was fighting our war, the State Department had in China a young man named John S. Service. His task, obviously, was not to work for the communization of China. Strangely, however, he sent official reports back to the State Department urging that we torpedo our ally Chiang Kai-shek and stating, in effect, that communism was the best hope of China.

Later, this man—John Service—was picked up by the Federal Bureau of Investigation for turning over to the Communists secret State Department information. Strangely, however, he was never prosecuted. However, Joseph Grew, the Under Secretary of State, who insisted on his prosecution, was forced to resign. Two days after Grew's successor, Dean Acheson, took over as Under Secretary of State, this man—John Service —who had been picked up by the FBI and who had previously urged that communism was the best hope of China, was not only reinstated in the State Department but promoted. And finally, under Acheson, placed in charge of all placements and promotions.

Today, ladies and gentlemen, this man Service is on his way to represent the State Department and Acheson in Calcutta—by far and away the most important listening post in the Far East. . . .

This, ladies and gentlemen, gives you somewhat of a picture of the type of individuals who have been helping to shape our foreign policy. In my opinion the State Department, which is one of the most important government departments, is thoroughly infested with Communists.

I have in my hand 57 cases of individuals who would appear to be either card carrying members or certainly loyal to the Communist Party, but who nevertheless are still helping to shape our foreign policy.

One thing to remember in discussing the Communists in our government is that we are not dealing with spies who get 30 pieces of silver to steal the blueprints of a new weapon. We are dealing with a far more sinister type of activity because it permits the enemy to guide and shape our policy. . . .

The FBI, I may add, has done an outstanding job, as all persons in Washington, Democrats and Republicans alike, agree. If J. Edgar Hoover had a free hand, we would not be plagued by Hisses . . . in high positions of power in the State Department. The FBI has only power to investigate. . . .

This brings us down to the case of one Alger Hiss who is important not as an individual any more, but rather because he is so representative of a group in the State Department. It is unnecessary to go over the sordid events showing how he sold out the Nation which had given him so much. Those are rather fresh in all of our minds.

However, it should be remembered that the facts in regard to his connection with this international Communist spy ring were made known to the then Under Secretary of State Berle 3 days after Hitler and Stalin signed the Russo-German alliance pact. At that time one Whittaker Chambers—who was also part of the spy ring—apparently decided that with Russia on Hitler's side, he could no longer betray our Nation to Russia. He gave Under Secretary of State Berle—and this is all a matter of record—practically all, if not more, of the facts upon which Hiss' conviction was based.

Under Secretary Berle promptly contacted Dean Acheson and received word in return that Acheson (and I quote) "could vouch for Hiss absolutely" — at which time the matter was dropped. And this, you understand, was at a time when Russia was an ally of Germany. This condition existed while Russia and Germany were invading and dismembering Poland, and while the Communist groups here were screaming "warmonger" at the United States for their support of the allied nations.

Again in 1943, the FBI had occasion to investigate the facts surrounding Hiss' contacts with the Russian spy ring. But even after that FBI report was submitted, nothing was done.

Then, late in 1948 — on August 5 — when the Un-American Activities Committee called Alger Hiss to give an accounting, President Truman at once issued a Presidential directive ordering all Government agencies to refuse to turn over any information whatsoever in regard to the Communist activities of any Government employee to a congressional committee.

Incidentally, even after Hiss was convicted — . . . it is interesting to note that the President still labeled the exposé of Hiss as a "red herring."

If time permitted, it might be well to go into detail about the fact that Hiss was Roosevelt's chief adviser at Yalta when Roosevelt was admittedly in ill health and tired physically and mentally . . . and when, according to the Secretary of State, Hiss and Gromyko drafted the report on the conference. . . .

According to the then Secretary of State Stettinius, here are some of the things that Hiss helped to decide at Yalta. (1) The establishment of a European High Commission; (2) the treatment of Germany — this you will recall was the conference at which it was decided that we would occupy Berlin with Russia occupying an area completely circling the city, which, as you know, resulted in the Berlin airlift which cost 31 American lives; (3) the Polish question; (4) the relationship between UNRRA [United Nations Relief and Rehabilitation Administration] and the Soviet; (5) the rights of Americans on control commissions of Rumania, Bulgaria, and Hungary; (6) Iran; (7) China — here's where we gave away Manchuria; (8) Turkish Straits question; (9) international trusteeships; (10) Korea.

Of the results of this conference, Arthur Bliss Lane of the State Department had this to say: "As I glanced over the document, I could not believe my eyes. To me, almost every line spoke of a surrender to Stalin."

As you hear this story of high treason, I know that you are saying to yourself, "Well, why doesn't the Congress do something about it?" Actually, ladies and gentlemen, one of the important reasons for the graft, the corruption, the dishonesty, the disloyalty, the treason in high Government positions — one of the most important reasons why this continues is a lack of moral uprising on the part of the 140,000,000 American people. In the light of history, however, this is not hard to explain.

It is the result of an emotional hang-over and a temporary moral lapse which follows every war. It is the apathy to evil which people who have been subjected to the tremendous evils of war feel. As the people of the world see mass murder, the destruction of defenseless and innocent people, and all of the crime and lack of morals which go with war, they become numb and apathetic. It has always been thus after war.

However, the morals of our people have not been destroyed. They still exist. This cloak of numbness and apathy has only needed a spark to rekindle them. Happily, this spark has finally been supplied.

As you know, very recently the Secretary of State proclaimed his loyalty to a man guilty of what has always been considered as the most abominable of all crimes—of being a traitor to the people who gave him a position of great trust. The Secretary of State in attempting to justify his continued devotion to the man who sold out the Christian world to the atheistic world, referred to Christ's Sermon on the Mount as a justification and reason therefor, and the reaction of the American people to this would have made the heart of Abraham Lincoln happy.

When this pompous diplomat in striped pants, with a phony British accent, proclaimed to the American people that Christ on the Mount endorsed communism, high treason, and betrayal of a sacred trust, the blasphemy was so great that it awakened the dormant indignation of the American people.

He has lighted the spark which is resulting in a moral uprising and will end only when the whole sorry mess of twisted, warped thinkers are swept from the national scene so that we may have a new birth of national honesty and decency in Government.

QUESTIONS

According to McCarthy, what was the evidence that the United States was losing the cold war? • Why had the United States failed to maintain the strong position it had at the end of World War II? • What kind of people worked in the State Department? • What policies did McCarthy accuse Alger Hiss of shaping? • Which of these did he consider high treason? • What should Americans do, according to McCarthy? • How do you account for the discrepancy between the number of Communists in the State Department cited by McCarthy in Wheeling and the number in the speech he finally entered in the *Congressional Record?*

DOCUMENT 3

Postwar Perceptions: Oral Histories

World War II changed Americans' perceptions of themselves and of the nation as a whole in many ways. When veterans returned home, they found possibilities that had not existed before the war. In interviews conducted during the early 1980s, five individuals recalled their experiences in the months and years just after the war. Their reflections disclose important changes that were under way in postwar America.

Laura Briggs

The war made many changes in our town. I think the most important is that aspirations changed. People suddenly had the idea "Hey, I can reach that. I can have that. I can do that. I could even send my kid to college if I wanted to." These were things very few townspeople had thought about before.

The war made us aware that there was a larger world outside of Jerome, Idaho. . . . I think everyone had more hope, more expectations for a better quality of life.

When the war was over we felt really good about ourselves. We had saved the world from an evil that was unspeakable. We had something no other country had. We were a God-sanctioned invincible holy power, and it was our destiny to prove that we were the children of God and that our way was the right way for the world. I think all of us felt that way. We were so innocent and naïve. We believed everything good about ourselves. Life was going to be glorious from now on, because we deserved it. Good times were going to go on and on; everything was going to get better. It was just a wonderful happy ending.

James Covert

My mother had a grocery store, and during the late Depression I remember so many of the people in the neighborhood would come in and receive credit. In fact, she had a little box where she kept a list of their charges. People would pay when they could, but it was always a big chore to get them to do it.

When the war started and people began to work, they actually plunked down money on the counter—hundreds of dollars, it seemed. I remember Saturday nights when my mother would count all the money and take it to the bank. I was fascinated seeing all that currency, the wads of money that would be going to the bank.

For the first time we began to have money. My mother had a great fear of a renewed depression, and she didn't trust banks anymore. She thought if they failed once they might fail again. So she would take silver dollars and put them in little packages, and we would use them for doorstops in our house. Silver dollars were better than paper money in case things got bad again. By 1945 we had a thousand dollars in one box as a doorstop in our house, where five years before we were completely impoverished.

While there wasn't that much to spend the money on during the war, it still changed our lifestyle and, more important, our outlook. You sensed

---

Mark Jonathan Harris, Franklin D. Mitchell, and Steven J. Schechter, *The Homefront: America during World War II* (New York: Putnam, 1984).

that prosperity was coming. You started to think you could do things. We used to go out to a restaurant now and then, where we would never do that before the war. We hardly ever went to picture shows during the Depression; now I did all the time. There was a feeling toward the end of the war that we were moving into a new age of prosperity. Affluence was already in people's minds, and there was a belief that the war would really end on a positive note. My mother saved enough money to buy a modest home. That was the first home we ever bought.

Yet other changes were also taking place. My mother had a neighborhood grocery store, but by the end of the war these Mom-and-Pop stores couldn't compete with the big supermarkets and the chain stores. People had cars and they began to go outside the neighborhood to shop. Society became larger, more impersonal. My mother actually had to leave and find a different kind of employment. For maybe ten years our life was working in a little grocery store, but by 1946 our little grocery store was gone and with it that sense of closeness we had experienced during the war.

Larry Mantell

Our ship was anchored in Tokyo Bay during the surrender. We were about a hundred yards off the port bow of the U.S.S. *Missouri*, where the official surrender took place. My parents had already been writing me that Congress had passed a bill establishing benefits to returning veterans. They were both very anxious to see me come back and go to school.

Before the war I had had no plans whatsoever to go to college. Financially, it was just out of the question. But the GI Bill changed everything. As a kid I had worked selling Cokes in the Coliseum and had always rooted for UCLA athletic teams, so I told my dad to find out what he could about UCLA. My high-school grades weren't good enough for me to be accepted, though, so my dad said, "Go to USC. It doesn't cost you anything." So when I returned to the States in October of 1945 I began preparing my application and establishing my transcripts for the University of Southern California.

When I left home I was a seventeen year-old boy, and since then I had been alongside people who had had their heads blown off. The first time we got hit I was on the bridge of the ship, and a man's arm was blown off. You go through some of those things and you wonder what are you going to be like. But when the war was over we knew that it had all been worthwhile because we had won. There was a lot of exuberance —like the excitement of marching in a Navy Day parade in New Orleans. As returning heroes, we were treated with tremendous generosity. While I stayed in New Orleans I never paid for a meal or a glass of beer or anything there.

I remember coming home and seeing a few of my friends who, for various reasons, didn't go into the service, or those who remained stateside and never had the experiences I did. I looked at them as a little less than me: You guys were fat cats staying here, making out with all the women, having all the fun, and you made money. Well, I felt I was better than they were. When the war ended and it was time to become a hero, the guys who had all the battle scars and had been through all this mess were the ones who seemed to get the most respect.

A good example of this is what happened when I went to buy a car. They didn't manufacture cars during the war years, and when the first ones came out in 1946 the lists were huge. When I got home I really wanted a car, though, so my dad suggested we offer the dealer a little extra money. I was about thirtieth down on the list and the car dealer was really offended by Dad's offer, but he elevated me way up the list because I was a veteran and had been overseas and helped keep this country safe. Within a week, I had a 1946 two-door black Ford and it cost me nine hundred dollars. People in shops had such respect for us. Your whole self-esteem was elevated.

And as a result of the GI Bill, ten days after I got out of the service I started as a freshman at USC. Almost everything important that happened to me later came from attending college there. I met my wife, my closest friends, my accountant, my attorney, my business partners. It was the war and going into the service, a coincidence of living, that absolutely changed my life. I don't know what I would have been if it hadn't been for that.

Don Condren

I got out of the service in the late fall of 1945 and returned to Amarillo [Texas]. After I graduated from high school I had gone to junior college for about a year and worked as a drugstore clerk until I was drafted. I had no idea what to study at junior college, though, or what to do for a living.

Being in the service had improved my expectations because all of a sudden I had the GI Bill, and I needed it. I could go to college and it would be paid for.

I read a number of articles in books and magazines that said we were becoming an increasingly technological society, that there was going to be a lot of opportunity for engineers. So I took engineering courses at the junior college in Amarillo; then I transferred to the University of Colorado, where I completed my degree. While at the University of Colorado I married, and after I graduated, my wife and I bought our first home on a GI loan. It cost ten thousand dollars. Sometimes I tell my kids I never even had a room of my own until after I was married.

I considered the GI Bill a good piece of fortune, but I didn't consider it charity. World War II was a popular war, so we all came home heroes. The people around us looked upon us with approval. They thought we deserved the GI Bill and were happy for us to have it.

I'm not sure whether I could ever have gone to college without the GI Bill. I doubt if I would have moved away from the Texas Panhandle. The GI bill had a major impact on the country. It set a whole new standard of improved education for a large number of people, a whole new standard of improved housing, A college graduate has higher expectations, and he finds ways to realize those expectations, or tries to. I think the GI Bill gave the whole country an upward boost economically and in every other way—at least in the late forties and early fifties.

Henry Fiering

We came out of the war the only country that wasn't destroyed. That put us in the number-one position in the world. We were the most prosperous nation in the world, and the people took advantage of it,

By the end of the war labor was well entrenched. The most important segments of American industry were organized. And they were organized for good. There was nothing that could dislodge the unions from the shops. Nothing. There was no power strong enough for that. So they had to be dealt with.

Moreover, the conversion period was not as traumatic as everybody was afraid it was going to be. The companies were eager to get on peacetime production, so they did it with a minimum of layoffs and dislocations.

The workers felt they were in a good bargaining position, so they went after some more things. From that time on, we saw the kinds of modern contracts we see today: continual improvement in wages, fringe benefits like holidays, vacation, medical plans, dental plans, all sorts of things that provided more security for people.

One of the effects of this improved standard of living was to change the thinking of people. During the Depression people were radicalized. They were convinced of the need for social change, that the system as it was wasn't good enough. But with increased economic security people began to think more moderately. They developed a stake in the country. They had something they owned which they hadn't before, and the radical ideas which they had embraced during the Depression suddenly became very alien to them. Because of their new position in society, they wanted stability, not change, They had brought about just as much change as they needed at that time. They were content to leave it at that.

QUESTIONS

What changes did these individuals notice in postwar America? • How did their expectations change? • How did veterans' benefits influence their lives? • From the perspective of these individuals, how did the end of the war influence political attitudes?

DOCUMENT 4

A POW in Korea

During the fierce battles of the Korean War, many Americans were captured and taken to prisoner of war camps. In the camps, POWs often received political in-doctrination. Nick Tosques spent two and a half years in a POW camp, as he re-called in an interview, excerpted here. Tosques's experiences reveal that cold war battlefields extended from combat zones to beliefs.

Nick Tosques
Oral History

I was drafted the first time in 1946. In 1947, after I'd put in about thir-teen months, the army had a reduction in force and I was let go. Then, in July 1950, shortly after the Korean War broke out, a notice appeared in the newspapers saying that anybody drafted between 1945 and 1950 who had served less than thirteen months was subject to be redrafted. I had put in just under thirteen months, and sure enough, . . . I was called back in again.

I was sent straight over to Korea. . . . The 555th, they called it the Triple Nickles, had just been hit hard. They'd been overrun and lost a lot of men and a lot of their guns. . . .

At that time, early September of 1950, they were still fighting in the Pusan perimeter. There were fire missions every day, and I had to learn real fast. . . .

I learned how to load the gun, I learned how to fire it, and I learned everything fast, because if you didn't, you didn't survive. The North Ko-reans kept punching holes in our line, and many times we'd have to fire at point-blank range. . . . [A]fter the breakout from the Pusan perimeter we went up with them almost to the Yalu River.

Up at the Yalu the word was, "You'll be having your Christmas din-ner in Japan, and then it's back home to the States."

Next thing we knew, we were back below the 38th parallel. And the only people going home were the guys with serious wounds. The Chi-nese had come into the war, and Christ did we take a beating. I never saw so much stuff go up in smoke during that retreat. Tons and tons of C rations, ammunition, equipment, gasoline. Anything we couldn't carry back with us we burned.

After a couple of months we were back on the offensive. In April of 1951 I got picked to go on ten days R and R in Tokyo. . . .

Rudy Tomedi, *No Bugles, No Drums: An Oral History of the Korean War* (New York: John Wiley and Sons, Inc., 1993), 224–34.

I'm supposed to go home in two weeks. A couple days later the Chinese started their spring offensive. They decided they were going to push us back below the 38th parallel again.

I was still thinking, Well, I'm going home.

All we were doing now was firing and firing and firing. Day and night. In shifts. But we couldn't stop them.

On the afternoon of the twenty-fifth of April our CO came out to the gun positions and said, "Pack up and leave. We're getting the hell out of here."

Up ahead we could see the guys . . . leaving their positions. They were jumping on trucks and heading back toward us. We hitched up our guns and jumped on our own trucks and joined them on the road, but I don't think we went more than a mile when we ran into a roadblock. The Chinese had gotten in behind us and knocked out an American tank and put it across the road. Both sides of the road dropped off into rice paddies, so when we came to the roadblock we had to stop. And as soon as we stopped the Chinese opened up from the hills all around us.

Machine-gun fire. Mortar fire. Rifle fire. It poured in on us like rain. We unhooked our guns, swung them around, and fired pointblank open the breech block, aim down the barrel, ram the shell in, and fire. And hope you hit something.

Some of the Chinese moved in close enough to throw hand grenades. There were explosions going off all around my gun. Somebody yelled, "Nick, look up!" I looked up and I saw the grenade coming, and the last thing I remember is taking a flying leap.

Next thing I knew, it was night. I don't know how long I was out, but it had been daytime when I jumped away from that grenade. I remember pinching myself. I thought I might be dreaming. All around me are dead and wounded men. The trucks are on fire. I didn't know which way to go, so finally I got up. . . .

Up the road a little ways I ran into three or four guys. . . . They were huddled together along the road. . . . But no matter which way we tried to go, we would hear Chinese talking. Out in the dark ahead of us and all around us.

So finally I said, "Look, get rid of your rifles, lie down, and play dead."

But what the Chinese did was go around and stick all the bodies with bayonets. Not to kill the wounded, but to see if anybody was still alive. They knew that someday there was going to be peace talks, and they wanted as many prisoners as they could get. . . .

It wasn't until daybreak that I realized the fix I was in. It didn't sink in right away that I was a prisoner. . . .

On the first day they brought in an officer who spoke English, and the interrogations started. During basic training every soldier is told: If you're captured, you give only your name, rank, and serial number. But you can say that for only so long. You see some of the other guys getting hit in the back or the kidneys with a rifle butt, and hit hard, and you start thinking about what else you can say without really telling them anything.

This Chinese officer asked me, "What outfit?" I didn't tell him. But when he said, "Those trucks, and those big guns, were you with them?" I said, "Yeah."

Only that. "Yeah."

Then he asked me where I was from. I said Washington. I didn't say Washington D.C., or Washington State. Just Washington.

He didn't press me. I saw that if I just gave him an answer, he'd move on. It didn't have to be an exact answer, just so it looked like I was cooperating. There were a lot of interrogation sessions, but I don't think anybody actually told them very much.

Over the next couple of days other prisoners were brought in, and when we got to be a fairly large group they told us we were going north to a POW camp. . . .

The march north lasted around sixty days. I was captured on the twenty-fifth of April and it was toward the end of June when we got to . . . North Korea. . . .

Camp . . . turned out to be just a collection of old Korean mud huts and a few wooden buildings. There was no fence. After we were there a few days, during one of the lecture sessions when they would ask if there were any questions, somebody asked about that.

"Why isn't there a fence? Where's the barbed wire?" And the interpreter said, "We don't need barbed wire. Your faces are the barbed wire."

The first thing they did was break us up into small groups. Ten men were put into each little room. Not in each hut, but in each room. The rooms were about the size of a large closet. You couldn't move without touching somebody.

They took our clothes and gave us thin blue uniforms. We were all filthy, nobody had had a bath for two months, but we were not allowed to bathe. Everybody had body lice. They were in your hair, in your clothes, all over your body, and there was only one way to kill them: one at a time, between your thumbnails.

Right away the interrogations started. They interrogated us every day, and also at night. They'd take us out in groups, sometimes at two or three in the morning. You never knew when they were coming for you.

They found out, though not from me, that I was from Washington D.C., and then I was interrogated something awful. Hour after hour. What street is the White House on? Where is this building located? Where is that building located? Like it was a big military secret. You could get it from a guidebook, what they were asking. But I couldn't remember where everything was. I'd never paid that much attention to the streets these buildings were on. And when I couldn't answer, *whap*, I'd get hit with a rubber hose on the back of the neck.

Pretty soon I was telling them anything, just to keep from getting hit. That building's here, that other building's there. What the hell, how are they going to know? Well, somehow they found out I was making the stuff up. Whap. The rubber hose again. I guess it never occurred to them that I was telling the truth when I said I couldn't remember. I was from Washington D.C., and in their minds everybody from Washington was supposed to know where all the government buildings were. And also what the government was doing.

Then there were the lectures. We were given lectures every day. "You're capitalists. Your government lies to you. The rich people don't care about you, that's why they sent you over here to die. Your government makes war to oppress the Korean people." That kind of baloney.

We had to learn about communism. The only way to live. The only way to go. How under communism everyone is equal. We had to listen to that stuff every single day. . . .

The mornings were for hard labor. We'd be marched up into the hills to chop wood for them. All the huts were heated with firewood. We had to cut down the wood, chop it into sticks, and carry these big bundles of sticks down to the camp.

The afternoon was study time. We'd study about how Mao Tse-tung and his bunch got rid of Chiang Kai-shek and all the capitalists in China. How capitalism was no good. How the working man was exploited. How communism was the only way to go. And we had guys who turned. Who fell for that baloney. Not right away. But it was pounded and pounded and pounded into us. Every day. Every day. Capitalism no, communism yes.

Like most of the others, I went along with it. Yeah, yeah, yeah. You're right. You're right. But in the back of our minds all we're thinking about is home. About getting back, going to work, and buying what the hell we wanted.

After each study session we'd be sent back to our huts to discuss communism, but what we'd do, we'd put one guy on watch and the we'd talk about anything but communism. What kind of work did you do at home? What kind of car did you drive? Did you have any girlfriends?

But you couldn't completely ignore the lessons, because in the mass study sessions they would ask what you learned. What are you studying? Do you know how your government lies to you? That your Harry Truman lies. That he will never get you home.

There were times when I did lose hope of ever getting back. After a few months in the camp they told us that peace talks were starting. But nothing happened. . . .

After that happens three or four times, what are you going to believe? Months go by, a year, two years, and we're still there. Some guys didn't even believe there were any talks, that the Chinese were just playing with our minds.

A lot of guys got very depressed. A few even committed suicide. It got to be too much for them. They finally lost hope permanently, and when that happened you were a goner. . . .

I remember the first time they told us the war was over. We didn't believe it. They had to keep repeating it, because by this time we didn't trust anything they said.

QUESTIONS

How was Tosques captured and where was he taken? • What did his Chinese interrogators want to know? • How did they treat him? • What did they say in their lectures? • Did Tosques agree with the lectures? • What did Tosques and other POWs talk about?

COMPARATIVE QUESTIONS

How does George Kennan's view of Communists differ from Joseph McCarthy's? How do Kennan's views of the internal dangers of the cold war differ from those of McCarthy? How do McCarthy's views of America differ from those of returning veterans? Do Nick Tosques's experiences bear out McCarthy's and Kennan's views about the threat of communism? How were the views of the individuals in these documents shaped by World War II?

CHAPTER 27

THE POLITICS AND CULTURE OF ABUNDANCE
1952–1960

During the 1950s, Americans bought homes, refrigerators, cars, television sets, and other goods at an unprecedented pace. Americans could not seem to get enough of anything. Many worried that prosperity had a dark side that threatened to undermine traditional values. Yet in the climate of the cold war, raising questions about the role of women, the justice of segregation, or the cold war itself seemed subversive to many people. The numerous achievements of the nation during the 1950s seemed to be creating new, unsettling problems. The documents that follow illustrate Americans' often conflicting faith in both the new and the tried and true.

DOCUMENT 1
Adlai Stevenson Explains a Woman's Place

The prosperity of the 1950s made it possible for a home to be a castle in new ways, and most Americans assumed that each castle would have its queen. Adlai Stevenson, governor of Illinois and Democratic presidential candidate in 1952 and 1956, crystallized widely held views of the proper place for women in his commencement speech to the young women graduating from Smith College in 1955. Stevenson's remarks reflected the common notion that American women — even those with a college education — were destined to marry and have children.

Smith College Commencement Address, 1955

I think there is much you can do about our crisis in the humble role of housewife.

Adlai Stevenson, "A Purpose for Modern Woman," *Women's Home Companion* (September 1955); reprinted in *Major Problems in American History Since 1945: Documents and Essays,* ed. Robert Griffith (Lexington, MA: D.C. Heath and Co., 1992), 204–7.

The peoples of the West are still struggling with the problems of a free society and just now are in dire trouble. For to create a free society is at all times a precarious and audacious experiment. Its bedrock is the concept of man as an end in himself. But violent pressures are constantly battering away at this concept, reducing man once again to subordinate status, limiting his range of choice, abrogating his responsibility and returning him to his primitive status of anonymity in the social group. I think you can be more helpful in identifying, isolating and combatting these pressures, this virus, than you perhaps realize.

Let me put it this way: individualism has promoted technological advance, technology promoted increased specialization, and specialization promoted an ever closer economic interdependence between specialties.

As the old order disintegrated into this confederation of narrow specialties, each pulling in the direction of its particular interest, the individual person tended to become absorbed literally by his particular function in society. Having sacrificed wholeness of mind and breadth of outlook to the demands of their specialties, individuals no longer responded to social stimuli as total human beings; rather they reacted in partial ways as members of an economic class or industry or profession whose concern was with some limited self-interest.

Thus this typical Western man, or typical Western husband, operates well in the realm of means. . . . But outside his specialty, in the realm of ends, he is apt to operate poorly or not at all. And this neglect of the cultivation of more mature values can only mean that his life, and the life of the society he determines, will lack valid purpose, however busy and even profitable it may be.

And here's where you come in: to restore valid, meaningful purpose to life in your home; to beware of instinctive group reaction to the forces which play upon you and yours, to watch for and arrest the constant gravitational pulls to which we are all exposed — your workaday husband especially — in our specialized, fragmented society, that tend to widen the breach between reason and emotion, between means and ends.

And let me also remind you that you will live, most of you, in an environment in which "facts," the data of the senses, are glorified, and values — judgments — are assigned inferior status as mere "matters of opinion." It is an environment in which art is often regarded as an adornment of civilization rather than a vital element of it, while philosophy is not only neglected but deemed faintly disreputable because "it never gets you anywhere." Even religion, you will find, commands a lot of earnest allegiance that is more verbal than real, more formal than felt.

You may be hitched to one of these creatures we call "Western man" and I think part of your job is to keep him Western, to keep him truly purposeful, to keep him whole. In short — while I have had very little experience as a wife or mother — I think one of the biggest jobs for many of you will be to frustrate the crushing and corrupting effects of specialization, to integrate means and ends, to develop that balanced tension of mind and spirit which can be properly called "integrity."

This assignment for you, as wives and mothers, has great advantages. In the first place, it is home work—you can do it in the living-room with a baby in your lap or in the kitchen with a can opener in your hand. If you're really clever, maybe you can even practice your saving arts on that unsuspecting man while he's watching television!

And, secondly, it is important work worthy of you, whoever you are, or your education, whatever it is, because we will defeat totalitarian, authoritarian ideas only by better ideas; we will frustrate the evils of vocational specialization only by the virtues of intellectual generalization. Since Western rationalism and Eastern spiritualism met in Athens and that mighty creative fire broke out, collectivism in various forms has collided with individualism time and again. This twentieth-century collision, this "crisis" we are forever talking about, will be won at last not on the battlefield but in the head and heart.

So you see, I have some rather large notions about you and what you have to do to rescue us wretched slaves of specialization and group thinking from further shrinkage and contraction of mind and spirit. But you will have to be alert or you may get caught yourself—even in the kitchen or the nursery—by the steady pressures with which you will be surrounded. . . .

Women, especially educated women, have a unique opportunity to influence us, man and boy, and to play a direct part in the unfolding drama of our free society. But I am told that nowadays the young wife or mother is short of time for such subtle arts, that things are not what they used to be; that once immersed in the very pressing and particular problems of domesticity, many women feel frustrated and far apart from the great issues and stirring debates for which their education has given them understanding and relish. Once they read Baudelaire. Now it is the Consumers' Guide. Once they wrote poetry. Now it's the laundry list. Once they discussed art and philosophy until late in the night. Now they are so tired they fall asleep as soon as the dishes are finished. There is, often, a sense of contraction, of closing horizons and lost opportunities. They had hoped to play their part in the crisis of the age. But what they do is wash the diapers. (Or do they any longer?)

Now I hope I have not painted too depressing a view of your future, for the fact is that Western marriage and motherhood are yet another instance of the emergence of individual freedom in our Western society. Their basis is the recognition in women as well as men of the primacy of personality and individuality. I have just returned from sub-Sahara Africa where the illiteracy of the African mother is a formidable obstacle to the education and advancement of her child and where polygamy and female labor are still the dominant system.

The point is that whether we talk of Africa, Islam or Asia, women "never had it so good" as you do. And in spite of the difficulties of domesticity, you have a way to participate actively in the crisis in addition to keeping yourself and those about you straight on the difference between means and ends, mind and spirit, reason and emotion—not to mention keeping your man straight on the differences between Botticelli and Chianti. . . .

In modern America the home is not the boundary of a woman's life. There are outside activities aplenty. But even more important is the fact, surely, that what you have learned and can learn will fit you for the primary task of making homes and whole human beings in whom the rational values of freedom, tolerance, charity and free inquiry can take root.

QUESTIONS

According to Stevenson, what problems did the West face? • Were these problems only for men? • What did Stevenson believe women should do about these problems? • Why, according to Stevenson, did women have a unique opportunity? • According to Stevenson, how were women different from men? • What reactions might this speech have ellicited from the graduating women?

DOCUMENT 2

Allen Ginsberg's "America"

The complacency of the 1950s that many Americans embraced stultified others. In his poem "America," Beat poet Allen Ginsberg expressed rage at the hypocrisy, blindness, and greed of the 1950s. Ginsberg's poem, written in Berkeley, California, on January 17, 1956, put into words the undercurrent of dissatisfaction that spread far beyond the Beats.

"America," January 17, 1956

America I've given you all and now I'm nothing.
America two dollars and twentyseven cents January 17, 1956.
1 can't stand my own mind.
America when will we end the human war?
Go fuck yourself with your atom bomb.
I don't feel good don't bother me.
I won't write my poem till I'm in my right mind.
America when will you be angelic?

Allen Ginsberg, "America," in *Collected Poems, 1947–1980* (New York: Harper and Row, 1984), 146–48.

When will you take off your clothes?
When will you look at yourself through the grave?
When will you be worthy of your million Trotskyites?
America why are your libraries full of tears?
America when will you send your eggs to India?
I'm sick of your insane demands.
When can I go into the supermarket and buy what I need with my good
    looks?
America after all it is you and I who are perfect not the next world.
Your machinery is too much for me.
You made me want to be a saint.
There must be some other way to settle this argument.
Burroughs is in Tangiers I don't think he'll come back it's sinister.
Are you being sinister or is this some form of practical joke?
I'm trying to come to the point.
I refuse to give up my obsession.
America stop pushing I know what I'm doing.
America the plum blossoms are falling.
I haven't read the newspapers for months, everyday somebody goes on trial
    for murder.
America I feel sentimental about the Wobblies.
America I used to be a communist when I was a kid I'm not sorry.
I smoke marijuana every chance I get.
I sit in my house for days on end and stare at the roses in the closet.
When I go to Chinatown I get drunk and never get laid.
My mind is made up there's going to be trouble.
You should have seen me reading Marx.
My psychoanalyst thinks I'm perfectly right.
I won't say the Lord's Prayer.
I have mystical visions and cosmic vibrations.
America I still haven't told you what you did to Uncle Max after he came
    over from Russia.
I'm addressing you.
Are you going to let your emotional life be run by Time Magazine?
I'm obsessed by Time Magazine.
I read it every week.
Its cover stares at me every time I slink past the corner candystore.
I read it in the basement of the Berkeley Public Library.
It's always telling me about responsibility. Businessmen are serious.
    Movie producers are serious. Everybody's serious but me.
It occurs to me that I am America.
I am talking to myself again.

Asia is rising against me.
I haven't got a chinaman's chance.
I'd better consider my national resources.
My national resources consist of two joints of marijuana millions of genitals
    an unpublishable private literature that jetplanes 1400 miles an hour
    and twentyfive-thousand mental institutions.

I say nothing about my prisons nor the millions of underprivileged who live
   in my flowerpots under the light of five hundred suns.
I have abolished the whorehouses of France, Tangiers is the next to go.
My ambition is to be President despite the fact that I'm a Catholic.

America how can I write a holy litany in your silly mood?
I will continue like Henry Ford my strophes are as individual as his automo-
   biles more so they're all different sexes.
America I will sell you strophes $2500 apiece $500 down on your old strophe
America free Tom Mooney
America save the Spanish Loyalists
America Sacco & Vanzetti must not die
America I am the Scottsboro boys.
America when I was seven momma took me to Communist Cell meetings
   they sold us garbanzos a handful per ticket a ticket costs a nickel and
   the speeches were free everybody was angelic and sentimental about
   the workers it was all so sincere you have no idea what a good thing
   the party was in 1935 Scott Nearing was a grand old man a real
   mensch Mother Bloor the Silk-strikers' Ewig-Weibliche made me cry
   I once saw the Yiddish orator Israel Amter plain. Everybody must
   have been a spy.
America you don't really want to go to war.
America it's them bad Russians.
Them Russians them Russians and them Chinamen. And them Russians.
The Russia wants to eat us alive. The Russia's power mad. She wants to take
   our cars from out our garages.
Her wants to grab Chicago. Her needs a Red *Reader's Digest.* Her wants our
   auto plants in Siberia. Him big bureaucracy running our fillingsta-
   tions.
That no good. Ugh. Him make Indians learn read. Him need big black
   niggers. Hah. Her make us all work sixteen hours a day. Help.
America this is quite serious.
America this is the impression I get from looking in the television set.
America is this correct?
I'd better get right down to the job.
It's true I don't want to join the Army or turn lathes in precision parts
   factories, I'm nearsighted and psychopathic anyway.
America I'm putting my queer shoulder to the wheel.

QUESTIONS

What did Ginsberg criticize about America? • How, according to the
poet, did Time Magazine run America's emotional life? • What did
Ginsburg identify as the nation's resources? • What affection did Ginsberg express for America? • What impression did television give about
Russians and Chinese? • How was Ginsberg going to "get right down
to the job"?

Rosa Parks Says "No": A Memoir

Racial segregation was the rule rather than the exception during the 1950s in the southern states, where the great majority of black Americans lived. Outside the South, Jim Crow laws were less common, but racial prejudice and discrimination were widespread. In Montgomery, Alabama, on December 1, 1955, Rosa Parks refused to leave her seat in a segregated bus, setting off what became a full-scale, nationwide assault on Jim Crow laws. Parks described her experience in her memoir, excerpted here.

Rosa Parks: My Story

I don't think any segregation law angered black people in Montgomery more than bus segregation. . . . Here it was, half a century after the first segregation law, and there were 50,000 African Americans in Montgomery. More of us rode the buses than Caucasians did, because more whites could afford cars. It was very humiliating having to suffer the indignity of riding segregated buses twice a day, five days a week, to go downtown and work for white people.

There were incidents all the time. Mrs. [Virginia] Durr [a white woman] says that I would tell her about them time and time again. Mr. [E. D.] Nixon [a black community leader] used to try to negotiate some small changes. I know Mr. Nixon said that at some point he went to the bus company about black people having to pay at the front door and then go around to the back door to enter. They told him, "Your folks started it. They do it because they want to."

Another time he went to see about extending the route of the Day Street bus. Black people in a little community on the other side of the Day Street Bridge had to walk across the bridge, about half a mile, to get to the bus. Mr. Nixon went down to the bus company to protest. He was always going down to the bus company to protest; sometimes he went by himself, sometimes he took someone with him. He himself did not ride the buses—he had his own car; but he was acting on behalf of the community. The bus company told him that as long as the people were willing to walk the half mile and then pay to ride the rest of the way downtown, they had no need to extend the bus line.

Jo Ann Robinson [a black woman] was an English professor at Alabama State College. Back in 1946 she had helped found the Women's Political Council. Over the years she'd had her share of run-ins with bus drivers, but at first she couldn't get the other women in the Council to get indignant. She was from Cleveland, Ohio, and most of them were natives of

Rosa Parks, *Rosa Parks: My Story* (New York: Dial Books, 1992).

Montgomery. When she complained about the rudeness of the bus drivers, they said that was a fact of life in Montgomery. She had often brought protests to the bus company on behalf of the Women's Political Council. Finally she managed to get the company to agree that the buses would stop at every corner in black neighborhoods, just as they did in the white neighborhoods. But this was a very small victory.

What galled her, and many more of us, was that blacks were over sixty-six percent of the riders. It was unfair to segregate us. But neither the bus company nor the mayor nor the city commissioners would listen. I remember having discussions about how a boycott of the city buses would really hurt the bus company in its pocketbook. But I also remember asking a few people if they would be willing to stay off the buses to make things better for us, and them saying that they had too far to go to work. So it didn't seem as if there would be much support for a boycott. The Montgomery NAACP was beginning to think about filing suit against the city of Montgomery over bus segregation. But they had to have the right plaintiff and a strong case. The best plaintiff would be a woman, because a woman would get more sympathy than a man. And the woman would have to be above reproach, have a good reputation, and have done nothing wrong but refuse to give up her seat. . . .

I was in on the discussions about the possible court cases. But that is not why I refused to give up my bus seat to a white man on Thursday, December 1, 1955. 1 did not intend to get arrested. If I had been paying attention, I wouldn't even have gotten on that bus.

I was very busy at that particular time. I was getting an NAACP workshop together for the 3rd and 4th of December, and I was trying to get the consent of Mr. H. Council Trenholm at Alabama State to have the Saturday meeting at the college. He did give permission, but I had a hard time getting to him to get permission to use the building. I was also getting the notices in the mail for the election of officers of the Senior Branch of the NAACP, which would be the next week.

When I got off from work that evening of December 1, I went to Court Square as usual to catch the Cleveland Avenue bus home. I didn't look to see who was driving when I got on, and by the time I recognized him, I had already paid my fare. It was the same driver who had put me off the bus back in 1943, twelve years earlier. He was still tall and heavy, with red, rough-looking skin. And he was still mean-looking. I didn't know if he had been on that route before—they switched the drivers around sometimes. I do know that most of the time if I saw him on a bus, I wouldn't get on it.

I saw a vacant seat in the middle section of the bus and took it. I didn't even question why there was a vacant seat even though there were quite a few people standing in the back. If I had thought about it at all, I would probably have figured maybe someone saw me get on and did not take the seat but left it vacant for me. There was a man sitting next to the window and two women across the aisle.

The next stop was the Empire Theater, and some whites got on. They filled up the white seats, and one man was left standing. The driver looked back and noticed the man standing. Then he looked back at us. He said, "Let me have those front seats," because they were the front seats of the black section. Didn't anybody move. We just sat right where we were, the four of us. Then he spoke a second time: "Y'all better make it light on yourselves and let me have those seats."

The man in the window seat next to me stood up, and I moved to let him pass by me, and then I looked across the aisle and saw that the two women were also standing. I moved over to the window seat. I could not see how standing up was going to "make it light" for me. The more we gave in and complied, the worse they treated us.

I thought back to the time when I used to sit up all night and didn't sleep, and my grandfather would have his gun right by the fireplace, or if he had his one-horse wagon going anywhere, he always had his gun in the back of the wagon. People always say that I didn't give up my seat because I was tired, but that isn't true. I was not tired physically, or no more tired than I usually was at the end of a working day. I was not old, although some people have an image of me as being old then. I was forty-two. No, the only tired I was, was tired of giving in.

The driver of the bus saw me still sitting there, and he asked was I going to stand up. I said, "No." He said, "Well, I'm going to have you arrested." Then I said, "You may do that." These were the only words we said to each other. I didn't even know his name, which was James Blake, until we were in court together. He got out of the bus and stayed outside for a few minutes, waiting for the police.

As I sat there, I tried not to think about what might happen. I knew that anything was possible. I could be manhandled or beaten. I could be arrested. People have asked me if it occurred to me then that I could be the test case the NAACP had been looking for. I did not think about that at all. In fact if I had let myself think too deeply about what might happen to me, I might have gotten off the bus. But I chose to remain.

Meanwhile there were people getting off the bus and asking for transfers, so that began to loosen up the crowd, especially in the back of the bus. Not everyone got off, but everybody was very quiet. What conversation there was, was in low tones; no one was talking out loud. It would have been quite interesting to have seen the whole bus empty out. Or if the other three had stayed where they were, because if they'd had to arrest four of us instead of one, then that would have given me a little support. But it didn't matter. I never thought hard of them at all and never even bothered to criticize them.

Eventually two policemen came. They got on the bus, and one of them asked me why I didn't stand up. I asked him, "Why do you all push us around?" He said to me, and I quote him exactly, "I don't know, but the law is the law and you're under arrest." One policeman picked up my purse, and the second one picked up my shopping bag and escorted me to the squad car. . . .

I wasn't frightened at the jail. I was more resigned than anything else. I don't recall being real angry, not enough to have an argument. I was just prepared to accept whatever I had to face. I asked again if I could make a telephone call. I was ignored. . . .

I called home. My husband [Parks] and mother were both there. She answered the telephone. I said, "I'm in jail. See if Parks will come down here and get me out."

She wanted to know, "Did they beat you?"

I said, "No, I wasn't beaten, but I am in jail."

She handed him the telephone, and I said, "Parks, will you come get me out of jail?"

He said, "I'll be there in a few minutes." He didn't have a car, so I knew it would be longer. . . .

[T]he word was already out about my arrest. Mr. Nixon had been notified by his wife, who was told by a neighbor Bertha Butler, who had seen me escorted off the bus. Mr. Nixon called the jail to find out what the charge was, but they wouldn't tell him. Then he had tried to reach Fred Gray, one of the two black lawyers in Montgomery, but he wasn't home. So finally Mr. Nixon called Clifford Durr, the white lawyer who was Mrs. Virginia Durr's husband. Mr. Durr called the jail and found out that I'd been arrested under the segregation laws. He also found out what the bail was. . . .

Mrs. Durr was the first person I saw as I came through the iron mesh door with matrons on either side of me. There were tears in her eyes, and she seemed shaken, probably wondering what they had done to me. As soon as they released me, she put her arms around me, and hugged and kissed me as if we were sisters.

I was real glad to see Mr. Nixon and Attorney Durr too. We went to the desk, where I picked up my personal belongings and was given a trial date. Mr. Nixon asked that the date be the following Monday, December 5, 1955, explaining that he was a Pullman porter and would be out of Montgomery until then. We left without very much conversation, but it was an emotional moment. I didn't realize how much being in jail had upset me until I got out. . . .

Everyone was angry about what had happened to me and talking about how it should never happen again. I knew that I would never, never ride another segregated bus, even if I had to walk to work. But it still had not occurred to me that mine could be a test case against the segregated buses.

Then Mr. Nixon asked if I would be willing to make my case a test case against segregation. I told him I'd have to talk with my mother and husband. Parks was pretty angry. He thought it would be . . . difficult to get people to support me as a test case. . . . We discussed and debated the question for a while. In the end Parks and my mother supported the idea. They were against segregation and were willing to fight it. And I had worked on enough cases to know that a ruling could not be made without a plaintiff. So I agreed to be the plaintiff.

Mr. Nixon was happy as could be when I told him yes. I don't recall exactly what he said, but according to him, he said, "My God, look what segregation has put in my hands." What he meant by that was that I was a perfect plaintiff. "Rosa Parks worked with me for twelve years prior to this," he would tell reporters later. "She was secretary for everything I had going—the Brotherhood of Sleeping Car Porters, NAACP, Alabama Voters' League, all of those things. I knew she'd stand on her feet. She was honest, she was clean, she had integrity. The press couldn't go out and dig up something she did last year, or last month, or five years ago. They couldn't hang nothing like that on Rosa Parks."

I had no police record, I'd worked all my life, I wasn't pregnant with an illegitimate child. The white people couldn't point to me and say that there was anything I had done to deserve such treatment except to be born black.

QUESTIONS

What did Rosa Parks think about segregation? • Was she the only black person in Montgomery who protested segregation? • Why did she say "No"? • Did all white people in Montgomery favor segregation? • Why was Mr. Nixon "as happy as he could be"?

DOCUMENT 4

President Dwight D. Eisenhower's Farewell Address

After eight years as president and a lifetime of service at the highest levels of the U.S. military, Dwight D. Eisenhower delivered his farewell address on nationwide television. In his address, excerpted here, Eisenhower surveyed American achievements during the 1950s and identified threats posed by those achievements. His assessment suggests the qualms that, for many Americans, mingled with confidence about the future.

Farewell Address, January 1961

This evening I come to you with a message of leave-taking and farewell, and to share a few final thoughts with you, my countrymen.

Public Papers of the Presidents of the United States : Dwight D. Eisenhower, 1960–61 (1961); reprinted in *American Military Thought,* ed. Walter Millis (Indianapolis: Bobbs-Merrill, 1966), 508–14.

Like every other citizen, I wish the new President, and all who will labor with him, Godspeed. I pray that the coming years will be blessed with peace and prosperity for all. . . .

We now stand ten years past the midpoint of a century that has witnessed four major wars among great nations. Three of these involved our own country. Despite these holocausts America is today the strongest, the most influential and most productive nation in the world. Understandably proud of this pre-eminence, we yet realize that America's leadership and prestige depend, not merely upon our unmatched material progress, riches and military strength, but on how we use our power in the interests of world peace and human betterment.

Throughout America's adventure in free government, our basic purposes have been to keep the peace; to foster progress in human achievement, and to enhance liberty, dignity and integrity among people and among nations. To strive for less would be unworthy of a free and religious people. Any failure traceable to arrogance, or for lack of comprehension or readiness to sacrifice would inflict upon us grievous hurt both at home and abroad.

Progress toward these noble goals is persistently threatened by the conflict now engulfing the world. It commands our whole attention, absorbs our very beings. We face a hostile ideology global in scope, atheistic in character, ruthless in purpose, and insidious in method. Unhappily the danger it poses promises to be of indefinite duration. To meet it successfully, there is called for, not so much the emotional and transitory sacrifices of crisis, but rather those which enable us to carry forward steadily, surely, and without complaint the burdens of a prolonged and complex struggle—with liberty the stake. Only thus shall we remain, despite every provocation, on our charted course toward permanent peace and human betterment.

Crises there will continue to be. In meeting them, whether foreign or domestic, great or small, there is a recurring temptation to feel that some spectacular and costly action could become the miraculous solution to all current difficulties. A huge increase in newer elements of our defense; development of unrealistic programs to cure every ill in agriculture; a dramatic expansion in basic and applied research—these and many other possibilities, each possibly promising in itself, may be suggested as the only way to the road we wish to travel.

But each proposal must be weighed in the light of a broader consideration: the need to maintain balance in and among national programs—balance between the private and the public economy, balance between cost and hoped for advantage—balance between the clearly necessary and the comfortably desirable; balance between our essential requirements as a nation and the duties imposed by the nation upon the individual; balance between actions of the moment and the national welfare of the future. Good judgment seeks balance and progress; lack of it eventually finds imbalance and frustration.

The record of many decades stands as proof that our people and their government have, in the main, understood these truths and have responded to them well, in the face of stress and threat. But threats, new in kind or degree, constantly arise. I mention two only.

A vital element in keeping the peace is our military establishment. Our arms must be mighty, ready for instant action, so that no potential aggressor may be tempted to risk his own destruction.

Our military organization today bears little relation to that known by any of my predecessors in peacetime, or indeed by the fighting men of World War II or Korea. Until the latest of our world conflicts, the United States had no armaments industry. American makers of plowshares could, with time and as required, make swords as well. But now we can no longer risk emergency improvisation of national defense; we have been compelled to create a permanent armaments industry of vast proportions. Added to this, three and a half million men and women are directly engaged in the defense establishment. We annually spend on military security more than the net income of all United States corporations.

This conjunction of an immense military establishment and a large arms industry is new in the American experience. The total influence — economic, political, even spiritual — is felt in every city, every State house, every office of the Federal government. We recognize the imperative need for this development. Yet we must not fail to comprehend its grave implications. Our toil, resources and livelihood are all involved; so is the very structure of our society.

In the councils of government, we must guard against the acquisition of unwarranted influence, whether sought or unsought, by the military-industrial complex. The potential for the disastrous rise of misplaced power exists and will persist.

We must never let the weight of this combination endanger our liberties or democratic processes. We should take nothing for granted. Only an alert and knowledgeable citizenry can compel the proper meshing of the huge industrial and military machinery of defense with our peaceful methods and goals, so that security and liberty may prosper together.

Akin to, and largely responsible for the sweeping changes in our industrial-military posture, has been the technological revolution during recent decades.

In this revolution, research has become central; it also becomes more formalized, complex, and costly. A steadily increasing share is conducted for, by, or at the direction of, the Federal government.

Today, the solitary inventor, tinkering in his shop, has been overshadowed by task forces of scientists in laboratories and testing fields. In the same fashion, the free university, historically the fountainhead of free ideas and scientific discovery, has experienced a revolution in the conduct of research. Partly because of the huge costs involved, a government contract becomes virtually a substitute for intellectual curiosity. For every old blackboard there are now hundreds of new electronic computers.

The prospect of domination of the nation's scholars by Federal employment, project allocations, and the power of money is ever present— and is gravely to be regarded.

Yet, in holding scientific research and discovery in respect, as we should, we must also be alert to the equal and opposite danger that public policy could itself become the captive of a scientific-technological elite.

It is the task of statesmanship to mold, to balance, and to integrate these and other forces, new and old, within the principles of our democratic system—ever aiming toward the supreme goals of our free society.

Another factor in maintaining balance involves the element of time. As we peer into society's future, we—you and I, and our government— must avoid the impulse to live only for today, plundering, for our own ease and convenience, the precious resources of tomorrow. We cannot mortgage the material assets of our grandchildren without risking the loss also of their political and spiritual heritage. We want democracy to survive for all generations to come, not to become the insolvent phantom of tomorrow.

Down the long lane of the history yet to be written America knows that this world of ours, ever growing smaller, must avoid becoming a community of dreadful fear and hate, and be, instead, a proud confederation of mutual trust and respect.

Such a confederation must be one of equals. The weakest must come to the conference table with the same confidence as do we, protected as we are by our moral, economic, and military strength. That table, though scarred by many past frustrations, cannot be abandoned for the certain agony of the battlefield. Disarmament, with mutual honor and confidence, is a continuing imperative. Together we must learn how to compose differences, not with arms, but with intellect and decent purpose. Because this need is so sharp and apparent I confess that I lay down my official responsibilities in this field with a definite sense of disappointment. As one who has witnessed the horror and the lingering sadness of war—as one who knows that another war could utterly destroy this civilization which has been so slowly and painfully built over thousands of years—I wish I could say tonight that a lasting peace is in sight.

Happily, I can say that war has been avoided. Steady progress toward our ultimate goal has been made. But, so much remains to be done. As a private citizen, I shall never cease to do what little I can to help the world advance along that road.

So—in this my last night to you as your President—thank you for the many opportunities you have given me for public service in war and peace. I trust that in that service you find some things worthy; as for the rest of it, I know you will find ways to improve performance in the future.

You and I—my fellow citizens—need to be strong in our faith that all nations, under God, will reach the goal of peace with justice. May we be ever unswerving in devotion to principle, confident but humble with power, diligent in pursuit of the Nation's great goals.

To all the peoples of the world, I once more give expression to America's prayerful and continuing aspiration:

We pray that peoples of all faiths, all races, all nations, may have their great human needs satisfied; that those now denied opportunity shall come to enjoy it to the full; that all who yearn for freedom may experience its spiritual blessings; that those who have freedom will understand, also, its heavy responsibilities; that all who are insensitive to the needs of others will learn charity; that the scourges of poverty, disease and ignorance will be made to disappear from the earth, and that, in the goodness of time, all peoples will come to live together in a peace guaranteed by the binding force of mutual respect and love.

QUESTIONS

What did Eisenhower identify as basic American goals and what was required to achieve those goals? • What did he see as the dangers to be avoided? • Why did he consider balance to be essential? • What was his view of "the military-industrial complex"? • What dangers did technology pose? • What disappointment did he express? • Do you think his concerns are relevant in the 1990s? • Why or why not?

COMPARATIVE QUESTIONS

How do Adlai Stevenson's notions about the proper activities for women compare with Rosa Parks's ideas and experiences? How do Stevenson's views about the promise of America compare with Parks's, Allen Ginsberg's, and Dwight D. Eisenhower's? Compare Eisenhower's warnings about the dangers faced by America with Ginsberg's and Parks's. How did the era's relative economic abundance shape the ideas and experiences of the individuals described in these documents?

CHAPTER 28

A DECADE OF REBELLION AND REFORM
1960–1968

D uring the 1960s, many Americans sought to make changes that many other Americans resisted. To those who wanted change, the times seemed right and the causes just. Presidents sympathetic to change occupied the Oval Office, civil rights demonstrators confronted Jim Crow laws, black power advocates called for racial pride and revolution, and women's rights leaders outlined proposals for gender equality. The possibilities for change seemed extraordinary. The widespread sense that the American dream could be more fully realized is revealed in the following documents.

DOCUMENT 1
President Lyndon B. Johnson Describes the Great Society

During the 1960s, both President John F. Kennedy and President Lyndon B. Johnson tended to see government as an agent of change. Both presidents believed the government should take an active role in creating a better society. In 1964 President Johnson outlined his plans for the Great Society in a speech to students at the University of Michigan. Johnson's speech, excerpted here, illustrates the confidence many Americans had in the powers of government.

Address at the University of Michigan, May 22, 1964

I have come today from the turmoil of your Capital to the tranquility of your campus to speak about the future of your country.

Public Papers of the Presidents of the United States: Lyndon B. Johnson, 1963–65 (1965); reprinted in *Recent America: The United States Since 1945,* by Dewey W. Grantham (Wheeling, IL: Harlan Davidson, 1987), 422–25.

The purpose of protecting the life of our Nation and preserving the liberty of our citizens is to pursue the happiness of our people. Our success in that pursuit is the test of our success as a Nation.

For a century we labored to settle and to subdue a continent. For half a century we called upon unbounded invention and untiring industry to create an order of plenty for all of our people.

The challenge of the next half century is whether we have the wisdom to use that wealth to enrich and elevate our national life, and to advance the quality of our American civilization.

Your imagination, your initiative, and your indignation will determine whether we build a society where progress is the servant of our needs, or a society where old values and new visions are buried under unbridled growth. For in your time we have the opportunity to move not only toward the rich society and the powerful society, but upward to the Great Society.

The Great Society rests on abundance and liberty for all. It demands an end to poverty and racial injustice, to which we are totally committed in our time. But that is just the beginning.

The Great Society is a place where every child can find knowledge to enrich his mind and to enlarge his talents. It is a place where leisure is a welcome chance to build and reflect, not a feared cause of boredom and restlessness. It is a place where the city of man serves not only the needs of the body and the demands of commerce but the desire for beauty and the hunger for community.

It is a place where man can renew contact with nature. It is a place which honors creation for its own sake and for what it adds to the understanding of the race. It is a place where men are more concerned with the quality of their goals than the quantity of their goods.

But most of all, the Great Society is not a safe harbor, a resting place, a final objective, a finished work. It is a challenge constantly renewed, beckoning us toward a destiny where the meaning of our lives matches the marvelous products of our labor.

So I want to talk to you today about three places where we begin to build the Great Society—in our cities, in our countryside, and in our classrooms.

Many of you will live to see the day, perhaps 50 years from now, when there will be 400 million Americans—four-fifths of them in urban areas. In the remainder of this century urban population will double, city land will double, and we will have to build homes highways, and facilities equal to all those built since this country was first settled. So in the next 40 years we must rebuild the entire urban United States.

Aristotle said: "Men come together in cities in order to live, but they remain together in order to live the good life." It is harder and harder to live the good life in American cities today.

The catalog of ills is long: there is the decay of the centers and the despoiling of the suburbs. There is not enough housing for our people or transportation for our traffic. Open land is vanishing and old landmarks are violated.

Worst of all expansion is eroding the precious and time honored values of community with neighbors and communion with nature. The loss of these values breeds loneliness and boredom and indifference.

Our society will never be great until our cities are great. Today the frontier of imagination and innovation is inside those cities and not beyond their borders.

New experiments are already going on. It will be the task of your generation to make the American city a place where future generations will come, not only to live but to live the good life. . . .

A second place where we begin to build the Great Society is in our countryside. We have always prided ourselves on being not only America the strong and America the free, but America the beautiful. Today that beauty is in danger. The water we drink, the food we eat, the very air that we breathe, are threatened with pollution. Our parks are overcrowded, our seashores overburdened. Green fields and dense forests are disappearing,

A few years ago we were greatly concerned about the "Ugly American." Today we must act to prevent an ugly America.

For once the battle is lost, once our natural splendor is destroyed, it can never be recaptured. And once man can no longer walk with beauty or wonder at nature his spirit will wither and his sustenance be wasted.

A third place to build the Great Society is in the classrooms of America. There your children's lives will be shaped. Our society will not be great until every young mind is set free to scan the farthest reaches of thought and imagination. We are still far from that goal.

Today, 8 million adult Americans, more than the entire population of Michigan, have not finished 5 years of school. Nearly 20 million have not finished 8 years of school. Nearly 54 million—more than one-quarter of all America—have not even finished high school.

Each year more than 100,000 high school graduates, with proved ability, do not enter college because they cannot afford it. . . .

In many places, classrooms are overcrowded and curricula are outdated. Most of our qualified teachers are underpaid, and many of our paid teachers are unqualified. So we must give every child a place to sit and a teacher to learn from. Poverty must not be a bar to learning, and learning must offer an escape from poverty.

But more classrooms and more teachers are not enough. We must seek an educational system which grows in excellence as it grows in size. This means better training for our teachers. It means preparing youth to enjoy their hours of leisure as well as their hours of labor. It means exploring new techniques of teaching, to find new ways to stimulate the love of learning and the capacity for creation.

These are three of the central issues of the Great Society. While our Government has many programs directed at those issues, I do not pretend that we have the full answer to those problems.

But I do promise this: We are going to assemble the best thought and the broadest knowledge from all over the world to find those answers for America. I intend to establish working groups to prepare a series of White House conferences and meetings—on the cities, on natural beauty, on the quality of education, and on other emerging challenges. And from these meetings and from this inspiration and from these studies we will begin to set our course toward the Great Society.

The solution to these problems does not rest on a massive program in Washington, nor can it rely solely on the strained resources of local authority. They require us to create new concepts of cooperation, a creative federalism, between the National Capital and the leaders of local communities. . . .

For better or for worse, your generation has been appointed by history to deal with those problems and to lead America toward a new age. You have the chance never before afforded to any people in any age. You can help build a society where the demands of morality, and the needs of the spirit, can be realized in the life of the Nation.

So, will you join in the battle to give every citizen the full equality which God enjoins and the law requires, whatever his belief, or race, or the color of his skin?

Will you join in the battle to give every citizen an escape from the crushing weight of poverty?

Will you join in the battle to make it possible for all nations to have in enduring peace—as neighbors and not as mortal enemies?

Will you join in the battle to build the Great Society, to prove that our material progress is only the foundation on which we will build a richer life of mind and spirit?

There are those timid souls who say this battle cannot be won; that we are condemned to a soulless wealth. I do not agree. We have the power to shape the civilization that we want. But we need your will, your labor, your hearts, if we are to build that kind of society.

Those who came to this land sought to build more than just a new country. They sought a new world. So I have come here today to your campus to say that you can make their vision our reality. So let us from this moment begin our work so that in the future men will look back and say: It was then, after a long and weary way, that man turned the exploits of his genius to the full enrichment of his life.

QUESTIONS

What did Johnson identify as the challenge of the next half-century? • What were the goals of the Great Society? • In what ways were they different from the past? • How could the Great Society be realized, according to Johnson? • What did he identify as the source of the power to shape civilization?

DOCUMENT 2

Martin Luther King Jr. Explains
Nonviolent Resistance

The civil rights demonstrations that swept across the South during the 1960s employed tactics of nonviolent resistance. Many white Americans, North and South, condemned the demonstrators as extremists and law-breakers whose ends may have been admirable but whose means were deplorable. Martin Luther King Jr. responded to those views in 1963 in a letter he wrote while in jail in Birmingham, Alabama, where he had been arrested for participating in demonstrations. King's letter, excerpted here, was directed to a group of white clergymen who had criticized the Birmingham demonstrations. King's letter set forth the ideals of nonviolence embraced by many civil rights activists.

"Letter from Birmingham Jail," 1963

My dear Fellow Clergymen,

While confined here in the Birmingham city jail, I came across your recent statement calling our present activities "unwise and untimely.". . . [S]ince I feel that you are men of genuine good will and your criticisms are sincerely set forth, I would like to answer your statement in what I hope will be patient and reasonable terms.

I think I should give the reason for my being in Birmingham, since you have been influenced by the argument of "outsiders coming in." I have the honor of serving as president of the Southern Christian Leadership Conference, an organization operating in every southern state, with headquarters in Atlanta, Georgia. We have some eighty-five affiliate organizations all across the South. . . . Several months ago our local affiliate here in Birmingham invited us to be on call to engage in a nonviolent direct-action program if such were deemed necessary. . . .

Beyond this, I am in Birmingham because injustice is here. . . . I cannot sit idly by in Atlanta and not be concerned about what happens in Birmingham. Injustice anywhere is a threat to justice everywhere. . . .

You deplore the demonstrations that are presently taking place in Birmingham. But I am sorry that your statement did not express a similar concern for the conditions that brought the demonstrations into being. . . .

Birmingham is probably the most thoroughly segregated city in the United States. Its ugly record of police brutality is known in every section of this country. Its injust treatment of Negroes in the courts is a noto-

Martin Luther King Jr., "Letter from Birmingham City Jail," in *Why We Can't Wait* (1963); reprinted in *Major Problems in the History of the American South,* ed. Paul D. Escott and David R. Goldfield (Lexington, MA: D.C. Heath and Co., 1990), 544–57.

rious reality. There have been more unsolved bombings of Negro homes and churches in Birmingham than any city in this nation. These are the hard, brutal and unbelievable facts. . . .

You may well ask, "Why direct action? Why sit-ins, marches, etc.? Isn't negotiation a better path?" You are exactly right in your call for negotiation. Indeed, this is the purpose of direct action. Nonviolent direct action seeks to create such a crisis and establish such creative tension that a community that has constantly refused to negotiate is forced to confront the issue. It seeks so to dramatize the issue that it can no longer be ignored. . . . So the purpose of the direct action is to create a situation so crisis-packed that it will inevitably open the door to negotiation. . . .

One of the basic points in your statement is that our acts are untimely. . . . My friends, I must say to you that we have not made a single gain in civil rights without determined legal and nonviolent pressure. History is the long and tragic story of the fact that privileged groups seldom give up their privileges voluntarily. . . .

We know through painful experience that freedom is never voluntarily given by the oppressor; it must be demanded by the oppressed. Frankly, I have never yet engaged in a direct action movement that was "well-timed," according to the timetable of those who have not suffered unduly from the disease of segregation. For years now I have heard the words "Wait!" It rings in the ear of every Negro with a piercing familiarity. This "Wait" has almost always meant "Never." . . . We have waited for more than 340 years for our constitutional and God-given rights. The nations of Asia and Africa are moving with jetlike speed toward the goal of political independence, and we still creep at horse and buggy pace toward the gaining of a cup of coffee at a lunch counter. I guess it is easy for those who have never felt the stinging darts of segregation to say, "Wait." But when you have seen vicious mobs lynch your mothers and fathers at will and drown your sisters and brothers at whim; when you have seen hate-filled policemen curse, kick, brutalize and even kill your black brothers and sisters with impunity; when you see the vast majority of your twenty million Negro brothers smothering in an airtight cage of poverty in the midst of an affluent society; when you suddenly find your tongue twisted and your speech stammering as you seek to explain to your six-year-old daughter why she can't go to the public amusement park that has just been advertised on television, and see tears welling up in her little eyes when she is told that Funtown is closed to colored children, and see the depressing clouds of inferiority begin to form in her little mental sky, and see her begin to distort her little personality by unconsciously developing a bitterness toward white people; when you have to concoct an answer for a five-year-old son asking in agonizing pathos: "Daddy, why do white people treat colored people so mean?"; when you take a cross-country drive and find it necessary to sleep night after night in the uncomfortable corners of your automobile because no motel will accept you; when you are humiliated day in and day out by nagging signs reading "white" and "colored"; when your first name becomes "nigger" and your middle name becomes "boy" (however old you are) and your last name becomes "John," and when your wife and mother are never given the respected title "Mrs."; when you are harried by day and haunted by night by the fact that you are a Negro, living constantly at tiptoe stance never quite knowing what to expect next, and plagued with inner fears and outer resentments; when you are forever fighting a degenerating sense of "nobodiness"; then you will understand why we find it difficult to wait. There comes a time when the cup of endurance runs over, and men are no longer willing to be plunged into an abyss of injustice where they experience the blackness of corroding despair. I hope, sirs, you can understand our legitimate and unavoidable impatience.

You express a great deal of anxiety over our willingness to break laws. This is certainly a legitimate concern. Since we so diligently urge people to obey the Supreme Court's decision of 1954 outlawing segregation in the public schools, it is rather strange and paradoxical to find us consciously breaking laws. One may well ask, "How can you advocate breaking some laws and obeying others?" The answer is found in the fact that there are two types of laws: there are *just* and there are *unjust* laws. I would agree with Saint Augustine that "An unjust law is no law at all."

Now what is the difference between the two? How does one determine when a law is just or unjust? A just law is a man-made code that squares with the moral law or the law of God. An unjust law is a code that is out of harmony with the moral law. To put it in the terms of Saint Thomas Aquinas, an unjust law is a human law that is not rooted in eternal and natural law. Any law that uplifts human personality is just. Any law that degrades human personality is unjust. All segregation statutes are unjust because segregation distorts the soul and damages the personality. It gives the segregator a false sense of superiority, and the segregated a false sense of inferiority. . . . So segregation is not only politically, economically and sociologically unsound, but it is morally wrong and sinful. . . . So I can urge men to disobey segregation ordinances because they are morally wrong. . . .

I hope you can see the distinction I am trying to point out. In no sense do I advocate evading or defying the law as the rabid segregationist would do. This would lead to anarchy. One who breaks an unjust law must do it *openly, lovingly* . . . and with a willingness to accept the penalty. I submit that an individual who breaks a law that conscience tells him is unjust, and willingly accepts the penalty by staying in jail to arouse the conscience of the community over its injustice, is in reality expressing the very highest respect for law.

Of course, there is nothing new about this kind of civil disobedience. . . . It was practiced superbly by the early Christians who were willing to face hungry lions and the excruciating pain of chopping blocks, before submitting to certain unjust laws of the Roman Empire. . . .

I must make two honest confessions to you, my Christian and Jewish brothers. First, I must confess that over the last few years I have been gravely disappointed with the white moderate. I have almost reached the regrettable conclusion that the Negro's great stumbling block in the stride toward freedom is not the White Citizen's Counciler or the Ku Klux Klanner, but the white moderate who is more devoted to order than to justice; who prefers a negative peace which is the absence of tension to a positive peace which is the presence of justice; who constantly says, "I agree with you in the goal you seek, but I can't agree with your methods of direct action"; who paternalistically feels that he can set the timetable for another man's freedom; who lives by the myth of time and who constantly advised the Negro to wait until a "more convenient season." Shallow understanding from people of good will is more frustrating than absolute misunderstanding from people of ill will. Lukewarm acceptance is much more bewildering than outright rejection.

I had hoped that the white moderate would understand that law and order exist for the purpose of establishing justice, and that when they fail to do this they become dangerously structured dams that block the flow of social progress. I had hoped that the white moderate would understand that the present tension of the South is merely a necessary phase of the transition from an obnoxious negative peace, where the Negro passively accepted his unjust plight, to a substance-filled positive peace, where all men will respect the dignity and worth of human personality. Actually, we who engage in nonviolent direct action are not the creators of tension. We merely bring to the surface the hidden tension that is already alive. We bring it out in the open where it can be seen and dealt with. . . .

In your statement you asserted that our actions, even though peaceful, must be condemned because they precipitate violence. But can this assertion be logically made? Isn't this like condemning the robbed man because his possession of money precipitated the evil act of robbery? . . .

You spoke of our activity in Birmingham as extreme. At first I was rather disappointed that fellow clergymen would see my nonviolent efforts as those of the extremist. I started thinking about the fact that I stand in the middle of two opposing forces in the Negro community. One is a force of complacency made up of Negroes who, as a result of long years of oppression, have been so completely drained of self-respect and a sense of "somebodiness" that they have adjusted to segregation, and, of a few Negroes in the middle class who, because of a degree of academic and economic security, and because at points they profit by segregation, have unconsciously become insensitive to the problems of the masses. The other force is one of bitterness and hatred, and comes perilously close to advocating violence. It is expressed in the various black nationalist groups that are springing up over the nation, the largest and best known being Elijah Muhammad's Muslim movement. This movement is nourished by the contemporary frustration over the continued existence of racial discrimination. It is made up of people who have lost faith in America, who have absolutely repudiated Christianity, and who have concluded that the white man is an incurable "devil." I have tried to stand between these two forces, saying that we need not follow the "do-nothingism" of the complacent or the hatred and despair of the black nationalist. There is the more excellent way of love and nonviolent protest. I'm grateful to God that, through the Negro church, the dimension of nonviolence entered our struggle. If this philosophy had not emerged, I am convinced that by now many streets of the South would be flowing with floods of blood. And I am further convinced that if our white brothers dismiss us as "rabble-rousers" and "outside agitators" those of us who are working through the channels of nonviolent direct action and refuse to support our nonviolent efforts, millions of Negroes, out of frustration and despair, will seek solace and security in black nationalist ideologies, a development that will lead inevitably to a frightening racial nightmare.

Oppressed people cannot remain oppressed forever. The urge for freedom will eventually come. This is what happened to the American Negro. . . .

But as I continued to think about the matter I gradually gained a bit of satisfaction from being considered an extremist. Was not Jesus an extremist in love—"Love your enemies, bless them that curse you, pray for them that despitefully use you.". . .Was not Abraham Lincoln an extremist—"This nation cannot survive half slave and half free." Was not Thomas Jefferson an extremist—"We hold these truths to be self-evident, that all men are created equal." So the question is not whether we will be extremist but what kind of extremist will we be. Will we be extremists for hate or will we be extremists for love? Will we be extremists for the preservation of injustice—or will we be extremists for the cause of justice?. . .

But before closing I am impelled to mention one other point in your statement that troubled me profoundly. You warmly commended the Birmingham police force for keeping "order" and "preventing violence." I don't believe you would have so warmly commended the police force if you had seen its angry violent dogs literally biting six unarmed, nonviolent Negroes. I don't believe you would so quickly commend the policemen if you would observe their ugly and inhuman treatment of Negroes here in the city jail; if you would watch them push and curse old Negro women and young Negro girls; if you would see them slap and kick old Negro men and young boys; if you will observe them, as they did on two occasions, refuse to give us food because we wanted to sing our grace together. I'm sorry that I can't join you in your praise for the police department. . . .

I wish you had commended the Negro sit-inners and demonstrators of Birmingham for their sublime courage, their willingness to suffer and their amazing discipline in the midst of the most inhuman provocation. One day the South will recognize its real heroes. They will be the James

Merediths[1], courageously and with a majestic sense of purpose facing jeering and hostile mobs and the agonizing loneliness that characterizes the life of the pioneer. They will be old, oppressed, battered Negro women, symbolized in a seventy-two-year-old woman of Montgomery, Alabama, who rose up with a sense of dignity and with her people decided not to ride the segregated buses, and responded to one who inquired about her tiredness with ungrammatical profundity: "My feet is tired, but my soul is rested." They will be the young high school and college students, young ministers of the gospel and a host of their elders courageously and non-violently sitting-in at lunch counters and willingly going to jail for conscience's sake. One day the South will know that when these disinherited children of God sat down at lunch counters they were in reality standing up for the best in the American dream and the most sacred values in our Judeo-Christian heritage, and thusly, carrying our whole nation back to those great wells of democracy which were dug deep by the Founding Fathers in the formulation of the Constitution and the Declaration of Independence.

QUESTIONS

According to King, what was the purpose of direct action? • Did he believe it was a good time to engage in direct action? • How did King describe segregation as affecting black Americans? • Why did he advocate breaking some laws and obeying others? • How did white moderates disappoint King? • What historical and religious examples did King invoke in his letter to the clergymen? • Where did King position himself and those who supported nonviolent tactics and direct action on the spectrum of black society?

DOCUMENT 3

Black Power

To some activists, the doctrines of nonviolence seemed self-defeating and dangerous. The violence that civil rights demonstrators repeatedly suffered convinced many younger activists that the strength of white racism made racial integration hopeless. In 1967 the Chicago office of the Student Non-Violent Coordinating Committee (SNCC) published a manifesto calling for black power. The SNCC leaflet, excerpted here, embodied ideas that appealed to many African Americans in the later 1960s.

---

[1]**James Meredith:** The first black student to attend the University of Mississippi, Meredith had to be escorted by U.S. marshalls to protect him from a rioting mob of segregationists in 1962.

Chicago Student Non-Violent Coordinating Committee Leaflet, 1967

Black men of America are a captive people

The black man in America is in a perpetual state of slavery no matter what the white man's propaganda tells us.

The black man in America is exploited and oppressed the same as his black brothers are all over the face of the earth by the same white man. . . .

We are not alone in this fight, we are a part of the struggle for self-determination of all black men everywhere. We here in America must unite ourselves to be ready to help our brothers elsewhere.

We must first gain BLACK POWER here in America. Living inside the camp of the leaders of the enemy forces, it is our duty to our Brothers to revolt against the system and create our own system so that we can live as MEN.

We must take over the political and economic systems where we are in the majority in the heart of every major city in this country as well as in the rural areas. We must create our own black culture to erase the lies the white man has fed our minds from the day we were born.

The black man in the ghetto will lead the Black Power Movement

The black Brother in the ghetto will lead the Black Power Movement and make the changes that are necessary for its success.

The black man in the ghetto has one big advantage that the bourgeois Negro does not have despite his "superior" education. He is already living outside the value system white society imposes on all black Americans.

He has to look at things from another direction in order to survive. He is ready. He received his training in the streets, in the jails, from the ADC[1] check his mother did not receive in time and the head-beatings he got from the cop on the corner.

Once he makes that first important discovery about the great pride you feel inside as a BLACK MAN and the great heritage of the mother country, Africa, there is no stopping him from dedicating himself to fight the white man's system.

This is why the Black Power Movement is a true revolutionary movement with the power to change men's minds and unmask the tricks the white man has used to keep black men enslaved in modern society.

Chicago Office of SNCC, *We Want Black Power* (1967); reprinted in *Black Protest Thought in the Twentieth Century,* ed. August Meier, Elliott Rudwick, and Frances L. Broderick, 2d ed. (Indianapolis: Bobbs-Merrill, 1971), 484–90.

[1]**ADC:** Aid to Families with Dependent Children.

The bourgeois Negro cannot be a part of the Black Power Movement

The bourgeois Negro has been force-fed the white man's propaganda and has lived too long in the half-world between white and phony black bourgeois society. He cannot think for himself because be is a shell of a man full of contradictions he cannot resolve. He is not to be trusted under any circumstances until he has proved himself to be "cured." There are a minute handful of these "cured" bourgeois Negroes in the Black Power Movement and they are most valuable but they must not be allowed to take control. They are aware intellectually but under stress will react emotionally to the pressures of white society in the same way a white "liberal" will expose an unconscious prejudice that he did not even realize he possessed.

What Brother Malcolm X taught us about ourselves

Malcolm X was the first black man from the ghetto in America to make a real attempt to get the white man's fist off the black man. He recognized the true dignity of man—without the white society prejudices about status, education and background that we all must purge from our minds.

Even today, in the Black Power Movement itself we find Brothers who look down on another Brother because of the conditions that life has imposed upon him. The most beautiful thing that Malcolm X taught us is that once a black man discovers for himself a pride of his blackness, he can throw off the shackles of mental slavery and become a MAN in the truest sense of the word. We must move on from the point our Great Black Prince had reached.

We must become leaders for ourselves

We must not get hung-up in the bag of having one great leader who we depend upon to make decisions. This makes the Movement too vulnerable to those forces the white man uses to keep us enslaved, such as the draft, murder, prison or character assassination.

We have to all learn to become leaders for ourselves and remove all white values from our minds. When we see a Brother using a white value through error it is our duty to the Movement to point it out to him. We must thank our Brothers who show us our own errors. We must discipline ourselves so that if necessary we can leave family and friends at a moment's notice, maybe forever, and know our Brothers have pledged themselves to protect the family we have left behind.

As a part of our education, we must travel to other cities and make contracts with the Brothers in all the ghettos in America so that when the time is right we can unite as one under the banner of BLACK POWER.

Learning to think Black and remove white things from our minds

We have got to begin to say and understand with complete assuredness what black is. Black is an inner pride that the white man's language hampers us from expressing. Black is being a complete fanatic, who white society considers insane. We have to learn that black is so much better than belonging to the white race with the blood of millions dripping from their hands that it goes far beyond any prejudice or resentment. We must fill ourselves with hate for all white things. This is not vengeance or trying to take the white oppressors' place to become new black oppressors but is a oneness with a worldwide black brotherhood.

We must regain respect for the lost religion of our fathers, the spirits of the black earth of Africa. The white man has so poisoned our minds that if a Brother told you he practiced Voodoo you would roll around on the floor laughing at how stupid and superstitious be was.

We have to learn to roll around on the floor laughing at the black man who says he worships the white Jesus. He is truly sick.

We must create our own language for these things that the white man will not understand because a Black Culture exists and it is not the woodcarvings or native dancing it is the black strength inside of true men.

Ideas on planning for the future of Black Power

We must infiltrate all government agencies. This will not be hard because black clerks work in all agencies in poor paying jobs and have a natural resentment of the white men who run these jobs.

People must be assigned to seek out these dissatisfied black men and women and put pressure on them to give us the information we need. Any man in overalls, carrying a tool box, can enter a building if he looks like he knows what he is doing.

Modern America depends on many complex systems such as electricity, water, gas, sewerage and transportation and all are vulnerable. Much of the government is run by computers that must operate in air conditioning. Cut off the air conditioning and they cannot function.

We must begin to investigate and learn all of these things so that we can use them if it becomes necessary. We cannot train an army in the local park but we can be ready for the final confrontation with the white man's system.

Remember your Brothers in South Africa and do not delude yourselves that it could not happen here. We must copy the white man's biggest trick, diversion, (Hitler taught them that) and infiltrate all civil rights groups, keep them in confusion so they will be neutralized and cannot be used as a tool of the white power structure.

The civil rights, integrationist movement says to the white man, "If you please, Sir, let us, the 10 percent minority of American have our rights. See how nice and nonviolent we are?"

This is why SNCC calls itself a Human Rights Organization. We believe that we belong to the 90 percent majority of the people on earth that the white man oppresses and that we should not beg the white man for anything. We want what belongs to us as human beings and we intend to get it through BLACK POWER.

How to deal with black traitors

Uncle Tom is too kind of a word. What we have are black traitors, quisslings, collaborators, sell-outs, white Negroes.

We have to expose these people for once and for all for what they are and place them on the side of the oppressor where they belong. Their black skin is a lie and their guilt the shame of all black men. We must ostracize them and if necessary exterminate them.

We must stop fighting a "fair game." We must do whatever is necessary to win BLACK POWER. We have to hate and disrupt and destroy and blackmail and lie and steal and become blood-brothers like the Mau-Mau[2].

We must eliminate or render ineffective all traitors. We must make them fear to stand up like puppets for the white men, and we must make the world understand that these so-called men do not represent us or even belong to the same black race because they sold out their birthright for a mess of white society pottage. Let them choke on it.

Pitfalls to avoid on the path to Black Power

We must learn how close America and Russia are politically. The biggest lie in the world is the cold-war. Money runs the world and it is controlled completely by the white man.

Russia and America run the two biggest money systems in the world and they intend to keep it under their control under any circumstances. Thus, we cannot except any help from Communism or any other "ism."

We must seek out poor peoples movements in South America, Africa and Asia and make our alliances with them. We must not be fooled into thinking that there is a ready-made doctrine that will solve all our problems.

There are only white man's doctrines and they will never work for us. We have to work out our own systems and doctrines and culture.

Why propaganda is our most important tool

The one thing that the white man's system cannot stand is the TRUTH because his system is all based on lies.

---

[2]**Mau-Mau:** A revolutionary tribal society in Kenya in the 1950s that engaged in terrorism in an effort to rid the country of Europeans.

There is no such thing as "justice" for a black man in America. The white man controls everything that is said in every book, newspaper, magazine, TV and radio broadcast.

Even the textbooks used in the schools and the bible that is read in the churches are designed to maintain the system for the white man. Each and every one of us is forced to listen to the white man's propaganda every day of our lives.

The political system, economic system, military system, educational system, religious system and anything else you name is used to preserve the status quo of white America getting fatter and fatter while the black man gets more and more hungry.

We must spend our time telling our Brothers the truth.

We must tell them that any black woman who wears a diamond on her finger is wearing the blood of her Brothers and Sisters in slavery in South Africa where one out of every three black babies die before the age of one, from starvation, to make the white man rich.

We must stop wearing the symbols of slavery on our fingers.

We must stop going to other countries to exterminate our Brothers and Sisters for the white man's greed.

We must ask our Brothers which side they are on.

Once you know the truth for yourself it is your duty to dedicate your life to recruiting your Brothers and to counteract the white man's propaganda.

We must disrupt the white man's system to create our own, We must publish newspapers and get radio stations. Black Unity is strength—let's use it now to get BLACK POWER.

QUESTIONS

According to this Chicago SNCC leaflet, what were the sources of strength for Black Power? • Who was the Great Black Prince, and what did he teach? • Who were the enemies of Black Power? • Why was it necessary to be "a complete fanatic"? • What "white thing" should be hated? • What tactics would bring about Black Power?

DOCUMENT 4

Equal Rights for Women

Justice and equality for women had far-reaching implications for social change. In 1966, the newly formed National Organization for Women adopted a statement of purpose—excerpted here—that identified the changes demanded by women's rights activists. The statement, drafted by feminist leader Betty Friedan, revealed the concerns of many American women in the 1960s.

National Organization for Women Statement of Purpose, October 29, 1966

We, men and women who hereby constitute ourselves as the National Organization for Women, believe that the time has come for a new movement toward true equality for all women in America, and toward a fully equal partnership of the sexes, as part of the world-wide revolution of human rights now taking place within and beyond our national borders.

The purpose of NOW is to take action to bring women into full participation in the mainstream of American society now, exercising all the privileges and responsibilities thereof in truly equal partnership with men.

We believe the time has come to move beyond the abstract argument, discussion and symposia over the status and special nature of women which has raged in America in recent years; the time has come to confront, with concrete action, the conditions that now prevent women from enjoying the equality of opportunity and freedom of choice which is their right as individual Americans, and as human beings.

NOW is dedicated to the proposition that women first and foremost are human beings, who, like all other people in our society, must have the chance to develop their fullest human potential. We believe that women can achieve such equality only by accepting to the full the challenges and responsibilities they share with all other people in our society, as part of the decision-making mainstream of American political, economic and social life.

We organize to initiate or support action, nationally or in any part of this nation, by individuals or organizations, to break through the silken curtain of prejudice and discrimination against women in government, industry, the professions, the churches, the political parties, the judiciary, the labor unions, in education, science, medicine, law, religion and every other field of importance in American society.

Enormous changes taking place in our society make it both possible and urgently necessary to advance the unfinished revolution of women toward true equality, now. With life span lengthened to nearly seventy-five years it is no longer either necessary or possible for women to devote the greater part of their lives to child-rearing; yet childbearing and rearing—which continues to be a most important part of most women's lives—still is used to justify barring women from equal professional and economic participation and advance.

Today's technology has reduced most of the productive chores which women once performed in the home and in mass-production industries based upon routine unskilled labor. This same technology has virtually

National Organization for Women Statement of Purpose; reprinted in Betty Friedan, *It Changed My Life: Writings on the Women's Movement* (New York: Random House, 1976), 96–102.

eliminated the quality of muscular strength as a criterion for filling most jobs, while intensifying America's need for creative intelligence. In view of this new industrial revolution created by automation in the mid-twentieth century, women can and must participate in old and new fields of society in full equality — or become permanent outsiders. . . .

There is no civil rights movement to speak for women, as there has been for Negroes and other victims of discrimination. The National Organization for Women must therefore begin to speak.

WE BELIEVE that the power of American law, and the protection guaranteed by the U.S. Constitution to the civil rights of all individuals, must be effectively applied and enforced to isolate and remove patterns of sex discrimination, to ensure equality of opportunity in employment and education, and equality of civil and political rights and responsibilities on behalf of women, as well as for Negroes and other deprived groups.

We realize that women's problems are linked to many broader questions of social justice; their solution will require concerted action by many groups. Therefore, convinced that human rights for all are indivisible, we expect to give active support to the common cause of equal rights for all those who suffer discrimination and deprivation, and we call upon other organizations committed to such goals to support our efforts toward equality for women.

WE DO NOT ACCEPT the token appointment of a few women to high-level positions in government and industry as a substitute for a serious continuing effort to recruit and advance women according to their individual abilities. To this end, we urge American government and industry to mobilize the same resources of ingenuity and command with which they have solved problems of far greater difficulty than those now impeding the progress of women.

WE BELIEVE that this nation has a capacity at least as great as other nations, to innovate new social institutions which will enable women to enjoy true equality of opportunity and responsibility in society, without conflict with their responsibilities as mothers and homemakers. In such innovations, America does not lead the Western world, but lags by decades behind many European countries. We do not accept the traditional assumption that a woman has to choose between marriage and motherhood, on the one hand, and serious participation in industry or the professions on the other. We question the present expectation that all normal women will retire from job or profession for ten or fifteen years, to devote their full time to raising children, only to reenter the job market at a relatively minor level. This in itself is a deterrent to the aspirations of women, to their acceptance into management or professional training courses, and to the very possibility of equality of opportunity or real choice, for all but a few women. Above all, we reject the assumption that these problems are the unique responsibility of each individual woman, rather than a basic social dilemma which society must solve. True equality of opportunity and freedom of choice for women requires such practical and possible innovations as a nationwide network of child-care centers, which will make it unnecessary for women to retire completely from society until their children are grown, and national programs to provide retraining for women who have chosen to care for their own children full time.

WE BELIEVE that it is as essential for every girl to be educated to her full potential of human ability as it is for every boy—with the knowledge that such education is the key to effective participation in today's economy and that, for a girl as for a boy, education can only be serious where there is expectation that it will be used in society. We believe that American educators are capable of devising means of imparting such expectations to girl students. Moreover, we consider the decline in the proportion of women receiving higher and professional education to be evidence of discrimination. This discrimination may take the form of quotas against the admission of women to colleges and professional schools; lack of encouragement by parents, counselors and educators; denial of loans or fellowships; or the traditional or arbitrary procedures in graduate and professional training geared in terms of men, which inadvertently discriminate against women. We believe that the same serious attention must be given to high school dropouts who are girls as to boys.

WE REJECT the current assumptions that a man must carry the sole burden of supporting himself, his wife, and family, and that a woman is automatically entitled to lifelong support by a man upon her marriage, or that marriage, home and family are primarily woman's world and responsibility—hers, to dominate, his to support. We believe that a true partnership between the sexes demands a different concept of marriage, an equitable sharing of the responsibilities of home and children and of the economic burdens of their support. We believe that proper recognition should be given to the economic and social value of homemaking and child care. To these ends, we will seek to open a reexamination of laws and mores governing marriage and divorce, for we believe that the current state of "half-equality" between the sexes discriminates against both men and women, and is the cause of much unnecessary hostility between the sexes.

WE BELIEVE that women must now exercise their political rights and responsibilities as American citizens. They must refuse to be segregated on the basis of sex into separate-and-not-equal ladies' auxiliaries in the political parties, and they must demand representation according to their numbers in the regularly constituted party committees—at local, state, and national levels—and in the informal power structure, participating fully in the selection of candidates and political decision-making, and running for office themselves.

IN THE INTERESTS OF THE HUMAN DIGNITY OF WOMEN, we will protest and endeavor to change the false image of women now prevalent in the mass media, and in the texts, ceremonies, laws, and practices of our major social institutions. Such images perpetuate contempt for women by society and by women for themselves. We are similarly opposed to all policies and practices—in church, state, college, factory, or office—which, in the guise of protectiveness, not only deny opportunities but also foster in women self-denigration, dependence, and evasion of responsibility, undermine their confidence in their own abilities and foster contempt for women.

NOW WILL HOLD ITSELF INDEPENDENT OF ANY POLITICAL PARTY in order to mobilize the political power of all women and men intent on our goals. We will strive to ensure that no party, candidate, President, senator, governor, congressman, or any public official who betrays or ignores the principle of full equality between the sexes is elected or appointed to office. If it is necessary to mobilize the votes of men and women who believe in our cause, in order to win for women the final right to be fully free and equal human beings, we so commit ourselves.

WE BELIEVE THAT women will do most to create a new image of women by acting now, and by speaking out in behalf of their own equality, freedom, and human dignity—not in pleas for special privilege, nor in enmity toward men, who are also victims of the current half-equality between the sexes—but in an active, self-respecting partnership with men. By so doing, women will develop confidence in their own ability to determine actively, in partnership with men, the conditions of their life, their choices, their future and their society.

QUESTIONS

What were the goals of NOW? • What was the "silken curtain"? • What social changes permitted advancing the "unfinished revolution"? • What changes did NOW seek? • What should women do? • Who did NOW consider allies? • Who were its opponents?

COMPARATIVE QUESTIONS

How do Lyndon Johnson's aspirations for the Great Society compare with the goals of Martin Luther King Jr., the Chicago SNCC, and the National Organization for Women? What are the differences between the Black Power movement's ideas and those of King? How do the tactics advocated by Johnson, King, SNCC, and NOW differ?

CHAPTER 29

VIETNAM AND THE LIMITS OF POWER
1961–1975

The war in Vietnam began almost unnoticed by most Americans, but by the mid-1960s it had become the dominating fact of American political life. American views of the war conflicted profoundly. Policy makers tried to devise a military strategy that would also win political support for the war effort. Generals grappled with the complexities of a guerrilla conflict. Officers struggled with maintaining military discipline in an unpopular war. Soldiers encountered the horrifying realities of combat. The following documents illustrate the vantage points of the secretary of defense and the commanding general in Vietnam, as well as of officers and soldiers in the field.

DOCUMENT 1
A Secret Government Assessment of the Vietnam War

Policy makers in Washington, D.C., directed the military operations of the Vietnam War more closely than any previous war in American history. Advanced technology made it possible for politicians and generals to communicate readily and to gather and analyze vast quantities of information. The political sensitivity of the war made that communication necessary. In October 1966, Secretary of Defense Robert S. McNamara drafted a secret memorandum for President Lyndon B. Johnson about the current status of the war in Vietnam. McNamara's memorandum, excerpted here, expressed the misgivings of one of the most influential political managers of the war—misgivings that remained confined to secret documents until the leaking of and subsequent publication of The Pentagon Papers in 1971.

Robert S. McNamara
"Actions Recommended for Vietnam," October 14, 1966

1. Evaluation of the situation. In the report of my last trip to Vietnam almost a year ago, I stated that the odds were about even that, even with the then-recommended deployments, we would be faced in early 1967 with a military stand-off at a much higher level of conflict and with "pacification" still stalled. I am a little less pessimistic now in one respect. We have done somewhat better militarily than I anticipated. We have by and large blunted the communist military initiative—any military victory in South Vietnam the Viet Cong [VC] may have had in mind 18 months ago has been thwarted by our emergency deployments and actions. And our program of bombing the North has exacted a price.

My concern continues, however, in other respects. This is because I see no reasonable way to bring the war to an end soon. Enemy morale has not broken—he apparently has adjusted to our stopping his drive for military victory and has adopted a strategy of keeping us busy and waiting us out (a strategy of attriting our national will). He knows that we have not been, and he believes we probably will not be, able to translate our military successes into the "end products"—broken enemy morale and political achievements by the GVN [government of Vietnam].

The one thing demonstrably going for us in Vietnam over the past year has been the large number of enemy killed-in-action resulting from the big military operations. Allowing for possible exaggeration in reports, the enemy must be taking losses—deaths in and after battle—at the rate of more than 60,000 a year. The infiltration routes would seem to be one-way trails to death for the North Vietnamese. Yet there is no sign of an impending break in enemy morale and it appears that he can more than replace his losses by infiltration from North Vietnam and recruitment in South Vietnam.

Pacification is a bad disappointment. We have good grounds to be pleased by the recent elections, by Ky's 16 months in power, and by the faint signs of development of national political institutions and of a legitimate civil government. But none of this has translated itself into political achievements at Province level or below. Pacification has if anything gone backward. As compared with two, or four, years ago, enemy full-time regional forces and part-time guerrilla forces are larger; attacks, terrorism and sabotage have increased in scope and intensity; more railroads are closed and highways cut; the rice crop expected to come to market is smaller; we control little, if any, more of the population; the VC political

Robert S. McNamara, "Actions Recommended for Vietnam," October 14, 1966; reprinted in *The Pentagon Papers,* ed. George C. Herring (New York: McGraw Hill, 1971), 554–62.

infrastructure thrives in most of the country, continuing to give the enemy his enormous intelligence advantage; full security exists nowhere (now even behind the U.S. Marines' lines and in Saigon); in the countryside, the enemy almost completely controls the night.

Nor has the ROLLING THUNDER program of bombing the North either significantly affected infiltration or cracked the morale of Hanoi. There is agreement in the intelligence community on these facts. . . .

In essence, we find ourselves . . . no better, and if anything worse off. This important war must be fought and won by the Vietnamese themselves. We have known this from the beginning. But the discouraging truth is that, as was the case in 1961 and 1963 and 1965, we have not found the formula, the catalyst, for training and inspiring them into effective action.

2. Recommended actions.   In such an unpromising state of affairs, what should we do? We must continue to press the enemy militarily; we must make demonstrable progress in pacification; at the same time, we must add a new ingredient forced on us by the facts. Specifically, we must improve our position by getting ourselves into a military posture that we credibly would maintain indefinitely — a posture that makes trying to "wait us out" less attractive. I recommend a five-pronged course of action to achieve those ends.

   a. Stabilize U.S. force-levels in Vietnam.   It is my judgment that, barring a dramatic change in the war, we should limit the increase in U.S. forces . . . in 1967 to 70,000 men and we should level off at the total of 470,000. . . . It is my view that this is enough to punish the enemy at the large-unit operations level and to keep the enemy's main forces from interrupting pacification. I believe also that even many more than 470,000 would not kill the enemy off in such numbers as to break their morale so long as they think they can wait us out. It is possible that such a 40 percent increase over our present level of 325,000 will break the enemy's morale in the short term; but if it does not, we must, I believe, be prepared for and have underway a long-term program premised on more than breaking the morale of main force units. A stabilized U.S. force level would be part of such a long-term program. It would put us in a position where negotiations would be more likely to be productive, but if they were not we could pursue the all-important pacification task with proper attention and resources and without the spectre of apparently endless escalation of U.S. deployments.

   b. Install a barrier.   A portion of the 470,000 troops — perhaps 10,000 to 20,000 — should be devoted to the construction and maintenance of an infiltration barrier. Such a barrier would lie near the 17th parallel — would run from the sea, across the neck of South Vietnam (choking off the new infiltration routes through the DMZ) and across the trails in Laos. . . .

   c. Stabilize the ROLLING THUNDER program against the North.
Attack sorties in North Vietnam have risen from about 4,000 per month

at the end of last year to 6,000 per month in the first quarter of this year and 12,000 per month at present. Most of our 50 percent increase of deployed attack-capable aircraft has been absorbed in the attacks on North Vietnam. In North Vietnam, almost 84,000 attack sorties have been flown (about 25 percent against fixed targets), 45 percent during the past seven months.

Despite these efforts, it now appears that the North Vietnamese-Laotian road network will remain adequate to meet the requirements of the Communist forces in South Vietnam—this is so even if its capacity could be reduced by one-third and if combat activities were to be doubled. North Vietnam's serious need for trucks, spare parts and petroleum probably can, despite air attacks, be met by imports. The petroleum requirement for trucks involved in the infiltration movement, for example, has not been enough to present significant supply problems, and the effects of the attacks on the petroleum distribution system, while they have not yet been fully assessed, are not expected to cripple the flow of essential supplies. Furthermore, it is clear that, to bomb the North sufficiently to make a radical impact upon Hanoi's political, economic and social structure, would require an effort which we could make but which would not be stomached either by our own people or by world opinion; and it would involve a serious risk of drawing us into open war with China. . . .

At the proper time . . . I believe we should consider terminating bombing in all of North Vietnam, or at least in the Northeast zones, for an indefinite period in connection with covert moves toward peace.

d. Pursue a vigorous pacification program. As mentioned above, the pacification (Revolutionary Development) program has been and is thoroughly stalled. The large-unit operations war, which we know best how to fight and where we have had our successes, is largely irrelevant to pacification as long as we do not lose it. By and large, the people in rural areas believe that the GVN when it comes will not stay but that the VC will; that cooperations with the GVN will be punished by the VC; that the GVN is really indifferent to the people's welfare; that the low-level GVN are tools of the local rich; and that the GVN is ridden with corruption.

Success in pacification depends on the interrelated functions of providing physical security, destroying the VC apparatus, motivating the people to cooperate and establishing responsive local government. An obviously necessary but not sufficient requirement for success of the Revolutionary Development cadre and police is vigorously conducted and adequately prolonged clearing operations by military troops, who will "stay" in the area, who behave themselves decently and who show some respect for the people.

This elemental requirement of pacification has been missing.

In almost no contested area designated for pacification in recent years have ARVN [Army of the Republic of Vietnam] forces actually "cleared and stayed" to a point where cadre teams, if available, could have stayed overnight in hamlets and survived, let alone accomplish their mission.

VC units of company and even battalion size remain in operation, and they are more than large enough to overrun anything the local security forces can put up.

Now that the threat of a Communist main-force military victory has been thwarted by our emergency efforts, we must allocate far more attention and a portion of the regular military forces (at least half of the ARVN and perhaps a portion of the U.S. forces) to the task of providing an active and permanent security screen behind which the Revolutionary Development teams and police can operate and behind which the political struggle with the VC infrastructure can take place.

The U.S. cannot do this pacification security job for the Vietnamese. All we can do is "Massage the heart." For one reason, it is known that we do not intend to stay; if our efforts worked at all, it would merely postpone the eventual confrontation of the VC and GVN infrastructures. The GVN must do the job; and I am convinced that drastic reform is needed if the GVN is going to be able to do it.

The first essential reform is in the attitude of GVN officials. They are generally apathetic, and there is corruption high and low. Often appointments, promotions, and draft deferments must be bought; and kickbacks on salaries are common. Cadre at the bottom can be no better than the system above them.

The second needed reform is in the attitude and conduct of the ARVN. The image of the government cannot improve unless and until the ARVN improves markedly. They do not understand the importance (or respectability) of pacification nor the importance to pacification of proper, disciplined conduct. Promotions, assignments and awards are often not made on merit, but rather on the basis of having a diploma, friends or relatives, or because of bribery. The ARVN is weak in dedication, direction and discipline. . . .

e. Press for Negotiations. I am not optimistic that Hanoi or the VC will respond to peace overtures now. . . . The ends sought by the two sides appear to be irreconcilable and the relative power balance is not in their view unfavorable to them. But three things can be done, I believe, to increase the prospects:

(1) Take steps to increase the credibility of our peace gestures in the minds of the enemy. There is considerable evidence both in private statements by the Communists and in the reports of competent Western officials who have talked with them that charges of U.S. bad faith are not solely propagandistic, but reflect deeply held beliefs. Analyses of Communists' statements and actions indicate that they firmly believe that American leadership really does not want the fighting to stop, and, that we are intent on winning a military victory in Vietnam and on maintaining our presence there through a puppet regime supported by U.S. military bases.

As a way of projective U.S. bona fides, I believe that we should consider two possibilities with respect to our bombing program against the

North, to be undertaken, if at all, at a time very carefully selected with a view to maximizing the chances of influencing the enemy and world opinion and to minimizing the chances that failure would strengthen the hand of the "hawks" at home: First, without fanfare, conditions, or avowal, whether the stand-down was permanent or temporary, stop bombing all of North Vietnam. It is generally thought that Hanoi will not agree to negotiations until they can claim that the bombing has stopped unconditionally. We should see what develops, retaining freedom to resume the bombing if nothing useful was forthcoming. . . . [A footnote:] Any limitation on the bombing of North Vietnam will cause serious psychological problems among the men who are risking their lives to help achieve our political objectives; among their commanders up to and including the JCS [Joint Chiefs of Staff]; and among those of our people who cannot understand why we should withhold punishment from the enemy. General Westmoreland, as do the JCS, strongly believes in the military value of the bombing program. Further, Westmoreland reports that the morale of his Air Force personnel may already be showing signs of erosion—an erosion resulting from current operational restrictions.

To the same end of improving our credibility, we should seek ways —through words and deeds—to make believable our intention to withdraw our forces once the North Vietnamese aggression against the South stops. In particular, we should avoid any implication that we will stay in South Vietnam with bases or to guarantee any particular outcome to a solely South Vietnamese struggle. . . .

3. The prognosis.   The prognosis is bad that the war can be brought to a satisfactory conclusion within the next two years. The large-unit operations probably will not do it; negotiations probably will not do it. *While we should continue to pursue both of these routes in trying for a solution in the short run, we should recognize that success from them is a mere possibility, not a probability.*

The solution lies in girding, openly, for a longer war and in taking actions immediately which will in 12 to 18 months give clear evidence that the continuing costs and risks to the American people are acceptably limited, that the formula for success has been found, and that the end of the war is merely a matter of time.

QUESTIONS

According to McNamara, what progress had been made in Vietnam? • How had American efforts influenced the morale of the North Vietnamese and Viet Cong? • How successful was pacification? • What actions did McNamara recommend? • What did he expect these actions to accomplish? • What were the goals McNamara hoped to achieve? • What prognosis did he make?

DOCUMENT 2

Military Commander Reassures Americans the End Is in View

The Vietnam War generated dissent unprecedented in previous American wars. Antiwar activists burned draft cards and tried to impede military production. Hawks argued that nuclear weapons should be employed to bomb the enemy back to the stone age. Doves declared that the United States should immediately and unilaterally withdraw from the war. To bolster eroding political support for the war, General William C. Westmoreland, Commander of U.S. forces in Vietnam, gave a public address in November 1967. Westmoreland's optimistic assessment of the war, excerpted here, reflected the desire of policy makers to assure Americans that the war was being won and would soon be over.

General William C. Westmoreland
Public Address, November 1967

With 1968, a new phase is now starting. We have reached an important point when the end begins to come into view. What is this third phase we are about to enter?

In Phase III, in 1968, we intend to do the following:

Help the Vietnamese Armed Forces to continue improving their effectiveness.

Decrease our advisers in training centers and other places where the professional competence of Vietnamese officers makes this possible.

Increase our advisory effort with the younger brothers of the Vietnamese Army: the Regional Forces and Popular Forces.

Use U.S. and free-world forces to destroy North Vietnamese forays while we assist the Vietnamese to reorganize for territorial security.

Provide the new military equipment to revitalize the Vietnamese Army and prepare it to take on an ever-increasing share of the war.

Continue pressure on North to prevent rebuilding and to make infiltration more costly.

Turn a major share of frontline DMZ defense over to the Vietnamese Army.

Increase U.S. support in the rich and populated delta.

Help the Government of Viet-Nam single out and destroy the Communist shadow government.

General William C. Westmoreland, "Address on Vietnam," *Department of State Bulletin*, December 11, 1967; reprinted in *Vietnam: A History in Documents*, ed. Gareth Porter (New York: New American Library, 1981), 352–54.

Continue to isolate the guerrilla from the people.

Help the new Vietnamese government to respond to popular aspirations and to reduce and eliminate corruption.

Help the Vietnamese strengthen their policy forces to enhance law and order.

Open more roads and canals.

Continue to improve the Vietnamese economy and standard of living.

Now for phase IV—the final phase. That period will see the conclusion of our plan to weaken the enemy and strengthen our friends until we become progressively superfluous. The object will be to show the world that guerrilla warfare and invasion do not pay as a new means of Communist aggression.

I see phase IV happening as follows:

Infiltration will slow.

The Communist infrastructure will be cut up and near collapse.

The Vietnamese Government will prove its stability, and the Vietnamese Army will show that it can handle Viet Cong.

The Regional Forces and Popular Forces will reach a higher level of professional performance.

U.S. units can begin to phase down as the Vietnamese Army is modernized and develops its capacity to the fullest.

The military physical assets, bases and ports, will be progressively turned over to the Vietnamese.

The Vietnamese will take charge of the final mopping up of the Viet Cong (which will probably last several years). The U.S., at the same time, will continue the developmental help envisaged by the President for the community of Southeast Asia.

You may ask how long phase III will take, before we reach the final phase. We have already entered part of phase III. Looking back on phases I and II, we can conclude that we have come a long way.

I see progress as I travel all over Viet-Nam.

I see it in the attitudes of the Vietnamese.

I see it in the open roads and canals.

I see it in the new crops and the new purchasing power of the farmer.

I see it in the increasing willingness of the Vietnamese Army to fight North Vietnamese units and in the victories they are winning.

Parenthetically, I might say that the U.S. press tends to report U.S. actions; so you may not be as aware as I am of the victories won by South Vietnamese forces.

The enemy has many problems:

He is losing control of the scattered population under his influence.

He is losing credibility with the population he still controls.

He is alienating the people by his increased demands and taxes, where he can impose them.

He sees the strength of his forces steadily declining.

He can no longer recruit in the South to any meaningful extent; he must plug the gap with North Vietnamese.

His monsoon offensives have been failures.

He was dealt a mortal blow by the installation of a freely elected representative government.

And he failed in his desperate effort to take the world's headlines from the inauguration by a military victory.

Lastly, the Vietnamese Army is on the road to becoming a competent force. . . .

We are making progress. We know you want an honorable and early transition to the fourth and last phase. So do your sons and so do I.

It lies within our grasp—the enemy's hopes are bankrupt. With your support we will give you a success that will impact not only on South Viet-Nam but on every emerging nation in the world.

QUESTIONS

According to Westmoreland, what were the features of the new phase of the war in 1968? • Why did he contend that "the end" was beginning to come into view? • What evidence of progress did he mention? • Did the progress indicate that phase IV was likely to begin soon? • Do you think Americans found Westmoreland's speech convincing? • Why or why not?

DOCUMENT 3

Military Discipline in an Unpopular War

Soldiers in Vietnam knew that they were fighting in a controversial war—one that did not have overwhelming public support at home, that seemed confusing and deadly in the field, and that seemed to be poorly supported by the Vietnamese army, government, and general population. The perceptions and experiences of American soldiers had important consequences for military discipline. In 1971 Colonel Robert D. Heinl Jr., a twenty-seven-year veteran of the Marine Corps, cataloged in an army publication the state of military discipline among troops in Vietnam. Heinl's article, excerpted here, illustrates the demoralization within the armed forces while peace negotiators huddled with representatives of North Vietnam and the fighting continued.

Robert D. Heinl Jr.

"The Collapse of the Armed Forces," June 7, 1971

The morale, discipline and battleworthiness of the U.S. Armed Forces are, with a few salient exceptions, lower and worse than at any time in this century and possibly in the history of the United States.

By every conceivable indicator, our army that now remains in Vietnam is in a state approaching collapse, with individual units avoiding or having refused combat, murdering their officers and noncommissioned officers, drug-ridden, and dispirited where not near-mutinous. . . .

Intolerably clobbered and buffeted from without and within by social turbulence, pandemic drug addiction, race war, sedition, civilian scapegoatise, draftee recalcitrance and malevolence, barracks theft and common crime, unsupported in their travail by the general government, in Congress as well as the executive branch, distrusted, disliked, and often reviled by the public, the uniformed services today are places of agony for the loyal, silent professionals who doggedly hang on and try to keep the ship afloat. . . .

While no senior officer (especially one on active duty) can openly voice any such assessment, the foregoing conclusions find virtually unanimous support in numerous non-attributable interviews with responsible senior and midlevel officers, as well as career noncommissioned officers and petty officers in all services.

Historical precedents do exist for some of the services' problems, such as desertion, mutiny, unpopularity, seditious attacks, and racial troubles. Others, such as drugs, pose difficulties that are wholly new. Nowhere, however, in the history of the Armed Forces have comparable past troubles presented themselves in such general magnitude, acuteness, or concentrated focus as today. . . .

To understand the military consequences of what is happening to the U.S. Armed Forces, Vietnam is a good place to start. It is in Vietnam that the rearguard of a 500,000-man army, in its day (and in the observation of the writer) the best army the United States ever put into the field, is numbly extricating itself from a nightmare war the Armed Forces feel they had foisted on them by bright civilians who are now back on campus writing books about the folly of it all.

"They have set up separate companies," writes an American soldier from Cu Chi, . . ." for men who refuse to go out into the field. It is no big thing to refuse to go. If a man is ordered to go to such and such a place he no longer goes through the hassle of refusing; he just packs his shirt and goes to visit some buddies at another base camp. Operations have

Colonel Robert D. Heinl Jr., "The Collapse of the Armed Forces," *Armed Forces Journal*, June 7, 1971; reprinted in *Vietnam and America: A Documented History*, ed. Marvin E. Gettleman (New York: Grove Atlantic, 1995), 323–31.

become incredibly ragtag. Many guys don't even put on their uniforms any more. . . . The American garrisons on the larger bases are virtually disarmed. The lifers have taken our weapons from us and put them under lock and key. . . . There have also been quite a few frag incidents in the battalion."

Can all this really be typical or even truthful? Unfortunately the answer is yes.

"Frag incidents" or just "fragging" is current soldier slang in Vietnam for the murder or attempted murder of strict, unpopular, or just aggressive officers and NCOs. With extreme reluctance (after a young West Pointer from Senator Mike Mansfield's Montana was fragged in his sleep) the Pentagon has now disclosed that fraggings in 1970 (209) have more than doubled those of the previous year (96).

Word of the deaths of officers will bring cheers at troop movies or in bivouacs of certain units. In one such division . . . fraggings during 1971 have been authoritatively estimated to be running about one a week. . . .

Bounties, raised by common subscription in amounts running anywhere from $50 to $1,000, have been widely reported put on the heads of leaders whom the privates . . . want to rub out.

Shortly after the costly assault on Hamburger Hill in mid-1969, the GI underground newspaper in Vietnam, *GI Says*, publicly offered a $10,000 bounty on LCol Weldon Honeycutt, the officer who ordered (and led) the attack. Despite several attempts, however, Honeycutt managed to live out his tour and return Stateside.

"Another Hamburger Hill" (i.e., toughly contested assault), conceded a veteran major, "is definitely out."

The issue of "combat refusal" an official euphemism for disobedience of orders to fight—the soldier's gravest crime—has only recently been again precipitated on the frontier of Laos. . . .

"Search and evade" (meaning tacit avoidance of combat by units in the field) is now virtually a principle of war, vividly expressed by the GI phrase, "CYA (cover your ass) and get home!"

That "search-and-evade" has not gone unnoticed by the enemy is underscored by the Viet Cong delegation's recent statement at the Paris Peace Talks that communist units in Indochina have been ordered not to engage American units which do not molest them. The same statement boasted—not without foundation in fact—that American defectors are in the VC ranks.

Symbolic anti-war fasts (such as the one at Pleiku where an entire medical unit, led by its officers, refused Thanksgiving turkey), peace symbols, "V"-signs not for victory but for peace, booing and cursing of officers and even of hapless entertainers such as Bob Hope, are unhappily commonplace.

As for drugs and race, Vietnam's problems today not only reflect but reinforce those of the Armed Forces as a whole. In April, for example, members of a Congressional investigating subcommittee reported that 10 to 15% of our troops in Vietnam are now using high-grade heroin, and that drug addiction there is "of epidemic proportions."

Only last year an Air Force major and command pilot for Ambassador Bunker was apprehended at Tan Son Nhut air base outside Saigon with $8-million worth of heroin in his aircraft. This major is now in Leavenworth. . . .

It is a truism that national armies closely reflect societies from which they have been raised. It would be strange indeed if the Armed Forces did not today mirror the agonizing divisions and social traumas of American society, and of course they do.

For this very reason, our Armed Forces outside Vietnam not only reflect these conditions but disclose the depths of their troubles in an awful litany of sedition, disaffection, desertion, race, drugs, breakdowns of authority, abandonment of discipline, and, as a cumulative result, the lowest state of military morale in the history of the country.

Sedition—coupled with disaffection within the ranks, and externally fomented with an audacity and intensity previously inconceivable—infests the Armed Services:

At best count, there appear to be some 144 underground newspapers published on or aimed at U.S. military bases in this country and overseas. Since 1970 the number of such sheets has increased 40% (up from 103 last fall). These journals are not mere gripe-sheets that poke soldier fun . . . at the brass and the sergeants. "In Vietnam," writes the Ft Lewis-McChord Free Press, "the Lifers, the Brass, are the true Enemy, not the enemy." Another West Coast sheet advises readers: "Don't desert. Go to Vietnam and kill your commanding officer."

At least 14 GI dissent organizations (including two made up exclusively of officers) now operate more or less openly. Ancillary to these are at least six antiwar veterans' groups which strive to influence GIs. . . .

By present count at least 11 (some go as high as 26) off-base antiwar "coffee houses" ply GIs with rock music, lukewarm coffee, antiwar literature, how-to-do-it tips on desertion, and similar disruptive counsels. . . .

One militant West Coast Group, Movement for a Democratic Military (MDM), has specialized in weapons theft from military bases in California. During 1970, large armory thefts were successfully perpetrated against Oakland Army Base, Fts Cronkhite and Ord, and even the Marine Corps Base at Camp Pendleton. . . .

Internally speaking, racial conflicts and drugs—also previously insignificant—are tearing the services apart today. . . .

Racial conflicts (most but not all sparked by young black enlisted men) are erupting murderously in all services.

At a recent high commanders' conference, General Westmoreland and other senior generals heard the report from Germany that in many units white soldiers are now afraid to enter barracks alone at night for fear of "head-hunting" ambushes by blacks. . . . All services are today striving energetically to cool and control this ugly violence which in the words of one noncommissioned officer, has made his once taut unit divide up "like two street gangs.". . .

The drug problem—like the civilian situation from which it directly derives—is running away with the services. In March, Navy Secretary John H. Chafee, speaking for the two sea services, said bluntly that drug abuse in both Navy and Marines is out of control.

In 1966, the Navy discharged 170 drug offenders. Three years later (1969), 3,800 were discharged. Last year in 1970, the total jumped to over 5,000.

Drug abuse in the Pacific Fleet—with Asia on one side, and kinky California on the other—gives the Navy its worst headaches. To cite one example, a destroyer due to sail from the West Coast last year for the Far East nearly had to postpone deployment when, five days before departure, a ring of some 30 drug users (over 10 percent of the crew) was uncovered. . . .

What those statistics say is that the Armed Forces (like their parent society) are in the grip of a drug pandemic—a conclusion underscored by the one fact that, just since 1968, the total number of verified drug addiction cases throughout the Armed Forces has nearly doubled. One other yardstick: according to military medical sources, needle hepatitis now poses as great a problem among young soldiers as VD. . . .

With conditions what they are in the Armed Forces, and with intense efforts on the part of elements in our society to disrupt discipline and destroy morale the consequences can be clearly measured in two ultimate indicators: manpower retention (reenlistments and their antithesis, desertions); and the state of discipline.

In both respects the picture is anything but encouraging. . . . Desertion rates are going straight up. . . .

In 1970, the Army had 65,643 deserters, or roughly the equivalent of four infantry divisions. This desertion rate (52.3 soldiers per thousand) is well over twice the peak rate for Korea (22.5 per thousand). It is more than quadruple the 1966 desertion-rate (14.7 per thousand) of the then well-trained, high-spirited professional Army. . . .

Admiral Elmo R. Zumwalt, Jr, Chief of Naval Operations, minces no words. "We have a personnel crisis," he recently said, "that borders on disaster.". . .

The trouble of the services—produced by and also in turn producing the dismaying conditions described in this article—is above all a crisis of soul and backbone. It entails—the word is not too strong—something very near a collapse of the command authority and leadership George Washington saw as the soul of military forces. This collapse results, at least in part, from a concurrent collapse of public confidence in the military establishment.

QUESTIONS

According to Heinl, why was the army in Vietnam approaching collapse?
• What were the sources of the problems? • What caused fragging,
bounties, combat refusal, and search and evade? • What, according to
Heinl, were the consequences of these practices in Vietnam? • How did he
describe sedition, racial strife, and drug abuse as influencing the military?

DOCUMENT 4

An American Soldier in Vietnam

*Hundreds of thousands of Americans served in uniform in Vietnam. Their expe-
riences varied enormously, depending on when and where they served and what
they were assigned to do. Arthur E. Woodley Jr., who served as a Special Forces
Ranger in Vietnam in 1968 and 1969, recalled in an interview more than a decade
later how the war changed him. Woodley's interview, excerpted here, reveals experiences confronted by many young Americans in combat in Vietnam.*

Arthur E. Woodley Jr.
Oral History of a Special Forces Ranger

I went to Vietnam as a basic naïve young man of eighteen. Before I
reached my nineteenth birthday, I was a animal. . . .

It began on my fourteenth day in country. The first time I was ever in
a combat situation at all. . . .

I was a cherry boy. Most cherry boys went on point. . . . I adapted so
well to bein' a point man that that became my permanent position after
this first mission.

We was in very thick elephant grass. We had sat down for a ten-
minute break. And we heard the Vietn'ese talking, coming through the
elephant grass. So we all sat ready for bein' attacked.

I heard this individual walking. He came through the elephant grass,
and I let loose on my M-16 and hit him directly in his face. Sixteen rounds.
The whole clip. And his face disappeared. From the chin up. Nothing left.
And his body stood there for 'proximately somewhere around ten, fifteen
seconds. And it shivers. And it scared me beyond anyone's imagination.

Then it was chaos from then on. Shooting all over. We had a approxi-
mate body count of five VC. Then we broke camp and head for safer ground.

Arthur E. Woodley Jr. interview, in Wallace Terry, *Bloods: An Oral History of
the Vietnam War by Black Veterans* (New York: Ballantine, 1984), 243–63.

After thinkin' about that guy with no face, I broke into a cold sweat. I knew it could've been me that was in his place instead of me in my place. But it changed me. Back home I had to defend myself in the streets, with my fist, with bottles, or whatever. But you don't go around shooting people. As physical as I had been as a teenager, there were never life-threatening situations. I had never experienced anything quite as horrible as seeing a human being with his face blown apart. I cried. I cried because I killed somebody.

You had to fight to survive where I grew up. Lower east Baltimore. . . . It was very difficult for us to go from one neighborhood to another without trying to prove your manhood.

It was a mixed-up neighborhood of Puerto Ricans, Indians, Italians, and blacks. Being that I'm light-skinned, curly hair, I wasn't readily accepted in the black community. I was more accepted by Puerto Ricans and some rednecks. They didn't ask what my race classification was. I went with them to white movies, white restaurants, and so forth. But after I got older, I came to the realization that I was what I am and came to deal with my black peers. . . .

Being from a hard-core neighborhood, I decided I was gonna volunteer for the toughest combat training they had. I went to jump school, Ranger school, and Special Forces training. I figured I was just what my country needed. A black patriot who could do any physical job they could come up with. Six feet, one hundred and ninety pounds, and healthy. . . .

We got to Cam Ranh in November 1968. And I got the biggest surprise of my life. There was water surfing. There was big cars being driven. There was women with fashionable clothes and men with suits on. It was not like being in a war zone. I said, Hey, what's this? Better than being home.

When I got there, my basic job was combat infantryman, paratrooper, 5th Special Forces Group. . . . We were like a unit of misfits who were sort of throwed together and made into a strike combat unit. We would go out and capture prisoners, destroy a certain village, or kill a certain party because it was necessary for the war effort.

I didn't ask no questions about the war. I thought communism was spreading, and as an American citizen, it was my part to do as much as I could to defeat the Communist from coming here. Whatever America states is correct was the tradition that I was brought up in. And I, through the only way I could possibly make it out of the ghetto, was to be the best soldier I possibly could. . . .

Then came the second week of February of '69.

This was like three days after we had a helicopter go down in some very heavy foliage where they couldn't find no survivors from the air. . . . We were directed to find the wreckage, report back. They see if we can find any enemy movement and find any prisoners. . . .

The helicopter, it was stripped. All the weaponry was gone. There was no bodies. It looked like the helicopter had been shot out of the air. It had numerous bullet holes in it. . . .

We recon this area, and we came across this fella, a white guy, who was staked to the ground. His arms and legs tied down to stakes. And he had a leather band around his neck that's staked in the ground so he couldn't move his head to the left or right.

He had numerous scars on his face where he might have been beaten and mutilated. And he had been peeled from his upper part of chest to down to his waist. Skinned. Like they slit your skin with a knife. And they take a pair of pliers or a instrument similar, and they just peel the skin off your body and expose it to the elements. . . .

The man was within a couple of hours of dying on his own.

And we didn't know what to do, because we couldn't move him. There was no means. We had no stretcher. There was only six of us. And we went out with the basic idea that it was no survivors. We was even afraid to unstake him from the stakes, because the maggots and flies were eating at the exposed flesh so much. . . .

It was a heavy shock on all of us to find that guy staked out still alive. . . .

And he start to cryin', beggin' to die.

He said, "I can't go back like this. I can't live like this. I'm dying. You can't leave me here like this dying.

It was a situation where it had to be remove him from his bondage or remove him from his suffering. Movin' him from this bondage was unfeasible. It would have put him in more pain than he had ever endured. There wasn't even no use talkin' 'bout tryin' and takin' him back, because there was nothing left of him. It was that or kill the brother, and I use the term "brother" because in a war circumstance, we all brothers.

The man pleaded not only to myself but to other members of my team to end his suffering. He made the plea for about half an hour, because we couldn't decide what to do. . . .

It took me somewhere close to 20 minutes to get my mind together. Not because I was squeamish about killing someone, because I had at that time numerous body counts. Killing someone wasn't the issue. It was killing another American citizen, another GI.

I tried my best not to.

I tried to find a thousand and one reasons why I shouldn't do this. . . .

I put myself in his situation. In his place. I had to be as strong as he was, because he was askin' me to kill him, to wipe out his life. He had to be a hell of a man to do that. I don't think I would be a hell of a man enough to be able to do that. I said to myself, I couldn't show him my weakness, because he was showin' me his strength.

The only thing that I could see that had to be done is that the man's sufferin' had to be ended.

I put my M-16 next to his head. Next to his temple.
I said, "You sure you want me to do this?"
He said, "Man, kill me. Thank you."
I stopped thinking. I just pulled the trigger. I cancelled his suffering.
When the team came back, we talked nothing about it.
We buried him. We buried him. Very deep.
Then I cried. . . .

Now it begins to seem like on every mission we come across dead American bodies, black and white. I'm seeing atrocities that's been done on them. Markings have been cut on them. Some has been castrated, with their penises sewed up in their mouth with bamboo.

I couldn't isolate myself from all this. I had gotten to the conclusion today or tomorrow I'll be dead. So it wasn't anything I couldn't do or wouldn't do. . . .

. . . [T]he Vietn'ese, they called me Montagnard[1], because I would dress like a Montagnard. I wouldn't wear conventional camouflage fatigues in the field. I wore a dark-green loincloth, a dark-green bandana to blend in with the foliage, and a little camouflage paint on my face. And Ho Chi Minh sandals. And my grenades and ammunition. That's the way I went to the field.

I dressed like that specifically as the point man, because if the enemy saw anyone first, they saw myself. They would just figure I was just another jungle guy that was walking around in the woods. And I would catch 'em off guard.

When we first started going into the fields, I would not wear a finger, ear, or mutilate another person's body. Until I had the misfortune to come upon those American soldiers who were castrated. Then it got to be a game between the Communists and ourselves to see how many fingers and ears that we could capture from each other. After a kill we would cut his finger or ear off as a trophy, stuff our unit patch in his mouth, and let him die.

I collected about 14 ears and fingers. With them strung on a piece of leather around my neck, I would go downtown, and you would get free drugs, free booze, free pussy because they wouldn't wanna bother with you 'cause this man's a killer. It symbolized that I'm a killer. And it was, so to speak, a symbol of combat-type manhood. . . .

Some days when we came back on a POW snatch we played this game called Vietn'ese Roulette on the helicopter. We wouldn't be told how many to capture. Maybe they only wanted one. But we would get two or three to find out which one is gonna talk. You would pull the trigger on one. Throw the body out. Or you throw one without shooting 'im. You

---

[1]**Montagnard:** A French term used to describe a member of a dark-skinned people living in the highland regions of North and South Vietnam.

place fear into the other Vietn'ese mind. This is you. This is next if you don't talk. . . .

I guess my team got rid of about eight guys out of the chopper one way or another, but I only remember pushing two out myself. . . .

With 89 days left in country, I came out of the field.

At the time you are in the field you don't feel anything about what you are doin'. It's the time that you have to yourself that you sit back and you sort and ponder.

What I now felt was emptiness.

Here I am. I'm still eighteen years old, a young man with basically everything in his life to look forward to over here in a foreign country with people who have everything that I think I should have. They have the right to fight. I've learned in this country that you don't have the right to gather forces and fight back the so-called oppressor. You have the right to complain. They had the right. They fought for what they thought was right.

I started to recapture some of my old values. I was a passionate young man before I came into the Army. I believed that you respect other people's lives just as much as I respect my own. I got to thinkin' that I done killed around 40 people personally and maybe some others I haven't seen in the fire fights. I was really thinkin' that there are people who won't ever see their children, their grandchildren.

I started seeing the atrocities that we caused each other as human beings. I came to the realization that I was committing crimes against humanity and myself. That I really didn't believe in these things I was doin'. I changed.

I stopped wearing the ears and fingers. . . .

I left Vietnam the end of '69. . . .

The same day I left Vietnam, I was standin' back on the corner in Baltimore. Back in the States. A animal. And nobody could deal with me.

I got out January '71. Honorable discharge. Five Bronze Stars for valor. . . .

I couldn't deal with goin' to school, because I wasn't motivated. The only friends I made were militant types, because they were the only ones could relate to what I was tryin' to say. I took all the money I saved up and bought weapons. Fifteen hundred dollars' worth. Rifles, guns. I joined the Black Panthers group basically because it was a warlike group. With the Panthers we started givin' out free milk and other community help things. But I was thinkin' we needed a revolution. A physical revolution. And I was thinkin' about Vietnam. All the time. . . .

I don't have a job now. But I would take any human service job, especially where I could show the black kids and the black people that we ought to stop looking toward the stars and start looking toward each other. That our greatest horizons is in our children. And if we don't bring our children up to believe in themselves, then we'll never have anything to believe in.

But they turn their backs on a lot of us Vietnam vet'rans. They say the only way to success is through education. I wanna go back in school and get my B.A., but I can't afford to. I gotta get out there and get a job. Ain't no jobs out there. So what I'm gon' do now? Only thing else I know how to do is pick up a gun. Then I'm stupid. I'm being stupid again. I'm not going forward. I'm going backwards. And can't go any further backwards. I done been so damn far back, I'm listenin' to the echoes in the tunnel.

One day I'm down on Oliver and Milton Avenue. Go in this grocery store. In my neighborhood.

This Vietn'ese owns the store.

He say, "I know you?"

I say, "You know me from where?"

"You Vietnam?"

"Yeah, I was in Vietnam."

"When you Vietnam."

"'68, '69."

"Yeah, me know you An Khe. You be An Khe?"

"Yeah, I was in An Khe."

"Yeah, me know you. You Montagnard Man."

Ain't that some shit?

I'm buyin' groceries from him.

I ain't been in the store since. I'm still pissed off.

He's got a business, good home, drivin' cars. And I'm still strugglin'.

QUESTIONS

According to Woodley, how did he become an animal? • How did he feel about killing? • What was his view of the war? • Why was he called Montagnard? • How did his views change after he came out of combat? • What happened after he returned home?

COMPARATIVE QUESTIONS

How does General Westmoreland's public assessment of the war compare with Robert McNamara's private evaluation? How does Colonel Heinl's view of the military in Vietnam differ from Westmoreland's and McNamara's? How does Arthur Woodley's experience in Vietnam compare with the goals of American policy described by McNamara and Westmoreland. How does Woodley's experience compare with Heinl's observations?

CHAPTER 30

THE DECLINE OF TRUST AND CONFIDENCE

1968–1980

T he powerful currents of change that swept the nation during the 1960s created even stronger countercurrents that dominated the politics of subsequent decades. Most of the activist groups that had worked for social change succumbed to bitter in-fighting, fracturing their unity and sapping their political vitality. Their opponents mobilized effectively to stymie what they regarded as further decay in American values. The Watergate affair, however, revealed quite un-American values employed routinely at the highest levels of the Nixon administration. As the documents that follow illustrate, the crosscurrents of the time raised questions about the nation's political institutions.

DOCUMENT 1

Congressman Henry B. Gonzalez Criticizes Chicano Radicals

The racial nationalism embodied in the slogans Black Power, Brown Power, Red Power, *and* Yellow Power *generated a powerful backlash within minority communities, especially among established leaders. Congressman Henry B. Gonzalez expressed his views of Chicano radicals in a speech on the floor of the House of Representatives in 1969. Gonzalez's speech, excerpted here, illustrates the conflict within minority communities over how best to define and achieve their goals.*

Speech before the House of Representatives, April 22, 1969

An ethnic minority is in a peculiar position. I happen to be an American of Spanish surname and of Mexican descent. As it happens my parents were born in Mexico and came to this country seeking safety from a violent

Congressional Record, 91st Cong., 1st sess., 1969.

revolution. It follows that I, and many other residents of my part of Texas and other Southwestern States happen to be what is commonly referred to as a Mexican American. That label sums up most of the elements of a vast conflict affecting perhaps most of the 5 million southwestern citizens who happen to bear it. The individual finds himself in a conflict, sometimes with himself, sometimes with his family, sometimes with his whole world. What is he to be? Mexican? American? Both? How can he choose? Should he have pride and joy in his heritage, or bear it as a shame and sorrow? Should he live in one world or another, or attempt to bridge them both?

There is comfort in remaining in the closed walls of a minority society, but this means making certain sacrifices; but it sometimes seems disloyal to abandon old ideas and old friends; you never know whether you will be accepted or rejected in the larger world, or whether your old friends will despise you for making a wrong choice. For a member of this minority, like any other, life begins with making hard choices about personal identity. These lonely conflicts are magnified in the social crises so clearly evident all over the Southwest today. There are some groups who demand brown power, some who display a curious chauvinism, and some who affect the other extreme. There is furious debate about what one should be and what one should do. There is argument about what one's goals are, and how to accomplish them. I understand all this, but I am profoundly distressed by what I see happening today. I have said that I am against certain tactics, and against certain elements, and now I find yet more confusion. Mr. Speaker, the issue at hand in this minority group today is hate, and my purpose in addressing the House is to state where I stand: I am against hate and against the spreaders of hate; I am for justice, and for honest tactics in obtaining justice.

The question facing the Mexican-American people today is what do we want, and how do we get it?

What I want is justice. By justice I mean decent work at decent wages for all who want work; decent support for those who cannot support themselves; full and equal opportunity in employment, in education, in schools; I mean by justice the full, fair, and impartial protection of the law for every man; I mean by justice decent homes; adequate streets and public services; and I mean by justice no man being asked to do more than his fair share, but none being expected to do less. In short, I seek a justice that amounts to full, free, and equal opportunity for all; I believe in a justice that does not tolerate evil or evil doing; and I believe in a justice that is for all the people all the time.

I do not, believe that justice comes only to those who want it; I am not so foolish as to believe that good will alone achieves good works. I believe that justice requires work and vigilance, and I am willing to do that work and maintain that vigilance.

I do not believe that it is possible to obtain justice by vague and empty gestures, or by high slogans uttered by orators who are present today and gone tomorrow. I do believe that justice can be obtained by those who know exactly what they seek, and know exactly how they plan to seek it. And I believe that justice can be obtained by those whose cause is just and whose means are honest.

It may well be that I agree with the goals stated by militants; but whether I agree or disagree, I do not now, nor have I ever believed that the end justifies the means, and I condemn those who do. I cannot accept the belief that racism in reverse is the answer for racism and discrimination; I cannot accept the belief that simple, blind, and stupid hatred is an adequate response to simple, blind, and stupid hatred; I cannot accept the belief that playing at revolution produces anything beyond an excited imagination; and I cannot accept the belief that imitation leadership is a substitute for the real thing. Developments over the past few months indicate that there are those who believe that the best answer for hate is hate in reverse, and that the best leadership is that which is loudest and most arrogant; but my observation is that arrogance is no cure for emptiness.

All over the Southwest new organizations are springing up; some promote pride in heritage, which is good, but others promote chauvinism, which is not; some promote community organization, which is good, but some promote race tension and hatred, which is not good; some seek redress of just grievances, which is good, but others seek only opportunities for self aggrandizement, which is not good.

All of these elements, good and bad, exist and all of them must be taken into account. The tragic thing is that in situations where people have honest grievances, dishonest tactics can prevent their obtaining redress; and where genuine problems exist careless or unthinking or consciously mean behavior can unloose forces that will create new problems that might require generations to solve. I want to go forward, not backward; I want the creation of trust, not fear; and I want to see Americans together, not apart. . . .

Unfortunately it seems that in the face of rising hopes and expectations among Mexican Americans there are more leaders with political ambitions at heart than there are with the interests of the poor at heart; they do not care what is accomplished in fact, as long as they can create and ride the winds of protest as far as possible. Thus we have those who play at revolution, those who make speeches but do not work, and those who imitate what they have seen others do, but lack the initiative and imagination to set forth actual programs for progress. . . .

Not long after the Southwest Council of La Raza[1] opened for business, it gave $110,000 to the Mexican-American Unity Council of San Antonio; this group was apparently invented for the purpose of receiving the grant. Whatever the purposes of this group may be, thus far it has not given any assistance that I know of to bring anybody together; rather

---

[1]**La Raza Unida:** From the Spanish, "the United Race," a Chicano party founded by Jose Angel Guitierrez in Texas and based on cultural pride and brotherhood.

it has freely dispensed funds to people who promote the rather odd and I might say generally unaccepted and unpopular views of its directors. The Mexican-American Unity Council appears to specialize in creating still other organizations and equipping them with quarters, mimeograph machines and other essentials of life. Thus, the "unity council" has created a parents' association in a poor school district, a neighborhood council, a group known as the barrios unidos—or roughly, united neighborhoods —a committee on voter registration and has given funds to the militant Mexican-American Youth Organization—MAYO; it has also created a vague entity known as the "Universidad de los Barrios" which is a local gang operation. Now assuredly all these efforts may be well intended; however it is questionable to my mind that a very young and inexperienced man can prescribe the social and political organizations of a complex and troubled community; there is no reason whatever to believe that for all the money this group has spent, there is any understanding of what it is actually being spent for, except to employ friends of the director and advance his preconceived notions. The people who are to be united apparently don't get much say in what the "unity council" is up to.

As an example, the president of MAYO is not on the Unity Council payroll; but he is on the payroll of another Ford Foundation group, the Mexican-American Legal Defense Fund. He is an investigator but appears to spend his time on projects not related to his defense fund work. This handy device enables him to appear independent of Foundation activities and still make a living from the Foundation. Of course, his MAYO speeches denigrating the "gringos" and calling for their elimination by "killing them if all else fails" do little for unity, and nothing for law, but that bothers neither him nor his associates.

As another example, the "Universidad de los Barrios" is operated by a college junior and two others. The "universidad" has no curriculum and offers no courses, and the young toughs it works with have become what some neighbors believe to be a threat to safety and even life itself. After a murder took place on the doorstep of this place in January, witnesses described the place as a "trouble spot." Neighbors told me that they were terrified of the young men who hung around there, that their children had been threatened and that they were afraid to call the police. After the murder, the "dean" of this "university" said that he could not be there all the time and was not responsible for what happened while he was away. This might be true, but the general fear of the neighbors indicates that the "university" is not under reliable guidance at any time. . . .

Militant groups like MAYO regularly distribute literature that I can only describe as hate sheets, designed to inflame passions and reinforce old wounds or open new ones; these sheets spew forth racism and hatred designed to do no man good. The practice is defended as one that will build race pride, but I never heard of pride being built on spleen. There is no way to adequately describe the damage that such sheets can do; and there is no way to assess how minds that distribute this tripe operate. But, Mr. Speaker, I say that those who believe the wellsprings of hate can be closed as easily as they are opened make a fearful mistake; they who lay out poison cannot be certain that it will kill no one, or make no one ill, or harm no innocent bystander. . . .

We see a strange thing in San Antonio today; we have those who play at revolution and those who imitate the militance of others. We have a situation in Denver where the local leader said, "This is our Selma,"[2] and not a week later a situation in Del Rio where the local leader said, "This is our Selma." But try as they might, Selma was neither in Denver nor in Del Rio. We have those who cry "brown power" only because they have heard "black power" and we have those who yell "oink" or "pig" at police, only because they have heard others use the term. We have those who wear beards and berets, not because they attach any meaning to it, but because they have seen it done elsewhere. But neither fervor nor fashion alone will bring justice. Those who cry for justice, but hold it in contempt cannot win it for themselves or for anyone else. Those who prize power for its own sake will never be able to use it for any benefit but their own; and those who can only follow the fashions of protest will never understand what true protest is.

I believe that a just and decent cause demands a just and decent program of action. I believe that a just and decent cause can be undermined by those who believe that there is no decency, and who demand for themselves what they would deny others. I have stood against racists before, and I will do it again; and I have stood against blind passion before and I will gladly do so again. I pray that the day will come when all men know justice; and I pray that that day has not been put further away by the architects of discord, the prophets of violence. I pray that these great tasks that face us in the quest for justice and progress will be taken up by all men; and I know that when all is said and done and the tumult and shouting die down those who only spoke with passion cast aside, and those who spoke with conviction and integrity will still be around. I am willing to let time be my judge.

QUESTIONS

According to Congressman Gonzalez, what conflict was felt by Mexican Americans? • How did he define justice? • What methods did he believe should be used to obtain justice? • What did he identify as "racism in reverse"? • What criticisms did Gonzalez have of those "who play at revolution"? • How might a Chicano member of La Raza Unida have responded to Gonzalez's arguments?

---

[2]**"Selma":** refers to the March 1965 demonstration for black voting rights that took place in Selma, Alabama, to which local police responded with brutal attacks injuring hundreds and killing three protesters.

DOCUMENT 2

Roe v. Wade *and Abortion Rights*

One of the important activities of the women's rights movement was setting up clinics to advise women about birth control, pregnancy, and abortion. In many states, abortions were illegal. In 1970 Sarah Weddington, a lawyer from the Women's Liberation Birth Control Information Center in Austin, Texas, filed suit in federal court to overturn the Texas antiabortion law. Weddington's client took the name Jane Roe in the legal documents to preserve her privacy. Jane Roe was actually Norma McCorvey, a pregnant young high school dropout who sought an abortion, an action opposed by Henry Wade, the district attorney of Dallas County. In 1973, a 7 to 2 majority of the U.S. Supreme Court decided the case of Roe v. Wade. *Justice Harry A. Blackmun wrote the majority opinion, the source of the following selection.*

Supreme Court Decision, 1973

We forthwith acknowledge our awareness of the sensitive and emotional nature of the abortion controversy, of the vigorous opposing views, even among physicians, and of the deep and seemingly absolute convictions that the subject inspires. One's philosophy, one's experiences, one's exposure to the raw edges of human existence, one's religious training, one's attitudes toward life and family and their values, and the moral standards one establishes and seeks to observe, are all likely to influence and to color one's thinking and conclusions about abortion.

In addition, population growth, pollution, poverty, and racial overtones tend to complicate and not to simplify the problem.

Our task, of course, is to resolve the issue by constitutional measurement free of emotion and of predilection. We seek earnestly to do this, and, because we do, we have inquired into, and in this opinion place some emphasis upon, medical and medical-legal history and what that history reveals about man's attitudes toward the abortive procedure over the centuries. . . .

Jane Roe, a single woman who was residing in Dallas County, Texas, instituted this federal action in March 1970 against the District Attorney of the county. She sought a declaratory judgment that the Texas criminal abortion statutes were unconstitutional on their face, and an injunction restraining the defendant from enforcing the statutes.

Roe alleged that she was unmarried and pregnant; that she wished to terminate her pregnancy by an abortion "performed by a competent, licensed physician, under safe, clinical conditions"; that she was unable

---

Roe v. Wade, 410 U.S. 113 (1973); reprinted in *Recent America: The United States Since 1945,* by Dewey W. Grantham (Wheeling, IL: Harlan Davidson, 1987), 438–42.

to get a "legal" abortion in Texas because her life did not appear to be threatened by the continuation of her pregnancy; and that she could not afford to travel to another jurisdiction in order to secure a legal abortion under safe conditions. She claimed that the Texas statutes were unconstitutionally vague and that they abridged her right of personal privacy, protected by the First, Fourth, Fifth, Ninth, and Fourteenth Amendments. By an amendment to her complaint Roe purported to sue "on behalf of herself and all other women" similarly situated. . . .

On the merits, the District Court held that the "fundamental right of single women and married persons to choose whether to have children is protected by the Ninth Amendment, through the Fourteenth Amendment," and that the Texas criminal abortion statutes were void on their face because they were both unconstitutionally vague and constituted an overbroad infringement of the plaintiffs' Ninth Amendment rights. . . .

It perhaps is not generally appreciated that the restrictive criminal abortion laws in effect in a majority of States today are of relatively recent vintage. Those laws, generally proscribing abortion or its attempt at any time during pregnancy except when necessary to preserve the pregnant woman's life, are not of ancient or even of common law origin. Instead, they derive from statutory changes effected, for the most part, in the latter half of the 19th century. . . .

Three reasons have been advanced to explain historically the enactment of criminal abortion laws in the 19th century and to justify their continued existence. . . .

It has been argued occasionally that these laws were the product of a Victorian social concern to discourage illicit sexual conduct. Texas, however, does not advance this justification in the present case, and it appears that no court or commentator has taken the argument seriously. . . .

A second reason is concerned with abortion as a medical procedure. When most criminal abortion laws were first enacted, the procedure was a hazardous one for the woman. This was particularly true prior to the development of antisepsis. . . . Abortion mortality was high. . . . Thus it has been argued that a State's real concern in enacting a criminal abortion law was to protect the pregnant woman, that is, to restrain her from submitting to a procedure that placed her life in serious jeopardy. . . .

The third reason is the State's interest—some phrase it in terms of duty—in protecting prenatal life. . . .

. . . [A]s long as at least *potential* life is involved, the State may assert interests beyond the protection of the pregnant woman alone. . . .

It is with these interests, and the weight to be attached to them, that this case is concerned.

The Constitution does not explicitly mention any right of privacy. In a line of decisions, however, going back perhaps as far as . . . [1891], the Court has recognized that a right of personal privacy, or a guarantee of certain areas or zones of privacy, does exist under the Constitution. . . .

This right of privacy, whether it be founded in the Fourteenth Amendment's concept of personal liberty and restrictions upon state action, as we feel it is, or, as the District Court determined, in the Ninth Amendment's reservation of rights to the people, is broad enough to encompass a woman's decision whether or not to terminate her pregnancy. The detriment that the State would impose upon the pregnant woman by denying this choice altogether is apparent. Specific and direct harm medically diagnosable even in early pregnancy may be involved. Maternity, or additional offspring, may force upon the woman a distressful life and future. Psychological harm may be imminent. Mental and physical health may be taxed by child care. There is also the distress, for all concerned, associated with the unwanted child, and there is the problem of bringing a child into a family already unable, psychologically and otherwise, to care for it. In other cases, as in this one, the additional difficulties and continuing stigma of unwed motherhood may be involved. . . .

On the basis of elements such as these, appellants and some *amici*[1] argue that the woman's right is absolute and that she is entitled to terminate her pregnancy at whatever time, in whatever way, and for whatever reason she alone chooses. With this we do not agree. . . . [A] state may properly assert important interests in safeguarding health, in maintaining medical standards, and in protecting potential life. At some point in pregnancy, these respective interests become sufficiently compelling to sustain regulation of the factors that govern the abortion decision. The privacy right involved, therefore, cannot be said to be absolute. . . .

We therefore conclude that the right of personal privacy includes the abortion decision, but that this right is not unqualified and must be considered against important state interests in regulation. . . .

Where certain "fundamental rights" are involved, the Court has held that regulation limiting these rights may be justified only by a "compelling state interest," . . . and that legislative enactments must be narrowly drawn to express only the legitimate state interests at stake. . . .

. . . The appellee and certain *amici* argue that the fetus is a "person" within the language and meaning of the Fourteenth Amendment. . . .

The Constitution does not define "person" in so many words. . . . All this, together with our observation. . . . that throughout the major portion of the 19th century prevailing legal abortion practices were far freer than they are today, persuades us that the word "person," as used in the Fourteenth Amendment, does not include the unborn. . . .

Texas urges that, apart from the Fourteenth Amendment, life begins at conception and is present throughout pregnancy, and that, therefore, the State has a compelling interest in protecting that life from and after conception. We need not resolve the difficult question of when life be-

---

[1]**amici:** from *amici curiae*, literally, "friends of the court"; people who are not party to the litigation but offer advice to the court on the litigation.

gins. When those trained in the respective disciplines of medicine, philosophy, and theology are unable to arrive at any consensus, the judiciary, at this point in the development of man's knowledge, is not in a position to speculate as to the answer.

It should be sufficient to note briefly the wide divergence of thinking on this most sensitive and difficult question. . . .

In areas other than criminal abortion the law has been reluctant to endorse any theory that life, as we recognize it, begins before live birth or to accord legal rights to the unborn except in narrowly defined situations and except when the rights are contingent upon live birth. . . . [T]he unborn have never been recognized in the law as persons in the whole sense.

. . . [T]he State does have an important and legitimate interest in preserving and protecting the health of the pregnant woman, whether she be a resident of the State or a nonresident who seeks medical consultation and treatment there, and that it has still another important and legitimate interest in protecting the potentiality of human life. These interests are separate and distinct. Each grows in substantiality as the woman approaches term and, at a point during pregnancy, each becomes "compelling."

With respect to the State's important and legitimate interest in the health of the mother, the "compelling" point, in the light of present medical knowledge, is at approximately the end of the first trimester. This is so because of the now established medical fact, referred to above, that until the end of the first trimester mortality in abortion is less than mortality in normal childbirth. It follows that, from and after this point, a State may regulate the abortion procedure to the extent that the regulation reasonably relates to the preservation and protection of maternal health. . . .

With respect to the State's important and legitimate interest in potential life, the "compelling" point is at viability. This is so because the fetus then presumably has the capability of meaningful life outside the mother's womb. State regulation protective of fetal life after viability thus has both logical and biological justifications. If the State is interested in protecting fetal life after viability, it may go so far as to proscribe abortion during that period except when it is necessary to preserve the life or health of the mother. . . .

To summarize and to repeat:

1. A state criminal abortion statute of the current Texas type, that excepts from criminality only a *life saving* procedure on behalf of the mother, without regard to pregnancy stage and without recognition of the other interests involved, is violative of the Due Process Clause of the Fourteenth Amendment.

(a) For the stage prior to approximately the end of the first trimester, the abortion decision and its effectuation must be left to the medical judgment of the pregnant woman's attending physician.

(b) For the stage subsequent to approximately the end of the first trimester, the State, in promoting its interest in the health of the mother, may, if it chooses, regulate the abortion procedure in ways that are reasonably related to maternal health.

(c) For the stage subsequent to viability the State, in promoting its interest in the potentiality of human life, may, if it chooses, regulate, and even proscribe, abortion except where it is necessary, in appropriate medical judgment, for the preservation of the life or health of the mother. . . .

. . . The decision leaves the State free to place increasing restrictions on abortion as the period of pregnancy lengthens, so long as those restrictions are tailored to the recognized state interests. The decision vindicates the right of the physician to administer medical treatment according to his professional judgment up to the points where important state interests provide compelling justifications for intervention. Up to those points the abortion decision in all its aspects is inherently, and primarily, a medical decision, and basic responsibility for it must rest with the physician. If an individual practitioner abuses the privilege of exercising proper medical judgment, the usual remedies, judicial and intraprofessional, are available.

It is so ordered.

QUESTIONS

What did Jane Roe seek from the court? • What did the state of Texas seek? • According to the court, why were criminal abortion laws enacted? • What was the basis of the court's declaration of the right of privacy? • Was that right absolute, according to the court? • Under what circumstances could states regulate abortions? • What were the different factors the justices had to weigh when considering their decision?

DOCUMENT 3

The Watergate Tapes: Nixon, Dean, and Haldeman Discuss the Cancer within the Presidency

President Richard M. Nixon used the powers of the presidency to break the law and spy on political opponents. When the burglars who broke into the office of the Democratic National Committee in the Watergate building on June 17, 1972, were caught and arrested, they quickly began to demand financial help from their employers in the Republican party. They also threatened to tell what they knew about other dirty tricks they had perpetrated. On March 21, 1973, John Dean, the president's counsel, met with Nixon in the Oval Office to inform him of the demands of the Watergate burglars and the dangers they posed to his presidency. Secret tape recordings of that meeting and others were made public in April 1974 by President Nixon. He announced in an address to the nation, that "I know in my own heart that, through the long painful and difficult process revealed in these transcripts, I was trying in that period to discover what was right and to do what was right." The transcript of the March 21 meeting, excerpted here, demonstrates instead deep involvement in criminal activities by Nixon and leading members of his administration. The transcripts of the Watergate tapes provided all Americans with a detailed, word-by-word portrait of the inner workings of the Nixon White House.

Transcript from Tape-recorded Meeting on March 21, 1973

D[ean]: The reason that I thought we ought to talk this morning is because in our conversations, I have the impression that you don't know everything I know and it makes it very difficult for you to make judgments that only you can make on some of these things and I thought that—

P[resident]: In other words, I have to know why you feel that we shouldn't unravel something?

D: Let me give you my overall first.

P: In other words, your judgment as to where it stands, and where we will go,

D: I think that there is no doubt about the seriousness of the problem we've got. We have a cancer within, close to the Presidency, that is growing. It is growing daily. It's compounded, growing geometrically now, because it compounds itself. That will be clear if I, you know, explain some of the details of why it is. Basically, it is because (1) we are being blackmailed; (2) People are going to start perjuring themselves very quickly that have not had to perjure themselves to protect other people in the line. And there is no assurance—

P: That that won't bust?

D: That that won't bust. So let me give you the sort of basic facts, talking first about the Watergate; and then about Segretti; and then about some of the peripheral items that have come up. First of all on the Watergate: how did it all start, where did it start? OK! It started with an instruction to me from Bob Haldeman[1] to see if we couldn't set up a perfectly legitimate campaign intelligence operation over at the Re-Election Commit-

---

Submission of Recorded Presidential Conversations to the Committee on the Judiciary of the House of Representatives by President Richard Nixon, April 1974.

[1]**Bob Haldeman:** H. Robert Haldeman, one of Nixon's top aides.

tee. . . . That is when I came up with Gordon Liddy.[2] They needed a lawyer. Gordon had an intelligence background from his FBI service. I was aware of the fact that he had done some extremely sensitive things for the White House while he had been at the White House and he had apparently done them well. Going out into Ellsberg's[3] doctor's office —

P: Oh, yeah.

D: And things like this. He worked with leaks. He tracked these things down. So the report that I got . . . was that he was a hell of a good man and not only that a good lawyer and could set up a proper operation. . . . Magruder called me in January and said I would like to have you come over and see Liddy's plan.

P: January of '72?

D: January of '72.

D: . . . So I came over and Liddy laid out a million dollar plan that was the most incredible thing I have ever laid my eyes on: all in codes, and involved black bag operations, kidnapping, providing prostitutes to weaken the opposition, bugging, mugging teams. It was just an incredible thing. . . .

So there was a second meeting. . . . I came into the tail end of the meeting. . . . [T]hey were discussing again bugging, kidnapping and the like. At this point I said right in front of everybody, very clearly, I said, "These are not the sort of things (1) that are ever to be discussed in the office of the Attorney General of the United States — that was where he still was — and I am personally incensed. " And I am trying to get Mitchell[4] off the hook. . . . So I let it be known. I said "You all pack that stuff up and get it the hell out of here. You just can't talk this way in this office and you should re-examine your whole thinking."

P: Who all was present?

D: It was Magruder, Mitchell, Liddy and myself. I came back right after the meeting and told Bob, "Bob, we have a growing disaster on our hands if they are thinking this way," and I said, "The White House has got to stay out of this and I, frankly, am not going to be involved in it." He said, "I agree John." I thought at that point that the thing was turned off. That is the last I heard of it and I thought it was turned off because it was an absurd proposal. . . . I think Bob was assuming that they had

---

[2]**Gordon Liddy:** G. Gordon Liddy, a former FBI agent who led a secret unit set up under the Nixon administration and nicknamed the "plumbers" because their mission was to stop the kind of "leaks" that had led to the publication of the *Pentagon Papers*.

[3]**Ellsberg:** Daniel Ellsberg, a former aide who had leaked the *Pentagon Papers* to the *New York Times* in 1971. In an attempt to discredit him, the Nixon administration hired men to break into Ellsberg's psychiatrist's office, steal confidential records, and leak them to the press.

[4]**Mitchell:** John Mitchell, Nixon's former attorney general, who ran the Committee to Re-elect the President, an organization that authorized the Watergate break-in.

something that was proper over there, some intelligence gathering operation that Liddy was operating. . . . They were going to infiltrate, and bug, and do this sort of thing to a lot of these targets. This is knowledge I have after the fact. Apparently after they had initially broken in and bugged the DNC they were getting information. . . .

P: They had never bugged Muskie[5], though, did they?

D: No, they hadn't, but they had infiltrated it by a secretary.

P: By a secretary?

D: By a secretary and a chauffeur. There is nothing illegal about that. So the information was coming over here. . . . The next point in time that I became aware of anything was on June 17th when I got the word that there had been this break in at the DNC and somebody from our Committee had been caught in the DNC, And I said, "Oh, (expletive deleted)." You know, eventually putting the pieces together—

P: You knew what it was.

D: I knew who it was. . . .

P: Why at that point in time I wonder? I am just trying to think. We had just finished the Moscow trip.

The Democrats had just nominated McGovern—I mean, (expletive deleted), what in the hell were these people doing? I can see their doing it earlier. I can see the pressures, but I don't see why all the pressure was on then.

D: I don't know, other than the fact that they might have been looking for information about the conventions.

P: That's right. . . .

P: What did they say in the Grand Jury?

D: They said, as they said before the trial in the Grand Jury, that . . . we knew [Liddy] had these capacities to do legitimate intelligence. We had no idea what he was doing. . . . We had no knowledge that he was going to bug the DNC.

P: The point is, that is not true?

D: That's right.

P: Magruder did know it was going to take place?

D: Magruder gave the instructions to be back in the DNC.

P: He did?

D: Yes.

P: You know that?

D: Yes.

P: I see. OK.

D: I honestly believe that no one over here knew that. I know that as God is my maker, I had no knowledge that they were going to do this.

---

[5]**Muskie:** Edmund Muskie, a Democratic senator from Maine who had hoped to run against Nixon in the 1972 election. Watergate hearings in 1973 revealed that his bid for the Democratic nomination had been sabotaged by the Committee to Re-elect the President.

P: Bob didn't either, or wouldn't have known that either. You are not the issue involved. Had Bob known, he would be.

D: Bob—I don't believe specifically knew that they were going in there.

P: I don't think so.

D: I don't think he did. I think he knew that there was a capacity to do this but he was not given the specific direction. . . .

D: So, those people are in trouble as a result of the Grand Jury and the trial. . . . Now what has happened post June 17? I was under pretty clear instructions not to investigate this, but this could have been disastrous on the electorate if all hell had broken loose. I worked on a theory of containment—

P: Sure.

D: To try to hold it right where it was.

P: Right.

D: There is no doubt that I was totally aware of what the Bureau was doing at all times. I was totally aware of what the Grand Jury was doing. I knew what witnesses were going to be called. I knew what they were asked, and I had to. . . . Now post June 17th: These guys . . . started making demands. "We have to have attorneys fees. We don't have any money ourselves, and you are asking us to take this through the election." Alright, so arrangements were made through Mitchell, initiating it. And I was present in discussions where these guys had to be taken care of. Their attorneys fees had to be done. Kalmbach was brought in. Kalmbach raised some cash.

P: They put that under the cover of a Cuban Committee, I suppose?

D: Well, they had a Cuban Committee and . . . some of it was given to Hunt's[6] lawyer, who in turn passed it out. . . .

P: (unintelligible)—but I would certainly keep that cover for whatever it is worth. . . .

D: . . . Here is what is happening right now. . . . One, this is going to be a continual blackmail operation by Hunt and Liddy and the Cubans. No doubt about it. And McCord[7]. . . . Hunt has now made a direct threat against Ehrlichman[8]. . . . He says, "I will bring John Ehrlichman down to his knees and put him in jail. I have done enough seamy things for he and Krogh, they'll never survive it."

P: Was he talking about Ellsberg?

D: Ellsberg, and apparently some other things. I don't know the full extent of it.

P: I don't know about anything else.

---

[6]**Hunt:** E. Howard Hunt, a former CIA agent who, along with Liddy, led the "plumbers."

[7]**"Cubans . . . McCord":** refers to the four Cuban Americans who, together with former CIA agent James McCord, were arrested in the Watergate break-in.

[8]**Ehrlichman:** John Ehrlichman, a top Nixon aide.

D: I don't know either, and I hate to learn some of these things. So that is that situation. Now, where are at the soft points? How many people know about this? Well, let me go one step further in this whole thing. The Cubans that were used in the Watergate were also the same Cubans that Hunt and Liddy used for this California Ellsberg thing, for the break in out there. So they are aware of that. How high their knowledge is, is something else. Hunt and Liddy, of course, are totally aware of it, of the fact that it is right out of the White House.

P: I don't know what the hell we did that for!

D: I don't know either. . . . So that is it. That is the extent of the knowledge. So where are the soft spots on this? Well, first of all, there is the problem of the continued blackmail which will not only go on now, but it will go on while these people are in prison, and it will compound the obstruction of justice situation. It will cost money. It is dangerous. People around here are not pros at this sort of thing. This is the sort of thing Mafia people can do: washing money, getting clean money, and things like that. We just don't know about those things, because we are not criminals and not used to dealing in that business.

P: That's right.

D: It is a tough thing to know how to do.

P: Maybe it takes a gang to do that.

D: That's right. There is a real problem as to whether we could even do it. Plus there is a real problem in raising money. Mitchell has been working on raising some money. He is one of the ones with the most to lose. But there is no denying the fact that the White House, in Ehrlichman, Haldeman and Dean are involved in some of the early money decisions.

P: How much money do you need?

D: I would say these people are going to cost a million dollars over the next two years.

P: We could get that. On the money, if you need the money you could get that. You could get a million dollars. You could get it in cash. I know where it could be gotten. It is not easy, but it could be done. But the question is who the hell would handle it? Any ideas on that? . . .

D: Now we've got Kalmbach. Kalmbach received, at the close of the '68 campaign in January of 1969, he got a million $700,000 to be custodian for. That came, down from New York, and was placed in safe deposit boxes here. Some other people were on the boxes. And ultimately, the money was taken out to California. Alright, there is knowledge of the fact that he did start with a million seven. Several people know this. Now since 1969, he has spent a good deal of this money and accounting for it is going to be very difficult for Herb. For example, he has spent close to $500,000 on private polling. That opens up a whole new thing. It is not illegal, but more of the same thing.

P: Everybody does polling.

D: That's right. There is nothing criminal about it. It's private polling.

P: People have done private polling all through the years. There is nothing improper.

D: That's right. He sent $400,000, as he has described to me, somewhere in the South for another candidate. I assume this was $400,000 that went to [George] Wallace.

P: Wallace?

D: Right. He has maintained a man who I only know by the name of "Tony," who is the fellow who did the Chappaquiddick study.

P: I know about that.

D: And other odd jobs like that. Nothing illegal, but closer. I don't know of anything that Herb has done that is illegal. . . .What really bothers me is this growing situation. As I say, it is growing because of the continued need to provide support for the Watergate people who are going to hold us up for everything we've got, and the need for some people to perjure themselves as they go down the road here. If this thing ever blows, then we are in a cover up situation. I think it would be extremely damaging to you and the—

P: Sure. The whole concept of Administration justice. Which we cannot have! . . .

D: That's right. I am coming down to what I really think, is that Bob and John and John Mitchell and I can sit down and spend a day, or however long, to figure out one, how this can be carved away from you, so that it does not damage you or the Presidency. It just can't! You are not involved in it and it is something you shouldn't—

P: That is true! . . .

D: What really troubles me is one, will this thing not break some day and the whole thing—domino situation—everything starts crumbling, fingers will be pointing. Bob will be accused of things he has never heard of and deny and try to disprove it. It will get real nasty and just be a real bad situation. And the person who will be hurt by it most will be you and the Presidency, and I just don't think—

P: First, because I am an executive I am supposed to check these things.

D: That's right.

P: Let's come back to this problem. What are your feelings yourself, John? You know what they are all saying. What are your feelings about the chances?

D: I am not confident that we can ride through this. I think there are soft spots. . . .

P: . . . But just looking at it from a cold legal standpoint: you are a lawyer, you were a counsel—doing what you did as counsel. You were not—What would you go to jail for?

D: The obstruction of justice.

P: The obstruction of justice?

D: That is the only one that bothers me.

P: Well, I don't know. I think that one. I feel it could be cut off at the pass, maybe, the obstruction of justice. . . .Talking about your obstruction of justice, though, I don't see it.

D: Well, I have been a conduit for information on taking care of people out there who are guilty of crimes.

P: Oh, you mean like the blackmailers?

D: The blackmailers. Right.

P: Well, I wonder if that part of it can't be—I wonder if that doesn't —let me put it frankly: I wonder if that doesn't have to be continued? Let me put it this way: let us suppose that you get the million bucks, and you get the proper way to handle it. You could hold that side?

D: Uh, huh.

P: It would seem to me that would be worthwhile. . . .

D: There are two routes. One is to figure out how to cut the losses and minimize the human impact and get you up and out and away from it in any way. In a way it would never come back to haunt you. That is one general alternative. The other is to go down the road, just hunker down, fight it at every corner, every turn, don't let people testify—cover it up is what we really are talking about. Just keep it buried, and just hope that we can do it, hope that we make good decisions at the right time, keep our heads cool, we make the right moves.

P: And just take the heat?

D: And just take the heat. . . .

[H. R. Haldeman joins the meeting.]

P: . . . You see, John is concerned, as you know, about the Ehrlichman situation. It worries him a great deal because, and this is why the Hunt problem is so serious, because it had nothing to do with the campaign. It has to do with the Ellsberg case. I don't know what the hell the— (unintelligible)

H[aldeman]: But what I was going to say—

P: What is the answer on this? How you keep it out, I don't know. You can't keep it out if Hunt talks. You see the point is irrelevant. It has gotten to this point—

D: You might put it on a national security basis.

H: It absolutely was.

D: And say that this was—

H: (unintelligible)—CIA—

D: Ah—

H: Seriously.

P: National Security. We had to get information [from Ellsberg's psychiatrist's office] for national security grounds.

D: Then the question is, why didn't the CIA do it or why didn't the FBI do it?

P: Because we had to do it on a confidential basis.

H: Because we were checking them.

P: Neither could be trusted.

H: It has basically never been proven. There was reason to question their position.

P: With the bombing thing coming out and everything coming out, the whole thing was national security.

D: I think we could get by on that.

P: On that one I think we should simply say this was a national security investigation that was conducted. And on that basis, I think. . . Krogh could say he feels he did not perjure himself. He could say it was a national security matter. That is why—. . .You really only have two ways to go. You either decide that the whole (expletive deleted) thing is so full of problems with potential criminal liabilities, which most concern me. I don't give a damn about the publicity. We could rock that through that if we had to let the whole damn thing hang out, and it would be a lousy story for a month. But I can take it. The point is, that I don't want any criminal liabilities. That is the thing that I am concerned about for members of the White House staff, and I would trust for members of the Committee. . . .

H: Well, the thing we talked about yesterday. You have a question where you cut off on this. There is a possibility of cutting it at Liddy, where you are now.

P: Yeah.

D: But to accomplish that requires a continued perjury by Magruder and requires—

P: And requires total commitment and control over all of the defendants which— in other words when they are let down— . . . Another way to do it then Bob, and John realizes this, is to continue to try to cut our losses. Now we have to take a look at that course of action. First it is going to require approximately a million dollars to take care of the jackasses who are in jail. That can be arranged. That could be arranged. But you realize that after we are gone, and assuming we can expend this money, then they are going to crack and it would be an unseemly story. Frankly, all the people aren't going to care that much.

D: That's right.

P: People won't care, but people are going to be talking about it, there is no question. . . .And my point is that I think it is good, frankly, to consider these various options. And then, once you decide on the right plan, you say, "John," you say, "No doubts about the right plan before the election. You handled it just right. You contained it. And now after the election we have to have another plan. Because we can't for four years have this thing eating away." We can't do it.

H: We should change that a little bit. John's point is exactly right. The erosion here now is going to you, and that is the thing that we have to turn off at whatever cost. We have to turn it off at the lowest cost we can, but at whatever cost it takes.

D: That's what we have to do.

P: Well, the erosion is inevitably going to come here, apart from anything and all the people saying well the Watergate isn't a major issue. It isn't. But it will be. It's bound to. (Unintelligible) has to go out. Delaying is the great danger to the White House area. We don't, I say that the White House can't do it. Right?

D: Yes, Sir.

QUESTION

What "cancer" did John Dean worry about? • Did Dean and Attorney General Mitchell entertain plans to break the law? • How did President Nixon obtain information about opponents? • Why did Nixon and Dean believe they were being blackmailed, and how did they plan to respond? • How much money was involved? • How would it be obtained, and how would it be paid to the burglars? • How had money left over from the 1968 campaign been used? • What were the "soft spots" that worried Dean? • Did Nixon declare his opposition to a cover-up? • Did he demand that all members of his administration strictly adhere to the law? • How did Nixon hope to use arguments about national security? • Did Nixon believe the Watergate break-in was important? • Consider the type of source you have just read. • How reliable is a written transcript of a taped conversation? • Does it make a difference if you read the conversation rather than hear it?

COMPARATIVE QUESTIONS

How does the concept of justice outlined by Henry Gonzalez compare with that of President Nixon and John Dean? How does the issue of women's rights in the Supreme Court's judgment in **Roe v. Wade** *compare with the question of Mexican American identity voiced by Gonzalez? What basic political strategies were suggested by Gonzalez,* **Roe v. Wade,** *and Nixon?*

CHAPTER 31

THE REAGAN-BUSH COUNTERREVOLUTION
1980–1991

P resident Ronald Reagan set out to get government off the backs of the American people, to reduce taxes, to balance the budget, and to restore good, old-fashioned values. The problems of the nation were, in large measure, caused by government. Private enterprise and individual effort, not government programs, were the only solutions that worked. Reagan believed his views represented 100 percent Americanism and that those who differed were either deluded or suspect. The following documents illustrate Reagan's concept of morality, how it was put into action by his administration in the Iran-Contra affair, and how other Americans had different notions.

DOCUMENT 1
President Ronald Reagan Defends American Morality

President Ronald Reagan portrayed America as the embodiment of morality. He attributed American morality to traditional values he associated with Christianity. Millions of Americans agreed with him and voted for him. Reagan drew upon his ideas of American morality in his speech—excerpted here—to the annual convention of the National Association of American Evangelicals in Orlando, Florida, in 1983. The speech illustrates Reagan's concept of history as a struggle between good and evil and his certainty that he was on the side of good.

Address to the National Association of American Evangelicals, 1983

Those of you in the National Association of Evangelicals are known for your spiritual and humanitarian work. And I would be especially remiss if I didn't discharge right now one personal debt of gratitude. Thank you for your prayers. . . .

So I tell you there are a great many God-fearing, dedicated, noble men and women in public life, present company included. And yes, we need your help to keep us ever mindful of the ideas and the principles that brought us into the public arena in the first place. The basis of those ideals and principles is a commitment to freedom and personal liberty that, itself, is grounded in the much deeper realization that freedom prospers only where the blessings of God are avidly sought and humbly accepted. The American experiment in democracy rests on this insight. . . .

Well, I'm pleased to be here today with you who are keeping America great by keeping her good. Only through your work and prayers and those of millions of others can we hope to survive this perilous century and keep alive this experiment in liberty, this last, best hope of man.

I want you to know that this administration is motivated by a political philosophy that sees the greatness of America in you, her people, and in your families, churches, neighborhoods, communities — the institutions that foster and nourish values like concern for others and respect for the rule of law under God.

Now, I don't have to tell you that this puts us in opposition to, or at least out of step with, a prevailing attitude of many who have turned to a modern-day secularism, discarding the tried and time-tested values upon which our very civilization is based. No matter how well intentioned, their value system is radically different from that of most Americans. And while they proclaim that they're freeing us from superstitions of the past, they've taken upon themselves the job of superintending us by government rule and regulation. Sometimes their voices are louder than ours, but they are not yet a majority.

An example of that vocal superiority is evident in a controversy now going on in Washington. And since I'm involved, I've been waiting to hear from the parents of young America. How far are they willing to go in giving to government their prerogatives as parents?

Let me state the case as briefly and simply as I can. An organization of citizens, sincerely motivated and deeply concerned about the increase in illegitimate births and abortions involving girls well below the age of consent, some time ago established a nationwide network of clinics to offer

Ronald Reagan, "Remarks at the Annual Convention of the National Association of Evangelicals," in *Speaking My Mind: Selected Speeches* (New York: Simon and Schuster, 1989), 169–80.

help to these girls and, hopefully, alleviate this situation. Now, again, let me say, I do not fault their intent. However, in their well-intentioned effort, these clinics have decided to provide advice and birth control drugs and devices to underage girls without the knowledge of their parents. . . .

Well, we have ordered clinics receiving federal funds to notify the parents such help has been given. . . . I've watched TV panel shows discuss this issue, seen columnists pontificating on our error, but no one seems to mention morality as playing a part in the subject of sex.

Is all of Judeo-Christian tradition wrong? Are we to believe that something so sacred can be looked upon as a purely physical thing with no potential for emotional and psychological harm? . . .

Many of us in government would like to know what parents think about this intrusion in their family by government. We're going to fight in the courts. The right of parents and the rights of family take precedence over those of Washington-based bureaucrats and social engineers.

But the fight against parental notification is really only one example of many attempts to water down traditional values and even abrogate the original terms of American democracy. Freedom prospers when religion is vibrant and the rule of law under God is acknowledged. When our Founding Fathers passed the First Amendment, they sought to protect churches from government interference. They never intended to construct a wall of hostility between government and the concept of religious belief itself.

The evidence of this permeates our history and our government. The Declaration of Independence mentions the Supreme Being no less than four times. "In God We Trust" is engraved on our coinage. The Supreme Court opens its proceedings with a religious invocation. And the members of Congress open their sessions with a prayer. I just happen to believe the schoolchildren of the United States are entitled to the same privileges as Supreme Court justices and congressmen.

Last year, I sent the Congress a constitutional amendment to restore prayer to public schools. Already this session, there's growing bipartisan support for the amendment, and I am calling on the Congress to act speedily to pass it and to let our children pray. . . .

More than a decade ago, a Supreme Court decision literally wiped off the books of fifty states statutes protecting the rights of unborn children. Abortion on demand now takes the lives of up to one and a half million unborn children a year. Human life legislation ending this tragedy will someday pass the Congress, and you and I must never rest until it does. Unless and until it can be proven that the unborn child is not a living entity, then its right to life, liberty, and the pursuit of happiness must be protected. . . .

Now, I'm sure that you must get discouraged at times, but you've done better than you know, perhaps. There's a great spiritual awakening in America, a renewal of the traditional values that have been the bedrock of America's goodness and greatness.

One recent survey by a Washington-based research council concluded that Americans were far more religious than the people of other nations; 95 percent of those surveyed expressed a belief in God and a huge majority believed the Ten Commandments had real meaning in their lives. And another study has found that an overwhelming majority of Americans disapprove of adultery, teenage sex, pornography, abortion, and hard drugs. And this same study showed a deep reverence for the importance of family ties and religious belief.

I think the items that we've discussed here today must be a key part of the nation's political agenda. For the first time the Congress is openly and seriously debating and dealing with the prayer and abortion issues — and that's enormous progress right there. I repeat: America is in the midst of a spiritual awakening and a moral renewal. . . .

Now, obviously, much of this new political and social consensus I've talked about is based on a positive view of American history, one that takes pride in our country's accomplishments and record. But we must never forget that no government schemes are going to perfect man. We know that living in this world means dealing with what philosophers would call the phenomenology of evil or, as theologians would put it, the doctrine of sin.

There is sin and evil in the world, and we're enjoined by Scripture and the Lord Jesus to oppose it with all our might. Our nation, too, has a legacy of evil with which it must deal. The glory of this land has been its capacity for transcending the moral evils of our past. For example, the long struggle of minority citizens for equal rights, once a source of disunity and civil war, is now a point of pride for all Americans. We must never go back. There is no room for racism, anti-Semitism, or other forms of ethnic and racial hatred in this country.

I know that you've been horrified, as have I, by the resurgence of some hate groups preaching bigotry and prejudice. Use the mighty voice of your pulpits and the powerful standing of your churches to denounce and isolate these hate groups in our midst. The commandment given us is clear and simple: "Thou shalt love thy neighbor as thyself."

But whatever sad episodes exist in our past, any objective observer must hold a positive view of American history, a history that has been the story of hopes fulfilled and dreams made into reality. Especially in this century, America has kept alight the torch of freedom, but not just for ourselves but for millions of others around the world.

And this brings me to my final point today. During my first press conference as president, in answer to a direct question, I pointed out that, as good Marxist-Leninists, the Soviet leaders have openly and publicly declared that the only morality they recognize is that which will further their cause, which is world revolution. . . .

Well, I think the refusal of many influential people to accept this elementary fact of Soviet doctrine illustrates a historical reluctance to see totalitarian powers for what they are. We saw this phenomenon in the 1930s. We see it too often today.

This doesn't mean we should isolate ourselves and refuse to seek an understanding with them. I intend to do everything I can to persuade them of our peaceful intent, to remind them that it was the West that refused to use its nuclear monopoly in the forties and fifties for territorial gain and which now proposes a 50-percent cut in strategic ballistic missiles and the elimination of an entire class of land-based, intermediate-range nuclear missiles.

At the same time, however, they must be made to understand we will never compromise our principles and standards. We will never give away our freedom. We will never abandon our belief in God. And we will never stop searching for a genuine peace. But we can assure none of these things America stands for through the so-called nuclear freeze solutions proposed by some.

The truth is that a freeze now would be a very dangerous fraud, for that is merely the illusion of peace. The reality is that we must find peace through strength.

I would agree to a freeze if only we could freeze the Soviets' global desires. . . .

A number of years ago, I heard a young father, a very prominent young man in the entertainment world, addressing a tremendous gathering in California. It was during the time of the cold war, and communism and our own way of life were very much on people's minds. And he was speaking to that subject. And suddenly . . . I heard him saying, "I love my little girls more than anything.". . . He went on: "I would rather see my little girls die now, still believing in God, than have them grow up under communism and one day die no longer believing in God."

There were thousands of young people in that audience. They came to their feet with shouts of joy. They had instantly recognized the profound truth in what he had said, with regard to the physical and the soul and what was truly important.

Yes, let us pray for the salvation of all of those who live in that totalitarian darkness—pray they will discover the joy of knowing God. But until they do, let us be aware that while they preach the supremacy of the state, declare its omnipotence over individual man, and predict its eventual domination of all peoples on the earth, they are the focus of evil in the modern world. . . .

But if history teaches anything, it teaches that simpleminded appeasement or wishful thinking about our adversaries is folly. It means the betrayal of our past, the squandering of our freedom.

So, I urge you to speak out against those who would place the United States in a position of military and moral inferiority. . . . I urge you to beware the temptation of pride—the temptation of blithely declaring yourselves above it all and label both sides equally at fault, to ignore the facts of history and the aggressive impulses of an evil empire, to simply call the arms race a giant misunderstanding and thereby remove yourself from the struggle between right and wrong and good and evil.

I ask you to resist the attempts of those who would have you withhold your support for our efforts, this administration's efforts, to keep America strong and free, while we negotiate real and verifiable reductions in the world's nuclear arsenals and one day, with God's help, their total elimination.

While America's military strength is important, let me add here that I've always maintained that the struggle now going on for the world will never be decided by bombs or rockets, by armies or military might. The real crisis we face today is a spiritual one; at root, it is a test of moral will and faith. . . .

I believe we shall rise to the challenge. I believe that communism is another sad, bizarre chapter in human history whose last pages even now are being written. I believe this because the source of our strength in the quest for human freedom is not material, but spiritual. And because it knows no limitation, it must terrify and ultimately triumph over those who would enslave their fellow man.

QUESTIONS

According to Reagan, what was the proper connection between religion and politics? • Whom did he identify as the domestic opponents of his views on this subject? • What did his opponents believe? • What examples did he give of threats to the Judeo-Christian tradition? • What made the Soviet Union the "evil empire"? • What did he believe that the government should do to defend against the evil empire? • Who opposed such efforts?

DOCUMENT 2

The Iran-Contra Hearings: Lt. Colonel Oliver L. North Describes Covert Operations

The Reagan administration engaged in a number of illegal, secret ventures to support anti-Communist movements in Central America and elsewhere. Under the direction of the highest levels of the administration, a covert foreign policy was carried out in violation of federal law and the administration's own public statements. Some of the details of these activities came to light in the Iran-Contra hearings before a congressional committee in 1987. In the following excerpt from those hearings, Lt. Colonel Oliver L. North began his testimony about his own involvement in selling arms to Iran—one of America's enemies—and using the proceeds to finance the Contras, anti-Communist forces fighting the government of Nicaragua, an expenditure that Congress had not authorized. Colonel North's testimony illustrates the contempt among the highest officials in the Reagan administration for the nation's processes of constitutional democracy.

Testimony at the Iran-Contra Hearings, 1987

Mr. Nields: Colonel North, were you involved in the use of the proceeds of sales of weapons to Iran for the purpose of assisting the Contras in Nicaragua?

Lt. Col. North: On advice of counsel, I respectfully decline to answer the question based on my Constitutional Fifth Amendment rights.

Chairman Inouye: Colonel North, you're appearing here today pursuant to subpoenas issued on behalf of the Senate and House Select Committees. I hereby communicate to you orders issued by the United States District Court for the District of Columbia at the request of the Committees providing that you may not refuse to provide any evidence to these Committees on the basis of your privilege against self-incrimination and providing further that no evidence or other information obtained under the oath or any information directly or indirectly derived from such evidence may be used against you in any criminal proceeding. I, therefore, pursuant to such orders, direct you to answer the questions put to you. . . .

Mr. Nields: Colonel North, you were involved in two operations of great significance to the people of this country, is that correct?

Lt. Col. North: At least two, yes sir.

Mr. Nields: And one of them involved the support of the Contras during the time the Boland Amendment[1] was in effect, and another one involved the sale of arms to Iran, is that correct?

Lt. Col. North: Yes, it also involved support for the Democratic outcome in the Nicaragua vote before and after the Boland Amendment was in effect.

Mr. Nields: And these operations—they were covert operations?

Lt. Col. North: Yes, they were.

Mr. Nields: And covert operations are designed to be secrets from our enemies?

Oliver L. North, *Taking the Stand: The Testimony of Lieutenant Colonel Oliver L. North* (New York: Simon and Schuster, 1987).

[1]**Boland Amendment:** adopted by Congress and signed by President Reagan in 1984, forbidding the CIA or "any other agency or entity involved in intelligence activities" from spending money to support the Contras.

Lt. Col. North: That is correct.

Mr. Nields: But these operations were designed to be secrets from the American people?

Lt. Col. North: Mr. Nields, I'm at a loss as to how we could announce it to the American people and not have the Soviets know about it. And I'm not trying to be flippant, but I just don't see how you could possibly do it.

Mr. Nields: Well, in fact, Col. North, you believed that the Soviets were aware of our sale of arms to Iran, weren't you?

Lt. Col. North: We came to a point in time when we were concerned about that.

Mr. Nields: But it was designed to be kept a secret from the American people?

Lt. Col. North: I think what is important, Mr. Nields, is that we somehow arrive at some kind of an understanding right here and now as to what a covert operation is. If we could [find] a way to insulate with a bubble over these hearings that are being broadcast in Moscow, and talk about covert operations to the American people without it getting into the hands of our adversaries, I'm sure we would do that. But we haven't found the way to do it.

Mr. Nields: But you put it somewhat differently to the Iranians with whom you were negotiating on the 8th and 9th of October in Frankfurt, Germany, didn't you? You said to them that Secretary of Defense Weinberger in our last session with the President said, "I don't think we should send one more screw" — talking about the Hawk [missile] parts — "until we have our Americans back from Beirut, because when the American people find out that this has happened, they'll impeach you" — referring to the President. . . .

Mr. Nields: . . . [M]y question is simple. Did you tell the Iranians with whom you were negotiating on October 8th and 9th that the Secretary of Defense had told the President at his most recent meeting, when the American people find out that this has happened, they'll impeach him? That's the entire question. Did you say that to the Iranians? . . .

Lt. Col. North: Mr. Nields, this is apparently one of the transcripts of tape recordings that I caused to be made of my discussions with the Iranians. I would like to note that for every conversation, whenever it was possible, I asked for the assistance of our intelligence services . . . to tape record and transcribe every single session, so that when I returned there would be no doubt as to what I said. . . . That is a bald-faced lie, told to the Iranians, and I will tell you right now, I'd have offered the Iranians a free trip to Disneyland if we could have gotten Americans home for it.

Mr. Nields: Question was: Did you say it?

Lt. Col. North: I absolutely said it. I said a lot of other things to the Iranians, to get—

Mr. Nields: And, when the Hasenfus[2] plane went down in Nicaragua, the United States government told the American people that the United States government had no connection whatsoever with that airplane. Is that also true?

Lt. Col. North: I, I, when I—when the Hasenfus airplane went down, I was in the air headed for Europe, so I do not know what the initial statements were, and I couldn't comment on them. . . .

Mr. Nields: It was not true that the United States government had no connection with Mr. Hasenfus, the airplane that went down in Nicaragua.

Lt. Col. North: No, it was not true. I had an indirect connection with that flight. . . .

Mr. Nields: . . . [I]n certain communist countries, the government's activities are kept secret from the people. But that's not the way we do things in America, is it?

Lt. Col. North: Counsel, I would like to go back to what I said just a few moments ago. I think it is very important for the American people to understand that this is a dangerous world; that we live at risk and that this nation is at risk in a dangerous world. And that they ought not to be lead to believe, as a consequence of these hearings, that this nation cannot or should not conduct covert operations. By their very nature covert operations or special activities are a lie. There is great deceit, deception practiced in the conduct of covert operation. They are at essence a lie. We make every effort to deceive the enemy as to our intent, our conduct and to deny the association of the United States with those activities. . . . The American people ought not to be lead to believe by the way you're asking that question that we intentionally deceived the American people, or had that intent to begin with. The effort to conduct these covert operations was made in such a way that our adversaries would not have knowledge of them, or that we could deny American association with it, or the association of this government with those activities. And that is not wrong.

Mr. Nields: The American people were told by this government that our government had nothing to do with the Hasenfus airplane, and that was false. And it is a principal purpose of these hearings to replace secrecy and deception with disclosure and truth. And that's one of the reasons we have called you here, sir. And one question the American people would like to know the answer to is what did the President know about the diversion of the proceeds of Iranian arms sales to the contras. Can you tell us what you know about that, sir?

---

[2]**Hasenfus plane:** Hasenfus was an American citizen on a covert, Contra-supporting mission for the CIA whose plane crashed in the Nicaraguan jungle in 1986. At the time, the Reagan administration denied any knowledge of or connection with Hasenfus.

Lt. Col. North: You just took a long leap from Mr. Hasenfus' airplane. As I told this Committee several days ago, and if you'll indulge me, Counsel, in a brief summary of what I said, I never personally discussed the use of the residuals or profits from the sale of US weapons to Iran for the purpose of supporting the Nicaraguan resistance with the President. I never raised it with him and he never raised it with me during my entire tenure at the National Security Council staff. Throughout the conduct of my entire tenure at the National Security Council, I assumed that the President was aware of what I was doing and had, through my superiors, approved it.

I sought approval of my superiors for every one of my actions and it is well-documented. I assumed when I had approval to proceed from either Judge Clarke, Bud McFarlane or Admiral Poindexter[3], that they had indeed solicited and obtained the approval of the President. . . .

Mr. Nields: Colonel North, you left something out, didn't you?. . .

Mr. Nields: You testified that you assumed that the President had authorized the diversion. Lieutenant colonels in the Marine Corps do not divert millions of dollars from arms sales to Iran for the benefit of the contras based on assumptions, do they? You had a basis for your assumption.

Lt. Col. North: I had the approval of my superiors. As I did for all the other things that I did, Mr. Nields.

Mr. Nields: You had something else, didn't you, sir? You had a specific reason for believing that the President had approved. You wrote memoranda, did you not, seeking the President's approval for the diversion?

Lt. Col. North: I did.

Mr. Nields: And indeed, you wrote more than one of them.

Lt. Col. North: I did.

Mr. Nields: How many did you write?

Lt. Col. North: Again, I will estimate that there may have been as many as five. . . .

Mr. Nields: And these five were written, I take it, on each occasion where there was a proposed sale of arms to the Iranians that you felt had reached sufficiently final form to seek the President's approval?

Lt. Col. North: Yes. . . .

Mr. Nields: And you sent those memoranda up the line?

Lt. Col. North: It is my recollection that I sent each one of those up the line, and that on the three where I had approval to proceed, I thought that I had received authority from the President. I want to make it very clear that no memorandum ever came back to me with the President's

---

[3]**"Bud McFarlane or Admiral Poindexter":** Robert "Bud" McFarlane was Reagan's national security advisor in 1985 and the man who first proposed the arms-for-hostages deal; McFarlane was succeeded in the post by Admiral John Poindexter.

initials on it. or the President's name on it, or a note from the President on it—none of these memoranda. . . .

Mr. Nields: . . . My question right now is, you sent these memoranda up to the National Security Adviser, is that correct?

Lt. Col. North: That is correct.

Mr. Nields: For him to obtain the President's approval?

Lt. Col. North: Yes. . . .

MR. NEILDS: Because you specifically wanted before proceeding on a matter of this degree of importance to have the President's approval?

Lt. Col. North: Yes. . . .

Mr. Nields: . . . [W]here are these memoranda?

Lt. Col. North: Which memoranda?

Mr. Nields: The memoranda that you sent up to Admiral Poindexter seeking the President's approval.

Lt. Col. North: . . . I think I shredded most of that. Did I get 'em all? . . .

Mr. Nields: Well, that was going to be my very next question, Colonel North, "Isn't it true that you shredded them?"

Lt. Col. North: I believe I did.

Mr. Nields: And that would include the copies with the President—with a check mark where the line says, "approved"?

Lt. Col. North: That would have included all copies of—I tried, as I was departing the NSC, a process which began as early as October, to destroy all references to these covert operations. I willingly admit that. . . .

Mr. Nields: Well, that's the whole reason for shredding documents, isn't it, Colonel North, so that you can later say, you don't remember whether you had them and you don't remember what's in them?

Lt. Col. North: No, Mr. Nields, the reason for shredding documents and the reason the government of the United States gave me a shredder—I mean, I didn't buy it myself—was to destroy documents that were no longer relevant, that did not apply or that should not be divulged. And again, I want to go back to the whole intent of the covert operation. Part of a covert operation is to offer plausible deniability of the association of the government of the United States with the activity. Part of it is to deceive our adversaries. Part of it is to ensure that those people who are at great peril carrying out those activities are not further endangered. All of those are good and sufficient reasons to destroy documents. And that's why the government buys shredders by the tens and dozens and gives them to people running covert operations—not so that they can have convenient memories. I came here to tell you the truth, to tell you and this Committee and the American people the truth. And I'm trying to do that, Mr. Nields, and I don't like the insinuation that I'm up here having a convenient memory lapse, like perhaps some others have had. . . .

Mr. Nields: There's been testimony before the Committee that you engaged in shredding of documents on November the 21st, 1986. Do you deny that?

Lt. Col. North: I do not deny that I engaged in shredding on November 21st. I will also tell this Committee that I engaged in shredding almost every day that I had a shredder, and that I put things in burn-bags when I didn't. So every single day that I was at the National Security Council staff, some documents were destroyed. And I don't want you to have the impression that those documents that I referred to seeking approval disappeared on the 21st, because I can't say that. In fact, I'm quite sure, by virtue of the conversations I remember about the 21st that those documents were already gone. They were gone by virtue of the fact that we saw these operations unraveling as early as the mid part of October with the loss of the Hasenfus airplane and the discussion that the Director of Central Intelligence had had with a private citizen about what he knew of a contra diversion, as you put it. And at that point, I began to, one, recognize I would be leaving the NSC—because that was a purpose for my departure, to offer the scapegoat, if you will; and, second of all, recognizing what was coming down, I didn't want some new person walking in there, opening files that would possibly expose people at risk. . . .

Mr. Nields: Were you considering the issue of damage to the President when you were destroying documents from your files?

Lt. Col. North: I was considering the issue of damage to the President when I was preparing documents. . . .

Mr. Nields: What do you mean by "damage to the President"?

Lt. Col. North: Well, . . . damage to the President can come in several forms. Domestic political repercussions, international ramifications where other countries won't even talk to us again, like, perhaps the consequence of these hearings, or cooperate with us. I can see the risks that it would put on other people. The lives of the hostages, the damage potentially to international agreements, and quite apart from any other kinds of damage physically.

Mr. Nields: Let's talk about political damage. Were you concerned about political damage?

Lt. Col. North: Of course. I think one of the responsibilities of a National Security Council staff officer is to be aware that that staff has to be concerned about the domestic political ramifications as well as the international relationships that are affected.

Mr. Nields: And, the President was then suffering domestic political damage, was he not, as a result of the publicity surrounding the Iranian arms mission? . . .

Lt. Col. North: Yes.

Mr. Nields: And, you were concerned about that?

Lt. Col. North: Always. . . .

Mr. Nields: . . . Are you here telling the Committee that you don't remember whether on November 21st there was a document in your files reflecting Presidential approval of the diversion?

Lt. Col. North: As a matter of fact, I'll tell you specifically that I thought they were all gone, because by the time I was told that some point early on November 21st that there would an inquiry conducted by Mr. Meese[4], I assured Admiral Poindexter—incorrectly it seems—that all of those documents no longer existed. And so that is early on November 21st because I believe the decision to make an inquiry, to have the Attorney General or Mr. Meese in his role as friend to the President conduct a fact-finding excursion on what happened in September and November in 1985. I assured the Admiral, "Don't worry, it's all taken care of."

Mr. Nields: You had already shredded them?

Lt. Col. North: I thought. That's right. . . .

Mr. Nields: And, you were aware, were you not, sometime during the day on Friday, November 21st, that the Attorney General's people were going to come in and look at documents over the weekend?

Lt. Col. North: That is correct.

Mr. Nields: And, you shredded documents before they got there?

Lt. Col. North: I would prefer to say that I shredded documents that day like I did on all other days, but perhaps with increased intensity, that is correct.

Mr. Nields: So that the people you were keeping these documents from, the ones that you shredded, were representatives of the Attorney General of the United States?

Lt. Col. North: They worked for him. . . .

Mr. Nields: And the fact that you shredded a whole stack of documents in the afternoon of Friday, November 21st, right after you had heard the Attorney General's people were coming to look at documents in the morning is a pure coincidence? . . . Is it your testimony that the documents that you shredded right after you found out that the Attorney General's people were coming in over the weekend to look at documents had nothing to do with the fact that his people were coming in to look at documents?

Lt. Col. North: No, I'm not saying that.

Mr. Nields: So you shredded some documents because the Attorney General's people were coming in over the weekend?

Lt. Col. North: I do not preclude that as part of what was shredded. I do not preclude that as being a possibility—not at all. . . .

Mr. Nields: . . . Did you tell Gen. Secord[5] that you and the President had joked about the fact that the Ayatollah was providing funds to the contras?

---

[4]**Mr. Meese:** Edwin Meese, the Reagan administration's attorney general from 1985 to 1988.

[5]**Gen. Secord:** Richard Secord, a former air force general, who was recruited by Oliver North to buy weapons with laundered money and convey them to the Nicaraguan Contras.

Lt. Col. North: I do not recall specifically telling Gen. Secord that joke, or story, but I did not joke with the President, if I may amplify on that. As I recall, there was a meeting in mid to late summer of 1986 in which the discussion focused on the fact that the Congress, both houses, had voted $100 million to aid the Nicaraguan resistance, and that the $100 million appropriations and authorizations had to be conferenced to be sent forward to the President. And, for whatever reason, the Congress was unwilling to send a coordinated bill forward for the President's signature. And, if my recollection is correct, the principle discussion focused on that issue as to what could be done to help or encourage the Congress to, indeed, send forward what both Houses had already voted to approve.

At the conclusion of that meeting, on leaving, at the door, as I recall, I said to the back of Adm. Poindexter, "It looks like the Ayatollah is going to have help the Nicaraguan freedom fighters a little longer," or words to that effect. It was an aside. I do not believe that the President could have heard it. And I exaggerated that to Gen. Secord. . . .

Mr. Nields: So, you're not denying that you said that to General Secord?

Lt. Col. North: Absolutely not. . . .

Mr. Nields: And you recall, do you not, being intimately involved in the shipment of 18 Hawks to Iran?

Lt. Col. North: I was—

Mr. Nields: In November of 1985.

Lt. Col. North: I was, indeed, intimately involved in the shipment of Hawks to Iran in 1985. . . .

Mr. Nields: Was the Attorney General aware in November of 1985 that 18 Hawk missiles had been shipped to Iran?

Lt. Col. North: I did not specifically address it to the Attorney General in November of 1985. I do remember discussions which included the Attorney General subsequent to this event. . . .

Mr. Nields: I'd like to return to . . . the question of who it was in the Administration that decided that the false version of the facts should be put forward. . . .

Lt. Col. North: I don't know. . . .

Mr. Nields: Did you discuss the wisdom of putting out a false version of the facts with Admiral Poindexter?

Lt. Col. North: I may have. I don't recall a specific discussion. Again, he and I knew what had transpired back in November of '85. He and I knew that this version of the document was wrong, intentionally misleading, showing a separation between the United States and Israel on the activity. . . .

Mr. Nields: . . . First of all, you put some value, don't you, in the truth?

Lt. Col. North: I've put great value in the truth. I came here to tell it.

Mr. Nields: So, . . . that would be a reason not to put forward this version of the facts?

Lt. Col. North: The truth would be a reason not to put forward that version of the facts, but as I indicated to you a moment ago, I put great value on the lives of the American hostages. I worked hard to bring back as many as we could. I put great value in the possibility that we could . . . and that we had established for the first time a direct contact with people inside Iran who might be able to assist us in the strategic reopening, and who were at great risk if they were exposed. And, so, yes, I put great value in the truth, and as I said, I came here to tell it. . . .

Mr. Nields: By putting out this false version of the facts, you were committing, were you not, the entire administration to telling a false story?

Lt. Col. North: Well, let, let—I'm not trying to pass the buck here. Okay? I did a lot of things, and I want to stand up and say that I'm proud of them. I don't want you to think, Counsel, that I went about this all on my own. I realized, there's a lot of folks around that think there's a loose cannon on the gundeck of state at the NSC. That wasn't what I heard while I worked there. I've only heard it since I left. People used to walk up to me and tell me what a great job I was doing, and the fact is there were many many people, to include the former assistant to the President for National Security Affairs, the current national security adviser, the Attorney General of the United States of America, the Director of Central Intelligence, all of whom knew that to be wrong. . . .

Mr. Nields: . . . My question to you is this: Isn't it true—and I'll put it that others above you, by putting out this version of the facts, were committing the President of the United States to a false story.

Lt. Col. North: Yes, that's true.

Mr. Nields: Did you ever say to any of those people, "you can't do that without asking the President"?

Lt. Col. North: No, I did not.

Mr. Nields: Did you ever say, "you can't do that, it's not true and you cannot commit the President of the United States to a lie"?

Lt. Col. North: I don't believe that I ever said that to anyone, no.

Mr. Nields: Did anybody else in your presence say that?

Lt. Col. North: No.

Mr. Nields: So none of these people—Director of Central Intelligence, two National Security Advisors, Attorney General—none of them ever made the argument, "it's not true, you can't say it"?

Lt. Col. North: No, and in fairness to them, I think that they had a darn good reason for not putting the straight story out, and their reasons might have been the same as mine, they may have been different. And you'd have to ask them. The fact is, I think there were good and sufficient reasons at that time.

Mr. Nields: Did anybody ask the President?

Lt. Col. North: I did not.

Mr. Nields: Do you know if anyone else did?

Lt. Col. North: I do not.

QUESTIONS

Did North testify that he had been involved with the sale of weapons to Iran to aid the Contras in Nicaragua? • Did he believe his actions were legal? • Why were his actions kept secret from the American people? • Did North believe he had the approval of his superiors, including the president? • Why did he contribute to false public statements about activities he participated in? • From his viewpoint, how did shredding documents and telling lies to the American people reflect his commitment to the truth? • Do you agree with North's position that lying to the American people was necessary in this case?

DOCUMENT 3

Activism in the 1980s

While the 1980s saw many victories for the conservative agenda, liberal opposition was by no means completely absent. Activists worked for change on a number of issues, ranging from gay rights to U.S. policy in Central America to protecting the environment. In a 1989 interview, excerpted here, Mindy Lorenz traced her route to activism as a coordinator of the Greens, an international environmental movement. Lorenz grew up in a household that supported the presidential candidacy of conservative Republican Barry Goldwater, became an antiwar activist at the University of Maryland during the 1960s, and taught art history at a college in California before devoting her time to the Greens. Lorenz's interview illustrates how some Americans reacted to the activities of the Reagan administration in Central America.

Mindy Lorenz
Oral History, 1989

I was living in Washington, D.C., at the time that Martin Luther King was killed, and those events had just an incredible impact on me. I went downtown the day after the shooting to bring living supplies into churches and saw armed soldiers on the corner. The day before I had been into D.C. and it looked like it always did, and then the next day it looked like an armed camp. Those events just tremendously influenced me. I was very idealistic—I still am—and the fact that people were being killed for their beliefs, especially Martin Luther King, Jr., I guess helped make the point that has been growing in my awareness all these years,

In Lauren Kessler, *After All These Years: Sixties Ideals in a Different World* (New York: Thunders Mouth Press, 1990), 97–100.

that there's a lot at stake when people are very serious about wanting things to change. . . . [Lorenz went on to get a Ph.D. in art history and began teaching at Claremont College near Los Angeles.]

Then in 1980 I saw a show on television about the church women, the American church women who were murdered in El Salvador. And it was like a bomb going off in my head, and I thought, "Oh my god, we're into it again." And I could just see all the issues coalescing in terms of what had been going on during the Vietnam War, and so I just sought out information on what kind of organized activities there were in anti-intervention circles, and quickly became active in CISPES [Committee in Solidarity with the People of El Salvador] in Los Angeles, and started organizing a campus chapter. The situation personally grabbed me because it just seemed like some of the lessons that I had learned about what our government should and shouldn't be doing in the world were just coming to a kind of crisis point once again. And so, I got involved in the sanctuary movement.

For me this was a real life-affecting set of activities because during the Vietnam War I wasn't meeting people from Vietnam. I wasn't meeting the people that we were directly involved in the bombing and experiencing the impact that things were having in their lives. But here with the Central American refugees, I was meeting the people who were directly affected by what we were doing and, boy, that was really intense for me. Very, very painful. But very important in consolidating my personal awareness that I couldn't just do this part-time, I couldn't do it on weekends, I couldn't just do it sometimes and then forget about it. Personal experience with the people deepened my commitment, and sort of led to my making a decision to leave academic life full-time. It was interfering with my ability to spend the number of hours that it took to do my job well, and also it was interfering with me feeling like I had the freedom of action to do what I needed to do with my political work and not worry about the ramifications with my job.

It was an intense kind of family dynamic. My daughter was nine or ten years old in the early eighties. It was difficult for a young kid to have to face her mother getting arrested and possibly spending time in jail. And meeting these people from Central America who were very strange to her and very threatening in many ways, having a lot of people around the house, and hearing about our house being under surveillance—it was very difficult.

My daughter's sixteen now, and she has a very different perspective on things from that of most people her age, and I think she feels very proud of that. But it's also hard for her because it separates her a lot from her peers.

It was in the midst of doing the Central America work that I realized that single issue politics seemed somewhat limited to me. I mean, they were important, and it needed to be done, but I guess my personal frame of reference was to try to develop a really comprehensive way of seeing the way the change needed to happen, knowing that some of it was definitely short-term emergency kinds of urgent issues.

At one point I read about the German Greens and just had a very superficial understanding of what their program was about. So I wrote for their program, their platform. Reading that, it was like another kind of light bulb going off, I read the program and I thought, "Oh, my god, here it is. This is it." It was saying everything that I had been thinking about, and they were already organized and already out there in a visible way, already running people for office on the basis of a platform that just seemed to address all this comprehensive relationship between nature and women and domination and the environment. It was all laid out. And almost immediately at an antinuclear rally I saw a banner saying "Greens," and it was like a miracle. I thought, "God, I can't believe it." I went to a meeting, and that was it. That was about five years ago.

I think the time that it takes for fundamental changes to happen is sometimes very discouraging. But I do feel that just on this very broad scale, I think the history of human cultures has been a slow progression toward, I guess we'd just have to call it the establishment of ever more democratic institutions.

I think that globally we're beginning to understand what it takes to have truly democratic institutions in a way that I don't think has been understood before. And I think the Greens model of understanding what it takes to have truly democratic institutions is the best I see in the world. It takes massive citizen participation, otherwise it's going to be a form of oligarchy or a form of fascism, or closer to the models in the past where you basically had a benevolent, centralized leadership and a rather passive and uninformed mass of people. And I think that has to change in order for a democracy to function. And I think more and more people are realizing that.

Electoral politics is undeniably an important aspect of the Greens movement everywhere in the world. It's not the only part of it, but I think that to be able to work both within the existing power systems and to work outside those power systems, to develop strategies so that both happen simultaneously and remain linked with each other is an important set of experiments that we have to carry out. And it's not an either/or, it can't be, because it's rather difficult to work outside of the system. Change has to come simultaneously in many areas, and I think the Greens are developing an analysis that really recognizes that complexity. It's not a matter of just dropping out and trying to ignore the power system, it just cannot be done.

For me, the core issue has always been domination, trying to recognize domination wherever it occurs, whether it's in family dynamics or interpersonal or a broader kind of social level. I don't know why I have felt that so staunchly over the years, but that's the struggle I had with my mother, it's the struggle I've had in my personal life in relationships with men, and I just see it as the basis of a tremendous amount of suffering in the world. And until we can individually and collectively organize ourselves to create institutions and structures that are based on core values of not dominating, not needing to competitively dominate, we're just going to keep doing the same stuff over and over again.

I talk to people all the time who say, "Oh well, you know, nothing ever came of the sixties." And they've been holding a kind of pessimism for twenty years because of that. But the sixties did lead to something. It wasn't just this intense period and then everything died. It was part of an evolutionary process. It's hard to talk to people about a long period of history. People just see the kind of devastation around us and say, "Well, you know, if you guys can't do something in the next five years, forget it. We're not gonna join." But I think what Greens end up realizing is how deep these things go, and unless you're in for the long haul and unless you're willing to really study the history of these issues, we will only continue to repeat the same failures.

Having that broader picture, for me, is what keeps me going on a day-to-day basis and helps to give me the courage. It is really the seat of my optimism, and I think if I were to lose that broader picture and understanding of things, I would feel very swallowed up in the immediacy of the suffering. The Greens have a spiritual and historical and theoretical understanding that I have not found in any other political group I have ever worked with. Being part of the organization has allowed me to live in a way that feels very integrated and just feels terrific.

QUESTIONS

How did Martin Luther King's assassination influence Lorenz? • How did she become involved in work with refugees from El Salvador? • How did her work with them influence her political outlook? • How did her political work influence her family? • Why did she become active with environmental issues? • What did she believe was the core issue?

COMPARATIVE QUESTIONS

Does Oliver North's testimony uphold the ideals defended by President Reagan in his speech to the National Association of American Evangelicals? Does Mindy Lorenz's work with El Salvadoran refugees agree with the ideals of Reagan and North? How did the three individuals view communism? How did they view democracy? How do their views of political morality differ?

CHAPTER 32

THE CLINTON ADMINISTRATION AND THE SEARCH FOR A POPULAR CENTER 1992–1997: PERSPECTIVES ON AMERICA

L ike all people, Americans situate themselves in the present by re-flecting on the past. They look at their lives, measure the changes they have experienced, and chart a future that remains unknown. What follows are five perspectives on America. Each of the individuals interviewed discussed how his or her life intersected major changes that occurred in American society in recent decades. And each person wonders what the future will hold.

DOCUMENT 1
A Chicago Steelworker and His Wife

Changes in the American economy since the 1970s have profoundly altered the lives of many Americans. The shift of the employment base from manufacturing to service industries, the rapid transfer of jobs to low-wage areas throughout the world, the trend away from manual and toward mental labor—these and other economic developments have created hard times for many American fami-lies. In the following interview conducted in the late 1980s, Ike Mazo and his wife, Susan Dudak, who live in Chicago, describe their experiences with eco-nomic change.

Ike Mazo

Oral History

This is the first time in four generations that I have it worse than my father. My father had steady employment when he wanted it.

You had a thirty-, forty-year period where a guy could come in off the street and get a job. And go on. There were always strikes and layoffs, but you always came back. You could plan your life financially. You could say, I'll take X amount of income and I'll buy a house. I can put away X amount of income, so I could send at least one of my kids to college.

That's changed for me. My wife has went to work. Incomewise, we're the same. Standard of living, we're not. My father had hospital benefits. He was paid something while he was off sick. We pay our own hospitalization, what little we have. If I break my leg right now, we're gonna lose this house.

I went into the Marine Corps at seventeen, I came out at nineteen. I volunteered, of course. Came out of that, all screwed up mentally. It wasn't what I expected. A seventeen-year-old kid had been exposed to combat films and glory and stuff such as that: everything you had been brought up with. I swallowed all of it: George Washington, cherry tree, and everything. You come out and it's all gone.

You always felt that this country could do no wrong. We were always the good guys, whoever we take on are the bad guys. I was pro-Vietnam, I was one hundred percent. It was really funny, because I came home and my father was involved in anti-Vietnam demonstrations (laughs). My twin brother, Mike, was the same way. I called him a hippie. He was workin' in the mills, but he was goin' to college at night. I wanted to sweep through there and kick ass, get it over with, get out. We had some good discussions (laughs).

I started readin' and readin' in depth. I started readin' the news more than the sporting page. You gradually start to change. Plus there was a great deal of influence around.

I got out at nineteen, when most people were bein' drafted. Prior to Vietman, I wanted to go to college. For two or three years after I came back, I got jobs here and there, and made a conscious decision to be a worker.

I was walkin' by Southworks, U.S. Steel, and saw the sign: HELP WANTED. This is 1972. You could literally walk across the street and get a job. So I got an apprenticeship as a boilermaker. That's what I am now, a journeyman boilermaker. The main reason I stayed at Southworks was

Studs Terkel, *The Great Divide: Second Thoughts on the American Dream* (New York: Aron, 1988), 172–77.

the satisfaction in bein' a griever. You know, the one people come to when they have grievances. That was the greatest experience in the world. Up until this time, you're a worker and they're the boss. They have no problem pointin' that out to you damn near every day. I would sit in there as a high school dropout and I'm up against this college-educated superintendent, and you're on one-and-one and you're as good as him.

My father didn't want me in the mills. He cussed me and my brother both. Said he fought for twenty years to stay out of the mills, and me and my brother were lookin' at it simply as a job. You had to have a job.

I would want my children to go to college. But I never shared that idea that you strive and work and struggle so your children can rise above your class, which is working-class. If they choose that, so be it. I don't know if my father wanted me to be a doctor, lawyer, but—I wouldn't want my kids in the mill.

What do I see for my kids? I really don't know. It's kind of frightening, scary. It's not only for my kids. It's that whole young group. You get enough of 'em out of work and those are the ones that'll trip across the picket line. If they've never worked, they don't have that tradition. They've never worked with that old guy next to 'em.

I had a very close friend who went across the [Chicago] *Tribune* picket line. What do I do? I go shun this guy? Don't have nothin' to do with him? My father said, Yeah, cut him off.

I don't think this guy will ever do it again. When we bought this house, I had a little get-together. He didn't wanna come. He was ashamed. I remember him tellin' me, "You're treatin' me like a piece of shit." I said, "What do you expect? If they break that strike and you're gonna be permanent there, they'll want your head right. They don't care about you."

When you come back from Vietnam, you're angry, chip on your shoulder. You go to work and you start gettin' treated a certain way. You don't wanna be a suck-ass, you don't wanna take that shit. So you try different things. I was gonna be so good at my job that no boss was ever gonna mess with me. Then you realize that's not the answer. Look what happened at Southworks. The logical answer is havin' unions, all around you. These young kids figure the time for a union has come and went. They figure they can make it on their own. Individualism and makin' it on your own is an admirable trait. But it don't work that way. They never had the one older guy tellin' the next guy come along what it's all about.

Why did Southworks close? U.S. Steel bought Marathon Oil. And they was gettin' millions of dollars every time they shut down a facility. They had until April to shut us down to get the writeoff for the previous year.

This was one of the most modern facilities around. They got caster there, they got electric furnace, they got the oxygen process. And thousands of guys were laid off. So how's the individual gonna make it on his own? When the mill closed down in '82, I was out of work for a year and a half. That's when my wife went to work. The kids are old enough, she likes her job. Even if I make considerably less at my new job—just got it five days ago—it's gonna be two incomes. This new job is a real pain. I'm hopin' they lay me off in thirty days.

I'm a journeyman with fourteen years experience. They're treatin' me like a dog. The reason I became a craftsman was for a certain amount of dignity. They don't want craftsmen at this place, they want animals. How they're gonna treat these kids that are goin' out there, I don't know.

I've heard it many a time: Them people don't wanna work. There's jobs out there for six dollars an hour and they won't take 'em. When I was in high school, they told you: Go out, work hard, make something of your life. Now they're tellin' you you're not a good citizen if you're not willing to accept less. The whole country's supposed to accept less. It's steadily comin' down. It's an attack on the living standard of workers, since Reagan. And the best way is to hit the unions.

I'm workin' harder, makin' less money, got less of a future. I was put outa work in the steel mills at the ideal age. With ten years in the work force, still in my thirties, that's the guy they wanna hire. But now I'm pushin' forty. I know the law says they're supposed to do it, but they just don't hire you. This guy I know is gonna be forty-five, great skills and work history—just went back at a plant—maintenance. My wife is working. Friends of mine have problems with it. That guy that crossed the picket line. He didn't have to do it, he wasn't that hard up. He was right there with me in the union. He didn't take no shit from anybody. But I know he felt low being at home. He felt it was a reflection on him. He's Mexican. His pride, his macho.

There's somethin' in my life that I always wanted to do. I'd like to be a cabinetmaker. I'm makin' a table there. Before I die, I would like to make somethin' and stick it in the window and say, "I made this." If I sell it, I sell it. If I don't, I don't. But what I've made has never been made before.

Susan Dudak

Oral History

My life-style's changed quite a bit. I'm not the little housewife I was when I was twenty-one, twenty-two (laughs), I loved it at the time when I had little babies and was the nice little homemaker. But you have to wake up.

I was never what they called in the sixties an activist (laughs). I was more of a sideline. I remember about eight, nine years ago, a friend of mine got married and did not change her name. It stirred up quite an upset in the family. Eight years ago, you didn't hear of women doing that.

Out of high school, I went to a beauty salon. I was a licensed beautician. I worked part-time while the boys were babies. When the steel industry started going bad, I had to stop and think twice. The boys were getting older, they were starting school. Okay, now what do I do?

I decided I needed more of a training. I joined a program in word processing, secretarial. Since then, I've landed a real decent job as a paralegal. I work with a lot of immigrants who are having a hard time.

Being away from home so much, the boys had to adjust. I think in the long run it's been good for them. They learned how to wash their own clothes and do all kinds of goodie things. That's the only way we've been able to make it through this whole mill shutdown, is by me going to work.

I worry about their future every day. Will we be able to put them through college, if that's what they want? Will they be out in the work force working for four dollars an hour? What kind of home can you buy on four dollars an hour? Ike's nephew, he's married, twenty-one, and working for four-fifty an hour.

Is that the next generation coming along after us? Will it be that way for our children in five, ten years? I don't have the answers for them. I don't know.

QUESTIONS

How did Vietnam affect Ike Mazo? • What expectations did he have about his job at the steel mill? • How did his experiences at the mill shape his ideas? • What did he think about unions? • What was his vision of the future? • How did the closing of the mill affect him? • How did it affect his wife, Susan Dudak? • What future did they foresee for their children? • How did Ike Mazo feel about being working class? • Would you describe Susan Dudak as a feminist? • Do you think she would describe herself as one?

DOCUMENT 2

An Illegal Immigrant in Los Angeles

Illegal immigrants entered the United States by the hundreds of thousands since the 1970s. They came seeking political asylum, or reunion with family members, but above all they were seeking work. Vidal Olivares, a truck driver in Los Angeles, described his experiences as an illegal immigrant from Mexico in an interview in the late 1980s, the source of the following selection.

Vidal Olivares
Oral History

My origins are in a *ranchito* in the state of Jalisco, but I came to the United States in 1976. I have gone back three times. I had no trouble passing the first time, because I had a friend's green card. We look very much alike and he loaned me his papers, so I passed for him. At this time I was a bachelor. I stayed for two years, and when I returned to Mexico I met my wife and we married. But again, for economic reasons—I didn't have a job—I returned to work here.

My brother always wants me to come home. He can tell me that because he has work. He's a truck driver for a big company there and makes good money. That's why he doesn't have any interest in coming here.

It's very hard, the life in Mexico. We hardly had the money to eat. I had to leave my wife. We were newlyweds, we had been together only about ten months, and when I left she was pregnant. I wanted to get together the money for her and for my baby that was to be born.

When I first came here I met this man who had just begun his business and began to work with him. When I came back he gave me work again. There was never any problem; I have always had the same job.

One comes here thinking he is going to see only Americans, but then you find that there are a lot of people who speak Spanish and understand you. Not long ago, I had an experience in Texas. I was thinking that I was going to a city of Americans, El Paso. I was wondering how I would ask for the street. When I stopped, I tried to ask in English and they said, "No, we don't speak English here."

The second time I came, I had no knowledge of the kid who loaned me his card before, so I had to pass with a *coyote*. It was a big problem. At the border there are these *cholos* or *rateros* that rob people. We managed to get by them because we were all men, thanks be to God, but they made us run. Aside from this we had to walk from seven o'clock at night until five in the morning. We arrived at where the *coyotes* had their car. Some of us had to get in the trunk and others inside. They took us to a house. It was a Wednesday, and they kept us there until Sunday—waiting! They gave us hardly anything to eat. This was the hardest time.

When my daughter was born my wife called me, but I couldn't return. I wanted to save the money. I stayed until my baby was a year old, trying to save money to build a house in my pueblo. I came back for her first birthday. I had been gone a year and nine months.

Marilyn P. Davis, *Mexican Voices, American Dreams: An Oral History of Mexican Immigration to the United States* (New York: Henry Holt & Co., 1990), 206–9.

Well, I met my daughter and again returned to the United States. Passing the third time was really easy. When I arrived a man asked if I wanted to go to Los Angeles. I said, "Yes, but first I want to eat breakfast."

He said, "No, right now it is easy. Come now, I will give you breakfast." And yes, he gave me breakfast in his house in Tijuana. From there we jumped over the fence, then we waited for a few minutes because there was a patrol. As soon as the patrol passed we quickly ran, it was only about 100 meters, and we jumped in the car. There were about five of us. Quickly they took us to a house very close by. I think it was Chula Vista or somewhere near there. In this house there were something like forty people. From there they put us in a big truck with wooden boxes closed with chains, the kind they put heavy machines in. It was easy; we arrived in Los Angeles at about three in the afternoon. At times one has good luck.

Later I wrote and asked my wife if she would come. I had a friend, a woman who said she would help me. I paid her; it wasn't free. She picked my wife and the baby up in Tijuana in a pickup. It was very easy. The only thing was, she charged me quite a bit, $500 for both of them.

But there is the risk. The first time I passed, I gave the kid $30 for gasoline and a little bag of marijuana, about $10 worth. The second time they charged $225. As I remember, the third time they charged $275, but it seemed cheap because it was so fast.

Now I have about five years here. When my mother died in December I returned again, but I stayed only a week. Now I have my family here, and then I can't leave my work. But it was easy to pass this time. Four times I have passed, and not once have I landed in jail. I know the *migra,* but only from a distance.

Not long ago, my boss suggested that I try to get my papers because I travel, driving a big truck all over California and Arizona. So I went to an attorney, and when he asked me about my daughter and my work he told me not to try to get my papers. In this class of work they don't give green cards. There really isn't any problem, except the fear one has at times. I have seen the patrols. I am very careful, but because it's a big truck, they have never stopped me. But yes, I am a bit fearful that one day they will.

For those of us who are raised in a pueblo in Mexico, here we find a life that is really nice, beautiful. One becomes accustomed to the life and doesn't want to return. Now that I have my family, I am planning to stay, if they let us. If someday they send me and my family back, we will return, because I like living here very much.

I think it is good that my children will speak both languages. My oldest daughter is four years old and goes to preschool. She can speak various words, count to thirty, and say the days of the week, all in English. At times she surprises me. I get home from work and she says, "Poppy, you have a happy face." She can sing in English too. My youngest daughter was born here. She is from the United States.

Bueno, when one is married and has his family here, he hardly has time to think of his family there; rather, he thinks of his children, his wife, and his responsibilities. He tries to learn how to live. My father and sisters and brothers are still there. When I go there I never tell them about how it is here. Here we live better than we do there, yet if you earn dollars, you spend dollars. I tell my sisters and brothers that it isn't like they think. Sure we live better, there are more conveniences, but we aren't rich. I write to my father and tell him not to believe that just because someone lives here they have a lot of money. With working we hardly have enough to pay at the market, the rent, and clothes, because it is very expensive. But one becomes accustomed to living here.

Well, to my way of thinking, I don't know if it's good or bad, but what I want now is that my daughters grow up here and learn English. That is, if they don't throw us out. When they are older we'll take them to know Mexico. If one day we can get our papers, then it's all the better. That's how I think. The life is better here, that's why I want to raise them here.

Thanks be to God, I have never had any bad experiences here. The American people have treated me well. Never have they treated me badly, that's why I'm happy here.

QUESTIONS

Why did Vidal Olivares come to the United States? • How did he get across the border? • How did his wife enter the country? • Where did he find work? • What connections did he have with Mexico? • Why didn't he become a U.S. citizen? • What was his hope for the future and what ambitions did he have for his children? • Do you think his experience is typical of immigrants coming from Mexico?

DOCUMENT 3

A Vietnamese Immigrant on the West Coast

Following the Vietnam War, hundreds of thousands of immigrants came to the United States from Vietnam and elsewhere in Southeast Asia. The following interview, conducted in 1983, describes the experiences of one immigrant, a man from central Vietnam who preferred to remain anonymous.

Anonymous Man
Oral History

On our third attempt, my wife, children, and I escaped by boat from Vietnam and arrived in Hong Kong, where we remained for three months. Then my brother, who came to America in 1975, sponsored us, and we arrived in America in 1978.

We stayed with my brother and his family for five months. Neither I nor anyone in our family spoke any English before our arrival in America. I realized that I must study to communicate. Even though my brother was in one place, I decided to move to the West Coast. For nine months we lived in one town, where my children went to school. My wife and I also attended school to learn English. Although we received public assistance, we were always short each month by $20, $30, or even $40. If the situation continued like this, we'd have no money for clothes for the family. Even then, what we bought were old clothes that cost 20 or 25 cents apiece.

We made a visit to one of my sisters who lived in a small city that was surrounded by a lot of farmland. I saw that many of the people worked as farmers. I thought, "Maybe it's better for us to move here because I am used to working hard. God made me a hard-working man."

In 1980 we moved to that farming town. As soon as we arrived, I started to grow vegetables in the small backyard of the house we rented. In the meantime, I also worked as a farm laborer. We earned $35 to $45 a day, and that made me feel at ease. During the day I worked outside; in the evening I worked in my backyard. We began to sell what we grew, and from this we earned $200 a month. We liked to have our portion of land to do something, but we did not have enough money to buy.

We received help from the Public Housing Authority. The new house we moved into has four bedrooms. Each month we pay $50. The rest . . . is paid for by the government. The owner who rents us the house likes me very much because we keep the house very clean. . . . I moved all of the fruit trees from the old to the new house, and also planted a larger garden of vegetables and herbs. We have very good relations with our neighbors. They like us very much. They hire us to work on their backyards. That's the reason our income has increased. I grew too much to sell only to our neighbors. I needed to find a market.

One day I went to the farmer's market. I didn't know how to do it. I brought my vegetables there but they chased me away. . . . The second time I went back, they chased me away again. But that time I asked, "Can you help me so I can sell vegetables like other people?"

That man told me, "Okay, you come with me; I'll show you how."

James M. Freeman, *Hearts of Sorrow: Vietnamese-American Lives* (Stanford, CA: Stanford University Press, 1989), 382–90.

He gave me an application form, his business card, and an appointment. He explained to me during the appointment how I should do it and what kind of product I should have. He told me, "I want to come and see your garden, if it fulfills the requirements."

I agreed. He came down to inspect everything and wrote down on a piece of paper all the vegetables I grew. Then he gave me a permit. I brought my vegetables to the market, and nobody chased me any more. We earned some more money. . . .

After two years of this, we can save some [a lot]. Then we decided to have a fish truck. I borrowed some from my brother because it costs $4,000 to $5,000 to have a fish truck. During my work as a fish merchant our income was better. . . .

I am very happy in America for three reasons. First, I am very proud that I can do many things that other people could not do. Even though I do not know English very well, I did not bother anyone in dealing with paperwork or with translations. I myself did everything. I am very pleased by that. My English is not fluent, but when I speak with American people, they understand me, even though my grammar is not very good.

Second, I am at ease about living in America. Americans treat Vietnamese very well. I suppose if Americans had to live in Vietnam as refugees, the Vietnamese would not help them as much as the Americans helped me. We are very happy to live in America. I have received letters from Vietnamese refugees living in other countries. I am able to compare my life with theirs. Life in the United States is much better than in other countries of the Free World.

Third, what I like most is freedom, to move, to do business, and the freedom to work. I have freedom for myself, to work, to live, freedom to do everything you want. You can apply for a job or you can do a small business. You can apply for a license for a small business with no difficulties, no obstacles.

Although in America we live with everything free, to move, to do business, we still have the need to return to Vietnam one day. This is our dream. In Vietnam, before the Communists came, we had a sentimental life, more . . . comfortable and cozy, more joyful. To go out on the street, in the market in Vietnam, makes us more comfortable in our minds, spiritually.

Here in America, we have all the material comforts, very good. But the joy and sentiment are not like we had in Vietnam. There, when we went out from the home, we laughed, we jumped. And we had many relatives and friends to come to see us at home. Here in America, I only know what goes on in my home; my neighbor knows only what goes on in his home. We have a saying, "One knows only one's home." In America, when we go to work, we go in our cars. When we return, we leave our cars and enter our homes. . . . We do not need to know what goes on in the houses of our neighbors. That's why we do not have the kind of being at ease that we knew in Vietnam. . . .

When my sister came to America, she did as I am doing now. She and her family grew vegetables. Now they have two Vietnamese grocery stores and are the most successful Vietnamese refugees in their area. . . .

Another sister lives in the same town as I do. She and her husband are old, but their children are doing very well too. So four of my mother's children are now in America; four remain in Vietnam.

To live in America means that our life has changed. In Vietnam my family was very poor. We had to work very hard. We didn't have enough food or clothes. Under the Communist regime we were not free to do anything. If we made more than we needed, then the rest belonged to the revolutionary government. They did not want us to become rich. We needed to use old clothes. If we had new clothes, that's not good under the new regime because it showed that we had the capitalistic spirit.

My family living in America has everything complete and happy, and a new chance. I hope that my children become new people. My daughter in the eighth grade is the smartest of my children; she always gets A's. My youngest boy, who is eight years old, always is first in math in his class. My two oldest sons are not so good, but are above average and are preparing for electronics careers.

But the children are different here in America when compared with Vietnam. There is this big difference. Children growing up in Vietnam are afraid of their parents. Even when they marry, they still have respect and fear of their parents. In America, when they become 18, they lose their fear. They depend on the law of the land and go out of the house.

The one most difficult problem is the American law, and the American way to educate children. This is a big obstacle for the Vietnamese family. In Vietnam, in educating our children, if we cannot get success telling them what to do, we would punish them with a beating. By doing so, they would become good people. Here we cannot beat the children. That's the reason there's a big obstacle for us. When a child doesn't want to study, but likes to play with friends, if they want to smoke marijuana, when they do such bad things and parents tell them not to do so, the first, second, and third time, if they still don't listen, then parents *put them on the floor and beat them.* By doing so, this is the best way to prevent them from doing bad things, to get them to become good people. But here we cannot do that.

In my opinion, the Vietnamese have a lot of bad children because of American law, which is not like Vietnamese law. There are so many Vietnamese teenagers who came to America and who became not good people because of American law. When parents beat the child, the police come and arrest the parent. In the Vietnamese view, this is *the most dangerous and difficult obstacle.*

This is the *one most important thing* I want Americans to realize about the Vietnamese. The problem with educating and rearing the children is difficult because of American law. There's a second important point. Vietnamese life is not like American life. The Vietnamese have *villages, neighbors, and sentiment.* The father-child and mother-child relationship lasts forever, until the parents are very old. Children have the duty to take care of their parents. When the children were young, parents had the duty to raise and educate them. When the parents are old, duty is reversed: children take care of the parents. This is not like in America, where adult children leave the home, and old parents go to the nursing home. I'd like Americans to know that. I have met and talked with a lot of old American people. They have said to me, "When we become old, we . . . live together. When we become sick, nobody knows. When the postman comes, makes a surprise visit, only then does someone know we are sick. Sometimes our children aren't close by, or they live in a different state."

I ask the old people, "Do your children give you money?"

They reply, "No." These children do not think very much about their parents. This is very different from Vietnam; when children are married, they stay at home. When the parents become old, the children are together and take care of them.

But there are good lessons to be learned in America, such as *public sanitation.* That is what I have learned from America. At home, everything is arranged orderly and clean. Also, my American friends say what they think. This is different from what a Vietnamese would do. The American way, that's what I want my children to do. When we have one, we say "one." When we have two, we say "two." If that is a cow, we say it is a cow; if it's a goat, we say it's a goat. Vietnamese can learn this from Americans. I don't want to say what Americans can learn from the Vietnamese.

QUESTIONS

How did this Vietnamese immigrant come to the United States? • What kind of work did he do? • What did he like about America, and what did he criticize? • How did his life in America differ from that in Vietnam? • What difficulties did he encounter in America? • What aspirations did he have for his children?

DOCUMENT 4

A Health Care Researcher and Activist in Washington, D.C.

Since the 1960s, more Americans than ever before attended college. College graduates benefitted from the opportunity to learn and to prepare themselves for their future. The influence of learning and reflection on political activity are illustrated in the following interview, conducted in the late 1980s, with Hisani, an African American resident of Washington, D.C., who grew up in Houston and Pittsburgh.

Hisani

Oral History

All the kinds of outward trappings of political consciousness, I had very early. But it was all on the surface for me then. I didn't understand what it meant to my life, and how long the path moving in that direction really would be. The frustration of seeing yourself move in circles — expending a considerable amount of time and energy, but not really seeing any progress made — made me question whether the route that I was taking was a route that was ultimately going to transform the system into a society that was more humane and actually addressed people's needs, their hopes, dreams and aspirations.

So there was a transition in my life from involvement in community organizations to something that tried to do more than just patch up the system. I had started studying Marxism by my last year in college, like many people were doing. I was at Howard University, and a lot was happening in Washington then. Washington was a learning environment by itself. I was active in the National Liberation support committee which introduced me to a whole new grouping of people. I met people who were also studying Marxism and who had gone through similar experiences as mine. We were looking for models in other countries and trying to approach the struggle in a more scientific framework. We felt that there were lessons we could learn from other cultures, other societies that had been involved in struggle, particularly African countries, but also China and Cuba and the Soviet Union. So I studied revolutionary movements and became involved, in organizations that looked at these countries and tried to see what could be applied to this country.

After graduating from Howard, I took two years "off" and worked for a while in a warehouse. It really felt like we needed to develop our ties with working people. I think that time, more than any other, helped me understand the people of the world and their problems. I had come from a middle class family and had what we used to call petit bourgeois values. So coming out of school and working really did help me understand what the working class was all about. It helped me become a little bit more realistic about life and the problems people were facing and how ingrained they were. It was almost as if I had felt we could legislate change and people could suddenly live a better life, and that it was just a matter of changing the people in government. Or, the other side was that there would be a revolution, a violent overthrow as in the other countries we had studied. We were just that naive about the apparatus of the state.

Lauren Kessler, *After All These Years: Sixties Ideals in a Different World* (New York: Thunders Mouth Press, 1990), 48–49.

But I came to realize that the transformation of a people, the transformation of society was much broader than just this balance of power or shift in the balance. Partly, the realization came during those two years I took off after school. But, while I feel like I came to some of this on my own, I also think it came from being involved in the organizations I was and am involved in, forward-looking groups that are really struggling to understand the nature of our society and the political process. I've been involved in essentially the same organization since 1975, the group that's evolved, through different formations, into the New Democratic Movement. And now there's a maturity to our work. . . .

I've got some friends, people I've come through the movement with, who just seem to have given up. And you wonder if there was some critical time when someone just wasn't there for them, someone who could have helped to guide them or offered their support. That's what I feel has helped me a lot. My husband is politically involved, and we're involved in the same organizations. And I'm with a support network of people. But there were times I felt alone too. I mean there were times when we made it difficult for people to stay in the movement. We ostracized people because they went on to school, or we criticized them because they weren't working class enough or black enough. So some people were just driven away, and they never recovered.

It's an important question, what keeps people active. For me, it's the association with people. But I know there's something more, because I've tried to be a support for people who just haven't been able to hang in there, who've looked for quick answers. Maybe it had something to do with the quality of the training and preparation I had coming through. I think I came through a generation of some of the best trained activists. The organizations I've worked with, the black youth organizations, have trained what are now some of the most highly respected black leaders. It was something about the experience we went through, the molding and shaping of our personalities, our commitment, and especially the process of study—what happened in China, what happened in African countries—we saw that and were able to internalize it at a much higher level than other people. So we understood that things in this country weren't about change tomorrow.

The Reagan years were hard, but not as devastating to me personally as to some others because I was involved in surviving in a whole other world, the world of academia. There were so many assaults that we saw on the standard of living, on civil rights gains that you could see slipping before your eyes, women's movement gains, the fight for abortion. It was difficult. But I think, again, that understanding the system helped. I mean, a president can only do so much. We saw the tug and pull with Congress, the balance of forces, and you realized that he could do only so much. I think that if it had gone on much more than eight years, we would have wondered if we could ever recover. Even now, we are looking at the

Supreme Court and realizing that Reagan has left a mark there that will be with us for generations to come. But beyond this, I think there is a recognition that change is still possible.

There were things that happened during that same time period that were cause for optimism. I watched [Jesse] Jackson's campaign grow from being not taken very seriously to, during the second campaign, really becoming a force—an instrument of change in the rules and the platform. So there's a potential for more lasting change. I mean, as long as you have some signs that there's a potential for things to get better, you can fight off demoralization. Once you can see that there's that potential, you can keep the demoralization from overtaking you.

I think that the sources of power in this country are very entrenched and intertwined with money—that's still my view, and my understanding of that relationship hasn't changed over the years. But it does seem to me now that we have to infiltrate those networks that wield the most influence and authority in society. I don't think it's only working from within the system, because the system in many cases is corrupt in how it's structured. You've also got to mobilize from outside. The linkages of people I've maintained that are outside all the official structures I operate within are extremely important to me.

But for me, having children has definitely made a difference. When you become responsible for someone other than yourself, you think twice about the choices that you make in life. My husband and myself, by ourselves, could just pick up and leave because we disagreed with something at work. But when someone else's life is dependent on yours, it forces you to be more responsible in a way that you may not have been. I almost think it makes you a lot more conservative in your thinking, more cautious. We've begun to think, to wonder and question: Are we more conservative now than we were or is it just aging, maturity that leads to cautiousness? I don't know.

My attitudes toward different institutions, like the church and the police, certainly have changed since college years. Part of it, I think, is that those institutions have changed, at least a little, for the better. And this reflects our successes. These are struggles that we waged and that we've seen, in some sense, come to fruition. It's nice to reflect on that. It gives you another sense that things can change, that people can make a difference. So there's something about that idealism of youth that you hold on to. I enjoyed college and the years after that. I enjoyed the opportunity to think about the world and envision what it could be like. That's a luxury that I don't really have any more. Now I have to think about all the interests and concerns of my family.

The vision is still with me, but I'm much more pragmatic in terms of how I see myself or us achieving it. When you transform a society, real people are affected, and those people can't just be bulldozed over; they've got to be won over. That's the way our society works. And as long as we're here, we have to play the game by the rules that most people have grown to expect.

So you see signs, and you take heart from them. But you can't say that it's going to happen in your own lifetime. For example, in my own work, I've been involved in health care, developing a health care system that guarantees everyone access to care regardless of their financial situation. Now, I don't think that's so far off. I think the struggle today is being fought and won in separate arenas—the struggle around health, around housing, around education—there are people in each of those arenas who are working for a better system. But because the problems are so complex and deeply ingrained, the process of getting there is taking longer than maybe I would like. But I see the forward motion. I don't envision an overthrow of one government and the installation of a new one, to solve all our problems. That idealism is no longer with me. But I definitely see the forward motion.

QUESTIONS

How did college influence Hisani? • What did she learn from working after college? • What has been important to her in remaining politically active? • What signs of optimism did she see? • What discouraging signs did she notice? • How did she believe that the changes she favored could be brought about? • What did she anticipate for the future?

COMPARATIVE QUESTIONS

Did these five individuals agree on certain characteristics of America? Did they perceive similar strengths and weaknesses? Did they share a vision of the future? Did they have common concerns? Did they have similar views about politics?

ACKNOWLEDGMENTS

Chapter 17 Swedish Immigrants on the Kansas Prairie, from Ida Lindgren diary entries in H. Arnold Barton, ed., *Letters from the Promised Land: Swedes in America, 1840–1914.* Copyright © 1975. Reprinted with the permission of University of Minnesota Press.

A Romanian Jew Immigrates to America, from Michael Gold, *Jews without Money* (New York: Liveright Publishing Corporation, 1930).

Chapter 22 Patriotism and World War I Posters, from Anthony R. Crawford, ed., *Posters of World War I and World War II in the George C. Marshall Research Foundation* (Charlottesville:University Press of Virginia, 1979). Copyright © 1979 by The George C. Marshall Research Foundation. Reprinted with the permission of The George C. Marshall Research Foundation, Lexington, VA 24450.

An American Pilot Describes the Air War, from Geoffrey L. Rossano, ed., *The Price of Honor: The World War I Letters of Naval Aviator Kenneth MacLeish.* Copyright © 1991 by U.S. Naval Institute Press. Reprinted with the permission of the publishers.

Chapter 23 Reinhold Niebuhr on Christianity in Detroit, from *Leaves from the Notebook of a Tamed Cynic.* Copyright 1929 by Reinhold Niebuhr. Reprinted with the permission of The Westminster Press/John Knox Press.

The Crash, from Edwin Lefevre, "The Little Fellow in Wall Street," *The Saturday Evening Post* (January 4, 1930). Copyright 1930. Reprinted with the permission of The Saturday Evening Post Society.

Chapter 24 Working People's Letters to New Dealers, from Gerald Markowitz and David Rosener, *"Slaves of the Depression": Workers' Letters about Life on the Job.* Copyright © 1987 by Cornell University Press. Reprinted with the permission of the publishers.

Woody Guthrie on Hard-Hitting Songs for Hard-Hit People, from the Introduction by Woody Guthrie, to Alan Lomax with Woody Guthrie and Pete Seeger, *Hard-Hitting Songs for Hard-Hit People* (New York: Oak Publications, 1967). Copyright © 1967 by Woody Guthrie. Reprinted with the permission of Woody Guthrie Publications.

Chapter 25 A Japanese American Woman Recalls Pearl Harbor, from Monica Sone, *Nisei Daughter.* Copyright 1953 and renewed © 1981 by Monica Sone. Reprinted with the permission of Little, Brown and Company.

Letters From Soldiers Overseas, from Annette Tapert, ed., *Lines of Battle: Letters from American Servicemen, 1941–1945* (New York: Times Books, 1985). Copyright © 1985 by Annette Tapert. Reprinted by permission.

Chapter 26 Postwar Perceptions, from Mark Jonathan Harris, Franklin D. Mitchell, and Steven J. Schechter, *The Homefront: America During the World War II.* Copyright © 1984 by Mark Jonathan Harris, Franklin D. Mitchell, and Steven J. Schechter. Reprinted with the permission of The Putnam Publishing Group, Inc.

A POW in Korea, from Rudi Tomedi, *No Bugles, No Drums: An Oral History of the Korean War.* Copyright © 1993 by Rudi Tomedi. Reprinted with the permission of John Wiley & Sons, Inc.

Chapter 27 Women's Place in the Home, from Adlai Stevenson, "A Purpose for Modern Woman," *Woman's Home Companion* (September 1955). Copyright © 1955

INDEX

314